TOWERS IN THE VOID

Towers in the Void

Li Yu and Early Modern Chinese Media

S. E. Kile

Columbia University Press   New York

This publication was made possible in part by an award from the James P. Geiss and Margaret Y. Hsu Foundation.

Columbia University Press
Publishers Since 1893
New York   Chichester, West Sussex
cup.columbia.edu
Copyright © 2023 Columbia University Press
All rights reserved

Library of Congress Cataloging-in-Publication Data
Names: Kile, S. E., author.
Title: Towers in the Void : Li Yu and Early Modern Chinese Media / S.E. Kile.
Description: New York : Columbia University Press, [2023] | Includes bibliographical references and index.
Identifiers: LCCN 2022045547 (print) | LCCN 2022045548 (ebook) | ISBN 9780231210041 (hardback) | ISBN 9780231210058 (trade paperback) | ISBN 9780231558242 (ebook)
Subjects: LCSH: Li, Yu, 1611–1680?—Criticism and interpretation. | LCGFT: Literary criticism.
Classification: LCC PL2698.L52 Z726 2023 (print) | LCC PL2698.L52 (ebook) | DDC 895.18/4809—dc23/eng/20230106
LC record available at https://lccn.loc.gov/2022045547
LC ebook record available at https://lccn.loc.gov/2022045548

Cover design: Chang Jae Lee
Cover image: Zhan Wang 展望, *Finitude/Infinitude #1* (Youxian/wuxian 有限/無限 #1), 2021, 610 x 205 x 210 cm., stainless steel. Photograph: Elodie (Yaxing 雅行) © Beijing Nanchizi Museum (Beijing Nanchizi meishuguan 北京南池子美術館)

*To my parents,
Dianna and Fred*

Contents

Acknowledgments ix
Conventions xvii

Introduction 1

PART ONE Textual Media

CHAPTER ONE
Cultural Entrepreneurship and Woodblock Print 33

CHAPTER TWO
Building with Words 78

PART TWO Spatial Media

CHAPTER THREE
Fictional Space in *Twelve Towers* 119

CHAPTER FOUR
Garden Space in *Leisure Notes* 162

PART THREE Corporeal Media

CHAPTER FIVE
Remodeling Fictional Bodies   199

CHAPTER SIX
Remodeling Real Bodies in *Leisure Notes*   237

Epilogue   274

Appendix: Li Yu's Oeuvre   281
Notes   299
Works Cited   335
Index   353

Acknowledgments

This is, is the most general sense, a book about disruption and media, and those dynamics have grown ever clearer working under pandemic conditions. The absence of conferences, lectures, dinners, and drinks made me acutely aware just how much our work is dependent on the social; conversely, finding myself at the end of this book I realize with new perspective just how much of ourselves is lodged in our books.

This book began at Columbia University, where hours-long conversations in Shang Wei's office sparked questions I have puzzled over in the years since. Shang Wei taught me to be attuned to the play within old books, and to follow connections across the usual boundaries of genre and materiality. Dorothy Ko taught me how to get beyond texts to understand things, and bodies, as constitutive of the social. But she also taught me how to listen to voices from the past through texts, and how to tell their stories. Her guidance, at crucial moments over the years, has transformed my work; most recently, she helped me see what this book does.

My committee members offered the earliest guidance on how to transform my dissertation into a book: Lydia Liu taught me how to understand media; Weihong Bao taught me how to find connections between modern media forms and earlier ones; and Sophie Volpp encouraged me to dig more deeply into the literary possibilities of Li Yu's writing. Every day, I draw on what I learned about poetry from Wendy Swartz, about asking the right questions from Bob Hymes, about how culture gets made from Jenny Davidson, and about how things speak from Jonathan Hay. I am grateful to Chengzhi Wang at the C. V. Starr East Asian Library for his support right up to the final days of this project. My fellow graduate students offered intellectual engagement and camaraderie: I thank Michael Gibbs Hill, Tom Mullaney, Yi-Hsien Wu, Satoko Shimazaki, and Christopher Rea for their accumulated wisdom. I was glad to share the journey with Allison Bernard, BuYun Chen, Kaijun Chen, Chad Diehl, Noga Ganany, Andrew Liu, Peng Liu, Joseph Scheier-Dolberg, Miryong Shim, Timothy Yang, and Yurou Zhong. During the dissertation-writing process, Daniel Asen and Greg Patterson offered advice and moral support.

I drafted part of this manuscript at Brown University, where I learned much from conversations both within the China studies community and from their interdisciplinary engagements. I would like to thank especially Cynthia Brokaw, Laura Hess, Dore Levy, Rebecca Nedostup, and Lingzhen Wang. These interdisciplinary adventures were further strengthened during my years at the Michigan Society of Fellows. The opportunity for sustained and intensive engagement with the intellectual community there enabled me to rethink my work and communicate it to a broader audience. Once communicated, it turns out, the work itself changes for the better. I thank Donald S. Lopez Jr. for nurturing such a vibrant community, and, in posing his usual last question of the day at our lunches, for modeling what broad and deep intellectual engagement can be. For their engagement with this project during those exhilarating years, I thank my fellow Fellows, junior and senior alike.

I completed the manuscript at the University of Michigan, where both the Department of Asian Languages and Cultures and the Lieberthal-Rogel Center for Chinese Studies have provided guidance, collegiality, and community. For keeping these two intellectual homes functioning, I thank Nikki Gastineau, Kim Larrow, Patrice Whitney, Ena Schlorff, and Carol Stepanchuk. For their insights and engagement, I thank the ALC China cohort, Bill Baxter, Ben Brose, Kening Li, Sonya Özbey, Xiaobing Tang, and Emily Wilcox, and LRCCS directors Mary Gallagher, Ann Chih Lin, and Twila Tardif. Juhn Ahn, Micah Auerbach, Deirdre de la Cruz, Chris Hill, and Reginald Jackson offered much timely advice and encouragement. Liangyu Fu has helped me track down countless sources at libraries around the world. From my first visit to Ann Arbor to a multicity research trip to Japan, Jonathan Zwicker has been an inimitable intellectual and culinary guide. I have learned much from the astute mentorship of David Rolston: he helped me begin to imagine my readership, and while reading multiple versions of chapters in progress he provided meticulous notes on the entire manuscript. Christi Merrill read several chapters, offered extensive feedback, and first prompted me to conceive of my own book as a garden, rather than as a linear argument—transforming this project in the process. Since I arrived at Michigan, Miranda Brown has been an unwavering source of support, encouragement, and timely advice, sharing her ample wisdom on scholarship, teaching, and the profession. Conversations about poetry and comparison with David Porter, both on land and at sea, have been formative and refreshing; his encouragement at the end to "trim the weeds" served as a guiding refrain during the revision process. I am grateful for such generous and thoughtful colleagues, and for the graduate students who took my seminar on Li Yu: it was a pleasure to talk through *Leisure Notes* with all of you. I thank my graduate students Hanyu Hou and Charlotte Chun-lam Yiu for conversations about this material, and Yihui Sheng for her invaluable research assistance.

A manuscript workshop toward the end of this project helped me to hone my argument, and, in the analogy that ran through our conversation, trim the weeds. For saving my future readers from a visit to an overgrown garden, I thank Wai-yee Li and Judith Zeitlin, and my colleagues Miranda Brown, Donald S. Lopez Jr., Markus Nornes, David Porter, David Rolston, and Youngju Ryu. I thank Scotti Parish for her guidance during the First Book Workshop, and Paize Keulemans and Shang Wei for their valuable comments on the introduction. Dorothy Ko read the entire manuscript with insight and enthusiasm, helping me to think through where digital media studies and the early modern period might meet.

Throughout this project I have been sustained by the engagement and enthusiasm of my field. Conversations at conferences have provided invaluable wisdom, perspective, and critiques. For their insights in those settings, I thank Nan Z. Da, Maram Epstein, Tobie Meyer-Fong, Robert Hegel, Rania Huntington, Paize Keulemans, Ling Hon Lam, Tina Lu, Ōki Yasushi, Jing Tsu, Sophie Volpp, Steve West, Ellen Widmer, and Xu Peng.

Several invitations to participate in workshops and give lectures enabled me to share more sustained sections of the project with a variety of audiences. I first thought through media and technology when Patricia Sieber invited me to the Institute for Chinese Studies at the Ohio State University, and conversations with her have continued to shape this project ever since; Lingzhen Wang's invitation to speak at the International Conference on Gender Research in Chinese Studies at Nanjing University offered a chance to situate Li Yu's idiosyncrasies in broader context. My approach to cultural entrepreneurship was informed by the workshop on Cultural Entrepreneurship in Modern China organized by Eugenia Lean and Christopher Rea, as well as by Warren Palmer's invitation to write for economists at the Wealth and Well-Being of Nations Miller Upton Forum at Beloit College. I thank Beloit College Press for permission to include in chapter 1 revised portions of my essay from the proceedings of that forum, "The Values of Entrepreneurship in Early Modern China" in the *Annual Proceedings of the Wealth and Well-Being of Nations, The Miller Upton Forum*, vol. 8: 97–113. My work on gardens grew in conversation with colleagues at the Lieberthal-Rogel Center for Chinese Studies at the University of Michigan, with Mengjun Li's students at the University of Puget Sound, and with Phillip Bloom and the community at the Huntington Library. I worked through questions of theater, performance, and language thanks to Judith Zeitlin's symposium on Chinese Opera in Visual and Material Culture at the University of Chicago, James Robson's invitation to the Harvard China Humanities Seminar, and Tom Hare's invitation to the Translation Series at Princeton. Ariel Fox and Tom Kelly are excellent coconspirators in the study of early modern media and stellar coorganizers of Ming-Qing conversations: I am grateful for their friendship and for their insights.

This book was made possible by many welcoming and supportive colleagues in China. I thank Zhang Hongsheng for hosting me at Nanjing University, and Cao Mingsheng for hosting me in Yangzhou and for introducing me to Huang Qiang. Ma Jueping was a vibrant source of intellectual debate, and she introduced me to Shen Xinlin, who answered many questions about Li Yu. Shen Xinlin, in turn, introduced me to Li Caibiao, the president of the Li Yu Studies Society in Lanxi, Zhejiang, Li Yu's ancestral hometown, and representatives of the cultural bureau in Rugao, Jiangsu, Li Yu's birthplace. I thank Shi Mei and Li Dan for teaching me how to use reference materials at Nanjing Library. During several trips to Beijing, I am thankful to have been hosted by Liu Yongqiang and Pan Jianguo of Peking University's Chinese Department. Wang Ying helped me navigate the libraries in Beijing.

The staff at the Peking University Library, the National Library, the Capital Library of China, and the Beijing Normal University Library have been extraordinarily helpful. In Shanghai, I am grateful for the guidance of the staff at the Shanghai Library, the Fudan University Library, and the Zhejiang Library. I would also like to extend my thanks to the staff at the C. V. Starr East Asian Library at Columbia University; the Harvard-Yenching Library; the Memorial Library Special Collections at the University of Wisconsin, Madison; the Chinese Rare Books collection in the Asian Division of the Library of Congress; the Chinese Academy of Social Sciences; the Museum für Ostasiatische Kunst (Köln); the Stanford University Library; the Tenri Central Library; the Bayerische Staatsbibliothek; and the Sonkeikaku bunko.

This research was funded by a Fulbright-Hays Doctoral Dissertation Research Abroad Fellowship; a Mellon/ACLS Dissertation Completion Fellowship; a Michigan Society of Fellows Fellowship; a Seed Grant from the Institute for Research on Women and Gender, University of Michigan; and a Faculty Research Grant, from the Lieberthal-Rogel Center for Chinese Studies, University of Michigan. Publication subventions were provided by the College of Literature, Science, and the Arts at the University of Michigan, the Lieberthal-Rogel Center for Chinese Studies at the University of Michigan, and the James P. Geiss and Margaret Y. Hsu Foundation. I am grateful to all of these institutions for their financial support.

Christine Dunbar at Columbia University Press has spent hours talking with me about this project over the years, and those conversations, in turn, shaped this book. I am grateful to her, Christian Winting, and Leslie Kriesel for their confidence in my project and their expertise in seeing it through. I thank Mary Bagg for her careful editing of the manuscript, and Do Mi Stauber for preparing the index. I would also like to thank the three anonymous reviewers for the Press for their enthusiasm; their recommendations made the final version substantially better. A photograph of Zhan Wang's cloud-scraping, transmedial rendition of a garden rock, *Finitude/Infinitude #1*, exhibited at the Beijing Nanchizi

Museum, graces this book's cover. I thank him, the museum, and Elodie for permission to use the photograph.

This journey began during my undergraduate days at Beloit College, and I would like to thank my teachers there: Yong Shin for teaching me my first words in Chinese; Steve Wright for teaching me how to write; Rob LaFleur for sharing his zeal for Chinese history; Daniel Youd for introducing me to Ming-Qing literature and for teaching me Classical Chinese as an overload; and Natalie Gummer for teaching me how to understand texts.

In Ann Arbor, I feel fortunate to have found a wonderful community of friends. For the delightful meals and friendship, I would like to thank Mrinalini Sinha and Clement Hawes; Elizabeth Bruch and Tunghui Hu; Jatin Dua and Sanne Ravensbergen; Varuni Bhatia and Toy Basu; Manan and Retika Desai; Aida and Ari Levy-Hussen; Joseph Lam and Amy Stillman; Cathy Sanok and Basil Dufallo; Andrea Zemgulys and John Monnier; Isabel Hofmeyr; Aliyah Khan; Amanda Armstrong-Price and Alana Price.

Without the sustained intellectual and emotional support from friends at crucial moments, I could not have been finished this book. I am deeply grateful to Erin Brightwell, my oldest friend in Ann Arbor, who has been there with celebratory baked goods and *wenyan* jokes every step of the way; to Laurence Coderre, a true *zhiyin*, who has shown up weekly for years now for our writing group of two, deadpanning our way to the finish line; to Linda Rui Feng, who whether memorizing poetry while running laps or twisting my arm to take a quick trip to Kauai, has taught me the art of a balanced life; to Tarek Dika and Constance de Font-Réaulx, who have since Society of Fellows days navigated the ups and downs of life with me; to Qiong Liu, whose boundless intellectual curiosity caused our paths to first cross in Nanjing and who has been a dear friend ever since; and to Nino Budabin McQuown and Rebecca Wenstrom, with whom I have shared two decades of adventures in the most loving and restorative friendship I could imagine.

My family has been a fount of support across this long journey. From teaching me to read to encouraging me to pursue my dreams, wherever they should lead, my parents gave me the tools to forge this path. Matthew and Chelsea have been constant sources of love, good fun, and delicious barbecue. Rita, Ashok, Amrita, Madhav, Kartik, and Arjun have welcomed me into their family with open arms, and it has been a pleasure to get to know them these past few years.

Madhumita Lahiri has shown me what it means to be fearless and yet deeply committed, in writing, and in life. She has encouraged me to run with my boldest ideas and to broaden my scope; and, near the end of this project, she helped me hone them for the world—no small task. She is my first and last reader, and my daily interlocutor on the supermundane. Amitav Frederick Lahiri-Kile, not yet a year in this world, suffuses every day with curiosity and adventure. I thank them both for sharing their lives and love with me. They fill my life with uncountable joy.

Conventions

The following abbreviations appear through the text:

DMB	*Dictionary of Ming Biography,* ed. L. Carrington Goodrich, with Chaoying Fang
ECCP	*Eminent Chinese of the Ch'ing Period,* ed. Arthur W. Hummel
GBXQCK	*Guben xiqu congkan*
HJAS	*Harvard Journal of Asiatic Studies*
LIC	*Late Imperial China*
LYQJ	*Li Yu quanji* (Zhejiang guji)

Citations of Li Yu's works refer to the best widely available reproductions of early editions using the following short titles. See the bibliography for full citations and the appendix for further information on early editions.

Chidu	*Chidu chuzheng,* Baobianzhai edition reprinted in *Siku jinhui shu congkan*
Chuanqi shizhong	*Liweng chuanqi shizhong,* Shidetang edition reprinted in *Li Yu quanji* (Chengwen)
Liancheng bi	Saeki holding reprinted in *Guben xiaoshuo congkan*

Rou putuan	Manuscript copy held at Institute of Oriental Culture, Tokyo University
Shi'er lou, SEL	Xiaoxianju edition reprinted in *Guben xiaoshuo jicheng*
Wusheng xi	Sonkeikaku holding reprinted in *Li Yu quanji* (Cheng Wen)
Xianqing ouji	Yishengtang edition reprinted in *Xuxiu siku quanshu*
Yijia yan	*Liweng yijia yan,* Yishengtang edition digitized by Library of Congress
Yijia yan chuji	*Liweng yijia yan chuji,* Yishengtang edition reprinted in *Siku jinhui shu congkan bubian*
Yizhong yuan	Shunzhi edition reprinted in *Zheng Zhenduo cang zhenben xiqu wenxian congkan*

My translations, especially of Li Yu's titles, are indebted to the work of Patrick Hanan, *The Invention of Li Yu* (Cambridge, MA: Harvard University Press, 1988). For the convenience of readers, I have cited whenever possible from published translations that converge with my interpretations of the texts. Unless otherwise indicated, however, all translations are my own.

I provide the Chinese text for all passages quoted in this book, as well as additional resources for the study of Li Yu, at liyu-resource.org.

TOWERS IN THE VOID

Introduction

Opening this book just now, what you've found likely seems unremarkable: sheets of high-quality paper, neat rows of uniform text, the whole package elegantly formatted and tightly bound. But imagine your surprise if you had opened its covers to find nothing at all—an empty space where a book should be.

In 1672, the enterprising literatus Li Yu 李漁 (1611–1680, sobriquet Liweng 笠翁) included a design for such an empty book in the first installment of his collected works, *Liweng's Independent Words, A First Collection* (*Liweng yijia yan chuji* 笠翁一家言初集). That collection arranged his works by genre, and under the genre heading "inscriptions" (*ming* 銘), you would have come across a brief piece titled "Inscription on *The Collected Works of Mr. Nonexistent*" (*Wuyou xiansheng ji ming* 烏有先生集銘).[1] It was prefaced by a note to explain that the *Collected Works* of this "nonexistent" author were meant to prompt you to pursue your own creative enterprises:

> I have newly made a box: on the outside it appears to be a case containing a book, but when you open it and look inside, it is completely empty. All of the things that one needs at a desk, like writing paper, brushes, ink, and seals, are stored inside. For that reason, I named it "Mr. Nonexistent," to call it what it is, in fact [*shi* 實].

If this man doesn't exist, whence his collected works? With someone else's old name, I name my new design. When the ancients made things in the form of something, they did not insist that the name and the thing were in full accordance with one another. By emptying out the interior [*xu qi zhong* 虛其中] to make a container, you can select materials as you wish. The things that you need at your desk come not from the hand of a maidservant or the back of a servant boy, but instead are easily obtained from the bosom of Mr. Nonexistent. The subtle principle of the world, from ancient times to the present, has always been that only that which is most nonexistent can give rise to that which most exists. My inventing this thing and naming it in this way has its roots in the natural principles of heaven and earth, and it is not the same as the marketing of perversions by the likes of gougers and chiselers.[2]

The box Li Yu made for *The Collected Works of Mr. Nonexistent* likely resembled a traditional cloth case for multiple stitched bound volumes—that is, precisely the sort of case that would have held Li Yu's own collected works, in which these inscriptions were printed. Inside this case, however, would be the tools required to begin creating a book of one's own: brushes, ink, paper, and seals. Rather than imply that books are infrequently read or even opened, as suggested by the empty "faux books" produced today to decorate our shelves or hide our valuables, Li Yu's design encourages reflection on the expected contents, emphasizing the value of the book precisely by emptying it. By literally "emptying out" (*xu qi zhong*) this by then commonplace medium, Li Yu prompts his readers to reflect on what a book is, and what the medium of the book ensures. In the process, he arrests the usual reading experience, wherein readers forget the material existence of the book, and the mediating function of its format, as they peruse its contained pages.

The design for this inscribed book reflects three elements that will recur in my analysis of Li Yu's work. First, in describing a literal emptiness (*xu* 虛) at the heart of this design, Li Yu makes emptiness—an often intangible or even otherworldly quality—materially producible, through a simple design that captures the play between the substantial and the empty. In doing so, he makes a connection between rarefied aesthetic principles and everyday objects. Second, in Li Yu's cultural production, there is frequent play across media with these notions of *xu* and *shi*, which here literally signify "empty" and "full," but elsewhere refer variously to artifice and reality, fiction and reality, or imaginary and materially substantial.[3] The coherence of Li Yu's cultural production, which Patrick Hanan fittingly characterized as "all of a piece,"[4] emerges through similarities across its conceptualization: for example, *xu* and *shi* are here applied to a fake book container, and elsewhere to the balance of elements in a play or the placement of a latticework in a garden window. Third, much as an emptied-out book might prompt one to write a real book into existence, the proposed materiality of the emptied-out book in this inscription also guides readers in making a "Liweng book-shaped storage box" for themselves. Despite the claim at the beginning of the note that "I have newly made [*zhi* 制] a box," the material existence of this reproducible design may have been limited to what we have just read: words printed on a page. When considered alongside the many unrealized designs and ideas that Li Yu included in his writings, the term *zhi* may denote "designed" instead of "made": designed, as so many of his ideas were, for the reader to try. It was through Li Yu's innovative stories and plays that he first gained fame (and financial security) across the new empire. His fiction features clever plot construction and bawdy humor; his plays are raucous and entertaining. Although Li Yu was a wordsmith first, he often wielded words so as to materially influence the worlds of his readers; he does so here in transporting the idea of a book-shaped storage box through the technology of woodblock printing.

The originality of Li Yu's approach is disguised somewhat by his use of terms common in aesthetic and ethical writing, such as the complementary pair *xu/shi*. The late-Ming world in which Li Yu came of age had reveled in the interplay between these categories, blurring the boundaries between reality and fiction, world and stage, waking and dreaming, and even life and death.[5] My approach foregrounds how Li Yu harnessed this creative energy and adapted it to transform everyday life: rather than seeing *xu/shi* as accessing notions of transcendence or ultimate truth, Li Yu reconceptualizes them as tools that people can use to shape their worlds. Li Yu worked in a wide range of media: from writing, theater, architecture, and interior design to print, fashion, and the human body itself. Although he lived before the age of mass media, Li Yu conceived of human experience as fundamentally mediated. In defining a medium,

I mobilize Marshall McLuhan's distinction between the media forms that make our world and shape our experiences, and the contents of those media forms.[6] Rather than make a living as a "content producer," as the common description of him as the first professional writer in Chinese history might imply,[7] Li Yu devised a practice of cultural entrepreneurship that attended to the media forms themselves, remodeling them to various ends. For example, the common term at the time for composing *chuanqi* 傳奇, the southern song-drama form in which he wrote, was "filling in the lyrics" (*tianci* 填詞) to set tunes. Not satisfied with simply gaining national fame as a gifted lyric-filler, Li Yu worked to transform the theater world: he offered the first comprehensive theory of theater as a multimedia form, scrutinized the writing of spoken parts in addition to arias, prioritized performance and the training of actors, and invented a pulley system to rig up and surreptitiously adjust stage lighting. Through analogies to building design and to the human body, he explained that structure (*jiegou* 結構)—the container—is just as important to a play as the lyrics that are "filled in." His insistence on the primacy of performance is also a reminder that mediation is the very core of the theatrical experience.

In the example that opens this introduction, Li Yu's design calls attention to the medium of the book itself: not as a transparent record of the thoughts and words of an author, but as a container of tools with which readers can transport themselves beyond their immediate situations. I propose that the analytic of media enables us to better understand what drives Li Yu's cultural entrepreneurship: namely, his relentless attention to how human experience is mediated. In this, his approach coincides surprisingly well with what McLuhan terms "extensions" of the body: for example, writing connects bodies; print multiplies the number of people writing can reach; clothing offers warmth and attractive visual patterns; architecture makes room for others inside a protective "skin"; theatrical performance makes present scenes from other times and places.[8] For Li Yu, a focus on these media always points to mediation, an in-betweenness that reprioritizes the social after highlighting the materiality of media forms.

There was no term for media as such in early modern China, but the linguistic and conceptual resonance between the English terms "media" and "mediation" is present in the modern Chinese terms as well: the matchmaker (*mei* 媒), who serves an intermediary role as a go-between, persists in the modern Chinese terms for both media and medium, *meiti* 媒體 and *meijie* 媒介. I argue that the most distinctive aspect of Li Yu's cultural entrepreneurship was his consistent focus on finding ways to combine and remodel the media of his time so that they might better transport parts of himself out into the world. In his preface to Li Yu's *Independent Words*, Bao Xuan 包璿 (fl. 1670) compares Li Yu's fame to that of his late-Ming predecessors, the celebrity writer Chen Jiru 陳繼儒 (1558–1639) and the radical philosopher Li Zhi 李贄 (1527–1602), noting that Li Yu had risen to fame completely on his own, whereas Chen and Li Zhi both gained fame first by association with famous officials—Chen with Dong Qichang 董其昌 (1555–1636) and Li with Jiao Hong 焦竑 (1540–1620).[9] Li Yu built up a diverse network of patrons and clientele and published his work largely through his own publishing house (Yishengtang 翼聖堂), the combination of which allowed him to support his large family, own several garden residences, and maintain a significant amount of personal autonomy, all without official success, inherited wealth, or traditional patronage.

Through his various enterprises, Li Yu emptied out, remodeled, and transformed the connective potential of the media around him. Li Yu's designs repeatedly ask us to separate media from their contents, thereby calling attention to how a medium, and its whole network of relationships, functions. I came to the concept of media because I found that no other rubric would allow for Li Yu's work in various fields to be analyzed as a coherent cultural intervention. Li Yu's focus on using the media available to him to reach people and get in between things made him a matchmaker and mediator extraordinaire in the early decades of the Qing dynasty. I thus propose that we should understand his entrepreneurship through his innovations in media.

In order to apply the concept of media to the study of early modern Chinese culture, I start by situating print within the broader media context of its time. The late Ming had seen a shift away from what had long been considered print's primary function: transmitting (*chuan* 傳) the words of previous generations. Li Yu focused primarily on the ability of print to connect contemporary people, explicitly emphasizing how it could collapse space in the present. As he articulated a shift in print's transmission—from the historical to the simultaneous, from the temporal to the spatial—he used it to commune with his readers, bringing people into conversation with one another and transporting readers into his garden. Li Yu is well known as an unapologetic author of fiction in a sea of anonymous stories, but he also experimented with new ways of organizing information in printed books, combining an original epistemological approach with technological breakthroughs. He altered the reading experience of the vernacular short story by introducing chapter breaks; he commissioned illustrations that interacted with his text in novel ways, and he pioneered a hypertext-like system of indexing that for the first time linked a subject index to particular parts of particular pages.

In recent years, scholars interested in book culture in China have insisted that the materiality of print media is an indispensable part of understanding a culture that placed such high regard on books; the educated people of late imperial China, after all, expended considerable energy pursuing technical excellence in meticulously rendered calligraphic strokes and multicolor illustrations.[10] Through these scholars' efforts, we have learned to look at the material forms of books themselves, attending to innovative advertising strategies, experimental layouts, and collaborative projects, and even thinking beyond literacy to understand how people in imperial China interacted with their books.[11] Although these studies have generally eschewed explicit comparison with other early modern print cultures, as a crucial stage in the worldwide development of communicative media, print nevertheless raises important questions about the role of technologies in cultural change.[12]

I hope to shake the medium of print loose from a teleological account by discussing it alongside other early modern media. Li Yu, after all, reimagined print through engagement with other media: language and writing, buildings and gardens, bodies and clothing. In expanding the scope of what counts as media, I am inspired by Francesca Bray's work on technology and gender in imperial China. Bray's broad and connective definition of technology—which she uses to study agriculture, domestic architecture, and human reproduction—emphasizes not just material objects but their associated intentions, connections, and processes.[13] Li Yu frequently uses construction metaphors to explain how bodies are made, positing the human body as alterable through human intervention. His metaphorical use of construction refers us to material processes, and not to the idea of social construction that is common in contemporary discourse. For him, the body is material in the same way that writing is material: subject to human agency, but not created by it.

Writing as a technology has been most frequently contrasted with a prior or persistent orality.[14] Building on pathbreaking work in this area, this book will consider *wen* 文 (writing) as a material form—a type of thing (*wu* 物)—despite the fact that it was often contrasted with the material and practical, as in the expression *kongyan* 空言 (empty words).[15] The technology of writing had a changing valuation in the history of China. In ancient China it had an ambiguous status, for it was fundamental to transmitting core teachings, but it was often depicted as a symbol of civilizational decline. By Li Yu's time, centuries of vigorous debate about the status of writing and literature had come to include strains of thought that valued it as morally beneficial (*dao* 道), or even beautiful. Theories of literature had long focused primarily on the expressive function of writing; Li Yu, with his idea of structure as the most fundamental element of a literary work, instead reimagined writing as a tool to be wielded consciously to carefully designed ends. Li Yu's combined experimentation in *wu* and *wen*—material designs and the differently material printed accounts of those designs in writing—created a multimedia experience of reading that engaged readers' bodies and built environments.

Li Yu's approach to writing as a tool included advocacy of universal literacy. Departing from his peers' elitist restriction on the term *wenren* 文人—literally, "literary people"—to apply only to the literati, Li Yu defines *wenren* simply as "anyone who can read."[16] He calls literacy a "key that unlocks every door," and he describes learning to read as a process of incorporating written characters. Whether it was to confer moral lessons or to entertain, commercial publishers had long targeted the uneducated with performance literature, plain language, illustrations, or helpful glosses. But it is only with Li Yu's work that reading is conceived of as a tool that might transform such readers into "literary people." In this shift, people learn to read in order to use literacy as a tool for their own ends. As a consequence, literacy—which had been inseparable from a classical education—is suddenly positioned as widely accessible and broadly relevant.

SUBSTANTIATING A MIRAGE TOWER

The hefty materiality of the analogies of writing as a tool and of literary composition as building construction show one way that Li Yu's intermedial thinking lent substance (*shi*) to his literary work, even as their use as analogies pulls tools and building construction toward the intangible realm of nothingness (*xu*). Li Yu's *chuanqi* play *Tower in a Mirage* (*Shenzhong lou* 蜃中樓, ca. 1659) showcases how he remodeled the media of writing, buildings, and performance in the realm of theatrical production to mediate between *shi* and *xu* in surprising new ways. This play is unusual for Li Yu in that it draws heavily on existing literature, weaving together material from two Yuan *zaju* 雜劇 plays that recount love matches between a dragon princess and a mortal man.[17] But Li Yu adds a crucial new element: early in the play, the dragon kings decide to have a mirage tower built out of the breath and spittle of aquatic creatures and situated on the Eastern Sea, so that the two dragon princesses can view the scenery without being seen by mortals. The play's titular mirage tower draws on the old legend that the *shen* 蜃—alternately described as a magical sea dragon or a giant clam—could emit a vapor that would create a mirage of a tower on the water, one that could be seen but never reached (see figure 0.1).[18] In Li Yu's dramatization, the construction of this tower turns to slapstick, as he transforms the magical sea dragon into the lowly ranks of shrimp, crab, fish, and a soft-shelled turtle, the last of whom retracts his head and plays dead so he won't have to keep blowing. Once the tower is finally constructed, it proves to be permeable: the Royal Lord of the East uses his walking stick to build a bridge to the tower from the mortal world (see figure 0.2 for the play's illustration of this scene).[19] Two mortal men then visit the tower, romance ensues, and they eventually end up happily married to the dragon princesses.

To understand the role architectural and literary structure play in mediating between *xu* and *shi* in Li Yu's work, let's first consider his unusual literary treatment of the phenomenon of the mirage tower in this play. He invokes the materiality of buildings and the labor that goes into constructing them in order to create a memorable new version of this phenomenon for readers. The closing verse of the play emphasizes this desire to substantiate this usually nebulous tower:

FIGURE 0.1 "Illustration of a giant clam" in the "Animals" section of the 1725 *Imperial Encyclopedia*. (Chen Menglei and Jiang Tingxi, eds. *Qinding gujin tushu jicheng*, Beijing, [1890 reprint of 1725 edition], Bowu huibian, Qinchong dian, 156: Shenbu huikao, 1.) C. V. Starr East Asian Library, Columbia University, New York.

FIGURE 0.2 Illustration to Li Yu's play, *Tower in a Mirage*, depicting the eponymous tower. (Li Yu. *Shenzhong lou*. Yishengtang edition, Kangxi period.) Zhou Xinhui, comp. *Zhongguo gudai xiqu banhua ji*. Beijing: Xueyuan chubanshe, 2000, 623.

二事雖難辨假眞	Though it's tough to tell false from true in these two stories,
文章鑿鑿有原因	This composition certainly has an origin and cause.
蜃樓非是憑空造	The mirage tower was not manufactured out of thin air;
僅作移梁換柱人[20]	I simply served as one who tinkered with a few pillars and beams.

On the surface, these lines refer to the fact that Li Yu has constructed his play using material from two earlier plays. But given the blurring in the last two lines between the tower as represented in the play and the title of the play as itself a tower, we can read them in two different ways. On the one hand, Li Yu uses the expression "manufactured out of thin air" (*pingkong zao*), which usually refers to creating fictional works—in other words, precisely the sort of writing in which he specialized.[21] He is thus using terms associated with buildings—"manufacturing (*zao* 造)," "pillars," and "beams"—to describe the process of playwriting. On the other hand, given the play's emphasis on the construction of this tower, followed by the revelation that the mirage tower is made out of newly solidified materials, we can also read it as insisting once again that this mirage tower has materialized through the power of writing. In both cases, his phrasing shows the *xu* (fictional, nonexistent) becoming more *shi* (real, substantial). What distinguishes Li Yu's approach to these terms is the way the medium of architecture interacts with the medium of writing to create effect of substantiation.

The mirage tower further serves a literal mediating function between the two worlds represented in the play. For readers, Li Yu includes an unusually detailed note regarding set design at the beginning of scene 5:

> Build in advance one finely crafted and delightfully exquisite mirage tower. Secretly install it in the greenroom, and don't let the people in the performance area see it. Wait until they are singing onstage and the smoke is released, and then suddenly carry it out. It is of paramount importance to move with astonishing speed, so that the audience will be surprised and amazed, not knowing whence it has come. That way, it will be in keeping with the sense of a "mirage tower." Actors must not be negligent! (8:3481)

This elaborate set design deviates from the standards of the day, and thus creates a novel experience for readers of the playscript as they imagine how an audience would react to the materialized mirage tower. This note appears at the beginning of the scene, as if to invite readers into the greenroom to await the revelation. Stage directions describe the construction of the tower with great fanfare, as the sea creatures suck smoke into their mouths at the stage door (*guimen* 鬼門) and then puff it out onstage as they sing, leading up to the tower's revelation (8:3484).

The tower was a tangible presence in a theatrical world where sets were almost invariably minimal. In plays of this period, most any building would be invoked through lyric and gesture, rather than visually depicted or physically constructed, its details left to spectators' imaginations. In this play, which straddles two worlds, this conventional minimalism in set design is largely maintained: the settings of the underwater world and the human one are not depicted through material structures onstage.[22] The only depicted place that receives a physical set design is this tower, which exists at the boundary where the underwater world meets the human world, and whose very name indicates the illusory matter of a mirage. By substantiating onstage only this mediating place, Li Yu offers a physical portal between two ephemeral theatrical worlds, arresting the dichotomy between this world and the other by constructing a place in between, one variously composed of sea-creature spit, wood, and words.

Li Yu thus explored the possibilities where language met other media: buildings, printed books, theater, and even the body. He considered writing a matter of substance and plentitude, rather than absence and lack. This materialist vision of writing has significant implications, not only for literature but also for theatrical performance. Rather than a "true/*shi*" actor-body underneath the "false/*xu*" character-body, in Li Yu's approach there are layers of media, such as makeup and clothes, piled upon the already cultivated medium of the trained human body. Because he approaches writing and theatrical production as both constituted by media that are defined by presence, his conception of playmaking also emphasizes the substantial presence of the actors and audience. Following Li Yu's materialist mediations, I suggest that the experience of the theater is best understood not as a dichotomy between true and false, but as an interplay among diverse but tangible media forms.

Patrick Hanan has offered an astute assessment of Li Yu's inventive literary personae and literary creations, characterizing Li Yu's work as comedy and emphasizing the "primacy of pleasure" and pragmatic morality in his life philosophy.[23] Yet Li Yu repeatedly frames his writings as guidance on "how to live" by suggesting real, practical applications that his often-outrageous content and jocular tone belie. Attempts to theorize the balance between the serious and the jocular in Li Yu's work have frequently relied on his own conceptual language: describing his work, for instance, as "between *ya* (refined) and *su* (vulgar)" forms or as "combining *fengliu* 風流 (romantic) and *daoxue* 道學 (moralistic)" approaches.[24] In doing so, such studies situate his work in between modes of distinction associated with particular social classes or extreme social typologies, presenting it as the blurring of boundaries between these categories that had been popular since the late Ming.

My attention to media specificity and intermedial experimentation in Li Yu's cultural production allows me to reevaluate the significance of his interventions and communicative strategies. I thereby shift our focus away from the terms in which he and his contemporaries conceived of the nature of his work toward its broader historical significance. Li Yu was attentive to how human life was constituted by learned techniques, and he delighted in play and ironic reversals; he did not dwell on the origins or ultimate significance of the human condition. His apparent lack of interest in those questions informs my own focus: this is a book about media and the human, but it does not seek to constellate those terms in conclusive philosophical form. Instead, I hope to model a new approach to thinking about media in the early modern world, one that is informed by historical narratives that would identify it as the heyday of the "age of print," but one that at the same time takes a more expansive view of media, thereby avoiding a teleological account of technological development.

Li Yu lived through a dynastic shift, a massive historical transformation that reminded him, over and over across his life, of the transitory nature of familiar mediating technologies—in his case, to the fragile materiality of books, buildings, and bodies that constituted culture as he knew it. The shifts of Li Yu's lifetime prompted him to look at the world with changed eyes; his experiments across media forms, in turn, are best understood as attempts to mediate the lived experiences of his readers in new ways. His early-Qing world was shaped by multiple historical conjunctures: a crisis of faith that followed the dynastic transition, a renewed emphasis on the possibilities of the human body, and a radical rethinking of value, particularly as pertains to movable versus inalienable goods. These circumstances coincided with widespread but short-lived experiments with fictional narrative that challenged the boundaries of the genre: with mediating frame narratives in *Idle Talk Under the Bean Arbor* (*Doupeng xianhua* 豆棚閒話); through explorations of the inner workings of the mind in *Further Adventures on the Journey to the West* (*Xiyou bu* 西遊補); and via a focus on the strange in *Liaozhai's Records of the Strange* (*Liaozhai zhiyi* 聊齋誌異).[25] This constellation could arguably offer a starting point from which to mediate far-flung early modern worlds, as points of connection among disparate cultural formations that are visible only from the vantage point of the present.

MEDIA MASTER OF THE EARLY QING

Li Yu's accomplishments as a master of media in the early years of the Qing dynasty are astonishing. He became one of the first professional writers in Chinese history, adroitly mobilizing his brand name. And unlike most author-publishers, he was able to get by printing and selling only his own writing and editing projects. In more abstract terms, he found new ways to commodify his ideas: he sold concepts and designs for a variety of products, both ordinary and luxurious, rather than the products themselves, and he undertook an intermedial approach to printed texts, working between writing, image, and woodblock printing to make books communicate with readers in new ways. What unites these practices, I argue, is his identification of a set of primary media—texts, bodies, and the built environment—which he then remodeled with reference to one another. The contours of Li Yu's cultural entrepreneurship and his radical challenge to traditional literati culture cannot be simply attributed to the dynastic transition: many others, after all, lived through it and remained far more conventional. I do believe, however, that the rupture of the transition was the decisive turning point for him. As mentioned above, Li Yu would claim in his later years that literacy is a key that unlocks every door; I suspect that it was the dynastic transition that first convinced him that *his* literacy could open more than one door—that is, be used profitably for more than the civil service examinations.

Li Yu's initially unremarkable life as a Ming subject aspiring to official success began with his birth into a merchant family in Rugao, Jiangsu Province in 1611.[26] His father and uncles were doctors who ran a pharmaceutical shop. His family had resided in Rugao for several generations, where business was more lucrative than in their relatively out-of-the-way ancestral home, Xia-Li Village in Wuzhou (near modern Lanxi in Zhejiang Province). The family had not produced a successful scholar for more than nine generations, but Li Yu was a precocious child; his family saw in him hope for success in the civil service examinations, so they made sure he received a classical education. Around 1630, Li Yu returned to his ancestral village to prepare for his first examination. He passed the county-level civil examination in 1635 with distinction in the Five Classics, attracting the attention of Xu Zhi 許豸, Zhejiang's Vice Education Intendant, who printed Li Yu's examination paper and circulated it widely. Li Yu then enrolled in the prefectural school in Jinhua to prepare for the triennial provincial examination, which he failed at Hangzhou in 1639. In 1642, when he set out for a second attempt, the Ming was nearing collapse. Military conflict forced him to turn back before he reached Hangzhou: fighting had broken out across the south.

During his preparations for the civil service examinations, Li Yu experienced firsthand the middle ground between merchants (*shanggu* 商賈) like his family and the literati (*wenshi* 文士) whom he aspired to join. Xu Zhi's support probably gave him real hopes of an illustrious official career, but instead he would end up negotiating disparaging remarks from contemporaries throughout his life: although he became famous as a popular author, playwright, and bon vivant, he never passed even the provincial examination that would have qualified him for an official position and a government salary. In 1645 and 1646, when Fang Guo'an 方國安 attacked Jinhua as a Southern Ming general and then a year later with the Qing military, Li Yu and his wife were alone in that devastated city: his father had died in 1630 and his mother in 1642.[27] Li Yu sought refuge in the mountains and then, when he found himself homeless, went to stay with Xu Xicai 許檄彩, the assistant prefect of Jinhua, as his clerk; this is the only time he would take up residence in another's home.[28]

The dynastic transition from the Ming to the Qing caused massive upheavals across China: many of the political and cultural authorities of the Ming were killed, took their own lives, or went into reclusion as devoted loyalists (*yimin* 遺民) to the Ming, refusing to serve under the Qing government. The refusal to serve two dynasties and be deemed a turncoat (*erchen* 貳臣) was a standard practice, one exacerbated in this instance by the Manchu identity of the new ruling family. The early decree requiring all men to shave their foreheads and wear a queue prompted many who remained devoted to the Ming to go into reclusion or take up tonsure as a Buddhist monk. Some who accepted official positions in the Qing nonetheless sought to share in the remembrance of the Ming by sponsoring loyalist projects, while other educated men who had been employed in the Ming government or were studying for the examinations gave up those pursuits and turned instead to alternative sources of income.[29] In the midst of this crisis, Li Yu, too, gave up the traditional pursuit of success through the examination system and embarked on a career as a writer of fiction and plays in the bustling city of Hangzhou. While most of Li Yu's peers produced wrenching, nostalgic writing about the dynastic transition, nostalgia is largely absent from his writing, save a few poems he wrote during the 1640s lamenting that he had to shave his head in the Manchu style.

Despite the general lack of explicit discussions of dynastic transition in Li Yu's work, it would fundamentally alter his future pursuits. Around 1647, Li Yu bought a small plot of land that he called Yi Hill Estate (Yishan bieye 伊山別業) near his ancestral village, Xia-Li Village, thinking he might live out his days in reclusion. There he designed a modest garden with seven named scenic features that he celebrated in poetry, styling himself a "literate farmer" (*shizi nong* 識字農). He would remain at his garden residence only three years, however, leaving abruptly around 1651, perhaps due to a scandal involving either his wife's family or his first for-profit writing.[30] In Hangzhou, Li Yu published his first *chuanqi* play, the long southern style of song-drama that dominated the contemporary stage. The play was titled *The Fragrant Companions* (*Lianxiang ban* 憐香伴), and its content might have forced Li Yu's abrupt departure from Yi Hill, for it depicts a tripartite romance among a young man, his wife, and another young woman.[31] The play likely drew on his own experience: in 1645, Xu Xicai had offered Li Yu a concubine named Miss Cao

曹氏, who had been widowed during the dynastic transition. Though he already had a wife, Li Yu accepted, and written records portray the relationship between his wife and concubine as intimate. In writing the character of the young unmarried woman in his first play, Li Yu did not even change her surname.[32]

As he moved his family and completed *The Fragrant Companions*, Li Yu reflected on the relationship between writing and property in his playful but insistent "Deed of Sale for a Mountain" (Maishan quan 賣山券):

> A mountain can be bought, but it cannot be obtained by amassing copper and silver coins. Coins can procure its trees and stones, but they cannot change its spirit; they can purchase its physical body, but they cannot change its name. On what do I rely to make this claim? I will tell you: I rely on the lofty integrity of my peculiar ways, and on my elegant verses. Their value is considerable, such that even when this mountain changes names, this expense of spirit can bring it back in the end. Although time passes and brings with it great changes, it will not have two masters.[33]

By insisting on the value of literary representation over land ownership, Li Yu declared his ability to produce value with his brush and his right to claim mastery over property owned by others. Li Yu had written about his initial attempts to purchase the hill, his establishment of his ownership by writing about its various named sites, and his small family's labor in the estate's upkeep. This concept of the superiority of "aesthetic ownership" dates back at least to the Tang dynasty, when purely economic ownership of a garden came to be seen as inferior to the social and cultural capital of properly consuming those gardens—that is, the legal right to property was ideologically subordinated to the right to the use and ownership of gardens by those with the time and sensibility to appreciate them.[34]

When he sold the estate, Li Yu drew reassurance from the same long tradition by which the dissemination of writings about a place would continue to mark it as belonging to the author, regardless of who the current owner might be. He developed this claim through a list of famous associations between particular places and specific historical persons, such as those between Red Cliff (Chibi 赤壁) and Su Shi 蘇軾 (1037–1101)

or between the Orchid Pavilion (Lanting 蘭亭) and Wang Xizhi 王羲之 (303–361). With this idiosyncratic deed of sale, Li Yu thus placed himself and his unknown estate among the ranks of some of China's best-remembered places and people, while relegating the future owner of the estate at Yi Hill to the status of a groundskeeper: "Although a new master may replace the previous one, he is little more than a hired clerk or garden keeper, there to preserve traces of the past."[35] As he wrote these words to establish his claim to the mountain, Li Yu was just beginning to establish his literary name, which would be shaped by the mountain in turn. That identity is indicated in both of the names by which he was most commonly known: "Fisherman Li" (Li Yu) and "Straw-Capped Old Man on the Lake" (Hushang Liweng 湖上笠翁). Much as the desire to associate the mountain with himself sought to erase all future transformations in the mountain's fate, so too did Li Yu capitalize on his identity as a recluse for the rest of his days, despite the more urban lifestyle of his following three decades.

Later Li Yu would make a living selling copies of his writings, and his success, in essence, came from commodifying this sort of cultural product—the cultural value of a hill, or a garden; an arrangement of rocks, or of flowers; the design of a window, or a chair. The practice of writing on objects—whether literally inscribing curios or writing about an object or place and then disseminating that writing through print—was, for Li Yu, crucial to claiming ownership over them. Near the end of "Deed of Sale for a Mountain," he wrote of inscribing a particular place with his mark—something that would tie the site to himself in a durable way.[36] Compared with commemorative steles or poems written on walls, which are distinguished by their site-specificity, separation from the site would ensure a lasting connection between it and himself.[37] In a move that foreshadowed his dynamic cultural entrepreneurship, Li Yu made the literary production of value explicit by declaring his ownership of this mountain even as he sold it.

The fall of the Ming spawned the closing of many of the publishing houses in the Jiangnan region. In Nanjing the some thirty-eight publishing houses of the late Ming had dwindled to a mere seven in the first decades of the Qing; in Hangzhou, only five of twenty-five houses remained.[38] The dynastic transition also brought to an end the centuries-long, empire-wide dominance of the Fujian publishing industry when many of its towns were destroyed in the fighting.³⁹ As far as can be determined from extant texts, there were only a handful of new short stories published each year in the early Qing, supplemented by new editions of well-known works by author-publishers like Feng Menglong 馮夢龍 (1574–1645) and Ling Mengchu 凌濛初 (1580–1644). Yet despite these challenges, there seems to have been a market for Li Yu's entertaining fiction and plays. During his years in Hangzhou (ca. 1651–1661), he wrote play after sensational play, and he published three collections of original fiction and a novel in quick succession.⁴⁰ Li Yu's plays and fiction are distinctive not only for their originality, parody, and lively dialogue, but also for the way that the author-narrator-commentator—who was identified with Li Yu by name—constantly interrupts, baits, and gleefully outsmarts the reader. His authorial voice pervades his fiction, just as the many metatheatrical elements of his plays draw attention to the fact that they are plays. He was the first literatus to identify himself by name as an author of fiction in his works: whereas claiming authorship of plays had become increasing respectable in the late Ming, the literati of Li Yu's time generally avoided claiming authorship of their fiction.⁴¹

In addition to *The Fragrant Companions*, we know that Li Yu wrote at least nine other *chuanqi* plays.⁴² Beginning around 1653, Li Yu published these southern dramas individually as he completed them, in two-volume finely illustrated editions (see the appendix for details). Eventually he published all ten as a set titled *Liweng's Ten Plays* (*Liweng chuanqi shizhong* 笠翁傳奇十種, Kangxi period). Li Yu frequently wrote of selling his works and advertised upcoming works in earlier ones. In a letter to a friend, Li Yu mentions that his second play, *Mistake with a Kite* (*Fengzheng wu*), "had been coursing among the people for some twenty years, and there's nowhere one can't find a copy of it."⁴³

Li Yu wrote his plays for both the stage and the woodblock. A versatile comedian, he knew how to get laughs out of the illiterate and the overeducated alike; rather than focusing upon the lyric possibilities of arias, he experimented with the usually conventional dialogue, condensing and charging it with layers of meaning. Some of his plays are reminiscent of the romantic comedies of the late Ming, with their comic mismatches and multiplying pairs of lovers, while others embark on newly theatrical paths: for instance, actors performing as actors who actually die in performance, or an actor transformed from one role-type to another onstage.

Although he would continue to write plays throughout his career, all of Li Yu's fiction was likely published between 1654 and 1658. He first published a collection of twelve short stories, *Silent Operas* (*Wusheng xi* 無聲戲), with exaggerated Chen Hongshou 陳洪綬 (1598–1652)–style illustrations. From the start, Li Yu's comic stories were remarkably original; at a time when most fiction was derivative, his stories staged the reversal of received wisdom: an ugly man fated to marry a beautiful woman; a male wife more devoted than a female; an illiterate woman capable of outsmarting a powerful man. He then published *Silent Operas, Second Collection* (*Wusheng xi erji* 無聲戲二集), which likely contained six new stories with such novelties as a morally upright actress and a man who pretends to sleep with his friend's wife and ends up dead. To reach an even broader readership, he soon published a twelve-story compilation from both of the *Silent Operas* collections, with new illustrations and an affordable price, under the title *Silent Operas, Combined Collection* (*Wusheng xi heji* 無聲戲合集).

In 1657 Li Yu published his only novel, the parodic erotic jaunt titled *The Fleshy Prayer Mat* (*Rou putuan* 肉蒲團), under a dedicated pseudonym. Anyone familiar with his writing, however, would have recognized his voice in that text, and Huang Qiang has found many examples of phrases matching verbatim those in his other works.[44] That novel's protagonist sets out to sleep with the most beautiful woman in the world; the clockwork logic of karmic retribution—in a parody of that rather lazy narrative device—means that his wife has already slept with an equivalent number of other men.

Finally, he published his third collection of short stories, called *Twelve Towers* (*Shi'er lou* 十二樓). I discuss *Twelve Towers* in its entirety in chapter 3, for in that collection Li Yu drew extensively on the resources, both conceptual and narrative, of the building as a medium to reconfigure the *huaben* 話本 vernacular short-story form. In *Silent Operas*, he drew more extensively on the possibilities of the body as medium, and I accordingly discuss its stories in chapter 5.

The textual history of *Silent Operas* remains a matter of scholarly debate as a result of the controversial sponsorship by Zhang Jinyan 張縉彥 (1599–ca. 1670) of the second collection, or "both collections," if *Wusheng xi erji* is parsed that way (see the appendix). Zhang, who was the Provincial Administration Commissioner of Zhejiang from 1654 to 1658, allegedly used *Silent Operas* as a platform for clearing his name from involvement in surrendering Beijing to the rebel Li Zicheng when he was a Ming official. Ultimately Zhang was exiled to Ningguta, on the northeast frontier, and this political association seems to have made it impossible to circulate a collection titled *Silent Operas,* or even its stories with their original titles, after around 1660.[45] Instead, the stories circulated as *Priceless Jade* (*Liancheng bi* 連城璧), a collection whose new story titles and different order seem to have been intended to distance it from the *Silent Operas* collections.

We can discern the implications of Li Yu's association with Zhang Jinyan from Li Yu's 1664 preface to *Liweng's Discourses on the Past, Expanded and Revised* (*Zengding Liweng lungu* 增定笠翁論古). There he claimed to have been writing fiction only to appease the public; he had, he claimed, always been more interested in history. This work responded directly to a 1663 change in the examination system, when the focus shifted from the eight-legged essay form to questions based on policy and discourse.[46] In the preface to what amounted to examination preparation material, Li Yu mentioned that imperial censors had been trying to rid the world of fiction in favor of more decent writing, so he vowed to "accordingly, take all of the works I have authored to date, and offer them up to the flames. Then, I will take the cinders that remain and fling them into the river out of fear that the extinguished ashes might catch fire once again."[47]

Li Yu did not follow through on this hyperbolic threat, but he would never write fiction again. He did continue to promote his existing collections, but he repackaged them to reduce their apparent fictionality. Sometime after 1660, Li Yu and his closest collaborator, Du Jun 杜濬 (1611–1687)—who wrote prefaces and commentary for most of Li Yu's fiction collections under the pseudonym Libationer of Slumberland (Shuixiang jijiu 睡鄉祭酒)—reordered and reissued the *Silent Operas* stories under the new title *Priceless Jade*, a title that emphasized fiction's moralizing qualities. The titles of both collections were further subordinated to a new title, *Famous Words to Awaken the World* (*Jueshi mingyan* 覺世名言), which disguised their novelty through association with Feng Menglong's famous Ming-era collections, such as *Constant Words* to Awaken the World (*Xingshi hengyan* 醒世恆言). Similarly, Du Jun's preface to *Twelve Towers*, dated 1658, was also revised to remove the term "fiction" (*xiaoshuo* 小說).

After several years of traveling between Hangzhou and Nanjing, Li Yu relocated with his family to Nanjing around 1661. His projects from his Nanjing period largely comprised collections of his own nonfiction prose, on the one hand, and collections of contemporary writings—letters, parallel prose, and administrative documents—on the other. During this period, he also oversaw the publication in installments of his collected works, *Liweng's Independent Words* (*Liweng yijia yan*), which contained his collected poetry and prose. He wrote two works on history—the primer *An Outline of History* (*Gujin shilüe* 古今史略, 1659) and the more original *Discourses on the Past* (*Lungu* 論古, 1661, revised and reissued in 1664)—and he also wrote essays and commentary for his compilations *A New Aid to Administration* (*Zizhi xinshu* 資治新書, published in 1663 with a second collection in 1667).

Li Yu's post-1660 projects involved dozens to hundreds of people both as producers and consumers. They consequently operated, I argue, as a kind of social networking technology. I suggest that Li Yu was responding to latent demand in the urban center in which he lived for cultural products that referred to the contemporary moment and articulated a kind of community. His later efforts off the page, notably, included orchestrating spaces for shared experiences, both through his theater direction and through the design of Mustard Seed Garden (Jieziyuan 芥子園), his garden residence and private theater. In contrast, his fiction and printed plays would have served primarily as private entertainments, creating fictional worlds in which readers might lose themselves, which must have been a welcome distraction from the political upheaval of those years.

Li Yu's career as a cultural entrepreneur was importantly shaped by his trips across the empire in search of patronage. In addition to his early travels throughout Zhejiang and Jiangsu Provinces, he traveled nearly every year between 1666 and 1675, visiting most of the important regions of his time, including two visits to Beijing. The most successful of these trips was to Shaanxi in 1668, where he acquired the funds to build Mustard Seed Garden on a three *mu* (half-acre) property near Zhengyang Gate in the southeastern corner of Nanjing. It served as a residence, garden, publishing house, and bookshop. He managed and worked out of Mustard Seed Garden for eight years, selling his own literary works (published by Yishengtang) as well as woodblock-printed stationery that he had designed.

The entertainment in Mustard Seed Garden centered on romantic plays performed by a troupe starring two young women who had been given to Li Yu as concubines, Qiao Fusheng 喬復生 and Wang Zailai 王再來. Li Yu directed their performance of his own plays as well as old plays he had adapted for the modern stage, at home and on tour. Qiao Fusheng had a natural aptitude for music and could easily repeat verses she had heard only once, and she trained Wang Zailai in turn. These two women had very different regional origins: Qiao was from Shanxi and Wang from Gansu. In their collaboration, then, they instantiated the kind of empire-wide connectivity that Li Yu's pages could only promise. For several years, Li Yu tells us, they would perform any time there was cause for celebration, entertaining some of the most distinguished cultural figures of their time. These two young women, I suggest, contributed significantly to Chinese drama by making possible the works we credit to Li Yu. Despite their talents, however, they lived constrained and abbreviated lives: they died, one after the other, in 1673 and 1674, each at the age of just nineteen.

In 1671 Li Yu published the text that is widely recognized as his crowning accomplishment, *Xianqing ouji* 閒情偶寄. This book's elegant title casually revels in the experience of leisurely (*xian*) sentiment (*qing*): happenstance, spare moments of pleasure, freedom from obligations of work and family alike. So leisurely are these sentiments that the second half of the title notes that they are only "casually" (*ou*) sent out (*ji*) into the world (an alternate reading of *ji* would have them "lodged" in this text). I will call this work *Leisure Notes*, maintaining the casual sentiment of this title at the expense of a literal rendering of each character.[48] *Leisure Notes* was designed to engage with each reader in a personalized way, prompting them to transform their lived environments in accordance with its designs while Li Yu's chatty authorial voice hummed across the pages. It comprises eight books (*bu* 部), each of which is divided into numbered and titled sections, and each section is divided into titled essays. The first two books, "Playwriting" (Ciqu bu 詞曲部) and "Performance" (Yanxi bu 演習部), are long discussions of the theater and have received the most contemporary critical attention. The next four books—"Exquisite Ingénues" (Shengrong bu 聲容部)," "Residences" (Jushi bu 居室部), "Furnishings and Fine Things" (Qiwan bu 器玩部) and "Food and Drink" (Yinzhuan bu 飲饌部)—instruct readers in refined practices of purchasing and consumption, whether consumables, furniture, buildings, or women. The final two books, "Horticulture" (Zhongzhi bu 種植部) and "Care of the Self" (Yiyang bu 頤養部), focus on the cultivation of ornamental plants and of the reader. The selling point of the collection was arguably Li Yu himself, and a publisher's note promised an insider's guide to his glamorous lifestyle.

Li Yu's central preoccupation in *Leisure Notes* is the development of new "methods" (*fa* 法) in each of these categories, which taken together constitute Li Yu's idea of the good life. His innovations are varied and wide-ranging: he suggests boring a hole in the wall of your study to bring the outhouse to you; or installing drawers in your desk to avoid waiting for a servant; or cutting an aperture between rooms which would allow one light to illuminate both. I propose that we read these new methods as technologies, for through these proposals Li Yu devises new ways of imagining, experiencing, and shaping the media and materials of his time. While modern ideas of technology generally tend toward acceleration and efficiency—that is, modernity's famous investment in space-time compression—Li Yu's technologies have ambivalent effects: innovations that speed up time or contract space coexist with equally technical descriptions of things that slow down or expand. To speed things up, you might follow his designs for an efficient lantern-wick trimmer, incense ash tamper, or evening-length play—or you might slow down, embracing the dilatory pleasures of his designs for crackle-glazed wallpaper, a mural that appears to be alive, or winding garden paths. The purpose of these technological innovations, then, is not simply to replace human labor or accelerate existing processes (though frequently they work toward those ends). Instead, across multiple media, *Leisure Notes* invites individual users to actively harness and manipulate everyday space and time through Li Yu's methods. And because these methods circulate via print, his text thereby forges new connections between writing and the material world. The result is a composite experience that is nonetheless transmitted (*chuan*) through the single medium of print.

I argue that reimagining the possibilities of such transmission through print was at the heart of Li Yu's cultural entrepreneurship. Because he worked in multiple fields, he was keenly attuned to the variations across different media forms even as they overlapped in their guiding critical terms.[49] For example, *xu qi zhong*, which translates to "emptying out the interior," signifies differently in a design for an empty book container, a work of fiction, and a window. Li Yu drew upon the existing cross-fertilization of critical vocabulary to engage with the materiality of the media in which he worked, including that of the human body, borrowing and mixing approaches from different media forms. His primary goal, however, was not to justify lower prestige art forms through the critical vocabulary of the elite arts. Instead, I argue, he did so in service of his novelty-focused interest in aesthetics.

His work as a whole is guided by an investment in innovation: telling new stories, finding new uses for things, showing people perspectives they had not considered before. His fiction abounds with characters who excel at improvising with whatever was at hand, finding new uses for materials, writing, or bodies, for he was perpetually creating new stories for the real things in his fictional worlds. In moving from fiction and drama to *Leisure Notes*, Li Yu retained his imaginative investment in creating new stories about extant things, setting the scene for readers to create new narratives within their everyday lives.

Li Yu was writing in the wake of the late-Ming obsession with novelty as evidence of authenticity, inspired by thinkers like Wang Yangming 王陽明 (1472–1529) and Li Zhi, who championed notions of innate knowledge (*liangzhi* 良知) and a child-like heart (*tongxin* 童心). These writers idealized the uneducated as naturally possessing a novel experience of the everyday. Li Yu built on this valorization but reversed its assumed origins: instead of claiming that culture would only destroy the quotidian experience of novelty, Li Yu wrote books that might help one realize everyday novelty. He celebrated, moreover, the production of new versions of his own writing: he adapted four of his stories into plays, and in the published version of these adaptations, he explicitly noted that his plays were more malleable than his fiction. In *Leisure Notes* he provided detailed instructions about how to adjust a play to the length of time available for performance, and he even offered to move in with you so that his plays could be updated constantly: "If heaven gave Liweng some extra years and a bushel of gold, so that he could buy some actors himself, write some verses himself, instruct them with his mouth and direct them with his body, then the theatricals would be renewed every day, and the comedy onstage would constantly change."[50] The service Li Yu proposed here has at least a kernel of sincerity behind it: he would have liked to see a new play performed every evening. Of course, no one could achieve this playful ambition of filling every moment with brand-new theatricals. The text of *Leisure Notes*, I argue, comes closest to offering such a service to each of its readers.

In 1677 Li Yu moved from Mustard Seed Garden, leaving his son-in-law, Shen Xinyou 沈心友, to manage the business, to his final residence, Storied Garden (Cengyuan 層園), on Hangzhou's West Lake. He had previously commissioned Wang Gai 王槩 (1645–1707), the son of his close friend Wang Zuoju 王左車, to produce a manual on the fundamentals of landscape painting for aspiring painters.[51] The result was a multivolume instructional guide to painting, richly illustrated with detailed images of varying size. Shen Xinyou oversaw the 1679 publication of this very popular book, *The Mustard Seed Garden Painting Manual* (*Jieziyuan huazhuan* 芥子園畫傳), and it is the primary reason that the Mustard Seed Garden is known today. In Hangzhou Li Yu continued writing and providing comments and prefaces until just months before his death, on the thirteenth day of the first month, 1680.

BUILDING *TOWERS IN THE VOID*

Towers in the Void is organized in three parts, corresponding roughly to books, buildings, and bodies. In part I, "Textual Media," I explore the particular strategies of Li Yu's writing, printing, and publishing. While all the chapters in this study rely on textual analysis of printed works, the two chapters in part I address Li Yu's work with words in more general terms, considering, as it were, his writing about writing (chapter 1), his printed arguments about print (chapter 2), and, in both chapters, the language he uses when discussing language itself. In part II, "Spatial Media," I explore Li Yu's engagement with the built environment, whether gardens or buildings, first in his fiction (chapter 3) and then in his nonfiction (chapter 4). In part III, "Corporeal Media," I analyze his arguments about the medium of the human body, in his fiction (chapter 5) and then in his nonfiction (chapter 6). Across these six chapters, I argue that the ideas he explores in fiction often refract those that he proposes for everyday life, even as his work with actually existing spaces and bodies informs his approach to them in fiction.

I use the notion of cultural entrepreneurship in chapter 1 to show how Li Yu made a brand of his name, focusing in particular on how he solved the problem of making easily reproducible products that nonetheless promised his personal touch. Through an analysis of the representation of the demand for paintings in his play *A Much-Desired Match* (*Yizhong yuan* 意中緣), I suggest that he resolves the problem of overwhelming demand with his design in *Leisure Notes* of a "Li Yu fan painting" that readers could reproduce themselves. The chapter concludes by discussing his experiments with the technology of the printed book.

In chapter 2 I situate Li Yu's writing about playwriting and the training of actors in the historical context of the dynastic transition. His experience of losing his books, I argue, led him to experiment with orality and performance, as well as with new ideas about how to use print to disseminate those ideas. I also show how metaphors of building construction and the creation of human bodies, when envisioned from the wreckage of the transition, suggested new possibilities for what words can do.

Using examples from Li Yu's last collection of *huaben* short stories, *Twelve Towers*, I focus in chapter 3 on the relationship between buildings and fictional stories. I argue that Li Yu created this collection by experimenting with ways to make a story's structure analogous a building's (for example, by dividing it into chapters akin to the levels, or storeys, of a building), and with ways to use a building as a narrative device. Unlike the characters of a story, who most readers do not expect to meet in life, buildings featured in a story invite a different relationship to the fictional—one that might prompt the realization of an actual building on their model.

In chapter 4 I explore Li Yu's approach to garden design in *Leisure Notes*, situating his innovations alongside those of the garden designer Ji Cheng 計成 (1582–ca. 1642). I argue that Li Yu took his inspiration from the narrative arts, especially fiction and prose, and diverged from Ji Cheng's more conventional emphasis on the inspirations of landscape painting. The result was a different experience of both time and space in the garden, for Li Yu's narrative approach detached the garden experience from the seasons, so that time could be sped up or slowed down as one wished.

Li Yu's reimaginings of the human body in his fiction, through metaphors that link the body to woodblock printing and architectural remodeling, propose outlandish but plausible alternatives to our usual embodied experience. I demonstrate in chapter 5 that Li Yu set up an anthropomorphized and fallible Creator (*zaohua* 造化, *zaowu* 造物) so that he could invite people, both as fictional characters and as writers, to intervene and improve upon the Creator's work. By presenting the remodeling of the human body in terms of building renovation, Li Yu nudged the human body closer to buildings, and thereby into a space between fiction and the real world.

In chapter 6 I consider the proposals for real human bodies in *Leisure Notes* by examining the terms and metaphors with which Li Yu discusses "body design," such as likening skin to silk. Although many of Li Yu's body designs pertain to women who were bought and sold, others focus upon the literati body of his reader, and his approach to bodies thereby crosses divides of gender and class. In emptying out preconceived notions about the body and reconsidering it as a malleable material form, Li Yu asks every reader to reconsider how one's body mediates one's experience of the world.

READING FROM THE OTHER END

In designing this study, I have not followed the linear progression dictated by chronology, nor have I hewed to established distinctions between genres. Instead, I have been inspired by Li Yu's invitation to readers to use his magnum opus, *Leisure Notes*, as they like. In his letters to his friends, he advises one person to begin with the books on women and houses, and another to start with those on women and care of the self.[52] The text's openness to its readers is enabled rather than constrained by its extensive table of contents, for the standardized, to-the-point advice found in genres like connoisseurship manuals has given way to the idiosyncratic experiences and design ideas of a casual essayist. As an experiment with the cross-fertilization of media forms, *Leisure Notes* draws on Li Yu's deep understanding of print to offer the reader a new literary form: whereas his earlier writing directed the reader on a private linear trajectory of discovery, *Leisure Notes* offers a representational space for readers to explore as they wish.

In writing this study of multimedia experimentation, I have been inspired by the aspiration of providing readerly autonomy, which I find not only in Li Yu's *Leisure Notes* but also in the design he proposes for gardens. In *Leisure Notes* Li Yu argues that a garden must offer multiple different yet intersecting paths:

> With garden paths, there is nothing more convenient [*bian* 便] than the direct, yet nor is there anything subtler [*miao* 妙] than the circuitous. Those who intentionally make winding paths for their splendid effect must also install a side door to allow family members to get on with household business. If you are in a hurry, open the door; if you are at ease, then close it. This way the refined and the vulgar both benefit from it, both being well served by this way of doing it.[53]

The interplay between "the convenient" (*bian*) and "the subtle" (*miao*) here proposes a balance in design that constrains human capacity even as it extends it. This mode of design is usually characterized as finding a middle way between the refined (*ya*) and the vulgar (*su*), as I mention above, but it can also be understood as a mode of experimentation and innovation in media in the early Qing. I argue, in part, that Li Yu produced books whose relationship to their readers would be analogous to that of his gardens and their visitors: through a design carefully equipped with multiple entry points and an array of possible paths, his texts allow readers to delight in surprise, distraction, and the aesthetics of circumlocution and delay, even as they learn new practical methods for optimizing their experience.

I have drawn throughout on the garden as a figure for media history, precisely because its multimedia design shaped communication, bodies, and environment in an exceptionally coordinated way. At the center of this text-garden you will find *Leisure Notes*, for although *Leisure Notes* has often been used by historians as a core source on many topics—furniture, architecture, footbinding, letter paper, decorative objects, and medicine—no one has considered this pivotal text as a composite whole.⁵⁴ *Towers in the Void* discusses *Leisure Notes* in its entirety, and it serves here as the fulcrum around which Li Yu's diverse efforts in other genres and fields constellate. At the same time, other readerly paths through this book will take you closer to Li Yu's drama, or his writings on bodies and gender, or his relationship to the professional garden designers of his time.

A book may seem like a serious, silent, and linear genre, yet that, too, is an effect of the historical interactions of media forms. In contrast to the commonplace weighty notion of reading, we might remember this poem that Li Yu sent to a friend:

有借予閒情偶寄一閱。閱不數卷。即見歸者。因其首論填詞。非其所尚故耳。以詩答之。

SOMEONE BORROWED MY *LEISURE NOTES* TO READ, BUT AFTER READING A FEW VOLUMES, RETURNED IT BECAUSE THE BEGINNING DISCUSSES PLAYWRITING, WHICH WAS NOT SOMETHING HE LIKED. I WROTE THIS POEM BY WAY OF REPLY.

讀書不得法
2 開卷意先闌

此物同甘蔗
4 如何不倒餐⁵⁵

No knack for reading books,
He feels disheartened the moment he opens it.
This thing is just like sugarcane,
Why not eat it from the other end?

PART I
Textual Media

CHAPTER ONE

Cultural Entrepreneurship and Woodblock Print

Li Yu was an adamant dabbler, seeking profit and renown in realms as diverse as fiction and gardening, theater and interior design. But he did not sell devices; rather he sold instructions for how to build them. He may have designed a few gardens, but he sold ideas for how to design many more. All of this happened via one essential medium: the woodblock print. A couplet included in Li Yu's collected works testifies to his belief in the power of print. Titled "The Carver" (Jijue shi 剞劂氏), it reads:

馳姓名於四海	Carrying names throughout the four seas,
壽文字於千秋[1]	Granting words life for a thousand autumns.

This couplet credits the woodblock carver with the life-giving (*shou*) quality of print. The names of authors and historical figures, along with all of the other words on every page of every book, survive and circulate thanks only to the work of the woodblock carver. Li Yu's acknowledgment of the role of the carver gestures toward the medium's specificity—that is, he foregrounds the techniques and labor that make print possible. The "four seas" encompasses the whole world, while "autumns" stands synecdochally for "years." The term *chi*, which I have translated as "carrying," denotes galloping on horseback. The compound term *chiming* 馳名 had much earlier come to mean "famous," and Li Yu's use of it here reinvigorates the verb by attributing it to the work of the woodblock carver—as though his carvings were horses galloping with mounted names throughout the land. The simplicity of this couplet belies the enormity of the task it describes. Printing was an astonishing technological feat: once the woodblock was carved, the text therein could be quickly and cheaply copied, and then widely disseminated.² In the Ming and Qing, references to woodblocks (*zi* 梓, lit. catalpa) or carving (*ke* 刻) would frequently be used as metonyms for the carving and printing process, eliding the work of the carver himself.³ In Li Yu's couplet, in contrast, the figure of the carver charges back onto the scene, highlighting his role in the medium that grants literary immortality.

Li Yu might be best known as a wordsmith (*wenjiang* 文匠), acutely attuned to the possibilities of rhetorical play and eager to test the boundaries of genres in which he wrote, but his innovations in print were also central to his cultural entrepreneurship. He was actively involved in the printing and distribution of his works both while living in Hangzhou (ca. 1651–ca. 1661) and Nanjing (ca. 1661–1677). Most of the first editions of his fiction and plays do not include reference to any publisher (though they do credit the painters and carvers of the illustrations), which suggests that Li Yu may have hired carvers and overseen the publication himself. This early obscuring of publication conditions is not surprising. Given the growth in the late Ming and early Qing of a readership that no longer solely comprised literati, and the increase in the number of educated men who had to cobble together a living, some literati publishers began to focus on what would sell commercially, even as they hesitated to associate the name of their publishing house with some of those works.⁴

We have more information about Li Yu's involvement with the publication of his works during his Nanjing years. Almost all of the extant first editions of his Nanjing period were published under the name Yishengtang.⁵ He covered the expenses for the publication of these works, including those of paper and block carving; prepared and kept all of the blocks; exercised authority over the content of the blocks right up until printing; and personally invited well-known literati to contribute prefaces and comments.⁶ Almost every print that came out of Yishengtang during Li Yu's Nanjing years seems to have involved Li Yu.

My attention to the conditions of publication for Li Yu's work is informed by recent studies of publishing in early modern China, which have challenged the assumed distinction between private (or literati) publishing, on the one hand, and commercial publishing, on the other. For instance, although there were some ten "literati publishers" of fiction active in Hangzhou in the early Qing, only two of them published under their own names: Li Yu and Wang Qi 汪淇, a Ming loyalist who also published for profit.[7] And when Li Yu moved to Nanjing, he likely found only one other literati publisher on the scene, Zhou Liangjie 周亮節 (1622–1670), who published several editions of the great novels but who was not himself an author of fiction.[8] Rather than distinguish between publishers based on whether or not a literatus was involved, I suggest that profitability is a better criterion. We see this clearly in the publishing of Li Yu and Wang Qi: both of these men advertised the works they published, and both earned enough to make a living from publishing. Li Yu was distinctive because he had authored many of the works he published, whereas Wang Qi focused on compiling, editing, and commissioning new works from others. Like Li Yu, Wang Qi was unashamed of profiting from sales; in the prefatory material to the third installment of his letter compilations, he happily informed his readers that profits from sales of the first two letter compilations had been sufficient to "turn his tadpole studio into a unicorn pavilion."[9]

As a publisher, Li Yu experimented with the medium of print, focusing his creative energy on versatility: Given the technical restrictions of woodblock printing—two-dimensional designs stamped in ink on sheets of uniformly sized paper—what variation was possible, in content and format and layout, so that a single book could engage readers across space and time?[10] Although woodblock printing was not new, scholars have argued that it was only in the late Ming that print finally surpassed manuscripts in importance, perhaps even, as Kai-wing Chow has argued, creating a print-based public sphere that could challenge state orthodoxy.[11] In this chapter, building on the substantial scholarship that concerns the print culture of this period, I show how Li Yu's intermedial approach allowed him to find new uses for an old medium. Because print has been more exhaustively studied than any of the other media in which Li Yu worked, my focus on print in this chapter forms a foundation for the analysis of other media forms in the chapters that follow. As a vehicle for preserving and transporting one's words, print offered easy reproducibility but presented a challenge: how to convey a personal touch.

Retaining a sense of presence, even in the author's inevitable absence from the scene of reading, was a key objective. Li Yu thought about how his printed books might compare with singular works of painting or calligraphy, and how they might carry his name throughout the land.[12] I argue that Li Yu used print as a social networking technology, and that he also developed the technology of the printed book so that it could be used by people with different skill levels, through a system of indexing that resembles what we now know as hypertext.

Li Yu has been a household name in China for the past four hundred years, and the business side of his endeavors is crucial to understanding his approach to media, for his focus on the market informs all of his work. Li Yu was involved with the distribution of his books beyond his bookshop, and he relied on some combination of book sales and patrons' support for his livelihood. He explored a variety of marketing strategies, from advertising upcoming books within the pages of earlier ones, to carrying books on journeys to sell in other places, to simply pleading with readers not to take his livelihood away by pirating his work. This chapter opens by looking at the way Li Yu made a brand of his name, disseminated it through print, and protected it by claiming the rights to his designs. I explore his ideas about technological reproducibility through discussions of the late-Ming celebrity Chen Jiru, who seems to have been an inspiration. Chen is arguably the nearest historical precursor to Li Yu, and I discuss in some detail Li Yu's representation of him in his play *A Much-Desired Match*. Through this central character, Li Yu dramatizes the challenge that was at the heart of his experiments with print: how to facilitate technological reproducibility and yet retain the sense of a face-to-face meeting with a famous figure.

Li Yu's solution, in part, developed through collaborative projects: the collections of letters, parallel prose essays, and administrative documents that he compiled in the middle period of his career (1660s). I demonstrate how Li Yu incorporated ever greater numbers of participants and readers into these collaborations. Through these collections, I argue, Li Yu curated a virtual literary sphere in which his friends, acquaintances, and aspirational supporters could converge. To appeal to a broad readership, he also updated the form of the book: his first letter collection, published in 1660, is to my knowledge the first Chinese book to include an index with page numbers.[13] In a time when the recently deposed Ming inspired popular fascination and nostalgia, Li Yu used the affordances of woodblock reproduction to collect the dissipated energies of the collapsed dynasty in a single, condensed place.

WHY ENTREPRENEURSHIP?

What did it mean to earn a living by selling one's writing in the early Qing? Confucian tradition divided men into the hierarchical social categories of literati, peasants, artisans, and merchants, associating trade with the lowest ranks of social life. This hierarchical division persisted as an ideal throughout the dynastic period. From the middle of the Ming dynasty, however, a commercial boom made merchants wealthier, while literati increasingly struggled to obtain an official position in the bureaucracy. Many men found themselves occupying positions that were neither literatus nor merchant: merchants could now purchase positions, whereas great numbers of scholars gave up on the examinations to pursue commercial enterprises.[14] Many of the most famous cultural figures from this period—such as the author-publisher Feng Menglong and the painter-writer Chen Jiru—supported themselves by selling their works. This blurring of distinctions between merchants and literati poses a challenge to historians, for most contemporary accounts of social practice purposely ignored this changing reality: intellectual exchange was consistently valorized as superior to mercantile exchange, and monetary or in-kind compensation for intellectual labor often went unmentioned.[15]

The fraught intersection between literatus and merchant offers rich insight on the shifting values of entrepreneurship in the early modern period. Many educated men became entrepreneurs: some broadened the scope of the literary market (as Feng Menglong did with his pioneering collections of vernacular short stories); others diversified their profitable activities from writing fiction, plays, joke books, and essays to producing painting manuals, albums of paintings, and exclusive illustrated editions. Even though they were making a living selling books, investing capital into developing new kinds of books, and building up brand names that would increase sales of those books, these men did not consider themselves merchants. At the same time, merchants who were engaged in more traditional sorts of trade, and especially those trading in salt, found that wealth could readily buy them social distinction.

These merchants began to participate enthusiastically in literati culture, even as the literati began—often furtively and in denial—to undertake the activities of the merchant and trader class.[16]

The analytic category that has been most often used to characterize these hybrid figures is "scholar-merchant" (*shishang* 士商). As Cynthia Brokaw explained, these *shishang* "insisted that they were a special kind of merchant . . . devoted not just to the petty search for profit, but to the spread of learning."[17] Yet as Kai-wing Chow has demonstrated, the *shishang* were responding to dire economic and political realities.[18] The figure of the *shishang*, produced in the urban milieu of the mid to late Ming, effectively collapses the two poles of the Confucian social hierarchy into a single social role. While most literati made a profit through established practices, such as writing epitaphs or prefaces, or selling paintings, what I call cultural entrepreneurship refers to those who creatively developed and expanded their products, took risks, and sought out new markets. This distinction, crucially, is not the same as that between literati who would admit to selling their writing and those who would not.[19] Li Yu provides a particularly compelling model of such entrepreneurship, for he promoted his work by associating it with his brand names: his name, "Fisherman" Li (Li Yu); the sobriquet (*hao*), "Straw-Capped Old Man on the Lake" (Hushang Liweng); the name of his bookshop-garden residence, Mustard Seed Garden (Jieziyuan), or that of his publishing house, Yishengtang. He used these brands to market a diverse array of cultural products, combining the pursuit of innovation with an emphasis on easily reproducible designs.

Just how was his work entrepreneurial? First, he constantly sought to diversify and innovate. During the 1650s, he published a new play or short story collection almost every year. From 1660, he shifted his focus to collections of letters, administrative documents, and regulated verse, each of which included writing that had been solicited from cultural figures throughout the empire. Near the end of his life, he wrote *Leisure Notes* (1671), a collection of essays full of designs and suggestions that promised to transform the reader's everyday life without significant cost. One essay teaches readers how to install a pulley system to rig stage lighting; another describes a design for retractable eaves that allow one to enjoy a garden, rain or shine. In genre, subject matter, and tone alike, Li

Yu challenged the limits of what was considered acceptable writing for educated men of his day.

Second, Li Yu's work is entrepreneurial for the creativity and flexibility with which he embraced market-oriented cultural production. Many of his fellow literati preferred to quietly receive remuneration for standard literary products like prefaces or calligraphy-adorned fans. Li Yu, however, exploited the commercial possibilities of the publishing business. He printed books at his garden residence in Nanjing, where he also marketed and sold books and notepaper. He further undertook a range of nonliterary commercial ventures, such as designing gardens and directing a theater troupe that he took on tour to the homes of wealthy patrons, risking an association with the still lowly social positions of garden designers and actors.

The third and most distinctively entrepreneurial aspect of Li Yu's work concerns how he used writing and print to interact with other media forms. Writing popular plays and fiction was a straightforward way to spread his brand, but he was adamant about both experimenting and diversifying, seeking not just to attach his name to a particular object in the world. He first attempted to do this by using language to claim a particular thing (as when he retained literary possession of his Yi Hill estate), allowing words to triumph over legal property rights. Crucial to the further development of his entrepreneurship, however, was finding a way to extend that claim to unique designs that he had not yet produced, and to entire categories of objects. For example, on multiple occasions in *Leisure Notes,* he argues that his designs should be named after him, such as the "Liweng Incense Chop" (Liweng xiangyin 笠翁香印) and the "Liweng *Materia Medica*" (Liweng bencao 笠翁本草).[20]

Li Yu stands out among his contemporaries for the sheer range of products he developed, and he nevertheless maintains and even extends earlier types of social hierarchy by producing and enforcing new modes of consumption. He experimented with the ability of writing and print to transport new kinds of cultural products to a broader reading public, and in doing so, he generated cultural objects that blur the boundaries between production and consumption. Instead of approaching its purchaser as a pure consumer, many of Li Yu's cultural products encouraged interactivity and personalization, demanding, for example, that you stop reading to go construct a window diorama. It's hard to get lost in a novel when Li Yu's narrator is constantly interrupting you, just as it's hard to live in a study with bare walls after you've read about Li Yu's wallpaper design, which was intended to make you feel like you live inside a teapot.[21] This approach solved the problem of efficiency: whereas Li Yu could only write so many books, once he disseminated designs rather than final products his brand expanded considerably. In this way, he invited consumers to share the labor of the production of culture, even while the final product retained his brand name.

SCALING CULTURAL PRODUCTION WITH EARLY MODERN TECHNOLOGY

Unlike Li Yu, most writers or painters in the early Qing relied on individual patrons for their livelihood, and their success always came with a new problem: an increasing demand for their products. Writing could be scaled up or down, from a commissioned eulogy for an individual recipient to a published play sold commercially to multiple buyers. But painting and calligraphy were less flexible; the prevalence of ghostpainting and slipshod production of inferior works testifies to this challenge of meeting demand.[22]

In exploring modes of cultural production that could be easily scaled, Li Yu was inspired most directly by the late-Ming writer Chen Jiru. Jamie Greenbaum has called Chen the first celebrity in Chinese history, noting his unprecedented complicity in creating demand for products associated with him outside of the traditional avenues of patronage and politics.[23] Even in the Qing, cultural observers began pointing to the similarities between Chen and Li Yu, and Li Yu himself frequently referenced Chen in his writing. He directly addresses their relationship in a short essay titled "Pork" (*zhu* 豬) in *Leisure Notes*. Situated after entries on flour and cellophane noodles and just before those on mutton and beef, the essay opens with a reference to the delectable, braised pork belly dish known as "Dongpo pork," after its alleged inventor, the famed Song-dynasty statesman and poet, Su Shi, sobriquet Dongpo 東坡. This essay is more concerned with the image it projects of the text's author than with the stated content of the entry—a characteristic of many of the essays in *Leisure Notes* that connects it to the *xiaopin* tradition. It fails to provide a recipe for the pork dish, but instead ruminates on the unusual extensiveness of Chen Jiru's and Su Shi's entrepreneurial activities, and their risks (Chen's sobriquet was Meigong 眉公):

> "Dongpo pork" is an instance of food becoming known to posterity through a man. If we hear this expression in a rush, it seems as though it is not the flesh of a pig at all, but rather the very flesh of Su Dongpo. Alas, what offense did Dongpo commit that we would cut his flesh to fill the bellies of the gluttons of the ages? There are so many things that a literary man cannot do, and celebrities who dabble in lesser skills must be especially cautious. Several hundred years later, things like cake and cloth were named after [Chen] Meigong. If we compare "Meigong cake" and "Meigong cloth" to "Dongpo pork," the former seems superior, but least fortunate of all is that that thing in the outhouse has come to be known popularly as a "Meigong toilet." Alas, what kind of thing is a toilet that it should be crowned with the name of a distinguished man?
>
> It's not that I don't know the flavor of meat, but I dare not speak freely on the matter of pork for worry that I might end up following after Dongpo.²⁴

Reflecting on how names (*ming* 名) get attached to things, Li Yu mentions his celebrity predecessors as a cautionary tale: he too, he asserts, could invent all the things that they did, but he does not wish to cheapen his literary name. Chen Jiru had grown famous in the late Ming primarily through his witty *xiaopin* essays, which offered readers memorable aphorisms from the perspective of a carefree and reclusive aesthete. His celebrity had also led to widespread forgery through spurious works and unauthorized editions.²⁵ Shen Defu 沈德符 (1578–1642), a contemporary observer, mentioned that Chen also designed patterned textiles, pastries, a folding chair, and a urinal, attaching his name to them to boost sales.²⁶ The writings of Qian Qianyi 錢謙益 (1582–1664), moreover, reveal that even wine and tea shops displayed Chen's portrait.²⁷ Unlike Chen, Li Yu explicitly linked his words to designs that readers could follow to produce his inventions, aiming to have his name attached to some things and not others. Even as he created a brand name and transmitted it throughout the land by means of novel stories and designs, he sought to retain some control over its associations. By gesturing toward the verbal quality of his branding practice, he reminds us that his interventions hover between literary representation and material reality.

The valorization of nonconformity that allowed both men to thrive was couched in the celebration of the individual and the discourse of the strange (*qi* 奇) in the late Ming, trends that developed out of Li Zhi's iconoclasm.[28] Late Ming cultural figures sought to distinguish themselves by outperforming one another according to the discourse of *qi*, which might denote an unusual work of art or a delightfully original story. In inventing a range of unconventional personae for himself, Li Yu was likely inspired by Chen's idiosyncratic persona, but his creative energy was not focused on cultivating or manifesting an authentic self. Instead, he focused on the media through which constructed things (including a constructed self) might be transmitted (*chuan*) to others, and on their precise relationship to the name (*ming*) of their creator. This focus is exquisitely dramatized in Li Yu's *chuanqi* play *A Much-Desired Match*,[29] which centers on the nature of fame and of the work of art, and questions the values of cultural production and reproduction. When he wrote this play, Li Yu was quickly becoming a cultural figure in his own right, and it can be productively read as a dramatization of the stress that came with successful cultural production in the fast-paced urban centers of his time.

A Much-Desired Match is a romantic comedy that depicts four well-known late-Ming figures: Chen Jiru and the famous painter and politician Dong Qichang, and two women painters, Lin Tiansu 林天素 (late Ming) and Yang Yunyou 楊雲友 (d. 1627).[30] The two men, complaining about increasing demands for their work from patrons, decide to find artists who will serve as ghostpainters. By the play's end, the painters have embraced falsehood in advertising: Dong and Chen each end up marrying a woman who forges their paintings for a living, thereby doubling the production capacity of their brands.[31] A "substitute brush" (*daibi* 代筆)—that is, ghostpainting—is at the center of this love story: at the play's end, Dong Qichang rejoices that he will no longer have to produce his own paintings:

DONG QICHANG [*sings*]:
  To the tune of "Liu yao ling"
  Now that I have someone to hold a sword at the head of the dais
    [*chuangtou zhuodao* 床頭捉刀],

It would be a fruitless endeavor to try to produce any more authentic "Orchid Pavilions."
Beginning today, I will no longer hold my own brush;
I'll hand them all over to this lady champion.³²

The expression Dong uses, "hold a sword at the head of the dais," is a reference to an anecdote in *A New Account of Tales of the World* (*Shishuo xinyu* 世說新語), in which the warlord Cao Cao 曹操 (155–220), concerned that he did not look imposing enough, had someone stand in his place to receive a Xiongnu envoy. The envoy, however, saw through the ploy and reported that the true hero was the man "holding the sword at the head of the dais."³³ While the expression *zhuodao ren* names the fake—Cao Cao is just pretending to be an attendant—in later usage the term comes to stand in for Cao Cao himself. In the midst of this scene titled "Encounter with the Real One" (Huizhen 會真), Dong even celebrates the idea that there will never be another authentic (*zhenben* 真本) "Dong Qichang" painting produced, borrowing the term "Orchid Pavilion," a frequently copied work attributed to the famed calligrapher Wang Xizhi.

The play's second scene is titled "Fleeing Fame" (Mingbu 名逋), which can be interpreted literally as "fleeing one's name," and it opens with Dong and Chen planning to spend the day in disguise at Hangzhou's West Lake. For our purposes, it could even be read as "fleeing one's brand," and it is a notion that recurs frequently in the play, as *mingbu* and as its synonym *taoming* 逃名. I propose that Li Yu's play literalizes the notion of fame in order to reveal its workings as a mechanism for cultural production. Over the course of the Ming dynasty the notion of a recluse became ever more closely bound up with the new category of the professional writer and other market-oriented cultural producers, especially that of the *shanren* 山人 (mountain man).³⁴ "Fleeing fame" was primarily associated with reclusion, and with an unwillingness to serve the state in an official capacity. Whereas "mountain man" had initially indicated someone who fled from government service by retreating to the mountains, by this point it had come to indicate someone who was capitalizing on the cachet of the recluse: not escaping fame but cultivating it. It is this shifting cultural moment—of making a name by "fleeing" from it—that Li Yu dramatizes.

The play depicts the verticality of fame—*gaoming* 高名, literally "towering name"—as connecting famous men like Dong and Chen in Hangzhou with friends and patrons all over the country. The constant knocks at their door come not from neighbors, but from runners from the distant capital seeking painting and calligraphy. These runners embody the collapse of horizontal space, and the resulting impossibility of escape: "One word from a literary man is worth a thousand gold, with a letter, the runner connects ten thousand *li*."[35] The artists grumble that the connected empire leaves them endlessly tangled up in social exchanges: "Who under Heaven *doesn't* know me?" (42). Hangzhou cannot serve as a retreat for Dong and Chen, not only because of their outsized fame but also because Hangzhou's West Lake is a bustling marketplace. As Chen Jiru laments: "I only regret that the root of fame cannot be fully eradicated, and instead has turned this mountain retreat into a marketplace" (36).

Li Yu's painters seek to flee this new kind of urban fame, which proves more difficult than avoiding government service. Dong Qichang ponders why he is able to refuse a summons from the imperial court but cannot manage to extricate himself from the constant demands of "written social intercourse" (39), calling himself a "servant of the written word" (*ziyong* 字傭) (33). He complains in specific terms about the media that burden him: in once instance, "painting scrolls" (*huajuan* 畫卷) and "poetry tubes" (*shitong* 詩筒) (33), and elsewhere, poetry, prose, calligraphy, and paintings (35). Chen comments that poetry and words are easy enough to dash off, but painting is much more difficult, and he wishes he had never studied it (40).

In singling out painting as the most challenging, Chen uses the expression "completed while leaning against a horse" (*yima er cheng* 倚馬而成) (40). This phrase comes from an anecdote about the scholar Yuan Hong 袁宏 (328–376) who allegedly demonstrated his literary prowess by composing a seven-page victory proclamation (*lubu wen* 露布文) "in one dash," while leaning against a horse.[36] The expression later came to indicate literary talent, but Li Yu uses it here to point to the interiority of literary composition, which is readily adaptable to even the strangest of circumstances. Although painters were frequently described as containing "hills and valleys in their hearts" (see chapter 4), painting entailed distinct demands: the availability of polychrome ink; a complex spatial distribution of elements (as opposed to the regular grid used for writing); and waiting for various brushstrokes to dry. A work of *wen* could be written down, printed, or reproduced by anyone, while still retaining the distinction of the original writer, whereas a painting can only be copied by someone whose skills match those of the original painter.

We can contrast Li Yu's dramatization of ghostpainting in *A Much-Desired Match* with the depiction of forgery in Wu Bing's 吳炳 (1595–1648) late-Ming *chuanqi* play *The Green Peony* (*Lü mudan* 綠牡丹). *The Green Peony* centers on the scholar Shen Zhong's literary competition to find a husband for his daughter, and much of the action stems from characters' attempts to pass off poetry composed by others as their own.[37] As characters deliberate over the authorship and authenticity of the poems, the truth is methodically revealed, and honest Gu Wenyu, who came in third, eventually wins. Gu connects the attempts to pass off the poetry of others as one's own with theatrical performance: "Fine lines require deliberation. Dare 'he who holds the sword' deny his name is Cao? Hard to pull off a performance in actor's garb."[38] The difficulty of connecting poems to poets in the midst of so many forgeries is encapsulated in the image of the green peony, which requires extra attention to distinguish its leaves from its petals. In striking contrast to this play, Li Yu's depiction of ghostpainting positions forgery as a solution rather than a problem.[39]

In another of Li Yu's plays, *As Heaven Would Have It* (*Naihe tian* 奈何天), he likewise connects physical imposture with writing under someone else's name. Toward the beginning of the play, a talented woman about to be married off to a disgusting man remarks: "Daddy, all of the verse and prose in your correspondence has been written on your behalf by your child. From today forward, you'll no longer have anyone to 'hold the sword' for you, you'll have to come up with them yourself."[40] She has been writing in her father's name for some time, in a manner reminiscent—in both practical and gendered terms—of the desired outcome of *A Much-Desired Match*. In that play Dong asks: "What if we each sought a "sword-wielder" to keep by our side? All that correspondence we aren't able to finish, we could ask them to write on our behalf. Now *that's* a long-term plan."[41] This shift from forgery as a dramatized problem to ghostpainting as a romantic solution allows for multiple skilled producers to work under a single brand name, simultaneously acknowledging the demands of less discerning recipients and the real skill of less famous artists. This broadening of possibilities also suggests connections to Li Yu's theory of literature, with each writer capable of producing works in different styles to fulfill different aims. No longer does a writer need to be limited to a single, authentic poetic voice, just as a painter need not be constrained to a single set of hands.

At the same time, this shift has also been facilitated by an inversion of values. For an artist like Dong Qichang, it would generally be assumed that his ghostpainters would be his inferiors, in artistic conception if not also in execution. In the original anecdote, however, there is no text to be forged. Instead, the site of imposture is simply the body, as Cao Cao stands to the side, while another man stands "in his place." Significantly, Cao Cao's disguise fails, and he is recognized as *himself in disguise*. *Zhuodao ren* thus came to refer specifically to Cao Cao without naming him. Furthermore, in the original instance, recognizing the disguise comes with no reward: Cao Cao has the envoy who saw through his disguise put to death.

But when this expression is taken up again in the late Ming and begins to be used to indicate imposture, there is slippage between a person's physical body and their writing. In the examples above, *zhuodao ren* can apply to a man in disguise or to an actor on stage, although the real topic of conversation is someone *writing* as another, rather than physically passing as another (which comes up only in a description of a bride assessing a prospective groom in *As Heaven Would Have It*). In *The Green Peony*, as in many cases of faked identity, one can still determine whether a person is who they claim to be, or whether they actually wrote what they claim to have written.[42] Writing seems to be conceived as a more adequate conveyor of truth than facial features, though physiognomy is still a telling sign. The literary tests that are carried out onstage in *chuanqi* plays like *The Green Peony* and Li Yu's *Mistake with a Kite* (*Fengzheng wu* 風箏誤) only work because the differences between people are exaggerated and the task is almost always one of distinguishing a barely literate person from one steeped in the classical tradition.

A Much-Desired Match differs from these plays in reversing the terms of the disguise. Rather than a rich but unskilled patron seeking credit for brilliant verses not his own, or a dimwitted man passing off a borrowed poem, in this play the true talent is located in the person behind the scenes, or, in the expression about Cao Cao, the man behind the face. In *A Much-Desired Match*, finally, there is no discrepancy in skill level between the famous artists and the women they marry: the use of *zhuodao ren* in this context puts the women in the position of Cao Cao, whose true features could not be concealed, and demotes the artists to the role of mere façade. In the play, paintings are commodities, for sale to undiscerning buyers. The men describe their art under such demands in clunky terms, likening their fingers to mallets (*chui* 槌) and their brushes to wooden beams (*chuan* 椽), whereas the women are depicted drawing on their abilities to produce excellent works of art (39). Thus, one way of reading this play would be to see the women as the true talents, the "substance" (*shi*) to the men's "names" (*ming*).

In *A Much-Desired Match*, then, Li Yu updates an old historical allusion for the busy urban art market, focusing in particular on the medium of painting and its laborious reproduction. Li Yu famously commissioned *The Mustard Seed Garden Painting Manual* (1679), named after his Nanjing garden residence. In his introduction to that text, Li Yu claimed to have little skill in painting.[43] Given his depiction of painting's cumbersome production process in *A Much-Desired Match*, that claim may have as much to do with his assessment of the scalability of that art form as with his skill. Although Li Yu commissioned an artist to produce the models included in the woodblock-printed manual, he nevertheless put his own brand name in the title (and featured "Mr. Li Liweng" across the top of the title page). Today, *The Mustard Seed Garden Painting Manual* is still widely known; Wang Gai, and the other artists who designed it, are arguably not. I propose that we can read this manual as one instance in which Li Yu interpellated his readers as his own ghostpainters, casting them in a reimagined and rebranded version of the model dramatized in *A Much-Desired Match*. The printed examples in the painting manual include representative works and styles of dozens of historical painters, and the impressive range showcases Wang Gai's curatorial and instructional skill. But Li Yu controls the brand: the entire process of a reader learning from those paintings remains a "Mustard Seed Garden" experience, and thereby associated with Li Yu's powerful name.[44]

TECHNOLOGICALLY REPRODUCIBLE AND SINGULAR: A LI YU FAN PAINTING

Doubling was depicted as a romantic and a practical solution to the problem of demand in *A Much-Desired Match*, but it was not a sufficient scale for Li Yu. At the heart of Li Yu's cultural production was woodblock printing, whose rapid reproducibility far outpaced that of painting. But he also reconceptualized print, making easily reproducible books work in new ways. The popular late-Ming genre of connoisseurship manuals had commodified knowledge about the proper consumption of luxury goods.⁴⁵ *Leisure Notes* does this too, offering new valuations of old luxury goods like paintings, bronzes, and tea, but it is also full of reproducible designs that commodify everyday life. One such product, developed at the intersection of innovation and technological reproducibility, is the "Li Yu fan painting."

In this Li Yu innovation, readers make the painting themselves by following the instructions in their purchased copy of *Leisure Notes*. Li Yu explains how to create a window shaped like a fan in the wall of a boat, completely sealing off every other opening, so that light can only enter through the fan-shaped window opening:

> It would be solid on four sides, and only the middle area would be left open [*xu*] and made into the shape of a folding fan. The solid [*shi*] sides would be constructed of wooden boards and covered with putty so that not a ray of light could shine through. The open part would be fitted with a wooden frame, curved on the top and bottom and straight on the two sides: this is why it is called a "folding fan" [*bianmian* 便面]. It should be left completely empty [*kongming* 空明], with absolutely no obstruction of any kind. The two sides of this boat should feature only two folding fans; beyond these folding fans, there should be no other objects. When you sit between them, everything on the two shores—the glint of the lake and mountain hues, the temples and pagodas, misty clouds, bamboo, and trees, as well as the woodcutters and shepherd boys traveling to and fro, old tipplers and sightseeing girls, men and their horses, too—will enter the folding fan and make a natural painting for you.⁴⁶

With these instructions, he markets unique "Li Yu fan paintings" for each reader that could be distributed without extra effort or individualized attention on his part: that is, a technologically reproducible painting that nevertheless retains something of the uniqueness of a painting produced on commission. In this passage, Li Yu obviously elicits labor and materials from his readers. Yet even as he interpellated them as producers, he also construed his readers as consumers of the world, teaching them to view the world differently, so that they might find and create paintings through their own perception. Although readers are encouraged to construct their own "Li Yu fan painting," their primary task is to learn how to *see* such paintings, placing leisurely consumption, rather than inspired composition, at the forefront of this design.

Li Yu thus managed to reproduce his fan paintings through a configuration of printed words. In designing these "natural paintings" (*tianran hua* 天然畫), he ultimately harnesses Heaven to wield the brush, updating the scene as the boat drifts along. Li Yu is not the first to speak of such "borrowed scenes"—there are numerous examples of poetry written about capturing distant scenes through garden windows—but he does so in a way that seems particularly prescient of our now familiar, and then unknown, technology of cinematography, with its use of a darkened chamber to frame and capture images.

In keeping with his focus on consumption, Li Yu creates a second viewing opportunity with the same design. "This window will not only entertain you," he writes, "but it will also entertain others; not only does it absorb [*sheru* 攝入] the entire exterior scene onto the boat, but it can also project [*shechu* 射出] all of the people on the boat, along with the tables, mats, cups, and plates, outside the window for the enjoyment of passersby."⁴⁷ Li Yu's dynamic prose charges the flattened space framed by the window. The term "project" (*shechu*), for instance, conjures a way to envision the party on the boat being sucked through the window. And his articulation of the window "absorbing" (*sheru*) the exterior scene anticipates—by two hundred years—the modern Chinese word "absorb-shadow" (*sheying* 攝影), which now denotes both "to photograph" and "to film." Yet Li Yu's window is more than an early modern preview of future technological innovations. Whereas photography and film present the viewer with a single framed image from a fixed point of view, Li Yu's window causes two images to be projected simultaneously onto both sides of a frame. Those on the boat enjoy a scenic landscape painting, while those on shore savor a fan painting of a lively party, each viewer becoming simultaneously the object of another's view. In such a two-way painting, no brush is required—Li Yu's readers need simply to go about their lives, framing and capturing them for the pleasurable consumption of others.

This proposal, with its emphasis on intersubjectivity, renders the fan painting theatrical, and surely Li Yu is drawing on his experience as a director here. Moreover, this design evokes the "fan with a painting on one side and calligraphy on the other" (38) that was requested of Dong Qichang in *A Much-Desired Match*. In that discussion, not only was painting singled out as the most laborious of creative arts, but the folding fan was mentioned as the most burdensome canvas because it required the decoration of both sides. With this two-sided, constantly changing version of a fan painting, Li Yu solves both the problem of originality and the problem of labor: he provides the design, disseminated through the convenient technology of woodblock printing, and his readers borrow a scene, conveniently available in nature itself. This "folding fan painting" is a good example of the "remodeling" (*gaizao* 改造) that I theorize throughout this book as it appears across Li Yu's work in different media. As an architectural term, *gaizao* could describe quite literally the opening of a window in the wall of a building or a boat, and that sort of remodeling is precisely what Li Yu is proposing. Rather than leave a window design as a window design, however, Li Yu uses writing to introduce another medium into the remodeling process, in this case that of painting. He thus remodels the very idea of painting by mixing it with building design, in a move that shifts focus to the medium of painting itself.

Having revealed his "folding fan painting" to be a window shaped like a folding fan, Li Yu makes a strategic request of his reader-makers: "I only hope that when you break out in song in the midst of your enjoyment, you will shout out 'Liweng' a few times, so that my dreaming spirit may join you: that way people will be happy, and I can share their happiness with them."[48] There are several occasions in *Leisure Notes* when Li Yu asks readers to think of him or shout his name, slipping his brand name into their everyday lives. I argue that his mobilization of a brand name in this manner is unprecedented: he uses it to claim technical designs that have yet to be realized (and many of which he never built for himself). In the process he develops a practice of cultural entrepreneurship appropriate to the early Qing, using only the technologies of his time. Once combined with each reader's own tools, labor, and time, this single essay produces any number of "Li Yu fan paintings" (windows), each one distinctive and original.

This design, which appears in a *Leisure Notes* essay titled "Capturing Scenes Is in the Borrowing" (Qujing zai jie 取景在借), is particularly emblematic of Li Yu's approach. The essay is accompanied by a two-page woodblock illustration—the only two-page illustration in the book.[49] That illustration itself is not labeled, but it resembles one of the ten quintessential scenes of Hangzhou's West Lake, "Autumn Moon on a Calm Lake" (Pinghu qiuyue 平湖秋月), picturing the Bai embankment and Solitary Hill. The woodblock illustration of the fan window in *Leisure Notes* (figure 1.1) and the West Lake scene print of "Autumn Moon on a Calm Lake" (figure 1.2) that appears in *Convenient Guide to the Lake and Hills* (*Hushan bianlan*) both include the moon-viewing platform and the causeway with a bridge leading to the island. West Lake was frequently depicted in paintings and albums, and this proliferation meant that readers likely knew how they were expected to appreciate such an illustration.[50] And yet the print shown in figure 1.1, spread across two half-folios in *Leisure Notes*, does not provide a close-up of a particular scene. Instead, it shows the fan-shaped lens through which readers will take in countless scenes, and it leaves space on the page for the pictured boat to float along. At the bottom of the right-hand page (slightly left of center), the fan-shaped window is clearly visible and displays three human figures. It is fitting that the only folding-fan-shaped scene actually pictured in the illustration is the scene aboard the boat, because this scene would be more consistent over the course of the trip than the scrolling frames of landscape scenes.

The novelty of this illustration of a Li Yu fan painting becomes even more apparent when compared with the illustration of a Dong Qichang painting in *A Much-Desired Match* (figure 1.3). In the fan window illustration, the men who intend to admire the scenery have themselves become a painting, miniaturized and clearly framed, whereas in the play illustration, the painters are depicted viewing a painting that is not looking back at them. When we view the illustration of the two-way fan

FIGURE 1.1 Illustration of the "fan-shaped window" in *Leisure Notes*. (Li Yu. *Xianqing ouji*. Yishengtang edition, 1671, 8:22b–23a.) Harvard-Yenching Library.

FIGURE 1.1 (continued)

FIGURE 1.2 Woodblock print of the scene "Autumn Moon on a Calm Lake" (Pinghu qiuyue 平湖秋月), in the eighteenth-century *Convenient Guide to the Lake and Hills* from Zhejiang Province (Zhai Hao et al. *Hushan bianlan.* Ed. Wang Weihan. 3 vols. Taipei: Chengwen Publishing Co., Ltd., 1983, 1:84.) Reproduced with permission of Chengwen Publishing Co., Ltd.

FIGURE 1.3 Illustration to scene 5 of *A Much-Desired Match*, depicting the inspection of a painting in the marketplace. (Li Yu. *Yizhong yuan*. Yishengtang edition, Kangxi period.) Zhou Xinhui, comp., *Zhongguo gudai xiqu banhua ji*. Beijing: Xueyuan chubanshe, 2000, 618.

window, we must first see ourselves as viewers of the illustrated boat, our view framed by the tiny window, and then we must put ourselves in the place of the boaters (*sheshen chudi* 設身處地) so as to look out at the scenes framed by the fan window. When we look at the play illustration, in contrast, we may remark on their connoisseurship, and even consider what it means to look at them looking at a painting, but we remain at a fixed point outside the depicted viewing. Had Li Yu illustrated his fan window design in the shape of a folding fan, as would be done later in *The Mustard Seed Garden Painting Manual* (figure 1.4), he would have enabled the tradition of virtual travel through paintings (*woyou* 臥遊), but there would be

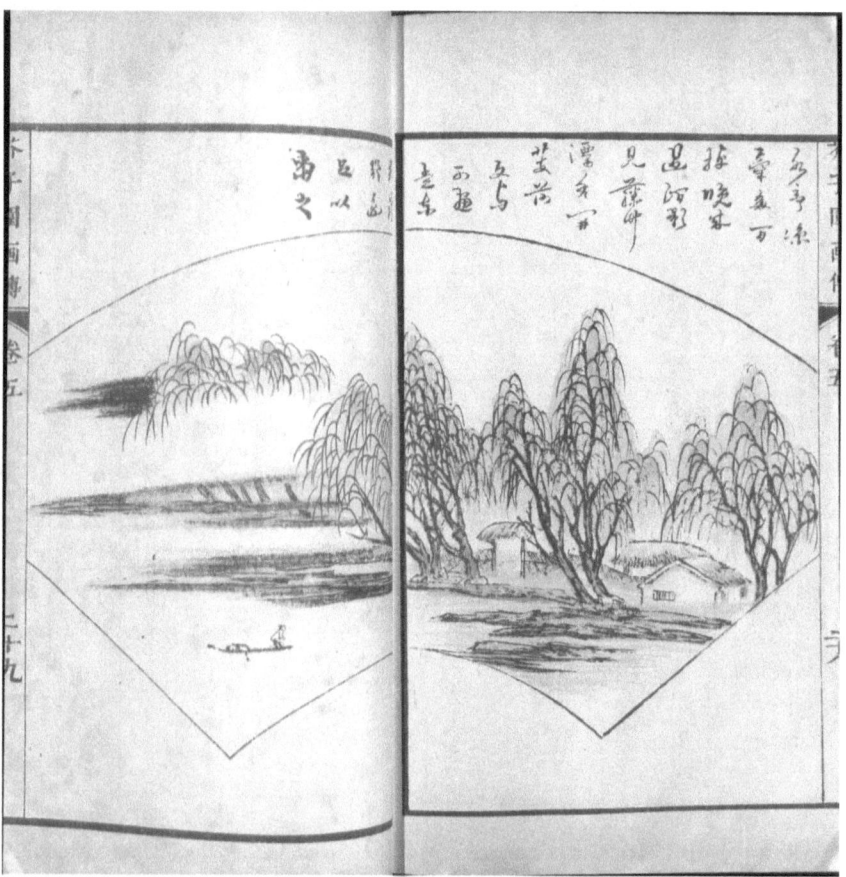

FIGURE 1.4 Illustration of fan painting from *The Mustard Seed Garden Painting Manual*. (Wang Gai. *Jieziyuan huazhuan*. 5 vols. [1679], 5:28b–29a.) University of Wisconsin, Madison, Memorial Library Special Collections.

no impetus to reverse the view, and the status of the two worlds—one real and the other painted—would remain unquestioned.[51] By placing the design within a larger scene, Li Yu's woodblock illustration instead draws viewers into the scene, and then shuttles them from one view to another.[52]

Li Yu's fan painting was just one of dozens of such designs in *Leisure Notes*. For each design, he offers a "method" (*fa*), carefully enumerating the steps required to create it. Again and again, from the meticulously designed "Liweng Incense Chop" (No more lumpy mounds of ash!) to his comprehensive guide to composing *chuanqi* (First come up with one good idea!), Li Yu borrowed readers' labor to redesign the stuff of their everyday lives: objects like chairs and drawers and even mundane activities like sweeping or walking could be "stamped" with his brand name. This combination of innovation and technological reproducibility deployed print for a new purpose. *Leisure Notes* offers a personalized, tailored, and interactive experience, requiring readers to provide their own resources to make (and perform in) their own "Li Yu originals." To use the metaphor for ghostwriting and ghostpainting that I discussed earlier, they must learn to "hold the sword" on Li Yu's behalf.

By borrowing his readers' labor, Li Yu turns his attention to the media of which such innovations are made as much as the innovation itself. For instance, with the fan window, Li Yu is emptying out the medium of painting: "only the middle area would be left open" (*du xu qi zhong* 獨虛其中). There is no trace of painting's expressive potential, nor any critical appreciation of brushwork or color. What remains of painting are its functions: as an aesthetic experience of looking and as a commodity that connects people. The influence of the theater medium is also felt in this two-directional looking, which places people in a landscape and values a work of art that is necessarily temporary. In keeping with his interest in reproducibility, Li Yu sought a new intermedial position—between writing, image, and woodblock-printed book—from which more people could access more images, all stamped with his name.

MASTER COPY

Now that Li Yu had figured out how to make his branded designs easily reproducible through woodblock print, he still needed to offer his readers a sense of a unique final product. To make a living from these designs, he had to claim the rights to each copy of his works. In the early Qing, profits on published works normally went to publishers, who might buy particular works from authors, but it was also easy for another publisher to carve new blocks on the basis of a popular existing book. Li Yu was the only person in this period who made a living by publishing only his own writing and editing. Other publishers who printed for profit relied at least in part on printing new editions of popular works, such as famous Ming novels or Confucian classics, while other writers of original works were mostly successful officials who sponsored their publication, whether or not it would be profitable. As we saw earlier, works of art were widely forged during this period, and Li Yu seems to have made a case for the value of a forgery good enough to deceive—a sign, he seemed to suggest, of unappreciated talent. With woodblock-printed works like his, however, he developed a different approach to attribution and remuneration, writing at length about his exclusive rights to sell copies of his works.

He ensured his profits, in part, by creating a network of his books, including notes about works in progress in each completed publication. Such notes served as advertisements; he would include a note in the table of contents of a short story collection, for example, to announce that a particular story would soon be adapted as a full-length *chuanqi* play. While scholars have argued that the well-written stories Li Yu adapted into *chuanqi* plays should not simply be read as sketches for future plays, his enthusiastic promotion of these stories' dramatic adaptations likely informed his readers' approach.[53] Opening the story collection to find an advertisement for a future theatrical version, readers may well have appreciated the story as a preview of the play to come. Li Yu placed his publications in anticipatory relations to one another through other marketing strategies as well: for instance, on the title page of some copies of the first edition of *Leisure Notes*, where he called it "Liweng's First Secret Book," he included a note on the line below, in smaller characters, that read: "The Second, *Independent Words*, To Be Released Soon."[54]

By explicitly linking his works within their published texts, Li Yu ensured that he would receive credit, if not profits, for his publications; publishers were pirating his works, despite his efforts, as early as the mid-1650s.[55] In a letter to a friend published in *Independent Words*, Li Yu wrote:

The only reason I moved to Nanjing was because people had been making trouble with my books, and there were numerous pirated editions [*fanban* 翻板]; I therefore violated the warning against uprooting a settled life to move again, thinking that a change of residence would allow me to obtain sustenance. I did not fathom that as soon as my new prints were out, the avaricious merchants of Suzhou would already be sprouting covetous intentions. Fortunately, I heard news [of their plans] first, and pled earnestly with Mr. Sun, an official of the Suzhou-Songjiang circuit, to put up a prohibitionary notice, putting a stop to their plans. Just as the Suzhou scheme was put down, a message suddenly arrived at the house saying that someone in Hangzhou had already completed a pirated edition and the new book would be on the market in a matter of days. . . . Alas! How much is that minuscule profit worth that these people will scramble after it like so many ducks?[56]

In this competitive and fast-paced publishing milieu, authors and publishers working for profit had to actively trace and prevent piracy, articulating what we now call intellectual property rights in the process. The fact that publishers in Nanjing and other cities throughout the southern Yangzi region were persistently pirating Li Yu's works gives us an idea of the popularity of his writing at the time. Notably, if other publishers were so eager to produce pirated versions of Li Yu's works, we might not be able to take Li Yu at his word that the profit to be gained from such an endeavor was indeed "minuscule." Although later in his life Li Yu was frequently on the road searching for patronage, during this period he seems to have survived mainly from his book sales.

As Li Yu sought to control what he claimed as his intellectual property, he not only moved to Nanjing but also began to supervise the carving of blocks and the printing of editions, as well as the marketing, sale, and distribution of his works. He explicitly discussed his conception of creative ownership in an essay about the notepaper he designed and sold out of his Mustard Seed Garden in Nanjing.[57] What is distinctive about Li Yu's notepaper, and what he owns, according to him, are his innovative writing-themed designs: "I already instructed my servants to make the notepaper according to my designs and sell it in the bookshop. Whatever money they acquire from sales, they turn over to the woodblock carvers to be used for the carving of blocks. In this way, from now on, this process will flourish continually. Its ability to give people something new to see and hear, and bring joy to the task of writing is truly without end."⁵⁸

In explicating for his readers the production and distribution process for his notepaper, including his servants' role as the producers and salespeople, Li Yu highlights his own unique role in production. Much as the painters in *A Much-Desired Match* claimed the paintings made by others in their style—and the fan window constructed by the reader of *Leisure Notes* remained a Li Yu fan window—Li Yu claims intellectual property rights over the notepaper based solely on his design, not on his labors for its production. Unlike those designs, however, his notepaper is reproducible by means of woodblock printing. As such, he implores readers to purchase these authorized copies rather than, as in other cases, to use his design idea to produce their own version. He explains the advantage of buying an authentic Li Yu notepaper rather than a knockoff:

> I have taken great pains to get this business underway, and it is difficult to enumerate the hardships involved. All of those sagely men who wish to obtain this writing paper may send someone to Nanjing to purchase it. I have been unable to carry out most of the many novel designs in this collection [*Leisure Notes*] in the world, so I use this one thing to convey the general idea. The place where the writing paper is sold is the same place that sells my books; everything I have ever written is assembled here. Those with peculiar penchants can purchase them here and take them with them; this is no different from taking Liweng back with them. Spiritual friendship [*shenjiao* 神交] over great distances depends entirely on this. At present, I can claim close friends throughout the land, why limit myself to those I meet face-to-face?
>
> > Inside the Cheng'en Temple in Nanjing, there is a sign with five words that read: "Mustard Seed Garden Famed Notepaper"— that is the place.⁵⁹

Li Yu's marketing strategy as expressed in this passage requires both the singular aura of a particular place—his bookshop in the Mustard Seed

Garden, inside the Cheng'en Temple in Nanjing—and the transportable spirit of his widely reproduced cultural products. The virtual connection that his products offer upon purchase—designated in this passage as *shenjiao*—is framed in the language that Li Yu and others used to describe print as a technology for building social networks. At the time of writing, Li Yu had spent the better part of a decade traveling the country in search of financial support, so it is understandable that he would have been invested in convincing his readers that his products could overcome the distance between them without requiring any travel at all. At the same time, the exigencies of piracy required him to demand that they travel to his particular shop for their purchases.

Li Yu does not argue for his rights to his cultural products based on the inherent value of their authenticity, as one might with a forged painting. Instead, he argues fervently against the unauthorized reproduction of his books and notepaper precisely because the pirated editions may be just as good. As the concluding section of his essay declares:

> Permission is granted to copy all the new styles in this book except the notepaper designs, which I get my servants to manufacture and sell as an alternative to making a living by my pen. These may not be reprinted [*fanzi* 翻梓], and I have already given public notice, warning people at the outset. If any bold fellows try to seize the market by reprinting the designs as they are, or else adding or subtracting a little here and there, or slightly altering their form, thus arrogating other people's achievements to themselves, grabbing others' profits while suppressing their names, they will be judged as contemptible as the Wolf of Zhongshan.[60] I shall accuse them in the courts wherever they are and plead that justice be done. As for those who reprint [*fanke* 翻刻] Hushang Liweng's books in the belief that their wealth and power will protect them, I don't know how many there are in the world, but they are living off my labor, and that is a situation I cannot tolerate. I swear that I will fight them to death, and hereby give notice to the authorities that this book marks a new policy on my part. In brief, Heaven and Earth endowed every person with a mind and it is up to each one of us to develop our own intelligence. I have done nothing to stultify their minds or prevent them from developing their intelligence and ingenuity. What

right do they have to take away my livelihood and prevent me from living off my own labor?[61]

Rather than encouraging the cultivation of an intimate and specialized knowledge, or a connoisseurship that distinguishes the real from the fake, Li Yu's printed books and his notepaper are portrayed here as reproducible cultural products, and even as templates that invite copying. The terms he uses here, *fanzi* ("to reproduce woodblocks") and *fanke* ("to reproduce carving"), refer to the carving of new woodblocks based on an existing woodblock-printed text. He thus argues that the labor of carving and printing of the paper are of secondary importance to his novel conception for the designs. His refusal to let any variation on his design be reproduced indicates a claim over a concept more than a product—a position that before modern copyright law was nearly impossible to enforce. Li Yu's vociferousness regarding his rights to his designs and written works draws on the literati practice of using language to claim moral and spiritual ownership of land—both in the absence of, and as superior to, financial ownership. He expanded upon this notion, using his style and writing to claim rights over every copy of his books and woodblock-printed notepaper. Because Li Yu depended directly on the profits from his cultural production to survive, he found a way to inscribe economic value within this literary conception of ownership: people should pay for his book to obtain the right to build their own "Li Yu fan painting."

TECHNOLOGY AND THE EDITED COLLECTION

Beginning in the 1660s, Li Yu undertook a series of collaborative projects that further expanded his use of print as a profitable and connective technology. He produced collections in several genres: his first was a collection of contemporary informal letters titled *A First Solicitation of Letters* (*Chidu chuzheng* 尺牘初徵, 1660, hereafter *Letters*; and possibly a second collection, *erzheng* 二徵, 1668?), followed by two collections of administrative documents (*A New Aid to Administration*, 1663; *Second Collection*, 1667) and *A First Solicitation of Parallel Prose* (*Siliu chuzheng* 四六初徵, 1671).[62] For each collection, Li Yu sought out contributions by posting notices, often in other publications. This shift to collections meant a sharp increase in the number of people associated with a given text. Li Yu's early plays and stories would feature a preface writer and a commentator or two. His collections, in contrast—featuring dozens of contributors who represented a broad spectrum of society from educated women to reclusive loyalist poets, and from prominent Qing officials to seal carvers—can be understood not only as experiments with print as a social networking technology but also with the book form as a medium for information storage and retrieval.

The importance of these works to Li Yu's publishing business can be discerned from a recently rediscovered book list he included in a letter to a potential buyer in Beijing (for more on the book list, see the appendix).[63] The two installments of *A New Aid to Administration* are listed first, followed by *A First Solicitation of Parallel Prose* and *Letters*. Next comes *Leisure Notes* and Li Yu's collected writings, followed by works on history and a dictionary. His plays and story collections are placed last. Since the list is not arranged in order of size, price, or chronology, I propose that Li Yu listed his edited collections first because of their perceived broad appeal, thinking they would convince potential buyers to read further. We can't be sure if the books listed first actually sold better, but we can extrapolate, perhaps, from the experience of his contemporary Zhou Lianggong 周亮工 (1612–1672), a Qing official and patron of artists, who noted that his own letter collections sold remarkably well.[64] I argue that the prominence of this genre can be attributed to the fact that they are highly networked books that offer social capital as well as insights from many leading cultural figures.

The gathering and publishing of contemporary writing gained exceptional currency during this transitional period, and collections proliferated as people rebuilt their disrupted lives.[65] Many early Qing collections offered loyalists a place to collectively mourn the loss of the Ming. Others provided more ambiguous spaces: the literatus-publisher Wang Qi, as Ellen Widmer has noted, professed loyalty to the Ming even as his profitable letter collections included contributions from Qing officials.[66] Li Yu's interest in the genre's social possibilities was also shared: Deng Hanyi's 鄧漢儀 three-volume *Poetry Survey* (*Shiguan* 詩觀), as Tobie Meyer-Fong has shown, aimed to forge new "transregional, and often explicitly transdynastic, social and literary communities" through its compilation of a diverse range of contributors.[67] Such printed collections were frequently the only place where men scattered across the new dynasty could encounter one another. Zhang Chao 張潮 (ca. 1650–1707) remarked in a letter from his own published compilation of friends' writings that "out of every ten friends" he was "only familiar with about half of their faces; the rest," he said, "fall into the category of 'spiritual friendship' [shenjiao]."[68] As we saw above, Li Yu, too, noted the necessity and utility of "spiritual communication" facilitated by print when face-to-face encounters were not possible. These comments show that edited collections in this period were broadly recognized as a way to transport people in spirit throughout the empire.[69]

As an entrepreneur looking to expand his cultural production beyond fiction and plays, moreover, Li Yu was the first to identify a latent demand for letter collections. Most edited collections at the time featured poetry, and Li Yu's *Letters* launched a new trend, inspiring several of his contemporaries to publish letter compilations of their own. In his editorial note at the beginning of *Letters*, he emphasizes the essential nature of the genre:

> Since the dynastic change, not only have splendid new collections of poetry and old-style prose come out in succession, but *chuanqi* and unofficial histories have also piled up on bookshelves and filled up carts. Yet there have been absolutely no new publications of letters. Spreading throughout the four directions are nothing but hackneyed words. Out of a hundred people, no more than one or two will author poetry, prose, *chuanqi*, or unofficial histories. Yet from the most esteemed Son of Heaven down to the lowliest commoner, not one can do without letters to communicate. No one can avoid writing letters: they are the essential stuff of writing.[70]

This editorial note showcases Li Yu's entrepreneurial thinking in action: surveying the book market, he notes that letters are absent. He goes on to build a case for their value, arguing that of all genres, they are the most ubiquitous in social life, including everyone from emperor to commoner. The term I have translated as "essential stuff" means literally "water and fire, beans and grain"—if any literary genre can be said to have real use value, Li Yu suggests, it would be letters. He aimed to promote letters as a universal genre, and he sought to reach a large readership through new textual designs that enabled a single publication to serve multiple audiences.

I suggest that Li Yu's letter collection operated as a social networking technology, not least because it mobilized certain unspoken advantages of the letter genre. The commonly collected genre of Li Yu's day, poetry, was often composed on a particular occasion in a social setting. Letters, however, are always written at a distance from the recipient. This distancing quality means that printed letters situate readers differently than poems do: whereas reading poems often carries a sense of displacement, or exclusion from the scene of their composition, letters are structured precisely around the absence of their addressee. I argue that by deploying this particular reader-relation of the published letter, Li Yu used the form of the letter collection to weave together writers from the Ming with his contemporaries in the early Qing, who could imagine themselves in the place of the recipient.

Li Yu's consistent emphasis on profit, practical value, and networking, combined with his decision to publish his own works rather than reissue reliably profitable texts, situates him between men like Zhou Lianggong, who sponsored their own publications and published whatever they wished, and men like Wang Qi, who regularly published new editions of already famous titles in addition to their own creative projects.[71] Li Yu's collection should thus be considered as analogous to collections from the 1660s to the 1680s—namely Zhou Lianggong's *Chidu xinchao* 尺牘新鈔 series (1662, 1667, and 1670), Wang Qi's *Chidu xinyu* 尺牘新語 (1671), and Huang Rong 黃容 and Wang Weihan's 王維翰 1681 collection, *Chidu lanyan* 尺牘蘭言—which were explicitly intended for scholars. Li Yu's *Letters* lacked nearly all remedial devices we see in letter-writing manuals, including arrangement by topic, use of generic rather than actual letters, and extensive annotation. Instead, *Letters* included mostly previously unpublished private correspondence of mostly contemporary figures, and it was well suited to a demand based primarily on an interest in the news these letters offered of the contemporary social world. That interest was shared, I argue, by his fellow publishers of collections for elite entertainment. In Huang and Wang's *Chidu lanyan*, for instance, they write: "*Cangju ji* 藏弆集 [Zhou Lianggong's second collection] and [*Chidu*] *xinchao* [Zhou Lianggong's first collection] were published in Nanjing, [*Chidu*] *chuzheng* [Li Yu's collection] and

[*Chidu*] *xinyu* [Wang Qi's collection] came out of Hangzhou, and all were snapped up with relish and became popular everywhere. Only Suzhou has failed to produce a printed collection of letters."[72] To the writer of this passage, Li Yu's collection was most valued as a collection of conversations about a particular place, and not as a model for writing letters. His collection included a significant number of letters from four members of a group of ten Hangzhou-based poets known as the "Hangzhou Ten" (Xiling shizi 西泠十子) who were influenced by Chen Zilong 陳子龍 (1608–1647): Lu Qi 陸圻 (1614–after 1688), Mao Xianshu 毛先舒 (1620–1688), Sun Zhi 孫治 (1618–1683), and Zhang Gangsun 張綱孫 (dates unknown). Published a couple of decades after Li Yu's letter collection, this note makes clear that the place of publication (and therefore place-specific content) was crucial to a collection's value.

The only element of *Letters* that resembles a manual is the index. Some contemporary scholars have argued that this index is the reason that no further installments of Li Yu's collection are extant, for they suggest that its function as a remedial tool likely put off educated readers. In Ellen Widmer's and David Pattinson's detailed studies of the letter collections that followed Li Yu's, both note that Li Yu's collection kick-started the trend in the 1660s for collections of contemporary letters, yet they depict his *Letters* as failing to satisfy customers with classical literacy by including remedial props.[73] In doing so, however, they miss a crucial component of Li Yu's design of this particular technology: to retain the collection's variety of readerships, the index is designed so that it can easily be discarded, removed, or ignored, leaving the reader with a very differently mediated experience of the collection depending on whether or not the index is consulted.

Li Yu's *Letters* was his attempt to reach the broadest possible audience with a single publication, and it was also his first experiment with soliciting manuscripts for a collection. In addition to predicting what kind of demand there would be for such texts, he used the project to connect himself with more people in more places. In other words, Li Yu experimented with using publishing as an interactive social technology. He solicited materials for his compilations from his extensive network of friends, as well as from influential cultural and political figures throughout the empire whom he had never met. *Letters* is divided into 12 volumes (*juan*) and contains 711 letters written by 178 named writers

(18 letters are anonymous). It opens with a preface by Wu Weiye 吳偉業 (1609–1672), a Ming *jinshi* (presented scholar) and acclaimed poet who held official positions in both the Ming and the Qing. Of the contributors whose dates are known, just under a third died in the Ming or during the transition, while slightly more than a third are younger than Li Yu (who was born in 1611). The collection includes literary figures, officials of both dynasties, and many writers who are otherwise unknown. Around forty of the contributors were Li Yu's close friends, but the majority are people with whom he has no other recorded social connection.

If you were a highly educated reader, you might start by thumbing through the standard tables of contents at the beginning of each volume where titles of letters, such as "Thanking a friend" (Xie you 謝友), would appear together with the name of the letter writer. You might immediately recognize many of the writers' names, such as Qian Qianyi, a poet and official who served in high positions in both the Ming and the Qing; the wild and witty poet and essayist, Ming *jinshi* Wang Siren 王思任 (1575–1646); and the Suzhou-based playwright and calligrapher, Ming *juren* (provincial graduate) Zhang Fengyi 張鳳翼 (1527–1613). You might note the founders of the Jingling 竟陵 school of poetry, Ming *jinshi* Zhong Xing 鍾惺 (1574–1625) and Ming *juren* Tan Yuanchun 譚元春 (1585–1637); Zhong Xing's name was frequently used to advertise books in the late Ming, including a letter-writing manual titled *Like Talking Face-to-Face* (*Ru miantan* 如面譚). You would also be pleased to find letters by the "Two Zhangs East of the River Lou" (*Loudong er Zhang* 婁東二張), Zhang Pu 張溥 (1602–1641) and Zhang Cai 張采 (1596–1648), both *jinshi*, who were the founders of the late-Ming political literary society known as the Revival Society (Fushe 復社); as well as by the influential Fushe member and poet, Ming *jinshi* Chen Zilong.[74]

Li Yu claims in the "editorial principles" (*fanli* 凡例) that unlike earlier collections arranged by subject, such as Shen Jiayin's 沈佳胤 (ca. 1630) *Sea of Letters* (*Han hai* 翰海), he has included letters in the order they were submitted. That policy, he notes, allows for such unusual phenomena as "commoners appearing before officials."[75] Perusing the table of contents, you might note that despite this ostensibly incidental ordering, there are some identifiable patterns, particularly in the first volume. That volume features primarily writers who had obtained the *jinshi* degree during the Ming dynasty, many of whom had died during the dynastic transition, and it includes some of the best known literary figures of the day, such as Wang Siren, Qian Qianyi, and Chen Zilong, as well as figures from earlier in the Ming like Jiang Yingke 江盈科 (1556–1605), who was associated with the Gong'an 公安 school of poetry.[76] Through a dense presentation of familiar names, the first volume knits together loyal officials of the Ming (who died by circumstance or by choice) with the generation of new officials populating the ranks of Qing officialdom (who appear in the volume's final third). In addition, you might meet some new friends: the first volume features letters written by famous men that were contributed by their recipients. Many of those less famous recipients, who were close friends of Li Yu, also contributed letters that were included less prominently in later volumes. This sequencing has the effect of staging a conversation that introduces these friends and justifies their presence in the collection: a *wenren* who picked up this collection to peruse at leisure would see familiar names addressing those who were less familiar and thereby assume that these "lesser" figures must also be worthy of reading.

In later volumes, too, you might identify some degree of order. It is sometimes possible to follow conversations among letters. Alternatively, letters by particular individuals are often grouped together, although a particular individual's letters also appear in multiple different volumes for no apparent reason. Letters are also occasionally grouped by social type, like women or Buddhist monks. Although women writers are not well represented in the collection, they are not relegated to the very end, as was usually the case in poetry collections. All twelve letters written by Li Yu appear at the end of the tenth volume. Finally, at the beginning of the twelfth volume, there is a note apologizing to his "refined and poetic readers" (*yaren yunke* 雅人韻客) for including letters in that volume that deal with correspondence among officials; tellingly, this more bureaucratic volume has the highest proportion of names that cannot be identified by contemporary scholars.[77]

For the most part, as an educated reader, you would find the format of the collection to be quite ordinary. The text is punctuated with standard marks for pauses and emphasis, and there are occasional "eyebrow" comments in the upper margin as well as a few interlinear comments in tiny characters placed in between the lines. The only unusual punctuation

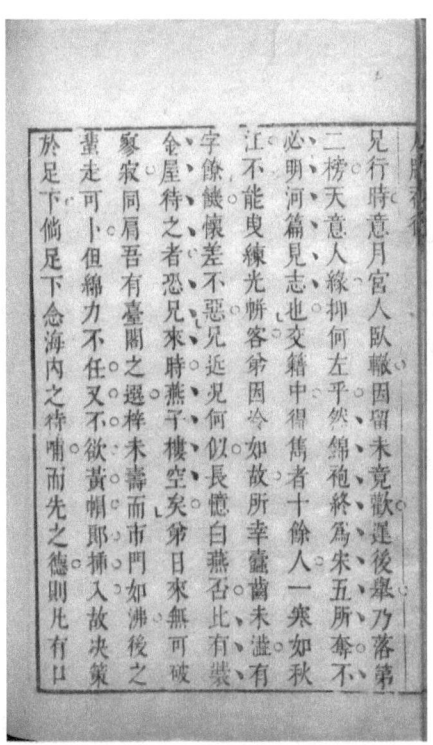

FIGURE 1.5 End of letter titled "To Shi Dequan" in *Letters*, with L-shaped dividing symbols in third, fifth, and sixth columns from the right. (Li Yu, ed. *Chidu chuzheng*. Baobianzhai edition, [1660], 4:6b.) Library of Congress, Asian Division, Chinese Rare Books.

you would come across would be a relatively unobtrusive L-shaped symbol, which is placed in the margin to the bottom left of a character to separate some letters into sections (figure 1.5). Li Yu excludes the familiar characteristics of the remedial manual, which used explanatory glosses and subject headings to aid the novice reader. He would include these reading aids in his later collection of the more challenging genre of parallel prose, but in the letter collection he chose to create new technologies for reading instead. Read in order, these letters would serve to invite you into the private social lives of a range of famous people.

If you wished to use the collection as a letter-writing manual, however, you would navigate the collection according to subject in an alternative approach anticipated by Li Yu's new technology of textual navigation.

Cultural Entrepreneurship and Woodblock Print 69

Li Yu provides detailed instructions in his editorial principles (*fanli*) about how to use the index to look up letters by category (*cha lei zhi fa* 查類之法):

> First, read [*yue* 閱] the list of subjects, and see [*kan* 看] to which category [*lei* 類] belongs the thing you want to look up [*cha* 查]. Next, look at [*yue*] the items and verify which category and item you are looking up. Each letter you look up will only require a single turn of the page and the letter will appear before your eyes [*bian zai mu qian* 便在目前]. You do not have to bother with looking up a second page. Each section is separated by an L-shaped symbol so that you only read [*yue*] the section that deals with your topic, and you do not have to read what precedes or comes after it. All of this is set up for those who are deficient in learning. What use would erudite scholars have for looking things up?[78]

Li Yu refines the technology of the printed book by enabling readers to quickly zoom in on the relevant parts of a letter. As far as I know, it is also the first use of page numbers in an index. Pages had long been numbered, but those numbers had never before served as a destination, for previous works would only have indicated the sequence of items within a volume. Li Yu thereby transforms the letters into reference material: the letter is no longer merely intercepted, for it has been redirected for new readers and intentions through Li Yu's technology of curation. The closest precedent to Li Yu's index can be found in Shen Jiayin's *Sea of Letters*, which was classified by topic.[79] Significantly, in prescribing how his readers are to interact with the text, Li Yu's explanation avoids using the word "read" (*du* 讀). Whereas erudite readers were encouraged in Li Yu's opening notice to "convene with the handwritten traces of like-minded friends," the people using the index are encouraged to "look" (*kan*), "look over" (*yue*), and "look up" (*cha*), so that the information they desire might "appear before their eyes." This plurality of approaches is indicative of the various forms of reading that had proliferated since the late Ming.[80]

Li Yu's index also significantly reorders the collection. For example, the index starts with utilitarian subjects like "Congratulations" and "Condolences," in keeping with the usual priorities of letter-writing manuals, and it situates "literature and art" near the end; in the body of the collection, by contrast, letters discussing "literature and art" appear most frequently at the very beginning of the collection, in keeping with literati values. In addition, some information is withheld from readers who use the index, which neither includes the writers' names nor indexes all of the letters. Index users may benefit from speed, but they may miss the author's name, which is only mentioned on the first letter, and they will also miss the many letters that were not indexed.

The index consists of two parts: a two-page list of subjects ("A First Solicitation of Letters: List of Subjects for Easy Reference" 尺牘初徵分類便查綱目) and a fifty-three-page index ("A First Solicitation of Letters: Index for Easy Reference" 尺牘初徵分類便查條目). The thirty-three general subjects in the initial list—such as "gifts," "paying visits," "current events," and "Buddhism and Daoism"—show the clear organizational plan for the index that follows.[81] The index divides these main subjects into 194 subcategories, with an additional 204 third-level divisions. In the index, each general subject—marked with a large open circle at the top of the column—is divided into subcategories, the titles of which are enclosed in cartouches and flush with the top of the column.

Imagine you are a remedial reader, looking at the right-hand page shown in figure 1.6. This page shows letters in two of the subcategories under "gifts": "objects," which starts on the previous page, and "money." Letter titles are listed two per column under the subheadings; following each letter title is the volume and page number, printed in smaller characters. Looking under the subject of "gifts" and the subcategory of "objects," you might choose the letter listed at the top of the third column from the right, "Replying again to Yanyuan" (You fu Yanyuan 又復彥遠). Under the letter, in smaller characters, you would see that the letter can be found on page 6 of the second volume (*erjuan diliu* 二卷第六). When a letter is divided into sections using the L-shaped symbols, as this one is, the relevant section is indicated immediately following the page number: here, you would learn that the "last section" (*moduan* 末段) is where you should look. Other examples include "beginning section" (*shouduan* 首段), "second section" (*di'er duan* 第二段), and so on. If there is a third-level category for the letter, as there also is in this case, the above information is followed by an open circle and a note indicating that "the above" (*yishang* 以上) fall into a particular category: in this

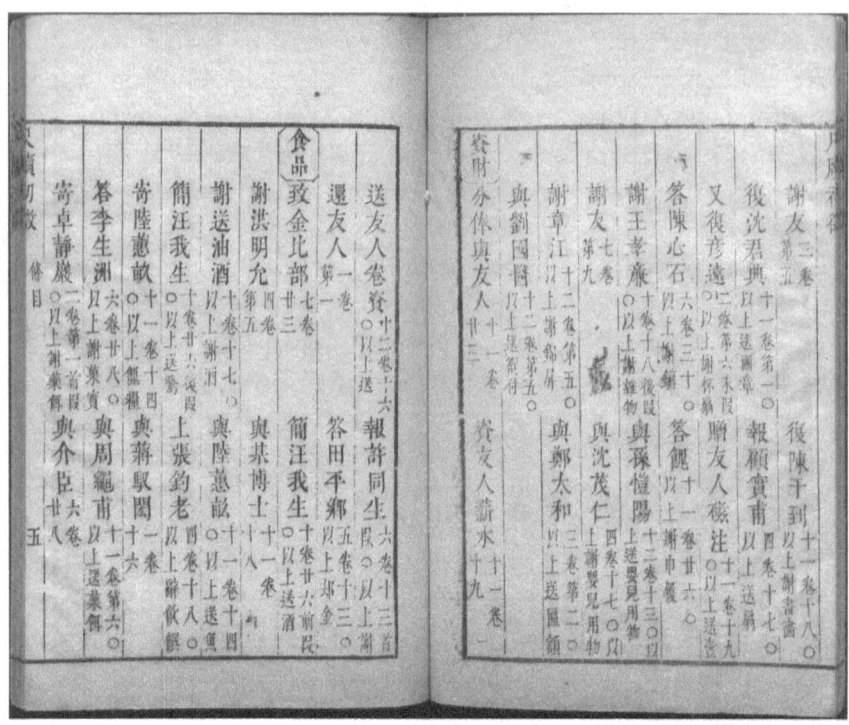

FIGURE 1.6 Pages with subheadings of the "Gifts" entry of *A First Solicitation of Letters:* Index for Easy Reference." (Li Yu, ed. *Chidu chuzheng.* Baobianzhai edition, [1660], 0:4b–5a.) Library of Congress, Asian Division, Chinese Rare Books.

case, "thanking for cups and fans" (*xie beishan* 謝杯扇). You could continue scanning this subcategory looking for particular items: children's toys, brushes, teapots, calligraphy.

A closer look at a multipart letter shows how the index functions. The ninth letter in volume 4, "To Shi Dequan" (Ji Shi Dequan 寄施得全), by He Weiran 何偉然 (1651 *juren*), is divided into four sections, with indexical references to the first section (2. Condolences / 8. Failing the exams), the third section (30. Leisure / 5. Concubines and female performers), and the fourth section (29. Literature and Art / 7. Printing poetry) (see figure 1.5). As this letter demonstrates, individual letters could span a broad range of topics and moods, and if you were limited to a single topic, it would be difficult to classify these letters. Although *chidu* are relatively informal, they only obliquely state the purpose of their composition, and in many cases that indication of the topic suffices to clarify the nature of the interaction. Even a less literate reader who begins by using the index may be tempted, once plunged into the middle of a letter, to read what precedes and follows the designated section. If you were using the index to console a grieving friend you might, after locating that portion of the letter, step back and take in the broader context, noting how the condolences resonate with the congratulations on passing the exam and the gift of a seal.

The index thus enables any reader to have a topic-driven reading experience, whether perusing literary conversations or reliving examination successes. Li Yu added more information to the index through the use of extensive subcategories, which he developed out of the letters themselves. He thereby offered a new approach to categorizing the genre of letters. In the process, his index became an epistemological and a technological intervention that reshaped understandings both of letter categorization and of woodblock-printed books.[82]

While he could have used these organizing methods to develop a letter collection arranged by subject, Li Yu seems to have wanted his book to allow two approaches to reading, and he uses the index in part to demarcate unusually fine gradations of meaning. For example, were you to select the subcategory "Marriage" under the first main category, "Congratulations," you would then have the third choice between "primary wife" or "concubine." For many entries, the index further distinguishes among examples based on the direction of the correspondence: by selecting "Congratulations," followed by "Birthday," you would then be able to choose between sending birthday wishes or replying to wishes sent. Second, Li Yu notes in the introduction that many letters cover more than one topic, rendering the usual mode of dividing a title into sections based on topic or genre unworkable. The L-shaped marks added to the letters resolve that issue, enabling different sections of a single letter to be listed separately in the index. Third, by adding page numbers to the index, rather than simply listing the volume or title of the letter, he allows your index-based reading to occur without fully opening the book: as page numbers were printed on the outer fold of each page of thread-bound books, you could simply glance at its outer edge to find the location of a letter. Fourth, because the index is bound as a separate volume (*ce*), you would find it easy to use as a reference while hunting through the collection for desired letters (easier, it is worth noting, than consulting indexes placed at the end, like in modern books). Li Yu's mode of categorization in the index was extensive—the multiplying subjects and subcategories and further divisions can feel dizzying—but it makes his collection eminently searchable.

Many collections of letters were published during the remainder of the seventeenth century, though none aimed at such a diverse readership as Li Yu's. This may be indicative of a demand among well-educated men for contemporary letters as reading material that could facilitate spiritual connections with likeminded friends. To assess the reception of Li Yu's index, we can compare it with an extant version of *Letters*, likely pirated, which appears to have been printed using altered original blocks or a very meticulously rendered copy.[83] This edition is dated twenty-four years after the first publication: it is attributed to Wang Qi on the opening page of most of the volumes, but to Li Yu on the first page of the ninth volume. This suggests that Li Yu's name had simply been removed (with a wood plane) from the blocks used to print earlier volumes, and then replaced. In this version, Li Yu's two user-friendly indices have been removed and replaced with a new table of contents that lists all the letters in the collection, in the order they appear. There are no authors' names listed, however, as in the most common format for tables of contents; in the place where a letter writer's name would appear is a single topic mentioned below some of the letters. The absence of the index makes this collection more difficult to use as a letter-writing manual, although that remains somewhat possible with the new table of contents. Alternatively, the absence of the index may reflect its relative difficulty and expense, for it comprised the most complex design and the most demanding carving of the entire collection.

The publication of *Letters* in Hangzhou in 1660 coincided with Li Yu's move to Nanjing, where he and his family would live until 1677. Just three years later he published a large, edited volume of contemporary administrative documents, *A New Aid to Administration*, out of his printshop in Nanjing. Li Yu would publish two collections of administrative documents in 1663 and 1667, and both of these collections were designed to serve multiple functions. On the one hand, they provided stories of compatriots serving throughout the empire, giving readers the pleasure of intimate contact with a community. On the other hand, the cases could also serve as instructional materials for newly employed officials. The first collection was arguably the most practical in its intent. It contained, for instance, model forms that an official could use for someone to report a death, accompanied by Li Yu's suggestion that "the model form to the left can be cut out and made a standard."[84] In its embrace of customization, this suggestion recalls his fan window design. Like his letter collection, his collections of administrative documents are user-friendly and meticulously organized, but with a crucial organizational difference. Whereas the letters were divided into subsections that were then labeled by topic, the cases themselves are not divided into subsections. Instead, the classificatory tables that divide the cases by category and subcategory anticipate readers who need specialized knowledge and shared experience, rather than, as with index for the letter collection, readers needing instruction.

Some people contributed both to his letter and his document collections, but the pool of potential contributors for his collections of administrative documents was limited to men who held, or had previously held, an official position. The preface to the 1663 *A New Aid to Administration* opens with a number of essays by Li Yu, who himself had never passed even the provincial-level examination, nor served as an official. In the process, it situates him at the center of a network of men who wielded administrative power in the early Qing, enhancing his status through the social networking properties of print.[85] Some contemporaries saw Li Yu's collecting of administrative documents as an improvement on the brash projects of his earlier years. In his preface to Li Yu's 1667 collection of administrative documents, for instance, Zhou Lianggong wrote: "Critics say that Liweng's profligate abuse of his talents in his early writings has been replaced by a dignified and righteous manner."[86] Given his longer pattern of print experimentation, however, we might understand these projects as yet another strategy within his ongoing cultural entrepreneurship, enabling him, as an outsider, to build a powerful social network.

Li Yu undertook a similar project of personal social elevation in his final edited collection, *A First Solicitation of Parallel Prose*, published in 1671.[87] The majority of submissions for that volume came from men who had held an official position, though Li Yu apologized for not including selections from a wider range of people. Even at this late stage of his career, Li Yu continued to advertise within his books to connect his print projects. In *Parallel Prose*, he expressed the hope that the first volume would serve as an advertisement, inviting submissions by mail for inclusion in the second collection, and he included prefatory material that listed the various works for sale at his garden residence and bookshop, the Mustard Seed Garden.

Each of these collections served a few distinct functions. First, for contributors, they provided a place on paper for people from all over the empire, creating a community that transcended each local place. Second, for readers, they presented communities of people getting on with life in the new dynasty: the readers imagined themselves a part of these communities even as they benefited from the educational aspect of each collected genre. Third, for Li Yu and his close friends, the collections situated them at the center of empire-wide social networks and broadened the scope of Li Yu's reputation. One of the immediate results of these publishing projects was that Li Yu expanded his reputation beyond that of an author of fiction and drama. In attaching his name to his vernacular fiction, he had already departed from the standard literati practice of publishing vernacular fiction anonymously, instead using the publication of fiction and plays to broadcast his name and shape an associated persona. As he aged, Li Yu could increasingly rely on that reputation—outrageous, entertaining, and deeply social—to advertise his collaborative texts, which offered readers access not just to Li Yu but also to many other influential people.

During the 1660s and 1670s, Li Yu also published a kind of collaborative writing that featured his own essays and collected works with comments from dozens of individuals. Some forty-three people commented on his *Discourses on the Past* (1664), nineteen on his *Leisure Notes* (1671), approximately eighty-four on his complete works, *Independent Words* (1672–1678), and fifteen on his *Singable Lyrics* (*Naige ci* 耐歌詞, 1678). Although such commentary had a rich history in the classics and more recently in fiction and plays, Li Yu's use of commentary was unusually extensive and varied. In contrast to the edited volumes discussed above, the contributors for these collaborations were all people Li Yu knew well. They included many who never held office; others who went into reclusion after the fall of the Ming; many individuals who served under the Qing and used their resources to support Li Yu's cultural production over the years; and others who are remembered as painters and seal carvers who frequented Li Yu's home. Including so many comments in his own writings served as a similar kind of social networking technology to his edited collections, for it gathered like-minded friends in a printed volume with Li Yu at the center.

In all, Li Yu produced edited collections of three distinct genres, and many more of his own works with commentary from his friends. A core of close friends and frequent patrons were featured in multiple projects, and these were supplemented by mailed submissions from across the empire. Each of the collections provided a print community that transcended locale while also potentially serving as reference material. Through these projects, Li Yu developed a reputation as a versatile cultural entrepreneur and cultivated a empire-wide support network. As a cultural entrepreneur, he was a hybrid figure, functioning between the well-to-do who could sponsor the publication of whatever they wished and the men who published a steady stream of older titles to make a living. Li Yu lived off of the proceeds of his publications and the support of connections he made through them, but he did not publish anything that did not feature his own creative touch.

In this chapter I have focused on how Li Yu's innovations in print capitalized on its reproducibility and expanded its range of functions. As he reconsidered the medium of painting with his "Li Yu fan painting" and argued for the rights to copies of his own works and notepaper designs, Li Yu's entrepreneurial savvy made it possible for him to retain his personal touch on products that could easily be reproduced. Although he described this process—*shenjiao*, or spiritual connection—in language long used for the communion that print, and even writing, was understood to facilitate, he remodeled this spiritual connection by experimenting, seeking to make what might seem like a second-best connection (*xu*) feel more substantial (*shi*). Language was a key part of that process, for Li Yu's energetic and jokey voice leaps off the page even today. In the next chapter, I look more closely at the role that writing played in Li Yu's efforts to enliven his printed works.

CHAPTER TWO

Building with Words

Periods of crisis often result in drastic shifts in collectively held values and in the way that people envision the world, thereby offering much fodder for creative thought. Such a shift was evident in the uncertain transitional period of the early Qing. Some paid with their lives for what they wrote, while many others who had been preparing their whole lives to seek government service found themselves scrambling to take up alternative vocations. In this tumultuous time, Li Yu used writing to build anew from the wreckage.

During the Ming dynasty, growing numbers of *wenren* had argued for the value of fiction and drama, whether by comparing their potential instructional power favorably to that of historical narrative, or by arguing that these genres' depiction of desire could show the human condition to its full extent.[1] By the end of the Ming, there was widespread interest in the art of creating fictional worlds through the composition of vernacular fiction and drama, and a significant amount of that creative energy went into producing commentary for, editing, and printing such works. The dynastic transition directed this energy toward the autobiographical, with writers increasingly using those literary forms to respond to contemporary events.[2]

In this chapter I explore how Li Yu reimagined writing in response to the disruptions of this transition. Li Yu's literary output suggests a new vision of what it might mean to create worlds on the page—seeking, and finding, ways to affect the world on the other side of writing's mediation. I argue that the experience of war made Li Yu particularly sensitive to the materiality of literary production. In his own lifetime, he saw not only his own poems, but also his collection of books, burned. In some of his earliest writing Li Yu grappled with questions raised through that material loss. That poetry, examined first in this chapter, asks: What is the value of the literary, and what kind of writing is valuable? How should writing be recorded and circulated? How do we deal with the fragility of writing media? I contend that in reconsidering these fundamental questions about language, writing, and print, Li Yu came to conceive of them as media that he could remodel and optimize according to his aims.

In remainder of the chapter I discuss the first three books of *Leisure Notes*, where those ideas culminate in Li Yu's treatise on playwriting and theatrical performance. There he proposed that talk—that is, the informal register of language associated with speech—contained as much literary potential as the more highly regulated language of poetry and arias. He further argued that the literary should be widely accessible, whether through clear written language or comprehensible oral performance. I argue that instead of equating the less valorized register of language with naturalness, as other thinkers did, he envisioned it as a particular kind of tool, technical in its design and a potential resource from which he could construct a highly complex literary form that did not require traditional literacy for its appreciation. Although there is much that is specific to playwriting in the treatise, a note in the table of contents indicates its applicability to writing in general.

In the final section of this chapter I show how Li Yu's recourse to metaphors of buildings and human bodies in his discussion of the structure of literary texts further reveals the technological quality of his approach, for by wresting the process of literary creation from its usual natural metaphors, Li Yu deposits it squarely in the hands of architects and builders. I argue that Li Yu thereby pulled writing toward the realm of the substantial (*shi*) world through a powerful combination of moves: not only did he shift literary creation from a natural to a technological activity, but he also emphasized the importance of a clear structure in writing. In the process, we see how Li Yu reenvisioned books within his book *Leisure Notes*.

A BURNING OF BOOKS

Although Li Yu is best known as a writer of fiction, plays, and essays, he was also a prolific poet, and it was in poetic genres that his earliest extant writings were composed. Poetry had an ambivalent status in the early Qing, for the hierarchy of literary genres had shifted: authenticity had become more strongly associated with genres like casual essays (*xiaopin*) and informal letters (*chidu*). Tina Lu has assessed the changed status of poetry in the late Ming, wondering whether "the ubiquitous use of poetry in social life had somehow cheapened it."[3] Nevertheless, as Wai-yee Li and Tobie Meyer-Fong have shown, poetry remained a preferred vehicle for many loyalists lamenting the fall of the Ming.[4] Although Li Yu counted Ming loyalists among his closest friends, his writing tended to point to the future—rather than gaze backward with nostalgia—by asking: What can we build? How can we remodel what we have? How can we improve upon existing genres? His early poetry reflects on his youth and the dynastic transition, in an earnest and emotional personal voice that is rare in his later work.

War has often been discussed, and rightly so, as a prime driver of technological development, and I propose that Li Yu's historical moment demonstrates how war can disrupt crystallized relationships to media forms. In the cultural context of the early Qing, such a disruption led to a reassessment of print's importance for writing and literature. In a childhood poem that dramatizes writing on a tree, Li Yu explores the relationship between the language of literary composition and the media of its recording. Although he published this poem several decades after the tumultuous dynastic transition of 1644, he opens with a note that positions it as a poem composed before that dramatic change:

	續刻梧桐詩	RECARVING THE PARASOL TREE POEM
	小時種梧桐	When I was young, I planted a parasol tree,
2	桐本細如艾	At first, it was as slender as a wormwood stem.
	針尖刻小詩	With the tip of a needle, I carved a small poem,
4	字瘦皮不壞	In characters so slight the bark did not crack.
	剎那三五年	In a flash, three, or five, years gone by,
6	桐大字亦大	The parasol is bigger now, the characters too.

	桐字已如許	If parasol and characters are both like this,
8	人長亦奚怪	Is it any surprise that people also grow?
	好將感嘆詞	I thought it right to carve a wistful lyric
10	刻向前詩外	Just beyond the previous poem.
	新字日相催	The new characters press in by the day,
12	舊字不相待	But the old characters don't wait for them.
	顧此新舊痕	Looking at these new and old marks,
14	而為悠忽戒	I guard against idleness and delinquency.[5]

The main theme of this opening poem is the passage of time, marked through the transformations of nature. This poem is unusual, however, in the temporal signaling of its speaker: instead of the following the convention of an old man with white and thinning hair lamenting that he has not done more with his life, it presents a voice that is unmistakably young. And rather than focus broadly on the changing of the seasons—generally represented as a cycle that becomes more familiar and seems to speed up with age—the poem focuses narrowly on evidence of growth and time passing that is external to the poet, who is still in the process of growing up himself. A primary level of awareness is found in the simple growth of a planted tree: year by year, season by season, the tree grows almost imperceptibly, until one day it suddenly appears significantly larger. A second level of awareness in this poem appears in the young poet's attempt to assess the tree's growth. He seeks to mark a particular moment in his life by carving text in the bark, but this action fails to serve the purposes of memorialization. Instead of marking their moment of inscription, the characters grow in step with the tree, thereby becoming a visual reminder of the gap between the poet and the moment of the poem's composition. A second poem carved on the same tree commemorates the boy's growing awareness of time, as he contemplates what it means that the words of the two poems will never touch. The gap between these two poems, given physical form by the growth of the tree, makes the poet determined to make good use of the allotted years of his life.

It is not only the tree, but also the characters carved into its bark that teach the child this lesson, for characters, and writing more generally, can record a particular moment of time as it passes by. Anxiety about the media of writing and their susceptibility to decay was common: silverfish feast; paper grows moldy. Here, however, writing grows along with a living thing, and thus becomes bound to the trajectory of time particular to the cycle of life and death. The introductory note explains that Li Yu's childhood poems had been previously published but were lost in the fires of war, and that this poem had been rewritten from memory. In quick succession, readers are thus taken from a recorded, and growing, poem etched into a tree's bark, to a printed volume, and from there to one lodged in the memory. Precisely because of the divergence between memory and reality—Li Yu can recall it but, as his note tells us, there is "not one copy left"—this poem attests to the simultaneity of persistence and erasure as a key element of dynastic change.

The weighty juxtaposition of the two poems on the tree bark and the single poem carved twice onto woodblocks (once in childhood, once later in life) presents us with opposing potentialities: the poems on the tree, with their temporality of life, would grow but never touch, whereas those printed on paper were static and risked being lost in the fires of war. In the former, the medium used for writing is vibrant, quite literally alive with prospects for the future. In the latter, the medium is more manipulable and transportable, yet it proves fragile, and even brittle, requiring memory to give it longevity.

But a question lingers: What is the poem that was first carved on the parasol tree? That earlier poem cannot be the one we're reading, as it encompasses both occasions of carving. Nor can it easily refer to the second poem carved on the tree, since it refers also to the time beyond that poem when the two are growing together (or rather, apart). Are we to regret the absence, and perhaps the loss, of that first poem, and the more innocent world to which it belonged? Of four carvings of at least three poems, the one we are reading is the only one that survived. Li Yu's focus remains on the medium—the tree, whether living or chopped down and converted into a woodblock—that will hold and transmit his words.

Li Yu's attention to the media of writing intensified in the midst of the dynastic transition. During that unstable period, educated men faced complex ethical quandaries as they dealt with the consequential tripartite loss, as Wilt Idema has noted, of "state, ideology, and career."[6] Undergirding every component of that loss was writing, which had—in a very material sense—been rendered suddenly unstable. Li Yu is often presented as a figure oblivious to these losses, whether because he would go on to pander to high officials or because his often-comedic fiction and plays only occasionally engaged recent events. Yet in a series of heptasyllabic poems in regulated verse, "Mourning My Books: Four Poems" (Diaoshu sishou 弔書四首), which he wrote early in the Qing, before the inauguration of his commercial career, he engaged the theme of writing threatened not just by time, but by war. There Li Yu proposed that the destruction of books would also mean the end of "those who read books"—*dushu ren* 讀書人 or *wenren*—with the emergence of a dominant orality (*tukou* 徒口) instead. Across these poems, the narrow focus on his own writing of his earlier poem expands to include the learned tradition as a whole.

	其一	I.
	鄴架羣書逐類分	I arranged all the books in my library by category,
2	總因世難靖狂氛	To provide a sense of calm in the midst of tumultuous times.
	蠹魚辟盡香成霧	The bookworms are exterminated, and the sweet fragrance has turned to smoke;
4	亥豕刊來墨是雲	The ink of characters that were set in print has turned to clouds.
	自昔康衡傳借苦	In bygone days, Kang and Heng suffered to pass down and borrow [books],[7]
6	虛勞袁峻手抄勤	In vain did Yuan Jun laboriously copy by hand.[8]
	輸他腹笥便便子	They've lost out now to men with their bellies stuffed with learning—
8	徒口猶能授典墳	Who can pass on the teachings of the ancient canon only by word of mouth.[9]

This opening poem of the "Mourning My Books" series depicts a systematically organized library dissolving in an instant into a cloud of smoke, which now must be interiorized in order to survive. The poem emphasizes the labor that went into writing, printing, and collecting the books and alludes to historical examples of men who endured hardship for their studies, materialized in the form of books. Print, which serves at once for preserving and transmitting text, no longer seems durable, and orality seems the only recourse.

Much as the final lines of "Recarving the Parasol Tree Poem" referenced how writing could be replaced by the alternative technique of memorization mentioned in that poem's preface, so too the final lines of this poem turn back to the preoccupations of this poem's title. The allusion in line 7 is to Bian Shao 邊韶 (ca. 2nd c. CE), a scholar from the Eastern Han, who is said to have had the following exchange with his students:

> Once Shao took a nap during the day, and his disciples privately made fun of him, saying, "Bian Xiaoxian, with that big belly of his, too lazy to read books, only wants to snooze." Shao furtively overheard them, and replied at once, "Bian is my surname, and Xiao my courtesy name. This big belly of mine? A case for the Five Classics. Only wanting to nap? Thinking on the classics. When I sleep, I dream together with the Duke of Zhou; when I'm still, I have the same will as Confucius. As for ridiculing one's own teacher, from which canonical work is that taken?"[10]

Bian Shao here represents learning that has been so internalized that he is no longer dependent on books: his "big belly" is now a storage "case" (*si* 笥) for literary knowledge, much as in Li Yu's poem the mouth becomes the mode of literary transmission. As his books go up in smoke, then, Li Yu turns mournfully to the body.

Yet even as Li Yu imagines literature stored without writing, he simultaneously positions himself as carrying on a tradition of preserving books during dynastic transitions. He does so by alluding to two figures: Wang Can (177–217), who lived during the violent years at the end of the Eastern Han and preserved the library of the eminent official Cai Yong 蔡邕 (132–192), and Fu Sheng, who is credited with preserving *The Book of Documents* (*Shangshu* 尚書) during the first Qin emperor's infamous "burning of the books and burying of the scholars" in 213 BCE.[11] These allusions appear in the next poem, which draws comparisons between the burning of the books and his own situation:

	其二	II.
	時流莫謂弔書迂	Contemporaries—do not say that my mourning books is misguided,
2	儂與前人性命俱	My nature is the same as the ancients.

	王粲再求誰付與	If a Wang Can comes asking again, who will give him [books]?
4	伏生肯授願為徒	If a Fu Sheng is willing to teach, I wish to be his student.
	太平有字飢堪煮	In peacetime, I have characters that I can boil to allay hunger,
6	喪亂無家口不糊	But in turmoil and without a home, I cannot feed myself.
	始信焚坑非兩事	I am starting to believe that the burning and the burying were not two separate things:
8	世間書盡自無儒	When all the books in the world are gone, the scholars will be, too.¹²

The poem thus establishes a dyadic relationship between scholars and books, asking what scholarly identity means in a world without books. It thereby hints at the poet's own concurrent—if symbolic—immolation.

The embodied interaction of writing is further emphasized in this second poem's use of the metaphorical expression "boiling characters" (*zhuzi* 煮字) that Li Yu uses nostalgically to describe writing-based livelihood in peacetime. The expression was usually a negatively coded reference to writing as a means of income. In Dong Sigao's 董嗣杲 (active 1260–1276) heptasyllabic poem, "Thinking of Home in the Autumn Chill" (Qiuliang huaigui 秋涼懷歸, third of three), for instance, "boiling characters" is associated with aging and obligation: "In my youth, I was sometimes carelessly ambitious in my writing. Nowadays, I labor steadfastly at boiling characters" 少年偶負投機愧 / 今日徒工煮字勞.¹³ In Li Yu's poem, in contrast, one can draw material sustenance from the writing life, except in wartime, when the poet becomes homeless. The connection to home also links writing for a living with plowing the land, as does Li Yu's use of the expression, "plowing with the brush" (*bigeng* 筆耕). Characters become seasonal sustenance in Li Yu's hands, making *shi* (real sustenance) out of *xu* (mere words) as long as circumstances allow. Whereas the first poem advocated oral preservation of texts, the final couplet of the second identifies scholars with material books, not with the contained knowledge that might be convertible to oral form.

The disruption of the dynastic transition provided Li Yu with an opportunity to reconsider the relationship of book learning to a scholar's physical body and his material possessions. In his play *A Much-Desired Match*, for example, Li Yu parodied common expressions for how literacy is embodied. In that play, one of the female protagonists, Lin Tiansu, is traveling in male attire when she is captured by bandits. These bandits decide to test their captive's scholarly competence. One of them proposes a test based on the expression used to praise fine writing: "a single character is worth a thousand pieces of gold" (*yizi zhi qianjin*$_1$ 一字值千金).[14] Interpreting the final character, "gold" (*jīn*$_1$ 金), for a homophonous unit of measurement, "catty" (*jīn*$_2$ 斤), the illiterate bandit takes the metaphorical expression literally and suggests weighing the scholar to see how many characters he knows, since "each character weighs a thousand catties" (*yizi zhi qianjin*$_2$ 一字值千斤) (177). His fellow bandit objects to this plan, pointing out that even a cursory knowledge of characters would result in an inordinately heavy person. Abandoning that plan, the bandits are next inspired by the common expression that "scholars have bellies full of ink" (178), proposing to hang their captive upside down from a tree to see whether ink flows out.

Whereas the first proposed test originated in a misunderstanding of a homophonic character by an illiterate person, this test originates in the literalization of a conventional phrase, one closely related to the classical expression "belly full of literature" (*manfu wenzhang* 滿腹文章), used to refer to an educated person. Both expressions liken knowledge acquisition to the visceral interiorization of written characters. By literalizing these established metaphors, Li Yu invites the play's readers and spectators to question what knowledge is and how it enters the body. The scene concludes when the bandits concur that "all the famous scholars can perform plays these days" (178) and ask the new captive to sing some lines from a play, which Lin Tiansu readily does. Memorization had been and continued to be a foundational element in traditional education, and plays, with their emphasis on performance, necessarily sought incorporation into the bodies of practitioners. For this reason, as we see in the next section, Li Yu's discussions of playwriting offer a particularly rich venue in which to consider how writing acquires embodied forms.

The third poem of the "Mourning My Books" series moves away from the second poem's historical allusions, instead focusing on the carefully organized library that was depicted in the first poem. In a triumph of brute military force over literary and political expertise, soldiers invade the poet's home and use his books and writing implements to cook food and warm wine. Their choice of fuel is motivated by resentment as much as exigency, for they blame the current state of the country on those very books.

	其三	III.
	將軍偶宿校書臺	Some officers happened to lodge at my editing terrace;
2	怒取縑緗入竈煨	In anger, they took up my books and put them in the embers of the kitchen stove.
	國事盡由章句誤	Blaming the state of affairs on those chapters and verses,
4	功名不自揣摩來	Believing that honor and rank don't come from intense study.
	三杯煖就千編絕	To warm three cups, a thousand tomes obliterated;
6	一飯炊成萬卷灰	To cook a single meal, ten thousand volumes turned to ash.
	猶幸管城能殉汝	Fortunate that my brushes can be sacrificed with you.
8	生同几案死同堆	In life, on the same desk, in death, on the same heap.[15]

This poem reworks the "boiling characters" of the second poem, taking the existing ambivalence of this expression into a decidedly negative vision of literary obliteration. This recasting is amplified by the opening image of the third couplet, for "warming three cups of wine" was once used to depict the rarefied experience of a garden.[16] Here, in wartime, it figures the inordinate destruction of books and literary community instead.

Li Yu concludes this series of poems by placing his body once again in the midst of this destroyed literary landscape:

	其四	IV.
	心肝盡貯錦囊中	I poured my whole heart into brocade purses of poetry;

2	博得咸陽片刻紅	They've all become a glint of red in Xianyang's wake.[17]
	終夜敲推成夢囈	Long nights deliberating over words now but slumberous delusions;
4	半生吟弄付飄風	Half a life intoning verse relinquished to the twisting winds.
	文多罵俗遭天譴	Writing that scorns convention meets the wrath of Heaven;
6	詩豈長城遇火攻	Is poetry some Great Wall that it should face attack by fire?
	切記從今休落筆	But keep this in mind—from now on I will cease putting brush to paper,
8	興來咄咄只書空	When inspiration comes, I will simply tut-tut and trace characters in the air.[18]

The series thus concludes with writing that emanates intimately from the body: in his phrasing, the heart and liver are poured into external purses, whose burning relegates such bodily extensions "to the twisting winds." In the fourth line, the measuring of literary works as "half a life" ties their value to the human lifetime, their loss appearing as a partial death. The poet's concluding oath emulates Yin Hao 殷浩 (306–356), who, after he was dismissed from office, spent his days tracing characters in the air. In the early days of a new dynasty, an allusion to the disgruntled Yin Hao would normally express the frustrations of an ambitious man.[19] In this series of poems, however, the allusion emphasizes the disembodied words by ending with the character for "emptiness" (*kong*, "air"). Just a few years later Li Yu would embark on a successful career of putting words to paper, one that nonetheless suggests an ongoing awareness of the fragility of that medium.

LITERARY BODIES

The only literary genre for which Li Yu composed a systematic guide is that of *chuanqi*, and as a consequence his most substantial conclusions about writing in general are found in his writing about playwriting. He drew on his personal experience writing plays and directing a household troupe in the first two books of *Leisure Notes*, "Playwriting" and

"Performance," as well as part of the third, "Exquisite Ingénues," and those books offer guidance on everything from plot construction to enunciation, from music to lighting. In the early Qing, Li Yu's theorization of theater was novel for its comprehensiveness: he included thoughts on less explored topics of performance, directing, and the training of actors, even as he developed a number of concepts that already had been discussed among late-Ming drama theorists, such as prosody, dialogue, and structure. In studies of the history of drama criticism, Li Yu is usually praised as heralding the end of an era that conceived of plays primarily as a literary form, despite his continued emphasis on singing (in modern terminology, *xiqu* 戲曲). His writing is also widely considered the beginning of a comprehensive notion of theater that included play scripts as well as the many elements of staged performance (in modern terminology, *xiju* 戲劇).[20]

By including playwriting as a subset of topics within a broader rubric of theatrical production, Li Yu's theorization of writing echoes the prospect of a world without books that we saw in his early poems, situating them as merely one of several literary media. In his theory of playwriting, however, he conceives of a more complex relationship between writing and orality, one that negotiated among colloquial speech; the composition of *chuanqi*'s highly regulated arias and spoken dialogue; and their performance by actors. The conclusions that he draws are at once contradictory and radical, for his impulse toward a democratization of literature is countered at every turn by his wish to control all aspects of its performance: playwrights should emulate speech, while actors should be taught to read; playwrights should prioritize the spoken parts of a play, while actors should perform those spoken parts in a more regulated way.

In trying to reconcile these imperatives, I argue, Li Yu's theorization of theater seriously contemplates the human body as a literary medium. In an essay on dialogue, he draws a striking connection between printing and performance, equating actors to woodblocks: "Each of my plays is seized by printers when I have barely set down my writing brush. Before the second half is drafted, the first half will have already been carved onto woodblocks. Not only will it have been carved onto blocks, but the fleet-footed among the actors will have already carved it onto their very guts and lungs, carved it onto their lips and tongues."[21] Bodies are here conceived of as a medium of transmission across a vast sphere of influence ("all-under-Heaven," *tianxia* 天下), a conception that elevates the significance of the actor's body even as it places it under someone else's control.

In *Leisure Notes*, Li Yu envisions a "universal theater" in which *chuanqi* can reach those who do not comprehend classical Chinese and who cannot read his books. Through this expansive category, he aims to produce a dramatic form suitable for broad circulation in both text and performance. In the middle of the opening essay in "Playwriting," Li Yu makes a bold claim for not keeping one's literary techniques a secret: "As I see it, literature [*wenzhang* 文章] is the common possession [*gongqi* 公器] of all under Heaven; it is not something that I can arrogate to myself."²² This statement goes beyond the simple claim that literary texts should be broadly circulated. The materiality connoted by the term *qi* ("possession"), which can be more literally rendered as "implement" or "tool," proposes that literary composition is a tool that anyone can learn to use.²³ Li Yu develops this claim through a circular logic that encourages playwrights to value nonliterary talk, while encouraging actors to learn and embody the classical language usually monopolized by the official class.

I argue that this characterization of literature was inspired by Li Yu's reconsideration of the value of books and the degree to which he saw literacy as an embodied skill. He develops these ideas about writing with reference to several interrelated terms concerning his enthusiasm about the ability of *wen* (writing) to create value. The primary terms he uses include: *wenzi* 文字, which indicates writing and written literature; *wenzhang*, which indicates literary works; *wenli* 文理, which includes both language (*wenci* 文辭)—especially written language—and the principles, argument, or sense conveyed by it (*yili* 義理),²⁴ and which Li Yu also uses to indicate "classical literacy;" and *wenren*, which usually refers to a classically educated literatus, but which Li Yu proposes might be interpreted more literally—a "*wen* person," or anyone conversant with *wen*. Like his contemporaries, Li Yu uses *wen* to refer to literature or even writing in general. He also uses it as shorthand for related concepts like literary works, prose (as opposed to poetry, and usually associated with the era of its ascendence, the Song dynasty), or the act of writing. Although he occasionally uses it as a synonym for *yu* 語 (language), he tends to differentiate it from *hua* 話 and other terms associated with speech.

Li Yu insisted that actors be taught to read and that they understand the lines they speak or sing. To "master" (*tong* 通) *wenli* means to be fundamentally transformed—both physically and mentally—by an ability to grasp deep principles. Such transformation is possible even for an uneducated person. The heroes of Neo-Confucianism, after all, were sometimes illiterate: Wang Gen 王艮 (1483–1541) is described as an "illiterate stove worker who didn't know even a single character" but was enlightened when he heard someone reading aloud.²⁵ Unlike strands of late-Ming thought that would lionize the uneducated, Li Yu instead proposes that literacy be widely adopted as a tool to be used for many different purposes. This is perhaps counterintuitive: we are accustomed, after all, to understanding the literary as precisely the arena in which language is appreciated and savored, not instrumentally deployed. I propose that Li Yu designed ways of writing that might broaden the reach of his texts, even as he developed a level of complexity that could simultaneously generate and sustain critical interest. He invited us, in the process, to reconsider the binary between instrumental and literary uses of language.

Li Yu suggests that *wenli* might be defined simply as "recognizing characters" for any purpose: a practical endeavor, rather than an obscure art. In an essay on the importance of teaching actresses to read, Li Yu claims that *wenli* can render the world accessible:²⁶

> There is a key that unlocks the door to all of the ten thousand things and events under Heaven. What is that key? It is found in two characters: *wenli*. Whereas regular keys open only a single lock, and one lock serves each door, *wenli* not only unlocks tens of thousands of doors, it also manages everything in the sky above and on earth below, in the ten thousand countries and the nine continents. It is so large that there is nothing outside of it, so small that it has no interior. As for anything you undertake to do or learn, there is nothing for which it does not hold the pivotal position, controlling all comings and goings.²⁷

Li Yu encourages us to understand *wenli* as a master key that not only provides access to all corners of the material world, but also lends people the power to manage (*si* 司) it. Although this grandiose vision originates in a rather narrow wish—for concubines and actresses to learn the literary arts—Li Yu broadens his call for literacy to include all people. As he explains: "This theory applies not only to married women and girls, but to all scholars, farmers, artisans and merchants under Heaven, those who follow the three teachings and the nine schools of thought, all the craftsmen and artisans—they should all look at it this way." Li Yu is enthusiastic about the efficiency afforded by writing, claiming that "if a builder could just recognize enough characters to keep his accounts, the buildings and wares that he produces would surely be different from those of an unlearned builder," resulting in "twice the result for half the effort" (*shiban gongbei* 事半功倍).[28]

Although *wenli* was generally associated with writing, it is best understood as a distinction between registers of language, and not merely between speech and writing. In Li Yu's training of actors, as I show, literacy is required, but writing is not the goal. In thinking about how to teach basic literacy, Li Yu distinguishes between the higher register of literary language (*wenli*) and "ordinary talk and common language" (*changtan suyu* 常談俗語), which he identifies here as the language of plays and novels, and which in modern terms is known as *baihua* 白話 ("plain speech"). In his method for teaching a concubine to read, texts composed in this lower register can teach character recognition to anyone who can talk:

> Avail yourself of a moment when she wants to read, and quickly find a play with a detailed plot or a novel with a seamless narrative. If you listen to her read it aloud, you will find that the book has ceased to be a book: it has become a wise teacher who guides her to the next level of proficiency without anger or threats. How can this be? The language in plays and novels is all ordinary talk and common sayings. When women read them, it is as if they have encountered something familiar. For example, in a given sentence of ten characters, she may know seven already, leaving three that she doesn't know. As she reads it off smoothly, she will naturally not miss any of them. . . . Those three characters are not taught by me: they are taught by plays and novels.[29]

Traditional education in classical texts required following a standard curriculum in a fixed sequence, but learning to read *changtan suyu* could be accomplished by simply reading a text aloud, and filling in the gaps as you went along.[30] If in the above passage literacy (*wenli*) was "the key that unlocks every door," here the metaphor has shifted: books in "ordinary" language unlock literacy by transforming themselves into "wise teachers." Li Yu's advocacy of universal literacy also contains the subversive potential of overturning class hierarchies by making writing "the common possession of all under Heaven." If anyone can learn to use characters for any purpose, and each and every character they learn has its utility ("Every character learned is a character that can be used"),[31] then Li Yu has offered a path to literacy that circumvents a traditional education in the classics—even as his newly literate reader might decide to study the classics nonetheless.

This unusual emphasis is dramatized in his short story "Tan Chuyu Expresses His Love in a Play; Liu Miaogu Dies for Honor after a Song" (譚楚玉戲裡傳情 劉藐姑曲終死節), which he adapted into a *chuanqi* titled *A Couple of Soles* (*Bimu yu* 比目魚) in 1661.[32] Both versions recount a forbidden romance between two teenage actors in the same troupe. They are the only members of the troupe who understand classical Chinese, so they are able to communicate privately during rehearsals by adding some classical constructions to their speech. Through this linguistic device, they declare their mutual affection and concoct a plan to change his role-type to that of the male lead (*sheng* 生), so that they may play opposite one another. The *chuanqi* version expands this plot to include written notes between them that could be read—but not understood—by their fellow troupe members. Both versions use the same vocabulary to describe the others' incomprehension: they are "not well versed in literary language" (*butong wenli* 不通文理), by which it is implied that they do not understand the arias in *chuanqi*.[33]

Despite these commonalities, the two versions represent *wenli* quite differently. In the short story, the narrator explains: "If he [Tan Chuyu] were to speak in ordinary talk and common language [*changtan suyu*], they would understand. However, if he adds in some 'thees and thous' [*zhi hu zhe ye* 之乎者也] then they would not be able to comprehend."[34] The narrator here suggests, using the common expression *zhi hu zhe ye* (four basic grammatical particles of classical Chinese), that ordinary speech (*changtan suyu*) can be transformed into *wenli* by adding particles. Their *wenli* conversation accordingly includes some of these particles. The first line reads "小姐小姐, 你是個聰明絕頂之人, 豈不知小生之來意乎?" (36–37), which includes the particles *zhi* and *hu*, as well as the literary construction *qibuzhi* 豈不知 ("how can you not know?"). Yet it is not fully converted to classical usages and grammar, with basic vocabulary and such decidedly nonliterary language as "*ni shi ge*" 你是個 ("you are a"). Although such a line would usually be translated into plain English, Patrick Hanan's delightful rendition achieves the intended effect: "O Mistress, Mistress, most intelligent creature as thou art, how canst thou not be aware of my purpose in coming?"[35]

In the play, however, Li Yu dramatizes the power of literary language to transmit secret messages in writing and in song, attributing one technique to each character. Tan Chuyu concocts a "secret classical" plan that will utilize difficult vocabulary and an ancient style of script: "Although the fools in this troupe may recognize a couple of characters here and there, none of them is well versed in literary language. If I make the meaning of the words a bit abstruse and include a good number of difficult characters, not only will everyone who sees it be entirely at a loss; even if they were to take the thing itself and deliver it into the hands of her parents, I'd venture even they would be unable to make out the slightest split seam."[36] Miaogu responds to his letter onstage, in a spontaneous song: "Let me compose an aria out of my response and sing it out loud for him to hear. Everyone will think that I am simply reciting the script; how would they know otherwise?" (10:4191). Whereas the characters in the short story version "literarize" their speech by merely adding particles,[37] Miaogu "takes" (*ba* 把) the "words with which she was going to respond" (*hui ta di hua* 回他的話), and "composes" (*bianzuo* 編做) an aria with them, transforming her "spoken words" (*hua*) into a highly regulated and more opaque form. Here is the beginning of her response:

【金絡索】	[*To the tune of* "Jin luosuo"]
來緘意太微,	The substance of your letter was most subtly conveyed;

知是防奸宄。	I am aware that this was for the purpose of protecting against malefactors.
兩下裏似鎖鑰相投，	It's as if we are passing a lock and key between the two of us.
有甚難猜的謎？	Is there any riddle that's too difficult to decipher?
心兒早屬伊，	My heart has long been yours, and
暗相期，	I've been furtively waiting for you;
不怕天人不肯依。	I fear not the judgement of Heaven or man.
你為我無端屈志增憔悴，	For me you have suffered endless wrongs and grown ever more laden with grief;
喫盡摧殘受盡虧。	You have endured ultimate humiliation and hardship.
好教我難為意，	It is difficult for me to achieve my desire:
恨不得乘鸞此際逐君飛。	I wish to mount the phoenix this instant and fly away with you.
怎奈道羽弱毛虧，	Alas, these feathers are feeble and damaged, and
去路猶迷。	The way out is yet unclear.
還須要靜待風雲會。[38]	We must calmly await an opportune moment.[39]

Whereas the lovers' secret messages in the short story would be easily comprehensible to the story's readers, the play version would be more challenging for illiterate members of the audience, in keeping with the references to the diction as a "riddle" and a "lock and key." Li Yu proposed that dialogue (*binbai* 賓白) could serve to translate arias, for, as he wrote in *Leisure Notes*, "arias can only transmit sound, they cannot convey the story" 止能傳聲, 不能傳情.[40] To demonstrate this point in the composition of this scene, Li Yu included an unusually lengthy exchange of spoken dialogue before the aria. The interruption of a long and highly accessible conversation with this aria would have reminded some listeners that they did not always comprehend the sung parts of *chuanqi*. This play about a play troupe thus shows the transformative power of *wenli*, for the actress character starts out using *wenli* for romantic purposes and is elevated into a playwright in the process.

In these examples, fictional characters use *wenli* as tools for secret communication in three different ways: they conceive of *wenli*, respectively, as specific empty grammatical particles, abstruse characters, and the transformation of "talk" into "song." But across all three strategies is an unspoken assumption: that everyone (*zhongren* 眾人) would be able to understand the spoken parts of the play and the everyday speech of the characters in the short story. This assumption is somewhat unusual, for the language used for short fiction and for the spoken parts of plays in this period, *baihua*, was not the same as a simple transcription of existing speech patterns. Rather, it was a standardized, empire-wide written form developed during the premodern period, and it served in literary texts, as Robert Hymes has argued, to "symbolize or emphasize conversationality" rather than "transcribe conversation." Similarly, *baihua* and *wenyan wen* 文言文 (the modern term for "classical Chinese"), as Shang Wei has argued, should be considered "two different registers of a linguistic continuum of written Chinese."[41] Li Yu's proposal, however, requires that the book written in *baihua* (his *changtan suyu*) clearly correspond to the aspiring reader's everyday speech, across the many regional variations in morphology and pronunciation. In this book that recommends that everyone should be able to read, Li Yu describes these printed sentences as coming "smoothly" out of the learner's mouth (*shunkou nianqu* 順口念去).[42]

Aiming to raise the status of dialogue in plays, Li Yu provides an extensive discussion of the relationship between speech and *changtan suyu*, and between *changtan suyu* and *wenli*. His discussion of playwriting in *Leisure Notes* proposes that dialogue—composed in what Li Yu calls *changtan suyu*—be equally valued with arias, not least because dialogue can transmit meaning when arias prove incomprehensible. Li Yu has an imaginary interlocutor point out that the primacy of arias is inherent in the very term for playwriting: "filling in lyrics" (*tianci*). The term for dialogue, the interlocutor continues, means "guest plain [talk]" (*binbai*). These literal translations of technical terms reference an existing tradition against which Li Yu rebelled: the earliest printed plays provided no dialogue at all, and even in the Ming, playwrights would often provide only cursory instructions, relying upon actors to improvise their lines. The entirety of play *writing*, in this tradition, entailed recording the arias. His imaginary interlocutor notes that dialogue is described as a "guest" and declares that "reversing the roles to make the host play guest would be like taking a tree to be greater than its root."[43] Li Yu, however, argues for the mutual dependence of arias and dialogue: "I have said that arias having dialogue [can be analogized], in terms of written language, to what the classics are to the commentaries; in terms of the pattern of material things, to what ridgepoles are to rafters; and in terms of the human body, to what the limbs and trunk are to the blood vessels" (523). The analogy to rafters and ridgepoles parallels the vertical dynamic of the tree-root analogy, but it reverses the valuation; the classics-commentaries analogy and the limbs–blood vessels analogy similarly emphasize the foundational nature of that which might be less obviously impressive. As the analogy to *wenli* culture suggests, if commentaries expound venerated truths revealed in the classics, so too might dialogue contribute to a shared cultural project.

In a move that would elevate *changtan suyu* to the status of *wenli*, Li Yu proposes that dialogue be promoted to the status of literary composition (*wenzhang*):

> Liweng treats dialogue as literary composition [*wenzhang*], expending effort to deliberate over every character. It has only ever mattered that dialogue was clear on the page, no one bothered to pay attention to whether it flowed smoothly out of the mouth. It is often the case that what is thoroughly lucid in the printed text [*keben* 刻本], becomes completely muddled when it is performed onstage. Is it possible that a single person's eyes and ears could be divided between sharp and dull? Because the author has only considered his brush and has not put himself in the position of others [*sheshen chudi*], allowing his mouth to take the place of the mouths of the actors and his ears to take the place of the audience, so that his heart and mouth are united, and from there he inquires after what makes for good talk and what is pleasing to the ear—this is the reason why there is such a clear distinction. (525)

Once again taking performance as the primary medium of *chuanqi*, Li Yu faults written and printed dialogue for not flowing smoothly out of the mouth. His language here emphasizes the body as a medium: Li Yu criticizes such playwrights for writing solely with their eyes and invites them to use their entire bodies, putting their ears and mouths in the place of others. This embodied writing process is transformative and exhilarating: "Li Yu may hold the brush in his hand, but his mouth is onstage. His body assumes all the movements of actors onstage, and his spirit circles round the four directions, examining plot elements and trying out sounds and tunes. If it's good, he immediately writes it down, if not, he puts down his brush" (525). In this dizzying production of performance-ready literature out of talk, the playwright's mouth separates from his hands: his body moves as all the actors move, and his voice articulates all the possible sounds. Notably, the emphasis remains on performance even at the moment of its writing.

Yet this new emphasis on dialogue only adds further regulations to the *chuanqi* genre. Li Yu's mouth may be gleefully onstage as he writes, but his own strict expectations for his new "literary composition" give free rein to almost no other mouths—for dialogue to claim universal literary status, it must be meticulously regulated. *Chuanqi* had long been recognized as requiring a fundamentally different approach to writing than earlier expressive forms used by literati. To write *chuanqi*, a literatus would need to compose in many different voices, including those belonging to different statuses and genders, and accordingly in a range of registers. Li Yu insists that playwrights must write in a way that is easily comprehensible, but he also demands that they carefully distinguish among the characters and role types. In this doubled requirement, a playwright must ensure that each line of verse contains a subjective representation of that character's personality.

We can compare this exuberant description of his proposed mode of playwriting to his lamentation of the existing writing practice. In an earlier essay in *Leisure Notes*, Li Yu argues that playwriting is the most difficult literary genre because it requires a unique combination of strict adherence to prosody in the writing of arias and lively imagination in constructing the total performance experience. Other genres also regulate structure, line length, and tonal pattern, but playwriting, he notes, also regulates sentence lengths, numbers of characters, tones, rhyme, and meter, as well as whether syllables are voiceless or voiced and pitches doubled or halved. He describes the restrictions of playwriting as an experience of haunting: "If you want to know the pitiable quality of the composition of this genre, how difficult it is to produce, I will tell you: the paper, ink, brush, and inkstone seem as though they do not belong to the writer but have been borrowed from someone else. Nor can the writer make good use of his own eyes, ears, and thoughts, as it seems like people are tugging at his elbows from all sides. It is not like poetry, rhapsodies, or old-style prose, which allow one to write swiftly and freely without being led along by gods or controlled by ghosts" (510–511). The tightly regulating rhyme schemes and metrical patterns of dramatic composition come to life as leading gods and controlling ghosts, turning the tunes of familiar arias into ominous forces, "leading along" and "controlling:" the playwright may choose his words, but he will always dance to an inherited tune. Li Yu's culminating vision for playwriting made the theatrical event a three-dimensional template on which the playwright must arrange dialogue so as to optimize the performance. Gone are the people pulling at his elbows and the ghosts leading him along: free to imagine every aspect of a performance, the playwright soars as the play stirs, the lifeblood of dialogue coursing through its veins.

If talk could be crafted into literature, the page was merely a temporary lodge. Even arias would need to be approached differently than if they were meant to stay on the page. Earlier playwrights, he argues, paid attention to prosody, but not to *wenzhang yidao* 文章一道, the "way of literature." A strong structure was missing from almost all earlier works, making them at once too literary and not literary enough. In the four essays on "Writing Arias" in *Leisure Notes*, Li Yu articulates how to transform the common idiom of everyday speech into a new literary form—something that is worthy of being called *wen*. By varying the significance of *wen* throughout these essays—from a category inclusive of *chuanqi* to its very opposite—Li Yu dislodges *wen* both from its classical and its expressive usages. Earlier theorists had also emphasized the range of registers in a *chuanqi*, noting that the lines of characters of lower status risked being too vulgar, whereas the lines of those of higher status risked being overly refined. Yet they had also postulated that the language of drama should be more direct and less allusive than poetry.[44] Li Yu, however, introduces new and specific gradations into the process of transforming everyday language into *chuanqi* dialogue. He instructs *chuanqi* writers to fit the language precisely to social distinctions among the play's characters and the actor's role types. He also suggests changing one or two characters to instantly transform "extremely coarse and extremely common [*su*] words" into "thoroughly new and thoroughly refined [*ya*] literature."[45] Thus, in Li Yu's conception, *ya* and *su* are not external, fixed categories between which the appropriate linguistic register must be found. Rather, he claims *ya*, or "refined," status for his artfully reworked and meticulously doled out expressions of the alleyways, hinting at his promotion of literate actors to literati in the essay "Teaching Arias": "All that is needed to transform a singer into a literatus [*wenren*] are the two words: 'can understand [*nengjie* 能解]'" (555).

In the final essay of this section, "Don't Overstuff!" (Ji tiansai 忌填塞), Li Yu warns that classical, historical, or poetic allusions should only be included if they also exist in everyday parlance: "And even if you occasionally happen to include something from a poem or the classics, these should be words [*yu*] that the ears are accustomed to hearing; language [*wen*] that is accustomed to being on the tip of the tongue. Although such language came from poetry or the classics, in fact it is no different from the talk of the streets and alleyways" (508). By using *yu* and *wen* interchangeably in this passage, Li Yu further dethrones *wen*. As he explains, in writing aria lyrics, "the words [*hua*] should originate in the talk of the streets and alleys; the events selected should be clearly and directly explained [*zhishuo mingyan* 直說明言]" (504). The terms used here are emphatically oral in their connotations, from the use of *hua* for "words" to the choice of *shuo* and *yan* to describe the language used to recount events in a play.

The ambivalent relationship between *chuanqi* and *wenzi* in these essays is compounded by the concomitant tension between *chuanqi* and books. The opening lines of the "Writing Arias" section compare the genres of *chuanqi* (here called *qu* 曲) with *ci* 詞 lyric poetry in terms of the length of their printed versions (*keben*) (504), yet Li Yu almost immediately returns to *chuanqi* in performance. He writes of the possible evaluations of the play by its performers (*yanzhe* 演者), spectators (*guanzhe* 觀者) (504), and audience members—literally "those who listen to singing" (*tingge zhe* 聽歌者) (505). Plays that do not adequately consider the question of performance, he warns, will be tainted by their dependence on books. Such plays are well known as so-called desktop plays (*antou xi* 案頭戲), and their book-dependent value was hotly debated in the late Ming.⁴⁶ For Li Yu, the "stench of books" (*shuben qi* 書本氣) wafting through the air indicates all that could go wrong with theatrical performance: "It's not that people in the Yuan did not read books and so the plays they wrote had not one whiff of pedantry [*shuben qi*]. It was that they had books but didn't reference them.... As for the plays of those who came later—their pages are covered in books [*manzhi jieshu* 滿紙皆書]" (504). One should read all kinds of books for inspiration, but at the moment of playwriting the books should be partly forgotten.

Through this strategic forgetting of the play's readership, the playwright can ensure that the play's plot and language remain easily comprehensible to its audience. Li Yu's image of "pages covered in books" is as unusual in classical Chinese as it is in English translation. This odd phrase identifies both an age-old literary problem—that of the inability of literature to equal or capture lived experience in all its glory—and a newer one, caused by the fall of the Ming dynasty. Li Yu's desire to distance his theory of playwriting from earlier literary works, and from books in general, speaks to a widely shared desire to change what books are, how they work, and who has access to them. The weirdness of the phrase prompts one to ask: What, if not books, might fill pages? Li Yu's answer is the living language of the everyday world. But as much as these plays were intended to capture the textures and shades of the everyday world in writing and print, they also sought to use the form of the *chuanqi* to bring those captured scenes back to life.

Whereas late-Ming thinkers had largely imagined the common people as having more direct access to truth, Li Yu envisages illiterate people as a potential audience.⁴⁷ This broadening of one's audience is partly a marketing move. He catered to a highly varied group of potential purchasers by finding ways to make the text speak to each of them in turn. He did so by drawing on the resources that he offered previously in *Leisure Notes*, where he explained how to differentiate characters' speech to reflect their role types. He further expanded his reach through inventive linguistic constructions like "pages covered in books." This construction is immediately comprehensible when spoken, as the diction and vocabulary are simple, yet it is also the sort of sentence that few had ever said before (or since)—thus modeling the clever inventiveness that translates flawlessly from page to stage that he has prescribed for his aspiring-playwright readers.

Near the end of the "Writing Arias" section, Li Yu declares: "Literature [*wenzhang*] is made for those who read books to look at, so it is not faulted for being deep. Plays [*xiwen*] are made both for those who read books [*dushu ren*] and for those who do not read books [*bu dushu ren* 不讀書人] alike to look at; they are also written for women and children who don't read books to look at. Thus, in plays, the shallow is valued, and not the deep."⁴⁸ These three consecutive claims, which occur on the final pages of the "Writing Arias" section, are deeply strange. By using the verb *kan* ("to look") for literate and illiterate people alike, Li Yu deprioritizes literacy, even as he notes that the *kan* literate people do with literature is fundamentally unlike the *kan* illiterate people do. By repeating the same character with such disparate implications, Li Yu valorizes a broad range of "looking," and he highlights that plays and books are both appreciated through "looking," despite the strong aural component of the former. And because three of the four categories of people he mentions are likely mostly illiterate, he prioritizes the "looking" experience of the illiterate over that of the expert reader. In addition, Li Yu equalizes the terms *dushu ren* and *bu dushu ren*, usually used to denote the status divide between literati (*wenren*) and everyone else, by equating the kind of looking that both groups do, which he terms *tongkan* 同看 ("to look together"). This kind of looking is hindered rather than aided by the ability to read. Furthermore, he uses two terms, *kan* and *du*, that are normally distinct verbs meaning "to look" and "to read," but when used in relation to books are understood as synonymous. In doing so, he further downplays the special status that is usually attributed to the ability to read, eroding the status distinction between *dushu ren* and *bu dushu ren*.

Li Yu follows up this equalizing claim with a much broader argument: that the sages of the classics might learn something from the fiction of his day. His phrasing here echoes that of Jin Shengtan 金聖嘆 (1608–1661), who had championed the moral and literary power of vernacular fiction, claiming that fiction shared rhetorical techniques and moral effects with the classics.⁴⁹ Li Yu's claim carries less of an ethical assessment. Instead, Li Yu continues his essay's dichotomy of deep and shallow, pondering how the sages would have written had they tried to write for everyone to "look at": "If, when literature [*wenzhang*] was first established, it had also been made for those who read books and those who don't, as well as women and children to look at together, then the classics and commentaries written by the sages that have been handed down from ancient times would also be shallow rather than deep, like the fiction of our day" (508). How might we understand this confounding comment within the larger context of *Leisure Notes*? Li Yu seems to indict the sages for excluding so many potential lookers, yet he also declares that an aspiration to inclusivity would have rendered the classics "shallow." Overturning traditional interpretations of the values attached to depth and shallowness, in classical Chinese and English alike, Li Yu causes the reader to wonder if the classics, too, could have been written as entertainingly as popular fiction. A few lines later in this essay, Li Yu recounts: "Someone asked: When literary men [*wenshi*] write *chuanqi*, it's no different from when they write books: they do so to display their genius. How can their genius be displayed in the shallow? I replied: He who can display his genius in the shallow is a true master of literature [*wenzhang*]" (508). Through wordplay once again appropriate to the multimedia environment of the theater, Li Yu here argues that *chuanqi* dethrones the established literary order. In his estimation, it is not just plays that would benefit from attention to the surfaces of language—all literature would.

We've seen how many of Li Yu's proposals in *Leisure Notes* subject received wisdom to a reevaluation; it is thus somewhat surprising that in his quest to develop a universally accessible dramatic form, he did not call into question longstanding stereotyped distinctions between north and south. Although northern plays were, by that time, rarely performed, these generic differences presented real issues for Li Yu. He worried, for instance, how one performer could take responsibility for all of the singing in a long southern drama, as was the generic requirement of the much shorter northern plays.

Many writers had transposed plays between regions while adapting to generic and musical differences, but Li Yu complicated the process by raising the issue of regional pronunciation in dialogue. In an essay titled "Characters Should Be Distinguished between North and South" (Zi fen nanbei 字分南北), he writes: "Northern tunes have characters [that represent] northern pronunciation, southern tunes have characters [that represent] southern pronunciation.... People only know that arias should distinguish between regions, they don't know that the dialogue should be adapted [*zhuan* 轉] along with the arias, and that they should not be treated as two separate pieces" (526–527). In a leveling of the aria-dialogue distinction in keeping with that in his earlier writing discussion, Li Yu here insists that the dialogue must be regionally translated at the same time that the arias are adapted, by using only characters that represent the regionally appropriate pronunciation. Li Yu laments, "The *chuanqi* written by our contemporaries often mix them [regional speech forms] together: even if they can separate them to use for the painted face [*jing* 淨] and the clown [*chou* 丑] roles, they don't know how to add gravitas for the male and female leads [*sheng* 生, *dan* 旦]. Or they can use them [regional speech] separately for men, but they don't know how to differentiate them for women" (527).

Li Yu's complaint here highlights the gendered nature of regional difference as it manifests in playwriting, a practice that Xiaofei Tian has traced to its development in the Six Dynasties.[50] Li Yu notes that playwrights frequently assigned lines to characters based on regional stereotypes: "Because northern characters are closer to the rough and heroic, it is easy to put them in the mouths of the bold and vigorous. Southern pronunciation is all rather sweet and charming, which makes it suitable to use for gentle and graceful people. Without the authors' realizing it, the sounds get all mixed together, in what is commonly known as a 'two-headed barbarian' [*liangtou man* 兩頭蠻]" (527). It is not clear what two-headed barbarians look like, but we now know what they *sound* like: when both accents are used at once, language shifts from the expressive to the monstrous. Li Yu emphasizes the importance of regional phonetic differences in nonrhyming dialogue, and he insists on doing so even when other playwrights and actors alike are already mixing regional speech. In attempting to elevate "speech" to the level of literary composition, Li Yu thus also seeks to standardize it and adhere to regional distinctions.

Although he advocates the inclusion of regional pronunciation, he criticizes the practice of using topolects (*fangyan* 方言, "regional words"): "Whoever writes *chuanqi* should not repeatedly use regional words [*fangyan*] as it will cause people to not be able to understand. Of late, whenever a painted face role comes onto the stage, playwrights always write a Suzhou accent. . . . They don't consider the fact that this kind of voicing can only be understood in Jiangsu and Zhejiang; beyond that, the audience will be at a loss. *Chuanqi* are the books of all under Heaven;

how could you design them for just those in the Jiangsu and Zhejiang regions?"[51] Rather than write in a *changtan suyu* that will be intelligible to all speakers, Li Yu insists that playwrights determine what is regional about their own speech so that they can write "speech" that will be comprehensible to "all under Heaven." The goal here is to produce plain literary languages that are nevertheless somewhat regionally inflected. They are not, however, authentic representations of regional speech, which has become somewhat jumbled across the bounds of class, gender, and personality. A playwright's characters must be able to speak as everyone under Heaven *should* speak, and yet that speech must evince regional distinction.

In an essay dedicated to the problem of dialect in theatrical performance, Li Yu criticizes the practice of the "painted face" roles speaking a motley assortment of regional dialects. He suggests that either the dialect should be selected based on the character's origins or the play's setting, or all dialect should be removed and replaced with Mandarin (*guanyin* 官音). Alternatively, the dialogue can be adapted to the performance locale: "Even if you use dialect, you can shift [*zhuan*] it according to the place. . . . If many can understand, everyone will laugh!" (563). The language of "shifting" (*zhuan*) here is reminiscent of the "flipping" (*fan* 翻) of scripts that was necessary to adapt them for performance in the north or the south. In both cases, Li Yu vacillates between two options in an effort to make the play more universally comprehensible: the first is to standardize the language of all characters; the second is to change the pronunciation as the plays are performed in different places. The former seeks universality through uniformity, the latter through adaptability.

Regional speech seems to function in quite the opposite way from the *wenli* with which we began. Whereas fluency in *wenli* enabled a secret message to be conveyed, the primary quality of the sounds (*shengyin* 聲音) of regional speech (*fangyan*) is precisely its limited circulation. In the end, the only language that Li Yu believes can travel with his plays is that which is written down, carefully standardized, and pronounced after being read: for him, this seems to have been true of dialogue as well as arias. These plays can "unite all under Heaven" (*tong tianxia* 通天下) in performance because they have made *binbai* into *wenli* (589).

In the end, Li Yu claims that *wenli* is the master key behind written and performed theater alike. When a performance genre sought to incorporate universally comprehensible literary texts into spoken or sung forms, it required further regulation: not only the appropriate training of the bodies and minds of the actors who would perform, but also the regulated pronunciation of those speech registers intended to resemble everyday speech. Through these considerations, in the end, the body once trained by Li Yu for performance emerges as a technology of literary reproduction: perhaps not as easily controlled as a woodblock print, but close enough.

CONSTRUCTING LITERATURE

For all of his criticism of written literature, Li Yu had no vision of an actor-centered, workshop-style theater. Before his works could be imprinted onto the lips and tongues of actors, he committed them to writing and to print, prioritizing a streamlined and easy-to-follow plot structure in addition to comprehensible language. He featured his essays on this topic first in *Leisure Notes*, attesting to his belief that such tight plotting was the most fundamental lesson for an aspiring playwright. Subsequent chapters will look at the interplay of writing, bodies, and buildings across Li Yu's work; here I begin by examining how he described the desired structural integrity of *chuanqi* using metaphors of bodies and buildings.

Early Qing writers frequently turned to nostalgic or fantastic modes to respond to the displacement of the dynastic transition, creating what Wai-yee Li has called "a new poetics of space" through their poignant usage of the term "no place" (*wudi* 無地).[52] In her analysis, many of these loyalists turned to the imaginary or the illusory as a form of "inner exile,"[53] as they saw no place for themselves in the real world. Whether immortal realms or imaginary mundane gardens, such writings tend to be tinged with loss—whether of the Ming state, actual land, career prospects, loved ones, or urban community. Li Yu's ideas about literary composition drew on the same sources of inspiration, for he too sifted through the loss of real places and focused, in response, on the space of the page. In loyalist writing, there is frequently tension between these media, with the present page disappearing in favor of the absent land: a poem may lament the poet's displacement even as it remains silent about the place it occupies on the printed page. Li Yu's work, in contrast, pondered not just a loss of a metaphoric "place" in the world or of a physical plot of land, but rather the loss of a different physical "place" (*di*): that of the surfaces of books themselves.

Although Li Yu did lose his home over the course of the dynastic transition, he was keen to recover and build on page-space as much as on plots of land, and he did so mostly with excitement rather than grief. He exclaimed, for instance, in an essay in *Leisure Notes* on achieving likeness in representation of characters in plays (Yu qiu xiaosi 語求肖似):

> Of all literary genres, that which is the boldest, the most unconventional and refined, that in the composition can most strengthen one's character, none surpasses playwriting. Without this genre, the talented would just about be killed by frustration and heroes would die of distress. I was born in the midst of suffering and misery, and I have dwelt in straitened circumstances from youth to adulthood, from maturity to old age, with never a moment's respite for my furrowed brow. Yet during those moments when I am composing plays, not only does my gloom lift and my anger dissipate, but I defiantly become the happiest person between heaven and earth. At such times, I feel as though there is no better way to enjoy wealth and rank and glorious luxury than this. There has never been in doing what one pleases in the real world [*zhenjing* 真境] anything that can exceed the bold and untrammeled quality of this illusory realm [*huanjing* 幻境]: If I wish to take office, then in an instant I attain glory; If I wish to retire from that office, then in the twinkling of an eye I can enter the forests and mountains again. . . . If I wish to become an immortal or a Buddha, then the Western Heaven and Peng Isle will appear before my inkstone and brush rest; if I wish to do my filial duty or demonstrate loyalty, then as to serving a sovereign or enabling my parents' long life, I could surpass [sage rulers] Yao and Shun and [long-lived legend] Peng Jian [彭籛].[54]

This passage, written late in Li Yu's career, echoes the *wudi* discourse of Ming loyalists in its contrasting of terms like "illusory realm" (*huanjing*) with the "realm of the real" (*zhenjing*) and the "realm of straitened circumstance" (*luopo zhi jing* 落魄之境). The usual relationship between the two realms, however, is transformed here by the mimetic powers of *chuanqi* composition. Instead of creating an illusory world to compensate for loss, Li Yu advertises the joys of the play composition process. Such composition proves better than the real world, just as illusory worlds should be, but it turns out not to be entirely illusory, because *chuanqi* can create an immersive social experience for writers, readers, actors, and audiences alike. Importantly, this happens through both the immateriality of the literary imagination and the material presence of things. The inkstone and brush rest mentioned toward the end of the passage highlight the media of which the illusory world is made, and the use of "before" in this reference further suggests a real, or imagined, performance of the created scene.

As Judith Zeitlin has shown, fictional worlds were widely understood to have real consequences in the seventeenth century because "once fictional characters or events have been created, they *cannot* be retracted or taken back. . . . They have entered the world of their readers and are no longer exclusively controlled by the author who invented them."[55] The tales of the strange (*zhiguai* 志怪) of Zeitlin's study as well as the many literary works that celebrated sublime passion (*qing*) during this period mingled our mundane world with the supernatural; when such stories dwell among us, they give our world an otherworldly dimension. Li Yu's "illusory realms," however, tended to feature the mundane. Consequently, I argue, there was only one boundary for them to cross: between the illusory and the real (*huan* and *zhen*) or, in the terms I've been developing in this book, *xu* and *shi*. Li Yu generates a sense of materiality for his illusory worlds by treating a literary work as a complex structure. His attention to plot construction, taken together with the analogies to buildings and bodies through which he expounded its importance in *Leisure Notes*, gave his plays a structural integrity that made them last in the real world.

Plot construction had increasingly become a concern of theorists as the *chuanqi* form developed over the course of the Ming and through the early Qing.[56] The combination of sheer length and multiple interwoven narrative threads made *chuanqi*, like full-length vernacular fiction, susceptible to prolixity and disorganization, and the handling of a long novel or play's elaborate structure was the most challenging component of the writer's craft.[57] With increased attention to overall structure and narrative coherence, the average number of scenes in *chuanqi* decreased steadily, from a sprawling 40 to 50 scenes in the early period (1465–1586), then 30 to 40 scenes in the late Ming (1587–1651), and finally 20 to 30 scenes in the early Qing (1652–1718).[58]

Though Li Yu was not the first writer to focus on structure in playwriting, he prioritized it above all other elements of playwriting and developed it to an unprecedented degree. My analysis here diverges from that of James Liu, who has characterized Li Yu's theory of literature as "technical" and his metaphors as reductive.[59] In contrast to this reading, I show how Li Yu condenses and intensifies the substance of *chuanqi* through practical suggestions and suggestive metaphors, proposing a tightly structured, lively play through a tightly structured, lively discourse on the play's form. I argue that Li Yu reimagines nature, the higher arts, and buildings, *in terms of* one another, rather than simply reducing one to the other. He conceived of these arenas as media in which he might work, and through which he might communicate, blurring the boundaries between the natural and the manufactured by combining elements of writing, architecture, and human bodies.

With his theory of "structure" (*jiegou*), Li Yu reimagines the technology of writing as a material tool, using memorable analogies to lend substance to the *chuanqi* form. As we saw, Li Yu argued for the indispensability of dialogue in *chuanqi* by likening the relationship between arias and dialogue in *chuanqi* to the commentarial tradition in the study of the classics, to architectural integrity, and to the functioning of the human body. In that series of analogies, he identified two crucial but distinguishable elements essential to each entity: as classics are to commentaries; as ridgepoles and roofbeams are to rafters; and as the limbs and trunk are to veins and arteries.[60] Written texts, material things, and the human body are thus presented as complex systems with identifiable and resonant governing structures. This is not an ancient correlative cosmology that would link the human body to the cosmos, but rather a technological practice that identified the primary media of experimentation as texts, bodies, and the material world, conceiving of them in interrelated terms.

By likening *chuanqi* arias to the classics and *chuanqi* dialogue to embedded commentary on those classics, Li Yu posits a connection between the most revered traditional texts, on the one hand, and new, risqué, and very popular plays, on the other. As David Rolston's study of fiction commentary has shown, writers of this period produced extensive commentaries for vernacular fiction and *chuanqi*, building on a commentarial tradition usually reserved for the most substantial texts.[61] Commentaries on the classics were usually interlinear, with two columns of commentary, carved in smaller characters, to one column of a classic text, carved in a larger font, interspersed throughout the work. Although Li Yu published many of his works with comments by his friends included in the upper margins, the analogy here does not refer to the widespread use of commentary in contemporary publishing. Instead, it indicates that the arias, which offer a more elevated experience, are crosscut with the clearer, more comprehensible, and lighter dialogue. Although the difference in size of the printed characters for the arias and dialogue is more moderate than that found between the classics and commentaries, with the same amount of space allotted to each character of both types, the dialogue characters are nevertheless noticeably smaller.

Much as the classics analogy dramatized the interdependence of *chuanqi*'s elements, so too the building analogy emphasizes their careful calibration. Here, the ridgepole, which occupies a building's highest point, and the sturdy roof beams are likened to arias.[62] The building requires careful measurements to ensure structural integrity, necessitating a level of complexity that rivals that of the rules concerning the composition of arias. The rafters, by contrast, are narrow beams of wood that slope from the ridgepole down to the eaves. In addition to being thinner than the roof beams, rafters tend to be uniform in shape and length when laid one next to the other over the roof beams. In material terms, then, although the rafters would fall to the ground without beams to support them, it follows that without rafters to support the roof tiles, the ridgepole and beams would provide only an open frame, and thereby fail to provide shelter from the elements. Taken together, however, these components of a building's roof create a habitable space. Dialogue fills in the spaces between the "roof beams" which would otherwise leave readers and spectators distracted—for instance, by the weather—and unable to focus their attention on the theater. Li Yu's final analogy separates the flesh and bones of a human body from the blood that courses through it: without dialogue, he implies, the play is no better than a corpse. He is certain that readers and spectators will sense the decay and refuse to waste their time on a play with only good arias to recommend it.

These analogies appear in an essay arguing for the importance of dialogue in *chuanqi*, and yet arias (and with them the classics, the ridgepoles and roof beams, and the human flesh and bones) retain a crucial structural significance in their respective media. Li Yu did not, after all, invent a spoken-dialogue-only theater—that would have to wait until the twentieth century. Instead, the two registers worked in tandem: arias provide a strong, substantial, and intricate structure that dialogue explicates, coheres, and animates. Attention to the varying affordances of *wen* allowed Li Yu to amplify the possibilities for each register in his conceptualization of the *chuanqi* form, which he then paired with a complex but streamlined plot structure.

The human body served a particularly rich metaphoric role in Li Yu's vision for literary creation, yet his discussion emphasizes the process of the body's creation rather than its attributes:

> When the Creator endowed us with form [*zaowu zhi fuxing* 造物之賦形], just as the semen and blood [*jingxue* 精血] were beginning to congeal, and before the fetus was formed, he first established the complete form of the body [*zhiding quanxing* 制定全形], making it so that a drop of blood was endowed with all the features of the five organs and the skeleton. Now suppose that he had not had a complete idea before he began, but rather had—from the top of the head to the bottom of the feet—proceeded to create us step by step. If that had been the case, people's bodies [*shen* 身] would contain countless scars where they had been cut off and then connected, which would obstruct the flow of blood and *qi*.[63]

Li Yu's metaphor mobilizes the drop of blood from which the body would be formed, and not the completed body. He thereby proposes taking the body as a model of the natural order at the moment before any of its component parts might be observed: none of the resulting attributes of the body, as a consequence, can be directly applied as guiding principles. This metaphor works both to support Li Yu's understanding of playwriting and to discount a skill—namely, the sophisticated prosody of playwriting—valued by theorists who preceded him. Using an analogy that resonates for us today, Li Yu suggests that sophistication produces creations akin to Frankenstein's monster, unless primacy is given, as he insists, to the extra-lyrical considerations of overall structure. By offering a negative example of a malformed body—cut off and then connected—he accentuates the force of the metaphor.

We can better appreciate the startling novelty of this analogy by considering the long tradition of invoking the body to discuss literature. In Liu Xie's 劉勰 (ca. 465–ca. 522) *The Literary Mind and the Carving of Dragons* (*Wenxin diaolong* 文心雕龍), for instance, bodies serve as natural models for literary creation. In an early example, the bilateral symmetry of the human body justifies the importance of parallelism in writing, sharply limiting the playwright's creative role: "When Creation unfurled the shapes [of things] [*fuxing* 賦形], the limbs of all bodies were in pairs. In the functioning of spirit's principle, no event ever occurs alone. And when mind generated literary language, giving thought to all manner of concerns and cutting them to pattern, by Nature parallelism was formed, just as [the concepts of] high and low are necessary to one another."[64] Later, Liu Xie used the human skeleton to encourage writers to ensure a strong underlying structure: "The way in which the words depend upon bone is like the way in which the skeleton is set in the [human] form [*ti* 體]."[65] This bodily analogy continued in Li Yu's time, as for instance in Xu Fuzuo's 徐復祚 (1560–after 1630) observation in *Discourse on Drama* (*Qulun* 曲論) about *The Story of Washing Silk* (*Huansha ji* 浣紗記, 16th c.): "its plot is meandering, without tendons or bones."[66] In contrast, in Li Yu's analogy, it is not immediately evident what particular quality the body is supposed to model.

The image of a human body formed from pieces resonates across the essays of *Leisure Notes*, indicating the unique challenge of the *chuanqi* form. For instance, Li Yu refers back to this body metaphor in the essay "Value Organic Unity and Witty Charm" (Zhong jiqu 重機趣), but he does so in oblique terms, referencing only the scars: "'Not having scars where it was cut off and then continued' refers not only to how one scene is connected onto another, or how one character is situated with relation to another, but you should also ensure that what comes earlier is carried on and what comes later is connected, linked together in a circulatory system."[67] As his return to this metaphor indicates, the organic quality Li Yu seeks for the plot of a play should be understood in relation to his reimagining of the work of the Creator. The image of nature gone awry implies that the human playwright might, in improving his playwriting skills, also improve upon Creation itself. If the ostensible point here is to offer an ideal organic model, that conventional emphasis is missing from the words we actually read. Through this dissonance between the expected comparison and the one provided, Li Yu provides his own improvement, hinting at the shortcomings of the Creator by showcasing a "bad creation" in this metaphor. With this double move, Li Yu manages to undermine the human body as ideal model even as he references it.

Whereas Li Yu's use of the body analogy elevated the playwright, comparing him to the exalted Creative Force of the universe, his likening of the playwright to a builder of houses associated him with a lower social status. In an analogy that desacralizes literary creation, Li Yu compares playwriting to the construction of a residence:[68] "A master builder's construction of a house is also the same. When the foundation has first been leveled, but before the frame has been erected, he first plans where to build the main hall, where to open doorways, what type of lumber he will use for the ridgepoles and roof beams. He must wait until the whole design is clear, and only then may he raise his hatchet."[69] This building analogy is developed through a fairly tight parallel structure that echoes the structure used to compare playwriting to the construction of the human body. This resonance manifests throughout: in the syntax used to broach each topic ("When the Creator bestows form" 造物之賦形; "When a builder constructs a building" 工師之建宅), in the parallel words chosen to structure each analogy ("before" *wei* 未, "first" *xian* 先; "if" *tang* 倘, "then" *ze* 則), and in the words used to describe each creative process ("predetermined structure" *chengju* 成局, "momentum" *shi* 勢, "build/create" *zao*) (496). The building analogy, however, diverges in providing an explicit goal of utility (*yong* 用): the function of a house, we are reminded, is to accommodate its occupants.

We can understand the significance of Li Yu's building analogy by comparing it with that used by the drama critic Wang Jide 王驥德 (?–1623), in his influential *Rules of Dramatic Prosody* (*Qulü* 曲律) in the late Ming. In a chapter titled "Discourse on Literary Structure" (Lun zhangfa 論章法), he wrote:

> Composing plays [*qu*] is like building [*zao*] a house. When a craftsman builds a house, he must first determine a design model: whether

there should be three, or five, or seven spans from the front gate to the reception hall, to the principle rooms, to the storied rooms; and again from the side-rooms to the studio, and as to such things as the granary, the kitchen and the washroom, the fence and the wall, the garden and pavilion—front and back, left and right, high and low, near and far—even the smallest detail must be conceived of fully in his breast—only then is he able to wield his axe.[70]

As Chen Duo has suggested, Wang Jide is referring primarily to the literary structure (*zhangfa*) of the plays, which he then explicitly ties to other literary forms, including *wen*, *cifu* 辭賦, and *geshi* 歌詩. In all of these cases, Wang proposes, "events already have a certain sequence," suggesting an older understanding of developing a literary form in keeping with the contours of an event. Wang Jide thus proposes that the expression of one's intent is most significant. Li Yu, in contrast, revises this older understanding to build what Chen Duo describes as a new way of thinking about theater as plot driven and always performance related.

Li Yu further analogizes writing fiction with designing buildings in order to explain what "fictionality" means. In the essay titled "Consider Fiction and Truth" (Shen xushi 審虛實) which is the final essay in the opening section on "Structure," he begins by dividing the material (*shi* 事) of *chuanqi* into four categories: ancient, modern, fictional, and real. He suggests that all *chuanqi* are made up, and he criticizes, as he does in "Avoid Satire" (Jie fengci 戒諷刺), those who seek to verify their dramatic plots through comparison with the historical record. And yet Li Yu asserts that plays set in the contemporary moment are much easier to write than historical plays, which must be verifiable against the historical record. In contemporary plays, a playwright may feel free to invent characters and events, since there is not yet a record in books—just the hearsay of news and gossip. He draws on the building metaphor to elaborate the "fictional," approaching this category through the notion of *xu*: "The fictional [*xu*] refers to 'towers in airy nothingness' [*kongzhong louge* 空中樓閣]. They are constructed according to your wishes and are without shadow or form."[71] By analogizing these made-up plays set in the present to "towers in airy nothingness," Li Yu uses his argument about fictionality to add a temporal element to a seemingly spatial building metaphor. To write a play set in the present, one builds it out there in the void; to write a historical play, one builds somewhere between the stage and the historical record.

In the late Ming, Li Zhi, the iconoclast and champion of vernacular literature, had argued fiercely for naturalness in playwriting. He contrasted the homophones *huagong* 化工 (works of Nature/the Creator) and *huagong* 畫工 (works of an artisan/painter) to argue that the Creator does not exhibit artifice. He further provided a natural example: "People see and delight in what heaven gives life to, what the earth nurtures, and the varieties of vegetation found everywhere. But when they search for Heaven's skill, no matter how they search, they cannot find a trace of it."[72] As we see from the above analogies, Li Yu's approach to dramatic composition blurs the distinction between these terms. He raises the status of artisanal work by drawing freely on architectural metaphors to offer models to would-be playwrights, while he brings the Creator down to earth by offering models of imperfect bodies as negative examples. By constructing them in parallel form, he refuses to distinguish between these natural and artificial metaphors, and he does not prioritize the unattainable model of nature over the vernacular model of architecture.

In Li Yu's writing, buildings and bodies and words all resonate against one another, whether in life or in metaphor. In later chapters I explore the implications of Li Yu's challenges to the Creator's infallibility and his proposals that nature might be improved by human creativity: nature is dethroned and replaced with a remodeled version of itself, acknowledged as produced and updated by human intervention. By modeling his plays after the human body, Li Yu would seem to be proposing writing as verisimilitude: *like* its organic model. But the building analogy positions the writer rather as a builder, lower in social status and fully human. Taken together, these analogies suggest that the architect is reimagined as capable of intervening, not just on literary composition but on the creation of human beings as well. The relationship among these three media—books, buildings, and bodies—is my focus in the next two sections of this book, for Li Yu reenvisions what is possible, not just for writing, but for the construction of the spaces and the bodies that mediate our lives.

PART II
Spatial Media

CHAPTER THREE

Fictional Space in *Twelve Towers*

How are books like buildings? Reading Li Yu's *Leisure Notes*, his contemporary Wang Zuoju commented: "Reading Liweng's books is like climbing a pagoda: each storey is invariably higher than the last."[1] Indeed, Li Yu's last collection of *huaben* short stories, *Twelve Towers* (ca. 1658), is carefully structured around the conceit of twelve specific buildings, one per story. Yet critics long dismissed this conceit as merely superficial. In one of the first modern reassessments of Li Yu's work, written in 1935, Sun Kaidi lamented: "Setting the theme with the title this way comes off as rather precious, but we may set this point aside without further discussion."[2] Half a century later, Patrick Hanan concurred: "The fact that each story is named for a building is merely a superficial bond."[3] Chen Jianhua recently proposed a link between the collection's buildings and Li Yu's expertise in garden design, and he has noted that in prefatory comments for the collection, Li Yu's friend Du Jun makes several comparisons between fictional narrative and garden design. For Chen, this interplay between cultural fields develops a new idea of fictionality that elevates the genre of fiction in China to a modern status.[4]

In this chapter I argue that Li Yu draws on his familiarity with architecture to transform the *huaben* short story collection. As I will discuss in chapter 4, he designed his own and others' gardens and would eventually include essays on home and garden design in *Leisure Notes*. Here, I propose that the conceit of his stories as buildings (*lou* 樓) was deeply informed by those nontextual activities, for that experience allowed him to reimagine the *huaben* collection as a garden. As Craig Clunas has shown, by the sixteenth century, buildings and rocks—and not plants—had become the fundamental elements of literati gardens.[5] I first examine the representation of a building in each story to understand how a building, as literary device, can cause a narrative to unfold. Second, I draw on the figure of a garden composed of buildings to offer an architectural explanation for the collection's formal innovations. Buildings in *Twelve Towers*, I argue, shape these narratives in several distinct ways, whether through their material affordances, their names, or their symbolism. These buildings are thus "actants," to use a term from actor-network theory; they make things happen. These functions are, in turn, revelatory, for they make fiction that hovers at the edge of reality, with its easily realizable buildings poised to remodel our world.

The first story in *Twelve Towers*, "Tower of Shared Reflections" (Heying lou 合影樓) includes a revealing phrase in the story's final line: the narrator mentions "towers in airy nothingness" (*kongzhong louge*), or as I have adopted it for the title of this book, *Towers in the Void*. Toward the end of chapter 2 we saw that this expression was commonly used to indicate appearance without substance, and in this first tower story Li Yu used it to emphasize fictionality (*xu*): "This account comes from one Mr. Hu's [lit. "Mr. Nonsense"] *Brush Notes*, but as that text is a manuscript that has not been carved on blocks for world-wide distribution, few have seen it. At present, I have made a work of fiction out of it, but people still won't believe it, saying that these twelve pavilions [*tingtai* 亭臺] are all 'towers in airy nothingness' [*kongzhong louge*]."[6] This jesting account of a work of fiction that originates in nonfiction problematizes both categories: according to the narrator, the true story—though undercut in the cheeky naming of its purported author—exists only in manuscript and has been lost forever, whereas the fictional story is dismissed as false even as it circulates widely.

We can begin to understand *Twelve Towers* by unpacking the phrase that Li Yu uses here. It can be traced back to Song Zhiwen's 宋之問 (ca. 656–712) poem, "Visiting Lotus Dharma Temple" (You fahua si 遊法華寺).[7] In that poem, which is filled with Buddhist motifs, "airy nothingness" brings to mind both the sky and the more technical term "emptiness," understood in Mahayana doctrine as all things lacking an independent existence. In later usage, this phrase tends to be synonymous with the English expression "castles in the air": dreams that will likely go unfulfilled, plans that will not come to fruition. But it could also suggest exceptionally clear understanding: a penetrating mind whose imaginative aerial viewpoint can grasp the entirety of an issue.[8] By bringing both of these senses of *kongzhong louge* into play, I foreground how the tower conceit enables Li Yu once again to recalibrate *xu* and *shi*, emphasizing both the fictionality and the nonfiction consequences of his towers in airy nothingness.

How does the notion of fiction as "towers in airy nothingness" change when a work of fiction not only features buildings but also names its stories after those buildings? Some of the best-known works of fiction and drama in the Chinese tradition—like *Dream of the Red Chamber* (*Honglou meng* 紅樓夢) or *Story of the Western Wing* (*Xixiang ji* 西廂記)— feature buildings in their titles. In these works, the titular structures either symbolize qualities of human characters or play a minor role as a setting: in *Dream of the Red Chamber*, the "dream" emphasizes the distance between the setting and the novel itself, whereas in *Western Wing* the building is a meeting place for the characters.[9] In Li Yu's collection, by contrast, the design of each tower fundamentally grounds its story: the building in each title provides a spatial structure to the story, and it also acts on and is acted upon by its characters. Moreover, unlike in other works, each building participates neither in a generic naming practice nor in a grand allegory. Whereas full-length novels might contain, as Andrew Plaks has argued for *Dream of the Red Chamber*'s Grand Prospect Garden (Daguan yuan 大觀園), the entire "aesthetic structure of encyclopedic allegory," the smaller rooms of *Twelve Towers* are humbler in their aims and more varied in their narrative functions.[10] Rather than fleeting encounters or encyclopedic allegory, they demonstrate how buildings mediate our everyday lives. Their operations include that which Keith McMahon has noted for architectural interstices in seventeenth-century fiction, in which "a gap" proves simultaneously to be "also a link or juncture."[11] And even as fictional buildings shape Li Yu's plots, the term "tower" in the collection's titles stands for the story itself, altering its medium. This collection of twelve "towers" no longer takes recourse to the familiar narrative forms of "stories" (*ji*) or "dreams" (*meng*) that announce their narrative quality, but rather insists that what we are reading is itself a tower. This move makes reading a story, as we will see, akin to ascending a tower's storeys.

These building actants are individually named but remain inanimate, which lends them a distinctive kind of fictional status. Although no one would believe that a person they met named Pan Jinlian was *that* Pan Jinlian, we do not associate the naming of a building with the same singularity. As a result, a named fictional building blurs the boundary between the fictional and the real to a greater extent than is possible for human characters. A focus on buildings as media allowed Li Yu to reshape the *huaben* genre, for *huaben* before the *Twelve Towers* collection had been defined by their purported historical relationship to the temporal art of oral storytelling. In chapter 4, I demonstrate how this innovative foregrounding of the narrative possibilities of fictional space in turn informed Li Yu's ideas about garden design.

WHERE STORIES TAKE PLACE

Following a brief prologue, the main story of a *huaben* almost invariably begins in a conventional way. It starts by listing the time and place in which events will unfold, as well as the name of a primary protagonist, along with other personal details like family members and line of work. The setting is usually drawn in broad strokes: we are told the dynasty, and possibly the reign period, as well as the city, province, or administrative district. Sometimes, as in the Tang capital Chang'an or Hangzhou's West Lake, a particular place acquires a thick pile of stories; other specified places become associated with a particular theme, such as that of Chengdu with ghosts.[12] In all of these situations, the stories lay out narrative trajectories over real geographical places, even when trips to Heaven or the Underworld or dreams invite detours into other realms.[13] As brief forays into an imaginary world, most *huaben* stories do not create immersive fictional universes, and their plausibility depends heavily on established doctrines or genres.

Li Yu published all of his fiction within the span of just a few years, from around 1654 to 1658. The eighteen stories of his earlier *Silent Operas* collections feature protagonists from a broad range of backgrounds, and despite Li Yu's signature penchant for comic inversion, the stories adhere to many conventions familiar from the late-Ming collections of Feng

Menglong and Ling Mengchu.[14] The *Silent Operas* stories are layered over the historical world that Feng and Ling had mapped out, and the plots of Li Yu's stories, like theirs, prominently feature a single protagonist and a major event. Just a few years later, however, his collection *Twelve Towers* marks a distinctive departure from earlier *huaben* fiction, for buildings become a newly significant element of each story.

Li Yu saw buildings as integral to our sense of self: "The extent to which people cannot do without houses is akin to the extent to which bodies cannot do without clothing."[15] In keeping with this view, the buildings in the *Twelve Towers* stories become as identifiable with his characters as were the beloved tokens of the protagonists created by earlier short story writers (like the "pearl-sewn shirt" of Jiang Xingge). This emphasis on fictional buildings has some precedent in the *huaben* tradition. For instance, the sixth story in Ling Mengchu's first collection, *Slapping the Table in Amazement* (*Pai'an jingqi* 拍案驚奇, 1628), features a character who goes into an upstairs room to look into someone else's house, and the fifteenth story centers on selling a house as well as spying from its upstairs windows.[16] Navigating architectural space was especially central to the plots of romances, both when a suitor is seeking a particular woman, and when a young man wants to glimpse the women's quarters. For instance, to see the party in Ling Mengchu's story, "Young Ladies Enjoy a Swing-Set Party," a young man peeps over a garden wall from horseback.[17] It is not incidental, perhaps, that more than half of Li Yu's "towers" depict romances, but as I demonstrate, he builds on this tradition to explore a wider range of human-building relationships.[18]

Readers who encountered *Twelve Towers* in Li Yu's time would have immediately noticed that these stories weren't following the rules of the genre. Since the late Ming, the most common titling style for *huaben* fiction had been descriptive couplets that summarized plot: each paired story would either be titled with half of a parallel couplet (as in Feng Menglong's collections), or an individual story would be titled with a full parallel couplet (as in Ling Mengchu's collections).[19] *Silent Operas* followed Feng Menglong's titling convention, using half-couplet titles to facilitate structural and thematic connections between paired stories.[20] In *Twelve Towers*, by contrast, each title comprised a mere three characters, and each named a building featured in a particular story as, for example, in the first three titles: "Tower of Shared Reflections," "Tower of Trophies" (Duojin lou 奪錦樓), and "Tower of Three Companions" (Sanyu lou 三與樓).²¹ This type of title offered a new shorthand for the story, and it downplayed the usual emphasis on the protagonist and the plot. Looking at the table of contents for a *huaben* collection, readers would usually have found titles that served as a series of plot summaries, marked by the rhythm of semantically parallel couplets. In the table of contents for *Twelve Towers*, however, they would first encounter a series of named, fictional buildings. By departing from generic expectations, Li Yu encouraged the association of his *huaben* stories with titling practices in two other genres: *chuanqi* plays, like *The Peony Pavilion* (*Mudan ting* 牡丹亭), which tend to be three characters long and often denote a place; and full-length novels like *The Plum in the Golden Vase* (*Jin Ping Mei* 金瓶梅) or *The Journey to the West* (*Xiyou ji* 西遊記). Like those novels' chapter titles, the individual chapters of *Twelve Towers* stories are titled with full couplets previewing each chapter's two main events.

The story titles of *Twelve Towers* are also akin to the placards that were generally affixed to buildings. Years later, Li Yu would write of these placards at length in *Leisure Notes*; almost all its illustrations were devoted to reproductions of placards from his own garden that were done in the calligraphy of his famous friends. Through their practices of naming, the placard-titles of *Twelve Towers* create sites that delineate the contours of the story collection. This place-making conceit can be compared to earlier collections where the use of a familiar setting, such as Hangzhou's West Lake, creates a place for each story as one trajectory mapped among others. In *Twelve Towers*, however, the building placard instead suggests a desire for singularity that paradoxically introduces reproducibility, since a building placard could easily be copied.

The story titles of the *Twelve Towers* collection are thus situated at the threshold between fictional content and the medium through which they circulate, the printed book.²² At once story title and building placard, the virtual entrance to each building serves as the written entrance to each story. In addition, each building functions both as a building within the diegetic space of the story, and, synecdochally, stands for the story itself. In Michel de Certeau's terms, the building can be conceived of as a place that becomes a space through the enactment of the story in or around it.²³ The implications are intriguing: unlike a title couplet describing the events that will unfold and the characters and places that will be involved, a building used as a title promises only a place. This place is both static (as a title) and dynamic (in its association with a particular spatial practice to activate it: the story itself). Unlike most other titular references to buildings, *Twelve Towers* is interested not just in the relations between a named place and particular events, but also in the relationship between a character and the various buildings in his or her life: these can range from personal identification with a building to the savvy deployment of a building in service of a scheme.

Li Yu's *Twelve Towers* experiments with the various functions of buildings in people's lives. Instead of a fantasy world apart from the everyday, it features multiple buildings that shape narratives and make introductions; that foil meetings and transmit messages; that provide privacy and enable spying. These buildings are explicitly constructed: sometimes by the narrator, sometimes by a character or characters. They are christened with placards that name their functions or mark them as extensions of their owner's ambitions or wishes, or that offer demands or predictions for their owners. By setting them together in a single collection, I argue, Li Yu presents them as though they were twelve pavilions of artfully varied heights and designs within a single garden.

Intellectuals in the late Ming and the early Qing were increasingly preoccupied with the relationship of garden space to textual and visual depictions of garden scenes, and Li Yu's experience as a garden designer made him particularly attuned to the possible ways of inhabiting garden and residential spaces. The formal structure of the *Twelve Towers* collection is fundamentally indebted to Li Yu's thinking as a garden designer, for the collection functions as a fictional garden in which the tropes and conventions of *huaben* fiction undergo substantial remodeling. Unlike the many literary representations of gardens and parks dating back to at least the Han, only a small fraction of the stories included in the *Twelve Towers* collection depict actual gardens.

In arguing for this collection to be interpreted as a literary garden, I suggest that instead of focusing only on the representation of buildings within these stories, we should consider how together the stories produce a three-dimensional fictional space reminiscent of a traditional garden filled with buildings of varying sizes. The preface to this collection, written by Li Yu's friend Du Jun, precisely encourages reading these multichapter stories as a level-by-level ascent through different buildings: "As the saying goes: 'Doing good is like ascending [a height; doing evil is like tumbling down].' With this collection, our Straw-Capped Man of the Way has formed a joyous connection with the entire world: hand-in-hand, you will stroll along with him and ascend these twelve towers. Doing so will cause you to suddenly forget that it is difficult to do good, and applaud instead how easy it is to ascend even to the heavens: his is a mighty achievement indeed."[24] This verticality of form is further enabled by the stories' content: Many of the stories proceed by narrating the new possibilities that arise when looking down from a height. In addition, as readers ascend the story chapter by chapter, they encounter the formal innovation of chapter breaks. The division of these stories into chapters differentiates them from earlier *huaben* fiction, including Li Yu's own. The chapter divisions are visually dramatic: the remainder of both sides of the last folio of each chapter is left blank, so that a new chapter always begins on a new page. (This division is much more pronounced in the early woodblock editions than in any modern edition or translation I have seen, in which the stories tend to be separated this way, but not the chapters within them.) By slowing down the reading process, these breaks force the reader to pause at each "storey" of a story; in the process, I propose, each chapter break generates an aesthetic viewpoint akin to a distinctive garden scene (*jing* 景).

While a few late-Ming story collections are also divided into chapters, their divisions are highly predictable, as for instance in the example of four long stories, each divided into ten chapters, of the erotic collection *Clapping to Dispel Worldly Dust* (*Guzhang juechen* 鼓掌絕塵, ca. 1629).[25] The stories of *Twelve Towers*, by contrast, are unusually variable in length, ranging from one to six chapters: in starting any particular story, the reader does not know exactly how many chapters await. The varying length correlates roughly to the range of storeys in the buildings of Li Yu's time. As Du Jun's prefatory comment explains, the reader is invited to see each chapter, or storey, of a particular story as offering a new perspective on unfolding events, and it is implied that upon arrival at the top level, the whole narrative will come into view.

In each story, the reader witnesses the building coming into being as an object of representation. Construction, design, and remodeling all play key roles within the diegetic worlds of the narratives, but the buildings play many other new kinds of signifying roles as well. In the first type of story (represented by the story number in parentheses), the eponymous buildings serve an intermedial expressive function, resonating with and reinforcing the narrative as it unfolds (3, 6). In the second type, the architecture of the building functions as a technology to facilitate or thwart human relationships (1, 2, 4, 7, 10). In the third type of story, the names of buildings play a role in shaping the plot and the characters' identities (5, 8, 9, 11). The final story of the collection (12) takes a different approach, offering a link between the fictional and real worlds through the interplay between the figure of the building and Li Yu's intrusion into the fictional world.

MEDIATING BETWEEN BUILDINGS AND FICTION

Of all the stories in the collection, the third, titled "Tower of Three Companions" (Sanyu lou, SEL3), is most explicit in its exploration of the many ways that stories as media might intersect with buildings as media. This three-chapter story about a three-storeyed building goes further than any other in its intermedial experimentation, mapping chapters onto storeys, as a family shapes and is shaped by a building. It centers on a father and son surnamed Tang, who are wealthy but parsimonious. The son expresses an interest in acquiring a finer house, and the residential compound they desire, which includes a tower, belongs to their neighbor Yu Suchen, a "lofty scholar" who takes great pleasure in designing gardens (*zao yuanting* 造園亭).[26] The Tangs wait for Yu Suchen to deplete his resources for his garden project, and eventually they purchase his entire estate. After the elder Tang dies, however, the family's fortunes change. The younger Tang has ongoing legal troubles, and when stolen silver is discovered on his property, he is arrested. Meanwhile, Yu Suchen's son, Jiwu, has become a successful official after his father's death. Working with a discerning local magistrate, Jiwu discovers that a friend of his father's had buried the silver under the tower so that Yu would someday find it. Once this mysterious friend arrives and confirms the origin of the silver, the property is returned to the Yu family.

The story's plot centers on the division and ultimate restoration of property, and the titular building under which the silver is found, the "Tower of Three Companions," features prominently. Over the course of the story's three chapters, that property is "divided into two compounds," with "the new owner getting nine tenths, and the former owner just one" (125). The narrator declares: "A new wall is built between them, and a new gate is opened" (124). The story ends when the split property is reunified and returned to the original owner's family after his death. The focus on a building's biography also allows for another innovative technique: the story of the building extends well beyond the death of the original protagonist, turning the story into an intergenerational tale.

Yu Suchen is imbued with an idiosyncratic disposition remarkably similar to Li Yu's, parroting lines that we might recognize from Li Yu's nonfiction writing.[27] Sun Kaidi first proposed that Yu Suchen is an autobiographical figure (*ziyu* 自寓), noting that Li Yu, too, had his first son after the age of fifty.[28] Yu Suchen is also obsessed with garden design: "Throughout his entire life, he had had no other interest than designing gardens and pavilions. Every day of the year, he worked at constructing his garden. The buildings he designed were invariably extremely elegant and refined, in every way different from ordinary gardens" (118–119). The singularity of Yu's obsession differentiates him from Li Yu, whose interests range across various media. Consequently, I approach Yu Suchen as a metaphorical figure for the act of authorship, rather than as a referential stand-in for the author-as-person: not Li Yu's double, but his designated explorer of writing and building as analogous arts. By depicting Yu Suchen as an avid garden designer, Li Yu directs our attention to the narrative's use of buildings.

Although building and remodeling are key plot elements across *Twelve Towers*, this is the only story in which the protagonist is a specialist in architectural design. Its plot thus relates closely to the topos of buildings in the collection's title, using enumeration to underscore the resonance between the literary and the architectural. Just as this collection of twelve stories is called *Twelve Towers* and composed of twelve named towers, so this building is called Three Companions, and is composed of three named storeys. The storeys are individually named and labeled with a placard: the first, the "Companion of Men" 與人為徒 (with its crooked railings and the bamboo furniture of an elegant garden); the second, the "Companion of Antiquity" 與古為徒 (filled with scrolls, books, and paintings); and the third, the "Companion of Heaven" 與天為徒 (furnished with a single Daoist classic and incense for meditation). These names allude to the Daoist classic *Zhuangzi*, where they describe the ideal progression of a perfected being.²⁹ The building serves as a material manifestation of its designer's philosophy of life, displaying it for others' appreciation. The building's durability beyond the human lifespan corroborates this life philosophy, even as it links it to the durability of the printed collection itself.

In addition to the interplay between the building, Tower of Three Companions, and its storeys, on the one hand, and the *Twelve Towers* collection and its stories, on the other, the narrative progression of the story's chapters also moves upward through the titular building. Each of the story's three titled chapters, I argue, correspond roughly to the building's three titled storeys. The posted names of the storeys have been introduced above; the titles of the three chapters are as follows:

Chapter 1: Before He Finishes Building His Garden Residence, [Mr. Yu] Is Forced to Sell; His Sights Set on Acquiring Property, [Mr. Tang] Gives out Largesse in Hopes of Future Gains (109)

Chapter 2: No Bandit's Lair nor Thievery, but a Strange Cache Suddenly Appears; Property and People Both Seek to Be Restored to the Previous Owner (129)

Chapter 3: An Old Adventurer Concocts a Plan to Deal with a Greedy Man; a Wise Magistrate Cracks a Tough Case with Care (151)

The three storeys—communing with men, antiquity, Heaven—map onto the narrative as it progresses through these three chapters. From socializing with a "friend from afar" on the first storey in chapter 1, the narrative then speeds up and distances readers from the characters in chapter 2, in a manner that correlates to the "Ancients" of the second storey. In the final chapter, it stages a celebration on the third storey, "Companion of Heaven," once the generous adventurer friend has returned and the property has been returned to its rightful owner: "That day, on the top floor of 'Tower of Three Companions,' he raised a cup of wine in thanks to Heaven" (165).

But how does the narrative arc of this story develop in relation to buildings? Toward the end of the first chapter, "Companion of Men," we learn that Yu Suchen sells his "halls and chambers, terraces and gazebo; pavilions and belvederes, pools and ponds" to his wealthy neighbor, retaining only a library (*shulou* 書樓) for himself (124). We already know that Yu is a fastidious designer constantly tinkering with his creations, but so far we have glimpsed his grounds only through the description of his crafty neighbors. Because they seek to undervalue the property prior to its sale, they describe Yu's carefully designed garden in resoundingly negative terms. Their disparagement nevertheless conveys the garden's refinement:

> It was built in a petty and contrived way that did not resemble in the least the grand mansions of the wealthy. The corridors meandered and twisted this way and that, making walking a drawn-out chore; the ornately decorated doors would do nothing to guard against robbery; the courtyard was the same size as the residential buildings, allowing vital energy to leak out: it's no wonder he was unable to amass wealth. Bamboo and flowers outnumbered hemp and mulberry trees, such that people would want to come by on outings and one would have to treat them to food and drink. Such a house stands only to be converted into a nunnery or temple; were one to want to make it into inner chambers in which to lodge his family, it would certainly not do. (123)

Even within this motivated criticism, Yu Suchen's skill and attention to detail is evident. If we read against the Tangs' dismissive perspective, as we are intended to do, we encounter delightful meandering paths, doors carved with exquisite openwork, a sizeable outdoor space, and clusters of stately bamboo and gorgeous flowers enjoyed for their aesthetic value alone, all of which would serve as an excellent venue for communing with guests. Li Yu thus skillfully offers a detailed picture of this elegant garden entirely within its criticism: we learn about the speaker at the same time as we learn about the garden. This accomplishment of two narrative aims at the same time is what he calls "close stitching" in *Leisure Notes:* a writing technique that he proposed for the writing of *chuanqi,* but that could be applied to other genres as well.

In the sale negotiations, Yu retains just a tenth of the original property, which has a single building that happens to be the one "with which he was most satisfied of all those he had designed in his lifetime" (124). Before the garden's sale, we know only that its first floor had served to lodge Yu's visitors. As soon as the sale takes place, however, we learn that "as it turned out, this library was actually the height of a small three-storey pagoda" (125). Thus, the narrative reveals the upper floors of the building to us only after we learn about sale of the rest of the garden. And Yu Suchen himself notes that when he owned the whole estate, he had not taken the time to appreciate the upper two floors. Consequently, we are told that the sale of the rest of his property enables Yu Suchen to fully realize his potential: "Living there, not only did Yu Suchen feel none of the pain of selling his garden, but in fact he felt that with that tumor removed, he had become a great deal more carefree" (128). The ability to consider situations from alternative perspectives, exemplified in the *Zhuangzi*, is crucial here: Yu Suchen is quickly able to adapt to his reduced circumstances, and even to enjoy them. This notion—that an artistic man, when limited to a single building, could become an even more refined version of himself—prefigures the portions of *Leisure Notes* that advise against extravagance.

Immediately preceding the first chapter break, the narrative zooms in on this building and up through its three floors. Having sold the rest of his property, Yu now focuses all of his attention on this building, "sitting inside it all day long, exactly in keeping with the implications of the titles" (127). The narrative thereby marks the culmination of Yu's social life, in which he had used only the first floor of "Tower of Three Companions." The narrowing narrative focus, and the removal of nine-tenths of Yu's property, thus prepares us to move up to the second storey, "Companion of Antiquity," as we begin the second chapter. There we find Yu Suchen happily ensconced in his "Tower of Three Companions," while the Tangs wreak havoc on their newly purchased garden:

> After Yuchuan and his son had purchased the garden, they could not avoid that unique disposition of the wealthy: that they simply must make some changes. Now, in such cases, it need not be the case that they replace rafters or pillars for it to seem different than before. Instead, just as with a fine landscape painting, even if they merely add a blade of grass here or remove a single tree there, it will fail to coalesce into a work of art. Naturally, after being subjected to such "renovations" [*zuozao* 做造], the garden lost its original quality: they wished to transform iron into gold with their touch; who would have thought that they would instead turn gold to iron? (129)

Whereas Yu Suchen is surprisingly content in his reduced circumstances, Tang Yuchuan grumbles about his partial acquisition. Instead of appreciating the progression through multiple levels of a house, Tang Yuchuan resents that vertical construction—as well as the act of reading—makes his shoddy remodeling of the garden increasingly visible. In voicing his complaint, Yuchuan gives us the first references to looking down from "Tower of Three Companions," from within the elevated vantage point of that story's chapter 2: "One garden cannot accommodate two families. He [Yu Suchen] stands at the top of 'Tower of Three Companions,' and I ask you, which of our rooms do not appear right before his eyes? He sees my wife, but I don't see his: no man would be willing to abide such a loss of dignity" (132). Chapter 2 thus shifts the narrative perspective not only spatially, through this reference to looking down, but also temporally, as we move from the worries of a single garden designer to intergenerational concerns. Once he ascends to the second storey of "Tower of Three Companions," Yu Suchen's priorities shift as well, and the second chapter recounts the surprise birth of a son when Yu is more than sixty years old.

In keeping with the second storey's claim to be a "Companion to Antiquity," chapter 2 features a proverb that promises retribution. The narrator explains that it is better when retribution is delayed, because it will have accrued interest (*lixi* 利息) (142). By the end of chapter 2, the Tang family has lost their property, the magistrate has been notified about the hidden treasure, and the Tang son has been imprisoned. The Tangs' only wish is that Yu Jiwu will accept the house and claim the treasure. This retribution meted out over the course of generations is visible only from the second floor of "Tower of Three Companions," and this extension of the timeframe beyond Yu Suchen's death is possible, I argue, because the central actant in the story is the building itself. The building has a particular relationship to the Yu family, and the story recounts their separation and ultimate reunion with that building. By playing with the form of the *huaben* story, Li Yu transcends the perspective of the individual character to consider a building's relationship to multiple generations instead. As one medium hovers over another (building over story, and story over building), drifting in and out of focus throughout the course of the narrative, we are left with the sense of entering a story that was also a building: that we ourselves had ascended the "Tower of Three Companions," storey by storey, and chapter by chapter.

The depiction of "remodeling" (*gaizao*) in this story foregrounds the connection between writing and building in two ways. First, Yu Suchen is described by his uncultured neighbors as a perfectionist obsessed with remodeling, despite his dwindling funds. For instance, when Tang Yuchuan's son becomes impatient about finalizing their planned purchase, Tang declares that Yu's perfectionism will be his undoing: "[Tang] Yuchuan replied: 'With each passing day, the likelihood that he'll sell grows surer, not to mention that the price falls as well. Cease your worries. The reason he never finishes building is that as soon as it is completed, he is dissatisfied, and he wants to tear it down and begin again. It is exquisite, but he wants to make it more refined still, so it has been delayed for some time. Just think of it as if he is remodeling [*gaizao*] for us, and for such a good price!'" (120). The notion of Yu's unending remodeling indicates both excellent taste and terrible judgment. Most obviously, Yu continually improves his works, but he gains nothing in the process. More subtly, through its links to the process of revising writing, this depiction of remodeling functions to draw our attention back to the text and the process of writing, and once again to lend substance (*shi*) to these fictional (*xu*) buildings: by depicting buildings as undergoing a revision process of constant change, Li Yu further blurs the boundaries between the fictional building he describes and the buildings that we (his readers) might build in our own gardens.

The layering of creative construction practices (*zao*)—of house and text—in this story creates a dynamic relationship between these two media forms. In many of Li Yu's stories, enterprising characters take on a director's role that resembles that of an author; in many of the stories in this collection, buildings are active participants in those plans. In this story, moreover, the character seems to perceive the fictional world from the perspective of an author. Yu Suchen has managed to design a building, and, by extension, a world, that delivers his wishes and executes his plans even after his death. When the structure and design of a fictional building exert this much influence on textual design, altering the form of the *huaben* narrative, it shifts the possibilities of fictional texts, rendering them more substantial and habitable. The result is a kind of fiction that draws nearer to the material world, populated not only by long-dead or made-up figures, but by buildings that could come to exist through readers' efforts.

The building in the sixth story, "Tower of Gathered Refinements" (Cuiya lou 萃雅樓, SEL6), also expresses the fictional narrative in intermedial form. This story describes a romantic and sexual relationship among three men, and then continues: "So they rented three storefronts along the banks of West River and removed the walls to join them together as a single store. In the middle they opened a bookstore, which was managed by Jin Zhongyu; to the left they opened an incense shop, which was managed by Quan Ruxiu; and to the right they opened a flower shop that also carried antiques and was managed by Liu Minshu" (323-324). Their joining of the three stores into one is described in remarkably similar terms as the merging of their three bodies: they "join them together as a single store" (*bing zuo yijian* 併做一間) much as "the three had joined together as one" (*bing zuo yiren* 併作一人) (323). Two of the men, Jin and Liu, are described as of similar age, status, and background, while the third, Quan, is described as young and beautiful ("although he was male, he was prettier than any girl").[30] The story does not explicitly state that the classmates Jin and Liu have a direct sexual relationship, but a three-way romantic relationship is strongly implied, with younger Quan—the "male favorite"—serving as a "tool" (*ju* 具) for facilitating physical intimacy between classically educated men: "In joining together with a 'male favorite' [*longyang* 龍陽], these two friends not only avoided any inkling of jealousy, but they even used him as a tool to facilitate a physical connection between themselves. People assumed that the two of them had added a third; what they didn't know was that the three had joined together as one" (322–323). The implications of a shared romance trouble the commentator, who wonders: "If brothers sleep with the same singing girl, or a father and son have an affair with the same maid, does that also facilitate their physical connection?"[31] Whether registering fears of incest or of repressed homoeroticism, this comment interrogates the usually rigid division between the desiring man and the man he desires, a division maintained in this period through the distinctions of age and status. In revealing that the desiring subject, even though an elite male, may be desired as a sexual object by his peers, the comment enmeshes these elite men in a larger erotic web.

In keeping with his lower status, the younger "male favorite" is in charge of selling incense, while Jin and Liu peddle the more durable wares, books and antiques. Despite the officially intermediary role of the "male favorite," his store is situated off to one side: he seems less a shared interest and more a pretext. The most significant building is located in the rear:

> Behind the shops there was a large building for which they inscribed a horizontal placard with the characters "Tower of Gathered Refinements." The elegance of its design and the refined quality of its furnishings require no further remark. Whenever there happened to be a moonlit evening with a gentle breeze, they would gather there to pluck strings, play the flute, and sing. All were possessed of such exquisite talent that anyone who heard them would feel their very soul take flight. (324)

This description of refined gatherings occurring "behind" (*houmian* 後面) the shops reiterates in spatial terms the physical relationship insinuated multiple times in this story. It even serves as the title of the first chapter: "The Flower-Seller Won't Sell 'Rear-Courtyard' Flowers [*houting hua* 後庭花]" (317). "Rear courtyard" was often used as a euphemism for anal intercourse, though in this story it is used non-euphemistically as well: it is, in this sense, a substantiated metaphor.

BUILDINGS AS MEDIA FOR SHAPING PLOT

Whereas "Tower of Three Companions" and "Tower of Gathered Refinements" deploy their buildings to resonate with and articulate the story's form, five of the stories in *Twelve Towers* develop their narratives precisely through the spatial and material constraints of architecture (1, 2, 4, 7, 10). I discuss three of them—1, 4, and 7—examining how the design of buildings both facilitates and thwarts the characters' plans.

In the first story of the collection, "Tower of Shared Reflections" (Heying lou, SEL1),[32] the plot is decisively shaped by its meticulously designed building. We meet two sisters who are married to men of opposite temperaments: a stodgy moralist, Guan, and an impassioned romantic, Tu. Living with them in a converted residential compound that had belonged to the sisters' deceased parents are Yujuan (Guan's daughter) and Zhensheng (Tu's son). The conversion of the property into two separate homes is described in great detail:

> All along the boundary between them, they built a high wall so that no one could see from one to the other. The rear garden had two pavilions on the water, one facing west that belonged to Inspector General Tu and another facing east that belonged to Supervisor Guan. Between them was a pond that matched exactly the two lines of the Tang poem: "From afar you know the gate is where the willows are / It seems cut off by lotuses with ne'er a path between."[33] It was easy enough to erect a wall along the boundary on land; in the deep water, however, a stone base could not be installed, so the top was connected, but the bottom was open. Now in principle, this "glittering stream between them" could serve as a natural moat better than even the Yellow River.[34] However, Supervisor Guan was a cautious man, and ... so he spared no expense in erecting stone pillars in the water, and laying a stone frame above the water's surface on which he built a wall to divide the two sides such that their lines of sight could not reach from one side to the other.[35]

The wall here is erected over the water precisely to obstruct direct view; no efforts are made, however, to curtail the visual properties of water which reflects otherwise occluded people. This description of the wall's construction itself immediately subverts the wall's purpose. Instead of obscuring sight and directing it elsewhere, the wall demands our attention, as it does that of the cousins, whose relationship becomes a central focus as the story unfolds: our gaze drifts, with theirs, to the open space beneath the wall and their reflections on the water. Even though the cousins have yet to glimpse one another, the passing allusion to a familiar Tang poem that describes unrequited love suggests a body of water designed to separate a pair of lovers.

Li Yu builds on earlier uses of garden walls through explicit references in "Tower of Shared Reflections" to two earlier literary works, the drama *Story of the Western Wing* and the Tang poem "A Summer Day at My Mountain Retreat" (Shanting xiari 山亭夏日), by Gao Pian 高駢 (821–887). He quotes from the poem:

綠樹陰濃夏日長	Green trees' shade is dense, the summer day is long;
樓臺倒影入池塘	The pavilion's image—upside-down—enters the pond.
水晶簾動微風起	Crystal curtains shift as a light breeze rises;
併作南來一味涼	And gives a whiff of cool fragrance from the south.[36]

This poem contrasts a cool and peaceful garden retreat with the summer heat waiting just beyond the dense shade of these trees. Poetry and fiction frequently commented on play with shadow and reflection in gardens: such descriptions would add a sense of movement to enclosed spaces.[37] The phrasing here also highlights the importance of optical illusion in garden design and the transitory quality of the garden experience. The scene in "Tower of Shared Reflections" doubles the reflected pavilion and adds a reflected cousin: "It was the height of summer, and the hot weather was oppressive. This boy and girl just happened to have the same idea, and both went to their waterside pavilions to enjoy the cool breeze. As they looked out, the light breeze gently moved, but not a ripple appeared on the water. The reflections of the two pavilions were very clearly there, upside-down in the water" (16). In keeping with the centrality of buildings to these stories, before the characters see the human reflections, they notice the reflections of the pavilions. The description of the buildings literally overshadows that of the characters.

In deploying the concept of "shared reflections," Li Yu's story effects a dramatic remodeling of an old conceit: that of the powerful portrait of a beloved. In the comments at the end of this story, the commentator (purportedly Du Jun; likely Li Yu himself) notes that the well-known lines from *Western Wing*, "'lover in a reflection' and 'beloved in a painting,' raise two excellent conceits for *chuanqi* and fiction."[38] But those lines were written some five hundred years earlier, he says, and since that time countless plays and novels featuring paintings of beautiful women had been written, but not a single one that featured a reflection. The commentator omits the obvious narrative advantages of the painting conceit, as it facilitates the representation of an entirely imagined interaction between two people with any amount of distance between them. The underexploited option of a reflection, in contrast, requires that a lover be simultaneously proximate and absent—a seemingly impossible situation.

We can read "Tower of Shared Reflections" as Li Yu's attempt to develop the conceit of a lover's reflection standing in for his physical body into a compelling narrative. He does so by manufacturing an unusual architectural environment, and this story is distinctive for the manner in which the design of the residential compound itself plays matchmaker for the two cousins. The narrator opens the story's prologue by claiming that even "walls made of iron or brass" cannot keep amorous young people apart, and that, consequently, "not only must they avoid revealing their physical form, but neither should they reveal their reflection" (6). This line at first appears to be a standard reference to the relationship between a person's form (*xing* 形) and its reflection or shadow (*ying* 影), where the latter simply reiterates the former. But as the story progresses it becomes a meditation on how architecture can be used to develop the simultaneous presence and absence required for the "revealed reflection" trope to function in fiction.

In the illustration depicting this line in the Min Qiji 閔齊伋 (1580– c. 1661) edition of *Western Wing*, only the reflection of the suitor, Student Zhang, is visible (figure 3.1). Viewers experience seeing only his reflection, just as Yingying does. The illustration to "Tower of Shared Reflections," however, shows both cousins, Yujuan and Zhensheng, as well as Yujuan's reflection from Zhensheng's perspective (figure 3.2). In doing so, it showcases the architectural structure as a facilitating mechanism, and presents Yujuan as doubled, or extended, by her reflection, rather than replaced by it.

In the story, after the cousins fall in love with each other's reflections, Yujuan's father rejects Zhensheng's marriage proposal and fills in the space beneath the wall. The brothers' mutual friend Lu Ziyou, whose name is homophonous with "there is a way," arranges a three-way wedding between Zhensheng, Yujuan, and Lu's adopted daughter, Jinyun, who is included in order to trick Yujuan's father into thinking Yujuan isn't involved. After the marriage, the buildings are renamed Towers of Shared Reflections, and the whole compound is once again redesigned so that each wife can occupy one of the pavilions. This redesign results in another doubling of women's images: "Not only did they tear down the wall and clear out the mud so that the two beauties could look at one another, but they also built an elevated bridge so that Zhensheng could easily go back and forth, making it so that the Milky Way no longer separated the Cowherd and the Weaving Maiden" (63). The combined reflections of this

FIGURE 3.1 This illustration to *Story of the Western Wing* depicts Student Zhang's reflection, but not his physical form. One of a set of twenty polychrome woodblock prints by Min Qiji. Reproduced with permission from Museum für Ostasiatische Kunst, Cologne. © Rheinisches Bildarchiv Cologne, Walz, Sabrina, rba_d012779_11.

story are doubly made by the pavilions: it refers both to those made by their physical shapes (the buildings' reflections) and those made possible by them (the characters' reflections).

Unlike the building in "Tower of Three Companions," which exists initially as a named building, this building is named only at the conclusion of the romantic plot. As a consequence, the story and the building shape each other. The story's title first appears within the story's text as a collection of the poems that the cousins have exchanged underneath the wall—*A Collection of Shared Reflections* (*Heying bian* 合影編). Zhensheng's father discovers this collection, which Zhensheng has had bound, and shows it to Lu Ziyou. In this moment of metacommentary, we have a bound collection of poetry within the diegesis of the story, sharing the title of the story we are reading, and displaying the titular building's

FIGURE 3.2 This illustration to "Tower of Shared Reflections" depicts a boy, a girl, and the girl's reflection as they gaze at each other's reflections in the water under the wall dividing their houses (Li Yu. *Shi'er lou.* Xiaoxianju, 1:1a.) Reproduced with permission from the Chinese Academy of Social Sciences.

prehistory as the title of another written work. We also get Lu Ziyou's comment on that collection, which simultaneously serves as a comment about the marketability of the story we hold in our hands: "Although the matter is greatly vexing, it nevertheless makes a great story. To fall in love with a reflection is the stuff of romance such as never has been seen before—it will certainly be passed on" (33). Jinyun also references the collection to reassure Yujuan that she will have a happy ending: "The poetry manuscript, *A Collection of Shared Reflections*, has already been made into a *chuanqi* play, and at present the grand reunion is about to take place" (50). By the end of the story, the phrase "shared reflections" has been applied to many things: the experience of seeing the two reflections in the water, an exchange of poetry, the production of a book of said poetry, and, finally, a *chuanqi* play adapted from the poetry collection. Only after all these uses is the name of the story finally adopted to name a building. By attaching this key phrase, "shared reflections," to the writing and the buildings, Li Yu further emphasizes the special bond between the worlds constructed in texts and those made by architecture.

This story also offers another instance of how Li Yu develops the fictional status of the buildings within his stories. It hinges on explicit interplay between the central terms I have been discussing: *xu* (the fictional, and here also virtual) and *shi* (the real). This interplay develops across the three chapters of the story, beginning as a *xu* relationship based on reflections alone (chapter 1), then a failed attempt at a *shi* relationship (he tries to visit her) (chapter 2), and finally, an arranged marriage when Tu explains that the virtual (*xu*) *is* real (chapter 3): "They may not have done the physical [*shi*] deed, but they do have a virtual [*xu*] love. Although their physical bodies may not have been joined together, that pair of reflections has already been husband and wife for the better part of a year. Presently their affection is real and their wishes heartfelt, so it will be truly [*shi*] impossible to wrench them apart" (33).

This virtual connection is derived from the reflections' meeting: "Now ever since he had encountered Yujuan, this young man's *hun* and *po* spirits had all attached themselves to his reflection. As a result, his reflection had grown extremely animated, while his physical body had come to resemble a corpse" (29–30). This plot thus proves that the "virtual," or the "fictional," has real effects: in this case, it has bound together as husband and wife two cousins who have not met since infancy. This sort of attachment is common in late-Ming romances, but here the entire relationship has been prescribed architecturally, in a revision of the old trope of glimpsing a potential lover through a chink in a wall. A solid (*shi*) building plays matchmaker to two cousins who fall in love with each other's reflections (*xu*), and their marriage transforms their relationship from the virtual to the physical, while the publication of the love poems and the renaming of the buildings emphasizes the possibilities of the virtual.

The fourth story in the collection, "A Tower for the Summer Heat" (Xiayi lou 夏宜樓, SEL4), also features architecture as a mechanism that propels a romantic narrative, but this time through height rather than reflection. Whereas in "A Tower of Shared Reflections" the lovers glimpse one another's reflections under a dividing wall, here the male suitor, Qu Jiren, looks over a compound wall from a tall tower outside. The male and female leads are each equipped with their own building, and this story constructs a relationship between two towers: the titular "Tower for the Summer Heat," in which female protagonist Zhan Xianxian is ensconced, and a taller tower in the distance, from which Jiren spies into her courtyard. Jiren's tower enables superhuman eyesight, while Xianxian's functions as an extended body: Jiren tells her the private information he has gleaned by spying on her, and she concludes that he can see her every move. (In the end, he admits to spying and they live happily ever after).

The story's first chapter introduces the titular tower and describes its multiple storeys:

> There were plenty of pavilions in the garden, but they all stood in the full sun and were useless for the purpose of escaping the heat. But there was also a spacious tower surrounded on three sides by a lotus pond and sheltered by sophoras and weeping willows that allowed not a ray of sunshine in all day long. The old adage warns us against climbing towers in summer, but this tower was well adapted to the season, a circumstance that had led Mr. Zhan to inscribe its name as *A Tower for the Summer Heat*. Much attracted by it, [Xianxian] received her father's permission to move in and live there. She made one part into a study and the other into a bedroom, and spent all of her time in the tower, never going downstairs.[39]

This building is named from the outset for its particular quality of being blocked from view on every side. The sightline that Qu Jiren will eventually use is foreshadowed in negative example: we read that not even a sliver of sunshine could seep through, an architectural problem to which the narrative responds (*Shi'er lou*, 178).

In the second chapter, we are suddenly transported into an unnamed building, described only as the tallest pagoda around, where Jiren uses a telescope to look into private courtyards. While the telescope is the most obvious technology at work here, the narrative pays special attention to the additional height that would be required to gain the necessary line of sight; by combining the telescope with the appropriate architecture, Jiren can not only see people behind the courtyard walls but also read a text lying in front of them. He attempts to look at Xianxian from the fifth or sixth storey, and he is depicted as climbing higher and higher: by the end, we can assume he has reached at least seven storeys—the dizzying heights of which surpass even the "tallest" tower-story of six chapters found in *Twelve Towers*.

This tower, and the story that contains it, thus affords a clear view in all directions, including of Xianxian writing a poem: "In the past he had stood on the fourth or fifth floors, and all he had to do was to level the telescope. But this time he assumed she would be at her table with the poem lying flat in front of her—she certainly wouldn't hang it on the wall, lest it be seen—and unless he stationed himself on high, he would not be able to look down upon the world of men and read it. So he kept climbing until he could go no higher, adjusted the telescope, directed it at the Tower for [the] Summer Heat—and examined Miss [Xianxian]" (*Shi'er lou*, 206–207; *Tower*, 24). Verticality emerges here as a solution to the architectural problem presented in this story. To get the right perspective, Jiren has to find a way to "position his body halfway up to heaven" (*zhishen tianban* 置身天半) (*Shi'er lou*, 207). A marginal comment to the story notes that Jiren excels at "putting himself in the place of another" (*sheshen chudi*) (206), which he demonstrates by finishing her poem for her. Li Yu usually used the expression *sheshen chudi* to discuss the writing process or theatrical role-playing, but here, it refers quite literally to "putting one's body in another place," for Jiren writes the poem for Xianxian only by "projecting" himself, using a tower and a telescope, into the tower she inhabits. Notably, the telescope does not simply enhance all of Jiren's facilities: instead, it pulls them apart, extending his eyes while deadening his ears, so that it mediates not only between Jiren and Xianxian but between his senses of vision and hearing.[40]

With *Twelve Towers*, Li Yu expanded the usually formulaic chapter-end prompts of chaptered fiction, which were meant to imitate a storyteller's hook between sessions, making them into a simulated conversation between the narrator and reader. Before the second chapter of "A Tower for the Summer Heat," he includes a long prompt goading readers to imagine the device that enabled Jiren's apparent omniscience—that is, to play at the author's job. At the end of chapter 2, he draws attention to the craft of fiction-writing itself. The break between chapter 2 and 3 occurs while the matchmaker is carrying the poem to the Zhan household, and this comment juxtaposes three spatiotemporal spans: the time required for Jiren to see into Xianxian's quarters; the time needed by the matchmaker to walk from his tower to the Zhan household; and the time taken by the author to tell the story: "But quick though the messenger may be, the author insists on a delay at this point, so that he can start a new chapter. Like [Xianxian's] poem, which was broken off [*ge* 隔] before it was completed, the story will be far more interesting than if it were told all in one piece" (*Shi'er lou*, 210; *Tower*, 26). By forcing the narrative and the matchmaker to go slowly on foot, this chapter break highlights the architectural practice of breaking (or dividing) space into smaller units. It does this through the use of the term *ge*, which can indicate a spatial as well as a temporal boundary. As such, it connects—in their *ge* separability—Xianxian's poem, this chapter, and the architectural arrangement that separates Jiren and Xianxian. Narrative time thus arguably becomes a component of narrative space, as the punctuated forward movement of the story works to emphasize the spatial dimensions of its key buildings. Here, instead of a one-to-one correspondence between chapter and storey, each chapter break offers a shuttle service between towers: from Xianxian's to Jiren's between the first two chapters, and back again with the matchmaker between the last two. I would suggest that this play with *ge* as it manifests in both building and chapter divisions leaves the story seeming quite far off to readers, as if we too were reading through a telescope from our own tower.

The apparent omniscience of one character that drives "A Tower for the Summer Heat" is repeated in the third story of this type, "Cloud-Scraping Tower" (Fuyun lou 拂雲樓, SEL7). Whereas the "false immortal" with "thousand-mile eyes" (*qianli yan* 千里眼) is the resourceful suitor in "A Tower for the Summer Heat," in "Cloud-Scraping Tower," it is the maid, Nenghong, who lodges in a tall tower to spy on the neighbors. She is able to accomplish a similar feat as Jiren, but without a telescope, mediated by a building alone. Her spying mechanism is nevertheless described using the same term that denotes the telescope's operations: "thousand-mile eyes" (424). As this parallel indicates, the building—not the telescope—is fundamental to the development of this conceit across stories.

Pei Yuan, the male suitor in "Cloud-Scraping Tower," had been compelled by his father to break off his engagement to Miss Wei and marry an ugly but wealthy woman. When that woman dies, he still wishes to marry Miss Wei, but the matchmaker reports that her father has refused. Pei kneels down before the matchmaker and implores her to ask Nenghong, Miss Wei's beautiful maid, to marry him instead. When the matchmaker speaks with Nenghong, Nenghong immediately mentions Pei's kneeling down—and this inexplicable knowledge convinces the matchmaker that Nenghong must be an immortal. Yet as their conversation proceeds, it becomes clear that Nenghong had not heard the conversation: all of her knowledge has been visually deduced. She has used the Cloud-Scraping Tower much as Jiren used his tower:

> The Weis' house faced the Yus' with only a wall in between [*ge*]. In the back garden was a tower named the Cloud-Scrap[ing Tower], which had a balcony for airing clothes that was encircled by a trellis. From inside it one could see out, but from outside nobody could see in. The day that Mother Yu returned from delivering the proposal, Nenghong had calculated that "that fellow Pei" would be waiting in front of her house, so she climbed up to the balcony to see what reception the messenger got. On arriving home, Mother Yu did bring a man inside, and Nenghong was able to get a full view of [Pei Yuan]. When she saw him sink to his knees, she assumed he was doing so for the young mistress, to persuade Mother Yu to

arrange not merely a marriage but an illicit rendezvous, and she was continually on her guard. (*Shi'er lou*, 426–427; *Tower*, 140)

Nenghong's superior visual perception, however, does not translate to improved comprehension, for the Cloud-Scraping Tower provides a full view but not a full understanding. The result is nonetheless fortuitous: when Nenghong learns that Pei Yuan had knelt for her rather than her mistress, she happily agrees to his proposal. On hearing the good news, Pei Yuan approaches the building with gratitude and bows in front of it as he would to the emperor (*wangque xie'en* 望闕謝恩) (*Shi'er lou*, 433). The Cloud-Scraping Tower thus becomes identified with Nenghong herself, and she is likened to the emperor in an expression that uses "palace" (*que*) as a metonym for him.

Part of the suspense that makes "A Tower for the Summer Heat" such an engaging story is the imperfection of Jiren's knowledge, since the telescope mediates his sensorium by solely enhancing his vision. The portrayal of Nenghong, by contrast, is that of a clever mind who coopts the conventional scholar-beauty love story to her benefit. Maids at least since Hongniang of *Western Wing* had been crucial to romance plots, facilitating the love lives of their sheltered mistresses, but they lacked the self-interested creative drive of Nenghong. In the second half of this story—the longest in the collection—almost every word spoken and every action taken by all characters are part of Nenghong's elaborate plan. As Nenghong builds scheme upon clever scheme, they are narrated chapter upon chapter, resulting in a sizeable tower built of airy nothingness, all according to her design.

Considered in this light, the Cloud-Scraping Tower, here again called a "sheer tower" (*weilou* 危樓), represents the social heights that Nenghong successfully scales through her unparalleled resourcefulness. The narrator judges her as a cunning usurper like Cao Cao or Wang Mang, who turned into a virtuous minister like Yi Yin or the Duke of Zhou, suggesting that her craftiness is ultimately forgiven (*Shi'er lou*, 490). If the Cloud-Scraping Tower symbolizes Nenghong's sharp-sightedness, it also materially facilitates it through its design: the diegetic tower gives her access to information out of which she constructs the remaining chapters of the story.

NAMED BUILDINGS AS FICTIONAL ACTANTS

Buildings were often named in traditional China, and there were varying approaches to selecting them, some of which involved divination. In the next type of story (5, 8, 9, 11), the name of a building has a significant influence on narrative development, more so than the structure's design. "Return-to-Right Tower" (Guizheng lou 歸正樓, SEL5) recounts how a building overcomes its rootedness and attracts sponsors from across the empire. The centrality of the building is signaled by the story's immediate decentering of the human protagonist: "Return-to-Right Tower" departs from *huaben* conventions by introducing its male protagonist with no name, no hometown, and no physical description. When the narrative finally discloses his name, it first offers the caveat that information about his identity became known only upon his repentance after a thirty-year life of crime, and then reveals that his name comprises components of the character for "thief" (Bei Qurong 貝去戎, comp. 賊 "thief"). Unlike some of Li Yu's other thief characters, Bei does not have a code of honor, but he does believe that once he has acquired a large amount of money, he must spread it around to avoid bad luck. He encounters a courtesan and is moved by her religious devotion, so he purchases a house that can be converted into two separate living quarters: a home for him and a nunnery for her.

The titular building of this story does not make an appearance until the third of four chapters, when Bei expresses a desire to reform. Once it appears, it quickly causes Bei to change his ways. He initially intends to use the site as an occasional residence and a place to store his stolen goods. Yet this plan, we learn, is contingent not only on the construction of the building—which is to be tall and secluded—but also on the name of the building, which was given by the previous owner "to signify that he was returning home for good" (*Shi'er lou* 288; *Tower*, 68). Bei's plans are foiled, however, when he discovers that the tower's placard has been altered by the addition of a single stroke. As the narrator tells us: "By a strange coincidence, one of those block characters sprang an odd trick of its own; the character for *rest* 止 suddenly acquired an extra stroke [i.e., 正, 'correct'], turning the name into Return-to-Right [Tower]" (*Shi'er lou* 288; *Tower*, 68). This "odd trick," whose agency the story first attributes to the block character itself, turns out to be transformative:

When Bei inspected the property, the name had read Return-to-Rest, but when, after choosing an auspicious day, he moved in, he looked up and noticed a tiny change that made all the difference in the world. It now bore an entirely different meaning. "Right is the opposite of wrong," he mused. "If I don't change my wrongful thinking, I'll find it hard to get back on the right path. Perhaps it's a miracle sent by the gods? After seeing me do one good deed, perhaps they wanted me to repent and added the extra stroke as an inducement?" (*Shi'er lou*, 288–289; *Tower*, 68)

Inspecting the added stroke, Bei finds that it is raised above the others and of an entirely different color, anomalous because it is "merely damp clay freshly deposited by the swallows" (*Shi'er lou*, 289; *Tower*, 68). He nevertheless interprets this as a form of divine writing and transforms himself as well as his building: "He converted his building into a Daoist chapel, and he and Pure Lotus pursued their separate vocations, seeking to return together as immortal and buddha, respectively. As his Daoist name he took Return-to-Right, since the gods had given it to him" (*Shi'er lou*, 290; *Tower*, 69).

In a story in which methods of swindling are described in great detail, it seems odd that Bei Qurong would himself be tricked by a building's placard. The narrative thereby highlights the substantiality of buildings, suggesting that their substance (*shi*) can make an honest man out of a thief. In the end, the building "Return-to-Right" is renovated by the character "Return-to-Right," which is recounted in the story of the same name. The proliferation of these two characters on the printed page might even make readers wonder about what substance with which the crowning line of the character 正 on the page in front of them is written: might it have been added by birds or gods? Is it really "right" at all?

Bei applies his longstanding ability to "disguise himself so thoroughly that someone he swindled one day was unable to recognize him the next" (*Shi'er lou* 242; *Tower*, 45) in order to transform this newly constructed extension of himself, the building. This technique of disguise—literally rendered to "change his head and face" (*gaitou huanmian* 改頭換面)—usually indicates a merely superficial transformation. Here, however, Bei transfers a corporeal technique to a building renovation, in yet another intermedial symbiosis. Instead of an owner naming a house after his own aspirations, as in "Tower of Three Companions," this house effectively names its owner.

The title of the next story, "Tower of Ten Nuptial Cups" (Shijin lou 十卺樓, SEL8) indicates a tale of ten weddings, and it narrates a building whose name predicts future events. The eponymous building, Tower of Ten Nuptial Cups, is first erected for an unremarkable young man, Yao Jian, by his doting father, to celebrate his engagement to the most beautiful woman in Wenzhou. An unorthodox but famously accurate fortuneteller—the illiterate "Crazy Drunkard" Guo, who exclusively channels the departed spirits of illustrious calligraphers—is able to satisfy his customers' aesthetic aspirations and future-oriented curiosity at once. But the name Guo offers, Tower of Ten Nuptial Cups, is so strange that the group gathered for the banquet tries to correct it:

> "There's just one problem: the character 'nuptial cup [*jin* 卺]' of 'Ten Nuptial Cups' should be 'scene [*jing* 景]' of 'scenic views.' Perhaps it means that this building is so expansive that one can gaze into the distance from the windows at the top and see ten different scenic views, and so it is called 'Tower of Ten Scenic Views.'" . . . They reverently entreated him, saying, "The meaning of the two characters 'Ten Nuptial Cups' does not make sense. We think that there must be an erroneous character. We hope that the great immortal might correct it." Crazy Drunkard again held the brush out and wrote four lines of poetry:
>
> > "Ten Nuptial Cups" was never wrong,
> > You, sirs, are wrong to doubt.
> > Another year you will fritter away,
> > 'Tis all a drunkard's riddle.[41]

The group finally converges on the only possible positive interpretation: that young Yao is destined to marry a wife and then acquire nine concubines.

As the story progresses, Guo's prediction proves true, though not in the way the group assumed. In marriage after marriage, Yao encounters a series of short-lived bedfellows: a beautiful "stone maiden" (*shinü* 石女), a bed-wetter, a pregnant woman, and six brides who fall ill and die. After nine marriages, "Father and son did not know who to blame, so they said that it must be that the house was not well built, and that they had fallen prey to some illicit plan of the builders that had caused things to come to this. They wanted to tear down the Tower of Ten Nuptial Cups and build a new building from scratch" (521). Fortunately for the tower, Yao's uncle explains there is no need for such destruction: since Yao has already gone through nine marriages, only a single marriage remains. The tenth marriage reunites Yao with the very first woman he had married: a "stone maiden" who seemed infertile. When, through the course of graphic narratorial detail, it turns out that she is now able to engage in sexual intercourse and bear children, the ten marriages of Guo's placard have come to pass, and the destruction of the building is never mentioned again. Although fortune tellers' predictions are common narrative devices, pairing that device with a building foregrounds the materiality of fortune-telling: when fate is linked to a building rather than a person, characters can consider destroying, renovating, or remodeling that building.

In "Tower of Returning as an Immortal Crane" (Hegui lou 鶴歸樓, SEL9), the notion of fate is again paired with an emphasis on human action. In that story, a circumspect husband, Duan Yuchu, names his own house so as to influence the future course of events—to construct his own fate, as it were. When he is conscripted for government service, Duan Yuchu "also attached a placard to the tower in which they lived, calling it Tower of Returning as an Immortal Crane. In doing so, he alluded to the story of Ding Lingwei's returning home as a crane to convey that he would certainly not return alive."[42] The inscription on the placard, "Returning as an Immortal Crane," alludes to the story of a man named Ding Lingwei 丁令威, who left home to seek immortality and returned only after a thousand years, stopping by in the form of a crane before soaring away.[43] This is just one of many measures that Duan takes to discourage his wife from missing him: he burns the clothes she has sewn for him, suggests she will take another husband once he is dead, and sends her a cruel "poem of separation." When he returns only eight years later, he finds his wife angry but healthy. Duan then explains himself and shows her that the poem, read backward, is actually a declaration of his devotion to her: his coldness was intended to ensure that she would not grow ill yearning for him.

At four chapters, "Tower of Returning as an Immortal Crane" is one of the longer stories in *Twelve Towers*, and much of the text is devoted to a narrative foil: a second couple, surnamed Yu, who share an unbridled passion. All of the chapter breaks follow Yu's exploits, not Duan's, and Yu moves from disappointment to disappointment: initially paired with the lesser beauty, Yu is sent on multiple assignments after his marriage, when he just wants to remain home with his wife. Meanwhile, Duan lives quietly in hostile Jurchen territory, and he sends his wife only a single letter with a cold poem. Through the narrative, Duan exists at a remove from the story's readers much as he does from his wife; his wife, too, remains mostly opaque, for the narrative does not dwell on her at home, except to comment briefly on her continued fidelity and her dissatisfaction. In this manner, the description of the love between Duan and his wife, as well as the description of their building, is signified primarily through textual absence, both within the story's world and in its formal unfolding.

At the end of the story, the commentator admires Duan's cunning pragmatism:

> The conception of this "tower" is quite profound and the path it takes quite winding: it is a variation on the age-old romance. Although the romantically inclined may not necessarily experience the same events, they still must adopt its approach to feelings. But when young romantics read it, they will without fail complain that it is too cold-hearted. I propose that without such coolness, the excitement [of love] cannot be dispelled. To suddenly see this after reading "Shared Reflections" and "Cloud-Scraping" is as if, in the extreme heat of midsummer, when sweat runs down in streams, someone were to offer you a melon that had been chilled at the bottom of a well, and you sliced it open and ate it. The pleasures of attaining such refreshing coolness are not superficial. (*Shi'er lou*, 619)

By calling this story a "tower" and describing it as taking a "winding path," the comment connects the story's narrative unfolding to the use of chapter breaks in a published book and to the use of spatial detours in garden design. The chapter breaks, described on several occasions as introducing a pause for heightened effect, work to dispel some of the excitement (*renao* 熱鬧) of the story, thereby giving the reader distance (*ge*) from which to observe the story's twists and turns.

This winding nature, moreover, is in keeping with the function of this story within the collection as a whole, for it offers the refreshing coolness of a long-married couple amidst the titillating scenes of courtship we find in "Tower of Shared Reflections," "A Tower for the Summer Heat," and "Cloud-Scraping Tower." All of those stories dramatize spying into the private rooms of other people, and we readers are positioned alongside these spies as they use forbidden knowledge to fulfill their romantic dreams. As an antiromance, "Tower of Returning as an Immortal Crane" is also an antitower story, in that we learn very little about its tower except for its naming.

Much as the protagonist of "Tower of Returning as an Immortal Crane" named his building to influence his fate, the protagonist of "Tower of My Birth" (Shengwo lou 生我樓, SEL11) constructs a building to transform his future: "Yin Hou had been a rich man his whole life, but he had never undertaken any construction projects. But because after marriage, he and his wife seemed unable to produce a son, he assumed that his house was unlucky, and beyond the buildings of his ancestral home, he constructed a small tower" (*Shi'er lou*, 666). Upon moving into this "little tower" (*xiaolou* 小樓) they have built, he and his wife conceive immediately and a robust baby boy is born ten months later. The father adopts a new sobriquet, "Little Tower," which neighbors had mockingly suggested for this building, and the couple name their child "Towerborn" (*lousheng* 樓生) (667). One day, however, the child goes out to play and does not return. The couple assume he has been eaten by a tiger. They do not conceive any more children, and eventually the father decides to try to find a son to adopt him in a bizarre final attempt to secure an heir.

Although it is not revealed until the story's final chapter, the son had been kidnapped and sold to the Yao family in another town. They raised him as their child, renaming him Yao Ji. Years later, after the elder Yaos have died, Yao Ji purchases the disguised Yin Hou as his adopted father. Yao then learns that Yuan soldiers have kidnapped all the local women, including the woman he hoped to marry, so he tries to locate her. But he finds that the abducted women are being sold in sacks by weight, so he cannot identify her. He purchases a sack that turns out to contain an elderly woman. She has befriended a young woman, whom she helps him identify, and who turns out to be his old love. The old woman turns out to be Yin's wife, and Yin and his wife take their adopted son and his fiancée to their home.

Much as the building had precipitated human reproduction, it now triggers familial recognition. The couple tell him about their lost child and offer him the child's bedroom:

> On arriving upstairs, Yao Ji examined the doors, windows, and furnishings—and was amazed. "This bedroom is the same one I had as a child, the one I see all the time in my dreams," he told [the "Little Tower" couple]. "But why [has it come over here] instead of [being] in my home?" "What makes you think it's the same?" asked [the "Little Tower" couple]. "From childhood on, whenever I drop off to sleep, I dream of a room whose doors, windows, and furnishings are *exactly* like these! One night I even asked a question in my dream. 'Whenever I dream,' I said, 'it's always of this room, never of anywhere else. Why is that?' And someone in my dream answered me: 'This is where you were born. That trunk over there contains the toys you used to play with. If you don't believe me, take them out and see.' I opened the trunk and found a great many toys—earthenware men and horses, cudgels, banners. When I looked at them, I felt as if I were meeting long-lost friends. On awakening, I compared the room of my dreams with the one I was in; they were entirely different, which puzzled me to no end. But as I came in here just now and looked about the whole scene struck me as exactly the same as in my dreams. I can't be dreaming *now*, can I, in broad daylight?"
>
> It was the [Little Tower couple's] turn to be astonished. "There *is* a trunk behind the bed-curtain that is full of our son's toys.[44]

By the time the family is reunited in the little tower, every one of its members—father, mother, son, and son's wife-to-be—has been bought and sold at least once. The little tower with its loving parents and its beautiful bride, not to mention its promise of sons soon to be born, has the feel of a dream. In fact, in the dramatic adaptation Li Yu did of this story, the second scene introduces the little tower as a dream of a lost childhood, complete with a bed set up onstage. Written only a few years after the dynastic transition, when many would have lost access to their childhood homes forever, this entire story serves as a dream of reunion that could only be brought about by outrageous coincidence (such as twice selecting the correct "bagged" person to purchase).

"Tower of My Birth" is the only story in the *Twelve Towers* collection that does not explicitly name its building in its text, even as its narrative revolves around it. By not naming its tower, and instead transferring the generic term "Little Tower" to name the couple, this story does two things. First, it shifts the loss of property during the transition from any particular building to the bodies of characters, suggesting that wherever those characters gather might serve as a place to rebuild the lost "little towers" of their dreams. Second, by not naming the building, Li Yu leaves a blank placard for readers to fill in with their own name: the "Tower Where I, the Reader, Was Born."

This breaking down of boundaries between the fictional (*xu*) and real (*shi*) worlds foreshadows the even more significant breakdown I discuss next, but it also relies once again on the substantial quality of a material building as a conduit. Through the mediation of this building, we can envision what it would take to reconstruct our lives after the transition and its losses, and then place ourselves in the position of the protagonist (*sheshen chudi*). Which of us doesn't have a "Little Tower" couple who doted on us back in the past, only to be lost? The figure of the transposable "Tower Where I Was Born" invites us to dream ourselves into this story, and to perhaps build the tower of our dreams anew. This retention of ambiguity is also in stark contrast to the treatment of fictionality in the story that precedes it, "Tower of Reverence for Ancestors" (Fengxian lou 奉先樓, SEL10), which repeatedly insists on its veracity and refuses to name its characters, pulling the story toward the world with truth claims rather than ambiguity.

BUILDING BETWEEN FICTION AND REALITY

By personalizing the voice of the narrator and commentator, and occasionally referring to himself as author in his stories, Li Yu broke with a tradition of modeling the narrator on the generic figure of the traditional storyteller. More subtly, as in "Tower of Three Companions," he linked the architect character to the author as architect, connecting building *in* a fictional world to the building *of* fictional worlds, in both cases using the term *zao* for the creative process of building. In addition to this thematic connection between author and character, Li Yu obliquely indicated his identification with his narrator, as for instance in the inclusion of his own poetry at the start of "Tower of Three Companions." In this section I trace some of the other ways Li Yu draws his fictional world toward actual existence (*shi*), focusing upon the last story in the collection, "Tower for Hearing My Faults" (Wenguo lou 聞過樓, SEL12). That story features the culmination of Li Yu's ongoing experiment in mixing media to break down the distinction between the fictional world (*xu*) and the real one (*shi*).

All the stories in *Twelve Towers* open with poems, of which seven seem to have been composed by Li Yu for the purpose of the story (despite his claim that he found one of them written on discarded cigarette rolling paper). Four stories contain poems previously composed by Li Yu in other contexts and included in his collected works; just one story opens with a poem written by another poet, attributed in the story to a "man of the Yuan," whom I have identified as Guo Kui 郭奎 (d. 1364).[45] By including his own poems in his fiction, Li Yu shifts the *huaben* short story toward the autobiographical. Whereas Feng Menglong and Ling Mengchu could take any classical anecdote and develop it into a piece of good vernacular fiction, complete with supporting verse, the early Qing witnessed a new trend of fictionalizing one's own experience. Most of the stories have commentary at their conclusion, which I believe was also written by Li Yu.[46] Li Yu thus steps into his stories in multiple ways, from including his own poetry without attribution to ultimately breaking down the boundaries (*ge*) in the final story between his roles as author, commentator, and narrator.[47]

To demonstrate how Li Yu uses a poem written for another context, I return to "Tower of Three Companions," the story discussed at the beginning of this chapter. The many resonances between Li Yu's self-description and the character Yu Suchen in that story create the sense that there are architects both inside and outside of the narrative, tinkering with its design. Sun Kaidi proposed that Li Yu identifies with this character's plight, noting that Li Yu opens this story with two of his own poems that marked the sale of his residence many years earlier:

賣樓徙居舊宅	"SELLING MY HOUSE AND MOVING BACK TO MY OLD RESIDENCE"
茅庵改姓屬朱門	My thatched hut has changed names, belonging now to a wealthier sort,
抱取琴書過別村	Clutching my instruments and books, I move on to another village.
自起危樓還自賣	I built this towering building myself, and I'll sell it myself as well,
不將蕩產累兒孫	So as to not burden my descendants with the infamy of losing the family fortune.[48]
賣樓	"SELLING MY HOUSE"
百年難免屬他人	In a hundred years, it's hard to avoid property falling into others' hands,
賣舊何如自賣新	But better than selling old property, is to sell the new property oneself.
松竹梅花都入券	The pines, the bamboo, and the plum blossoms, are included with the deed,
琴書雞犬尚隨身	At least my instruments and books, chickens and dogs, are still here with me.
壁間詩句休言值	Those lines of poetry on the wall—say nothing of their value!
檻外雲衣不算緡	Those wisps of cloud beyond the rail—don't calculate their price!
他日或來閒眺望	Another day perhaps, in an idle moment, I'll come for another look,
好呼舊主作嘉賓	And they'll call this former owner to be an honored guest.[49]

These poems belong to a tradition, dating back to the Tang, of laying claim to lost property through poetic description. As we saw in the introduction, the true owner of an estate was thus understood to be the person with the proper poetic sensibility to appreciate it.[50] There are several commonalities between these early poems and the story they introduce: a talented perfectionist who loves to design houses has to sell the house he built to a wealthier man, and a moral apology is offered by encouraging people not to leave their houses to their descendants. In the second poem, a broader perspective emerges, noting the transience of wealth and revisiting the theme of selling a home immediately after building it. Both poems note the sorts of possessions that are portable, but the second poem adds to the pathos, for it explicitly mentions the intangible experiential pleasures of living in one's own construction and imagines the tragic irony of becoming a guest in one's own home.

Given this tradition of claiming true ownership through one's capacity for appreciation, Li Yu's story may also be read as a claim to the building that he had sold many years earlier: counter to the Tang tradition and Li Yu's own poem, both of which highlight transience, the story demonstrates how a house might be lastingly possessed. The more unusual theme here is the insistence on trying to sell for the benefit of one's progeny, which appears at the end of the first poem and which is developed at length in the story, a theme that encourages us to view the loss of property from beyond the span of a single life. There are strong Daoist overtones in this story, from the description of the top floor as a place for Daoist meditation, to this strategy of being contented with the small and of choosing the lower position. In the broadest sense, "Tower of Three Companions" vindicates Li Yu the poet-builder, by expanding the time covered in the account to well beyond his death.

Throughout the collection, Li Yu occasionally allows his narrator to speak in the first person as the author. In "A Tower of Three Companions," Li Yu does not explicitly model the fictional character on himself: although he uses poems that would be easily recognizable from his collected works, he describes the poet as a "a lofty man [*gaoren* 高人] of the Ming who wrote them upon selling his home and parting with his property" (110). In the subsequent story, "A Tower for the Summer Heat," Li Yu opens with his own poetry and claims his authorial role: these are poems "that your humble servant wrote as a child" (171).

In the final story of the collection, Li Yu fully breaks down the barrier between himself and his nominally separate narrator (in other words, creating a narrator who speaks of himself as an author of fiction). As a result, the final story, "Tower for Hearing My Faults," reorganizes the relationships among the reader, the text, and the author. We are directed, first, toward its author and the real buildings of his past, and then to a fictional building prepared for us readers, now recast as patrons. Li Yu explicitly attributes the opening poem of this story to himself:

甲申避亂	"SEEKING REFUGE FROM THE TURMOIL IN 1644"
市城戎馬地	The city is a battleground;
決策早居鄉	I have resolved to go stay in the country before it's too late.
妻子無多口	We're a small family, just my wife and kids;
琴書只一囊	I've just one bag of my zither and some books.
桃花秦國遠	The Peach Blossom Spring is far from the state of Qin;
流水武陵香	The flowing waters carry the scent of Wuling.
去去休留滯	Away, away—be not detained;
回頭是戰場	Glance back and there's the battlefield.⁵¹

This poem is similar to those that Li Yu attributes to an anonymous "lofty man of the Ming" in the beginning of "Tower of Three Companions." But Li Yu explains that "Seeking Refuge from Turmoil in 1644" describes his personal experience of the dynastic transition. He then proceeds to include lines from his other poetry, as well as most of the poems from a series about his mountain estate. Although Li Yu uses one of his names when describing his series of poems (Li Daoren 笠道人 "Straw-Capped Man of the Way"), he does not tell us that these other poems describe his own real-life garden residence (726). Rather, he changes the name of the series from "The Ten Conveniences of Yi Garden" 伊園十便 to the generic "The Ten Conveniences of a Mountain Studio" 山齋十便, thereby enabling the series to be applied to any studio on a hill (725). In inviting readers to visit his garden in spirit (*lingren shenwang* 令人神往) (725), Li Yu offers a virtual journey to his garden, and he also promotes a general association between himself and gardens, elevating himself as a recluse to emulate. In the story, he specifically proposes similarities to the famous recluse poet Wang Wei's Wangchuan villa and Shan Stream 剡溪.

Li Yu uses different first-person pronouns for his different roles in the text. As commentator, for instance, he uses primarily the singular formal (classical) first-person pronoun *yu* 予 ("I"), which occurs in the post-story comments to the second, sixth, and ninth stories.[52] In most stories, the commentator speaks from a position of authority relative to the author/narrator, who, in turn, speaks from a position of authority relative to the story's characters. But at the beginning of the twelfth story, "Tower for Hearing My Faults," the author/narrator immediately attributes the opening poem to himself, and, for the first time in the entire collection, he uses this pronoun in the narrative proper: "This poem is one that I [*yu*] wrote just before the tumult when I took refuge in the countryside" (722). He goes on to use that pronoun twice more, speaking of the relative merits of the countryside in times of turmoil.[53]

A few lines after this initial barrage of the personal pronoun, the narrator quotes Li Yu's preface to a series of his poems, and in doing so he uses the same *yu*-I: "The Man of the Way says: 'I [*yu*] receive the natural benefits of the mountains and waters and enjoy the sincere offerings of the flowers and birds. The conveniences of such a life are so many that they cannot be counted. How could you say anything to the contrary?'" (726). Through these commentator-specific *yu*-I's, a string of pronouns links the narrator to the poet to the named author, collapsing the distance between them and producing a jarring effect for his readers.

In the post-story commentary, the same first-person pronoun appears again in much the same way that it had been used in earlier stories, except that now the implied speaker can no longer be differentiated from the narrator. In the process, Li Yu interpellates his readers into a new role as well: instead of generic readers or listeners in the usual simulated storytelling convention, readers become potential patrons of Li Yu, along the model of the "various gentlemen" featured in the collection's final story. The story proper depicts all of the influential gentlemen of the city pooling their resources to purchase a house just outside the city for their beloved friend who wishes to be a recluse. That character returns to the city expecting to stand trial, yet as he approaches town "all these gentlemen come to meet him bearing wine." The commentator concludes: "In my [*yu*] opinion, thanks for these donations are not due to the academician, nor to the magistrate, but only to the various gentlemen. The Old Fool could not but be grateful to them" (778). The *huaben* narrator's usual mode of address is *kanguan* (看官 "dear readers" or "dear audience") or *guanzhe* (觀者 "dear spectators"), and both terms offer readers a single identity: that of an audience solely concerned with the quality of the story and their experience of its telling. Here, in contrast, Li Yu uses the term *zhugong* (諸公 "you gentlemen"), which carries with it broader social responsibilities and relationships. Although Li Yu rarely uses this term in his writing, both in this collection and elsewhere, the term proliferates with the appearance of this new "I" (*yu*) at the start of "Tower for Hearing My Faults."[54] This new narrator begins to address readers as "you gentlemen" (as in "if you gentlemen don't believe me" and in a suggestion that "you gentlemen take a look at the poems"). I propose that once readers have been established as possessing this new status, Li Yu then weaves together the gentlemen depicted in the story with those interpellated as its readers.

The same address opens the post-story comment, which by this point clearly encourages identification between those depicted in the story and those who read it. The always opinionated commentator singles these unnamed fellows out for praise: whereas two individuals had each contributed a third of the thousand taels required to purchase a house for Yu, he is more impressed by those gentlemen who contributed some small amount without necessarily seeking anything in return. This fictional account offers perhaps the fullest description of Li Yu's own desired patronage model, in which he would avoid being bound to any particular patron by being celebrated and supported by all of his readers. This last "tower in airy nothingness" continues to conjure real buildings into being: in 2018, the Nanjing government rebuilt Li Yu's Mustard Seed Garden on its original site.

In this chapter I have demonstrated the range of narrative functions played by the buildings in Li Yu's *Twelve Towers* to show how he conceived of buildings as media for shaping human action, as named actants in stories that interact with characters, and as narrative devices that—through their constructability—pull fiction toward the real world. I have also proposed formal connections between the structure of buildings and Li Yu's innovative use of chapters in this collection. I argue that as a material medium, buildings lend substance to fictional narratives, and that the figure of the builder or architect, when likened to that of the author, serves to narrow the gap between the real world and the fictional one. As several scholars have observed, Li Yu himself appears much more prominently in this collection than in his earlier collections. I link this substantiation of his persona to the narrated construction of a building, and his wish to bring his real-life patrons closer to his fictional ones: to build them with his words.

At the beginning of this chapter, I discussed in detail Li Yu's structural changes to the *huaben* genre. Although the thematic resonances across paired and larger groups of stories in the late-Ming *huaben* collections invite closer attention to the relationships among stories, I have discussed the stories of *Twelve Towers* largely without regard to their position in the collection. That is not because I find the collection's sequence irrelevant or accidental. Quite the contrary: by envisioning this collection as a garden containing a variety of buildings of various heights (corresponding, in turn, to story lengths), I propose that Li Yu carefully designed the overall structure so that it could be read along different paths. In the literary garden constituted by the *Twelve Towers* collection, different towers might be glimpsed from the tops of others, but not necessarily from the ones adjacent to them. The first story, inspired by *Western Wing*, firmly grounds the collection in the intertextual fictional universe, while the final story, where Li Yu conjures patrons and himself emerges from the page, constructs a "tower in airy nothingness" so high it breaches the real world. The scheming maid Nenghong (SEL7, six chapters high) might peer over stories five (four chapters) and six (three chapters) to take a look at the telescope-wielding Jiren spying on Xianxian (SEL4, three chapters). Or she might look in the other direction and advise reclusive "Old Fool" Gu, the protagonist of the final story, how to build a tower out of airy nothingness that provides very real sustenance. Li Yu's intermedial design allows buildings to transform what a collection of stories can be, and by the end of the collection, the last two stories press at the threshold between the fictional and the substantial by incorporating both author and reader. Through this construction, the building motif loosens up the strict parallel structure of earlier *huaben* collections, opening up a range of garden paths for readers to meander.

CHAPTER FOUR

Garden Space in *Leisure Notes*

During the dynastic transition in the mid-1640s, Li Yu first designed, constructed, and commemorated in writing a garden of his own. By then, gardens had a long history of functioning as an aestheticized space apart from the larger public world and family responsibilities. Li Yu's poems on Yi Garden, the rural retreat that comprised his earliest design efforts, attest to his satisfaction with living far from the bustling city, delighting in the natural world.[1] Although he left that retreat three years later to pursue a career as an urban entrepreneur, he continued to design gardens for himself, and also sought prospective clients for his garden design services. Two decades later, he included many ideas about garden and interior design in *Leisure Notes*, particularly in book 4, "Residences" (Jushi bu), which features sections on buildings, windows and railings, walls, placards, and rockery. This particular combination gives Li Yu an unusual position in the garden history of this period: as a garden proprietor who also advertised his services for hire and sold books filled with his ideas, he forged a place for himself between literatus and artisan. But more important is the influence his experience as a prolific writer had on his conception of garden design, which, as it began to be valorized in the late Ming, tended to be described as an extension of painting.[2] Even as Li Yu mobilizes familiar aesthetic principles in his essays on garden design in *Leisure Notes*, he uses them in a manner reminiscent of, and inspired by, his work as a creator of fictional worlds in his stories and plays. In chapter 3 I proposed that Li Yu drew on his thinking as a garden designer in his fiction collection *Twelve Towers*, innovating on the *huaben* form through the narrative possibilities of buildings. In this chapter I demonstrate that the converse was also true: that Li Yu's work in garden design—both in his practice and in his extensive written descriptions of those designs—drew on the narrative and structural possibilities he explored in his fiction and plays.

Conceived of in terms of media, the garden poses a different kind of problem from that of the intermedial experiments with fiction discussed in chapter 3. Despite the slippage between oral storytelling and written text, before Li Yu's *Twelve Towers* there was a broad consensus about what a *huaben* story was, and what it was made of (i.e., words). By contrast, attempts to define a traditional garden tend to slip imperceptibly into a cycle of remediation: a microcosm of nature, an expensive indulgence, a solitary retreat, a social gathering place, fodder for paintings or poetry, utopias existing only on the page.[3] This is true whether we consider them from an aesthetic or a materialist perspective. The abstract aesthetic categories through which gardens were appreciated were shared with other media: with poetry, paintings, and calligraphy that laid out their ideals in verbal and visual form.[4] Craig Clunas's study of the discursive construction of gardens in the late Ming proposed that "the garden" as a concept is not described by, but rather emerges from, texts and paintings that depict them as a part of a strategy in a taste-making competition.[5] The body, too, gained meaning through its mediation by the garden: Stephen West has described how the elite aesthetics of the Tang gave way, in the Song, to a "new space in which subjectivity was fashioned not by ethics, ontological insight, or literary negotiation, but rather by materiality and bodily perception."[6] In the late Ming, theater also became part of what defined a garden, for gardens were the setting for theatrical performances and often the setting for the diegetical drama as well. (The definitional energies also worked in reverse, for theater was often referred to as the "Pear Garden" [*liyuan* 梨園], after the Tang dynasty academy for performing arts.) And as Wai-yee Li has noted, "both theater and garden thrive on illusions and perceptual manipulations; both combine individual imagination with social conviviality."[7] Thus, through interactions and overlaps with writing, painting, theater, and the body, gardens were understood with reference to their relationship to a variety of other media, even as the media emphasized changed over time.

Discussions of garden aesthetics entail many pairs of concepts that describe visual effects. In addition to *xu* and *shi*, the "empty" and the "substantive" themes I have been developing, where seeing the substantive form of the garden leads to an emotional response, these include "emotion" (*qing* 情) and "scene" (*jing* 景), "mood" (*yi* 意) and "situation" (*jing* 境), and "following" (*yin* 因) and "borrowing" (*jie* 借).[8] Because many of these terms evolved from literary criticism through painting criticism before they were taken up to address gardens, the specificity of the garden frequently risks being overshadowed by other forms. Scholarship on Li Yu's garden aesthetics has tended to discuss them in these general terms, but also separately from his work in other fields.[9] In a departure from the latter tendency, Song Shiyong and Zhang Caixia have proposed that Li Yu's garden design and his theory of theater share a common project: that what he terms "speaking for another" (*daiyan* 代言) in the theater is the equivalent of "standing in for mountains and water" (*daishan* 代山, *daishui* 代水) in the garden. They point to several shared principles, such as "valuing the natural" (*gui ziran* 貴自然), seeking the marvelous and novel, and prioritizing transformation.[10] These connections are enticing, encouraging us to think across Li Yu's creative work in different media forms, but this study leaves many substantial differences between the two unexplored. In Jonathan Chaves's study of poems inscribed on paintings (*tihua shi* 題畫詩), he finds that "the imagistic sphere of the poem and that of the painting . . . at certain times overlap and at other times cover mutually exclusive ground," thereby indicating how practitioners were fully aware of the divergences between these media even though they were frequently conflated in critical discourse.[11]

In this chapter I build on these approaches to engage—in media-specific terms—with the interplay between *shi* and *xu* in Li Yu's garden design. To do so, I offer an extended comparison to a treatise by the garden designer Ji Cheng, who was writing a generation earlier. Whereas Ji Cheng's conception of garden design proceeded with reference to painting and poetry—designed to capture lyrical moments and scenes—Li Yu's, I argue, intersected with his work in theater and fiction writing.[12] Before the early Qing, fiction was not a medium in which the lyric ideal associated with the garden was explored. The most extensively narrated fictional garden to date was the one at the center of the debauched world of the late-Ming novel, *Jin Ping Mei*, aptly characterized by Mary Scott as having a "corrupt, uneasy quality."[13] In Li Yu's own fiction, the most prominent garden is found in the *Silent Operas* story "A Ghost Loses Money, and a Living Person Repays a Gambling Debt" (鬼輸錢活人還賭債), where it entices young men into gambling.

Li Yu's plays, which were performed in his own and others' gardens, are plot-driven comedies, rather than poignant meditations on beauty or the meaning of existence. It should come as no surprise, then, that Li Yu's approach to garden design as an author of fiction, a dramatist, and a theater director should differ from the approaches of designers more invested in the lyrical tradition. The interplay between *xu* and *shi*, which we have seen Li Yu develop in other media, also materializes in his garden design. Li Yu combines and inverts these categories, developing new designs as well as new ways of reproducing those designs in text. The issue of illusion was all the more fraught in the early days of the Qing dynasty, but Li Yu's writing on garden design does not, for the most part, engage the discourse of displacement common among Ming loyalists, for he approaches garden sites as spaces for creative expression, rather than as illusory escapes from an inhospitable new dynasty.

The professional garden designers of Li Yu's time designed hundreds of gardens over the course of a career; Li Yu designed far fewer. In the most conservative estimate I have seen, the garden historian Cao Xun has proposed that beyond his own three estates—Yi Garden, Mustard Seed Garden, and Storeyed Garden—Li Yu can be definitively said to have designed only one other garden, which he made for Zhang Yong 張勇 (1616–1684), the Provincial Military Commander in Zhangye, Gansu.[14] Cao argues that Li Yu did not design any gardens in Beijing, noting that all records of those gardens postdate Li Yu; in addition, Li Yu's patron, a Han official, would not have been allowed to build a garden in the inner section of Beijing.[15] But in his published letters, Li Yu advertised his services as a garden designer to his patrons, and, although evidence is scant, he has long been credited with designing several such gardens around the country, including the famous Half-Acre Garden (Banmu yuan 半畝園) in Beijing.[16] These biographical facts allow us to read his essays about garden design as informed by his own tangible work. At the same time, in numerous essays in *Leisure Notes*, Li Yu recorded his idiosyncratic approach to garden design, interior decoration, and horticulture. These essays show Li Yu grappling with the material constraints afforded by actual garden construction, and they prove that he had practice shaping spatial experience through design.

Before discussing Li Yu's approach to garden design, I want to clarify how I frame it in terms of *xu* and *shi*: for one must decide whether to prioritize recovering descriptions of the gardens he designed (in his terms, *shi*) or analyzing the designs as he committed them to writing in *Leisure Notes* (*xu*). In this chapter I do not evaluate the poems Li Yu wrote on his own gardens or explore descriptions of gardens later attributed to him (notably, he did not mention anywhere the other gardens he purportedly designed). Instead, I rely on his textual descriptions of garden design through an analysis of *Leisure Notes*. His ideas there were based on some experience—these are not *purely* gardens-on-paper. But, as with my discussion of the fan window and of the inclusion of his poems on Yi Garden in *Twelve Towers*, I focus on how he uses *Leisure Notes* to transmit (*chuan*) garden designs to his readers.

I take this approach because it seems to me that Li Yu thought that writing was the most substantial (*shi*) way to record (*ji* 記) and transport (*chuan*) his garden and his garden ideas into the world. A standard prose record (*ji*) of a garden would describe its various sites in detail, and in doing so, it would offer descriptive minutiae of the pleasures and possibilities contained therein; as attempts to preserve the details of a particular garden, records (*ji*) thus refer at every turn to the absent, substantial garden. Although this could and did serve to link gardens in the cultural imaginary to their owners, as Li Yu attempted with his writing about his Yi Hill Estate, these records did not necessarily transfer the full *experience* of that garden to readers. Whereas the record as a genre retained a dichotomy between the *shi* garden and its *xu* description, I argue that Li Yu reversed these terms by muting references to his own garden and allowing it instead to overlap with readers' imagined (and actual) future gardens, which could be built based on his designs. Thus Li Yu's Mustard Seed Garden will be of interest to me primarily for the way in which it emerges obliquely through *Leisure Notes*: that is, in portable form, disseminated (*chuan*) in the service of his overall brand.

The rhetoric used by Li Yu and his friends helps clarify how this works. In 1671, in a letter to his patron, the literary luminary Gong Dingzi 龔鼎孳 (1616–1673), Li Yu solicited employment as a garden designer:

> I have often said to people: "I know nothing of designing temples or halls, but I do have ample understanding of the arrangement of springs and rocks. What a shame that I have not had a chance to use this knowledge myself, nor have others been able to make use of it. Sometime in the future, I will die with these unfulfilled ambitions, making it so that the Creator has made this person in vain [xu]—also a regrettable matter for the ages. So I had no recourse but to write *Leisure Notes*, entrusting all my talent to empty words [tuo zhi kongyan 托之空言].... I hope that I can finally bring to fruition [shi] what had previously only been committed to empty words [kongyan]."[17]

These comments equate "emptiness" (*xu*, and also *kong*) with the written word, distinguishing writings about garden design from its actual practice and couching Li Yu's complaint that his garden design skills had not yet been put to use in an advertisement for his recently completed magnum opus, *Leisure Notes*. I propose that we read his claim of "entrusting all my talent to empty words" (*tuo zhi kongyan*) within his wider pattern of usage. As we saw in the third chapter's discussion of *Twelve Towers*, Li Yu resignifies "towers in airy nothingness" to show that words are capable of substantiating buildings. Even as he refers to this distinction between "empty" words and "substantial" gardens in the standard terms of the day, his practice suggests that the "empty words" of fiction and design can be more enduring than any specific actual garden.[18]

A marginal comment to this letter by Li Yu's famous literary friend You Tong 尤侗 (1618–1704) goes further in equating the experience of visiting Mustard Seed Garden with that of reading *Leisure Notes*: "Whoever enters Mustard Seed Garden sees that which he has never seen before. Whoever reads the book *Leisure Notes* hears that which he has never heard before. If Li Yu were to have a chance to exhibit the 'hills and valleys' in his breast in the famous Garden of the Urban Recluse, who knows what sorts of wondrous views he might create?"[19] Here, the difference between *Leisure Notes* and Mustard Seed Garden is rendered one of a sensory distinction between sight and hearing: the garden is seen, while the book is heard. By drawing a literal parallel between Li Yu's text and his garden, and by distinguishing them based on the sense they engage rather than their substance or lack, You Tong further raises the status of *Leisure Notes*. He extensively develops this comparison in the preface he wrote for it:

> His *Leisure Notes,* in several volumes, uses crafty skill to make playful magic. He joins the ranks of actors and takes to the stage. He puts the bodies of beautiful women on display to put forth his theories. He also comments on architecture and touches on "mist and flowers;" the matter of nourishment can also be seen. Everything, no matter how small, finds its place. Now although he has mastered the secret of the genius, patching up Heaven's work with his brush, I fear that by engraving in the emptiness [*kong*] and painting in shadows, expounding the obscure and angling after the strange, he may have violated a taboo established by the Creator.
>
> But Liweng is by no means just spouting empty words; in fact he has already put these skills into action. He lives in Nanjing, among mountain towers and waterside pavilions, ornate railings and patterned stone inlay, which fascinate and enchant with a splendid scene.[20]

You Tong offers a different characterization of Li Yu's *kongyan*: instead of being a worthy alternative to a garden visit, here the *kongyan* are substantiated by Li Yu's practical experience with orchestrating garden space. But rather than be subordinated to the experience of visiting Li Yu's garden in Nanjing, Li Yu's actual garden (Mustard Seed) serves primarily to justify his right to create such a marvelous garden experience on paper—as if inventing a fantastical garden experience would challenge the Creator, but creating a garden experience in the material world would not. These are not just airy words composed of emptiness and shadows; rather they are airy words substantiated by material innovation.

I argue that Li Yu's attempt to record his garden designs in writing should in itself be considered an intermedial experiment. Although his experience as a garden designer is crucial to my argument, a substantial proportion of his writing about garden design seems to have been produced *in lieu of* actual gardens. If we agree with Cao Xun's argument that far more gardens are attributed to Li Yu's design than he ever actually designed, then we can see the genius and the "true" (*shi*) success of Li Yu's career, as it were, as a garden designer—for, whether or not he ended up designing many gardens himself, he certainly became a strong enough *brand* of garden designer that gardens were attributed to him long after his death.

GARDEN DESIGN BECOMES AN ART

Until the late Ming, most writing on gardens was either by the proprietor or his guests, with scant reference to the laborers involved in their original construction. As a consequence, the ideal aesthetic experience of the garden was filtered through the poetic dispositions of these privileged men.[21] By the Wanli period (1563–1620), some elite garden proprietors began to analogize the design of garden space to the expressive style of painting, potentially raising its status from an artisanal craft to an art form. For example, Huang Zongxi's 黃宗羲 (1610–1695) biography of the professional garden designer Zhang Lian 張漣 (courtesy name: Nanyuan 南垣, 1587–1671) situates garden design in a teleology of media improvement: "Many are the endeavors throughout history in which the later surpasses the earlier: thus, the culinary arts began with heated stones, jadework began with a hammer and a wheel. It is the same with the figures and the landscapes of painters: since the Han and Tang, the images of Lord Śākyamuni and his famed disciples were depicted through painting, and only after that did they slowly open up [*tong*] and become molded clay, cast metal, and dry lacquer."[22] The culmination of landscape painting as an art form, Huang concludes, was found in the art of garden design, and he credits Zhang Nanyuan with being the first to successfully transform a landscape painting into "sculpted" (*su* 塑) form. Literati painting had undergone a similar elevation in status during the Song dynasty, when it borrowed from the critical language of expressive theories of poetry such as "the breath of life and its reverberation" (*qiyun* 氣韻) and "conveying the spirit" (*chuanshen* 傳神) to make a case for the value of painting as a means of literati expression of the "hills and valleys" (*qiuhe* 丘壑) in their hearts.[23] Central to critical understandings of both poetry and painting became their ability to contain both external scene (*jing*) and subjective affections (*qing*) within a single work of art. Since the Tang, representations of gardens had been replete with such ideals, but without reference to the actual conception and construction of garden space. Although in poems and records from the Tang onward, writers frequently described garden scenes as "picturesque" (*ruhua* 如畫), the expressive potential of garden design itself was not widely celebrated until the late Ming.

This shift in the status of garden design took place largely in the writing of elite men. The designers who produced these gardens, in contrast, were for the most part remembered only by extant gardens and how others wrote about them. A small corpus of writings from the late Ming, mostly biographical accounts of famous garden designers, evinces fascination with garden design as an art and analogizes it with painting, even as it hierarchizes these media and highlights the chasm between garden designers and literary men.[24] For example, Wu Weiye's biography of Zhang Nanyuan emphasizes that Zhang, while exceptional as a garden designer, was a mediocre painter. In that biography, garden design remains inferior to writing and painting, even as Wu praises it in terms of painting: "adding" (*tian* 添) trees and rocks, "applying shades of texture" (*cun* 皴) to the rocks, or "applying colors" (*xuanran* 渲染) of mists and clouds.[25] Just as a literati painter was said to have "hills and valleys" in his heart awaiting expression on the canvas, Wu describes Zhang as "silently taking into his heart" all of the surrounding rocks. Once the rocks are absorbed into his heart, Zhang has no further need to look at the site: he merely instructs workers in detail as he visits with the proprietor. Despite the admiration with which Wu describes Zhang, we can infer his exclusion from the elite literary world from Zhang's need for a famous patron like Wu to record and transmit his accomplishments.

Li Yu's self-positioning as a garden designer should further be understood within the ambivalence of literati toward the designers of their leisure spaces, in part because of the romantic (*fengliu*) disposition popular among many late-Ming literati, which celebrated unstudied artistry as well as friendships that flouted class distinctions. When, in the late Ming, writing on garden designers started to characterize their process as expressive art, it also emphasized authenticity of character, inspired by the ideas of the radical thinker Li Zhi. For example, in Wu Weiye's biography, Zhang Nanyuan is described as being dark-skinned, short, and plump, a far cry from the lithe, pale masculinity idealized by the literati. Even the most skilled designer was depicted as being naturally—and artlessly—suited to garden design: in a repeated trope, the garden designer enters his trade by chancing upon a poor attempt at piling up rockery and bursting into laughter at the shoddy result.[26]

Li Yu's writing on garden design in *Leisure Notes* constitutes one of the two earliest extant works on garden design written by men who themselves designed gardens. The first was written by Ji Cheng, who initially worked as a professional painter.[27] Ji Cheng's illustrated book, *Fashioning Gardens* (*Yuanye* 園冶), published in 1631, provides much practical advice: offering guidance on site selection, reviewing dozens of designs for latticework windows and openwork walls, and teaching about various types of rocks. But in keeping with the aestheticization of the garden, it also contains poetic descriptions of the ideal aesthetic experiences that gardens offer, and it abounds with allusions to historical figures. The disjunction between these two writing styles is jarring. Ji Cheng alternates between these registers throughout his treatise, as though to demonstrate that the provider of customizable designs and guide to local rock hunting is also capable of literary style.

When Li Yu published the next sustained work on garden design, *Leisure Notes*, forty years later, he approached it from his background as a writer: "My other talent is designing gardens. I arrange them in a manner suitable to the lay of the land, not limiting myself to preconceived ideas. I have each and every rafter brought out for me to cut personally. In this way, I cause those who pass through them and enter their buildings to have an experience akin to reading my books—although they may lack great erudition, they are in fact rather unconventional."[28] Li Yu does not specify a genre for his "books" here, but by 1671 he had published vernacular fiction, plays, and essays. I propose that his conception of garden design draws on his writing in these genres, rather than the garden's traditional associations with poetry and painting, as we see in Ji Cheng's treatise. Connections to these genres can be glimpsed in his proposals for the material and spatial composition of a garden, as well as in his writing about the garden in terms of a narrative trajectory.

To a certain extent, the garden design writings of both Ji Cheng and Li Yu codify existing literati values and are expressed in similar terms.

Both men declare that two garden design principles are essential: "following the lay of the land" (*yindi* 因地) and "borrowing scenes" (*jiejing* 借景). Ji Cheng characterizes the task of the garden and the garden designer in precisely these terms: "When it comes to gardens, skill is in following [*yin*] [the land] and exquisiteness is in borrowing [*jie*] [scenes]; excellence is in attaining just the right arrangement" 園林巧於因借, 精在體宜.[29] Li Yu, similarly, boasts that this is precisely the area in which he excels: "to design in a way that follows the lay of the land to attain the right arrangement" 因地制宜.[30] Both, moreover, dismissed the advice of geomancers who would insist on a particular orientation, as well as the general practice of having all buildings face south. Both valorize the simple (*pu* 樸) and the natural (*ziran* 自然); both guide readers away from the vulgar (*su*) and toward the elegant (*ya*); both celebrate the picturesque (*ruhua*) qualities of garden scenes, as well as their illusory potential (*bianhuan* 變幻); and both seek a balanced effect that combines Heaven's ingenuity (*tianqiao* 天巧) with tasteful human intervention (*rengong* 人工). Both writer-designers, finally, consider a reliance on established methods or designs (*chengjian* 成見, *chengfa* 成法) to be a key problem in contemporary design. *Leisure Notes* also contains the only extant Qing reference to Ji Cheng's text: Li Yu recommends the openwork wall designs in *Fashioning Gardens*, stating that he has nothing to add to their exhaustive treatment there.[31]

Despite sharing an aesthetic vocabulary, however, the two designers conceive of their art in quite different ways. Ji Cheng's treatise oscillates between the elegant realms of practical design and lyrical expression, and a view of the ideal garden is achieved only through lyrical flourishes. Li Yu's proposals, in contrast, largely avoid extensively listing particulars; this is the case when such particulars were associated with exorbitant cost, as in rocks from specific locations, and when they appeared as a catalog of options from which a reader, or client, might select. Where Ji Cheng provides detailed descriptions of rock varieties, Li Yu offers a single description of how to piece together rockery so as to forego purchasing a large rock; where Ji Cheng proffers dozens of latticework and railing patterns, Li Yu simply advises that lattices should be sturdy, and not too ornate. Some of these differences can certainly be attributed to their distinct positions in the history of garden design. Ji Cheng was a professional garden designer who had designed gardens for many patrons, and in his text he codified a field of knowledge that had not previously been recorded in writing. Li Yu, in contrast, was an idiosyncratic cultural entrepreneur who may have designed just one garden beyond his own, but who had many creative ideas for gardens that could be.

Sidestepping these not insubstantial differences, I focus here on the connections between Li Yu's fiction, plays, and the essays expressing his ideas about garden design. Ji Cheng's *Fashioning Gardens*, characterized for its association of garden design with painting and poetry, will surface as a foil. Scholarship on Chinese gardens has often argued that the Chinese garden represented a real version of the patterns of nature because Chinese thought does not prioritize abstract ideals. We may find evidence for such a claim in Ji Cheng's assertion that he is "turning fiction into reality."[32] In contrast, Li Yu's ideas about the garden point to media that themselves not only celebrate fiction and play-acting, but do so in a way that seeks to remake the ostensibly natural. By approaching the literary representation of the Chinese garden through an exploration of two overlapping yet divergent literary representations of garden design, I offer a new perspective from which to consider the garden's significance.

ROCKERY FROM PAINTING, ROCKERY FROM ESSAYS

Writing is the principal analogy that Li Yu uses in describing the practice of garden design, an emphasis that distances his work from Ji Cheng's even when they otherwise agree. Both men point to piling up rockery as the most complex design element. Ji Cheng, however, suggests that the spatial arrangement of a garden can be easily derived from that of a painting, and of nature: "If you pursue intensely the meaning of the forested mountains, dallying with your affinity for the trees and flowers will come easily."[33] Li Yu, by contrast, calls design of rockery "another branch of study [*xuewen* 學問]"[34] and compares the piling up of rockery to the essay composition (*wenzhang*) of the great prose masters of the Tang and Song dynasties: "This is just like the principle of essay composition: the overall structure [*jiegou*] is difficult to achieve, but to elaborate details point by point is easy."[35] As a consequence, Ji Cheng's rockery emulates the concreteness often claimed for all Chinese gardens, steeped first in nature, while Li Yu's rockery proceeds through the abstractness of an argument, modeled after the essays of the past.

Li Yu deploys other comparisons for the piling up of rockery, but in all cases his comparisons are to abstract human practices: in the course of a single essay, he compares the construction of rockery to essay composition, painting and calligraphy, and a monk's patchwork cassock in turn. The language he uses for seams, long important for the conception of a "seamless" narrative, links his work in several media to sewing; this analogy is often implicit in his verb choices, where it functions metonymically. By mentioning sewing, Li Yu connects his practice of garden design to the suturing of what is not already joined; he may claim to prioritize "borrowing views" that already exist as a substitute for painting, but he writes of creating new objects through the connection and then erasure of seams.

In the final third of the essay, Li Yu shares concrete instructions for piling up large rockery structures using a mixture of earth and stone. In Li Yu's hands, these materials have passed through several layers of metaphor in order to remove any "signs of patching and chiseling."[36] The analogy to writing reaches its rhetorical pinnacle when Li Yu muses about whether one must wait for the ancient prose masters to be reincarnated and then transformed into strongmen (*lishi* 力士) who can take on the task.[37] Playful and confounding, this suggestion is nevertheless remarkable for how it renders writing and rockery construction seamlessly convertible. Li Yu's solution to the challenge of making large rockery look "no different from a real mountain" is to find a way to write in its crevices.[38] The result is a rockery hill that is as coherent as an essay, with human genius rather than nature's mysteries serving as the blueprint.

Emerging from this analogy, Li Yu proposes that soil be used liberally to fill in spaces between rocks: translated across media, soil serves the connective function of "empty" functional words (*xuci* 虛詞) to the stones' "substantial" notational words (*shici* 實詞). By planting trees whose roots are indistinguishable from the color of the rocks, Li Yu's method eliminates signs of human intervention in this mountain's creation. In its final lines, the essay emphasizes that these materials—earth, rocks, living trees—are exactly the stuff of which real mountains have always been formed. The terse final line brings out this point: "Earth and rocks have always been near one another, and if a rocky mountain contains no earth, no vegetation will be able to grow on it: it is a bare mountain [*tongshan* 童山]."[39] The celebration of the natural material here operates as a cover: after all, given Li Yu's dominant metaphor, these trees and hills have grown out of the "fertile soil" of words.

Ji Cheng's approach to rockery, in contrast, affirms the valorization of the natural that is usually central to Chinese garden design. He observes that rocks bring with them the fullness of their natural expression: "rocks are not like plants and trees; after they are picked, they are born again [*fusheng* 復生]."[40] He thereby highlights the life-force inherent in rocks: unlike plants and trees, which wilt and wither, transplanted rocks resonate with a new space. This perspective can be traced back at least to the Song dynasty, when rock collecting became a craze, and Emperor Song Huizong's collection attained notoriety.[41] The admiration of rocks was rooted in claims about life: people cannot usually come back to life, and vegetation is bound to a seasonal cycle, but rocks maintain a full existence.

Through the analogy to essay writing, Li Yu's rockery is prized for its placement, rather than for the natural qualities celebrated in the tradition of rock mania: just as a list of words is subordinated to an essay, his rocks become valuable only when they are woven together with living trees and plants. What is more, rockery's value is proclaimed from a distance, not from the close proximity of a rock lover's adoring gaze. This distancing suggests a detached form of engagement that prioritizes the overall structure of the work, especially when the rockery is framed with a window. We might take the metaphor one step further and consider the parallels: the artistry of an essay holds up when reframed in print, whereas the brushstrokes of a calligraphic composition invite close scrutiny in its original context.

Both Ji Cheng and Li Yu develop their discussions of rockery with reference to other media, and in both cases, the referenced media of painting and writing often imply the tacit insertion of a brush between designer and garden. At the conclusion of Wu Weiye's biography of Zhang Nanyuan, the writer Zhang Chao comments that the art of rock piling is more challenging than painting and even poetry, and he offers some more media-specific reflections on garden design as an art.[42] Whereas the biography emphasized the painterly qualities of rock piling and even called rock piling an "art" (*yi* 藝), Zhang Chao lists its many material constraints: the need to adhere to the contours of the particular plot of land and rocks, to use more or fewer materials based on availability, to limit expenditures based on a budget, to accord with of the proprietor's temperament, and to execute the work through hired hands. His comments give unprecedented credit to the garden designer, whom he depicts as creating art despite many limitations and constraints. In the process, Zhang Chao turns the traditional hierarchy on its head: if painting was often considered a spontaneous expression of the heart, or a response to the surrounding environment, artisanal work was seen as craft, busying the hands more than the heart. By elevating garden design to a branch of knowledge (*xuewen*) worthy of study, Zhang Chao suggests that it is well suited to artistic expression. In a sense, Zhang Chao's claims resonate with Li Yu's: he finds garden design exceedingly difficult because it is akin to a theater staged only through its setting, without any plot or characters, or even a predetermined hour for performance. The garden designer works with a cluttered canvas, borrowing the hands of laborers with averted eyes while accommodating the desires of the proprietor, and yet he still manages to produce transformative arrangements. Without seasonal imagery or heartfelt words, he makes art with only a small tract of land and some rocks.

As a writer who also designed gardens, Li Yu was invested in elevating garden design but also in wresting credit for gardens away from professional garden designers, reclaiming it for writers and, perhaps, for his readers. Consequently, he characterizes most professional garden designers as more akin to illiterate spirit writers than artists, wielding their instrument to marvelous effect in spite of themselves. *Leisure Notes*, in addition to advertising Li Yu's own skills in garden design, counsels proprietors to insist on personally directing the design process. Li Yu's opening essay in the section on rockery divorces the garden's expressive properties from human intentions: not only does he compare the figure of the garden designer to a spirit writer, but he also suggests that the proprietor of the garden cannot intentionally shape the design. Instead, the garden will inevitably reflect the true character of the garden's proprietor. Writing in an age when physiognomy suggested that one's body could perfectly reflect one's character, Li Yu here describes the garden's expressivity as a kind of expanded body—a notion I revisit in chapters 5 and 6. Li Yu's garden comes to be understood as a body turned inside out: the hills and valleys of the heart, which had previously been expressed through the brush in painting, can now be put on view in the garden. In the process, the expressive potential of garden design comes to surpass that which he claims for writing.

SUBSTANCE AND EMPTINESS IN THE GARDEN

I now turn to tropes and ideas from fiction that inform Li Yu's garden design in subtler ways, grounding this discussion in the concepts of *shi* and *xu*. The tropes I examine include clutter; metafiction; the literalization of *xu* (emptiness) and *shi* (substance), which I discussed in the previous chapter in fictional, dramatic, and theatrical contexts; and the notion of fiction as comprising all "that which is within the realm of the eyes and ears" (*ermu zhi nei* 耳目之內).

In Li Yu's essays on residential space we find an attention to aspects of the material world that poetic and painterly depictions tended to neglect. In fiction, these less savory elements of daily life such as clutter, garbage, human waste, and foul odors had long received extensive descriptions: one of Li Yu's first moves as a fiction writer is to invite readers into a marriage bed reimagined as foul-smelling darkness, sniffing along with a shocked young bride.[43] As we have seen in Zhang Chao's comment, the art of garden design is characterized by its dependence on the particulars of a plot of land and the available materials. As a result, it must constantly make artistic use of the *shi* substances of the material world in a way that writing and painting, though also material practices, do not—for their materials, like ink and paper, are much more processed. When assessing the material environment of a site, Li Yu applies what I would characterize as a sensibility drawn from his fictional mode of depicting the world.

Whereas Ji Cheng oscillates between design options and the literary realm, Li Yu devotes space in his essays to the clutter and dirt that were so often omitted from idealized literary depictions of residences. Early in his writing on design, Li Yu decried the detritus of everyday life and championed waste management as crucial for achieving the desired aesthetic: everyone, he observes, has "old stationery and discarded paper, dirty inkstones and bald writing brushes" lying around.[44] He wonders: "If even these most cultured of objects can make a person appear uncultured, then what of other things?"[45] His solution involves making better use of domestic space: installing side rooms to hold old objects, opening up cupboards in walls, adding drawers to desks, and even adding cabinets inside a dropped ceiling.[46] These designs, importantly, open up concealed empty spaces (*xu*) within the solid (*shi*) parts of a home, whether walls, ceilings, or furniture. A decluttering philosophy and home organization system in one, these designs take place out of sight. In the process, they bring the interior of the home into the purview of garden aesthetics, for Li Yu's reader must attend to the less savory aspects of his domestic space, which, especially in urban environments, would form a continuous residential space with the outdoor sections of the garden. (The final touch of his waste management system goes so far as to encourage a bamboo urinal in the study, which will ensure that the scholar will not lose his inspiration while running back and forth to the outhouse.) As these writings on interior space indicate, Li Yu pays attention to the entire material environment of any site, revealing the detritus that other writers on spatial design tacitly ignore.

This usage of the empty within the substantial appears to be indebted to his creative thinking about residential space more than a decade earlier, for the plot of another of Li Yu's short stories had turned decisively on the workings of spaces hidden inside walls. In his *Silent Operas* story "A Handsome Youth Tries to Avoid Suspicion But Arouses It Instead" (美男子避惑反生疑), an incorruptible prefect suspects an innocent young man of having an affair with his neighbor, a married young woman, because he is initially unable to imagine what happens in the unseen space inside a house's walls.[47] It is not until trinkets are discovered to have moved between households that there is substantial evidence (*shi*) to confirm that suspicion. Once the prefect becomes attuned to the space inside walls (*xu*) in his own home, however, he realizes mice have been carrying valuables from one household to another, rather than lovers furtively exchanging tokens.

Li Yu's garden design is further distinguished by its self-referential quality, which I would describe as his fictional sensibility: the metafictional elements that draw attention to the constructedness of fiction. Much as the narrator in *Twelve Towers* frequently mentions between chapters that the story was composed by an author, many of Li Yu's visual effects in the garden emphasize their artifice, rather than nature or painting or a transportive experience. We saw in the previous chapter that he sometimes conflated the roles of author, narrator, and commentator through his use of personal pronouns and the inclusion of his own poetry in his fiction. I argue that some of his garden designs similarly foreground their authorship: while offering readers a path along which to experience the garden, the designs point to him as designer as insistently as the personal pronouns pointed to his authorship toward the end of *Twelve Towers*.

A comparison with Ji Cheng's painting-oriented design practice will help demonstrate how Li Yu's approach differs. Whitewash plays a special role in garden design, as it transforms *shi* (substance) into *xu* (emptiness), allowing material elements to take on an immaterial quality, even if only as a visual effect. Conceiving of gardens as akin to paintings, Ji Cheng approaches a whitewashed wall as a blank canvas: "Towering crags usually rest against a wall. You can take a whitewashed wall to be paper, and the rocks as a painting. The cracks in the rocks' surface can be made following the cracks in the rockface, after the style of the old master painters. You should cultivate pine and cypress from Yellow Mountain, ancient plum, and lovely bamboo. If you gather them together in a round window, it will be just as though you were traveling in a mirror."[48] Ji Cheng's conception here reverses the established representational standard: real rocks, against the whitewashed backdrop, cease to appear as concrete and natural, and instead resemble the brushstrokes of a painting.

In painting criticism, the brushstrokes of the masters were understood to express more than mimetic representation: because they recreate these brushstrokes in three dimensions, garden designers' reworking of the natural is also, Ji Cheng suggests, a lofty form of artistic self-expression. He uses this brushwork analogy throughout his treatise, describing Longtan rocks 龍潭石 as "like brushwork on a painting" (*ruhua*)[49] and suggesting that one consult iconic landscape paintings when choosing rocks.[50] In the last line of the passage, Ji Cheng pulls the rocks and surrounding trees into the round window frame, while the overall image pulls the viewer into the picture from the other side as well: once properly staged, the blank wall enables "traveling in a mirror," thereby encouraging a virtual stroll. The collapsing of the three-dimensional space of the garden into that of a framed—and thus two-dimensional—view prioritizes a distanced aesthetic experience of the garden as a painting-like image over the embodied experience of strolling among the rocks.

Like Ji Cheng, Li Yu uses whitewash to create the effect of emptiness (*xu*) on a material surface (*shi*), but his designs create optical illusions that seem to flout the rules of nature, thereby drawing attention to the design itself. For instance, Li Yu uses a whitewashed wall to work "emptiness" into a latticework window design, through what he terms the "Elusive Technique" (Duoshan fa 躲閃法). This design features thin pieces of wood slanting in a zigzag fashion across the front of a window (figure 4.1). The vertical board that secures them at intervals is painted to match the walls, and, as a result, the zigzag boards appear to float in midair.[51] Rather than directing our eyes into a scene beyond, as did Ji Cheng's craggy mountain and gnarled trees, Li Yu's use of whitewash

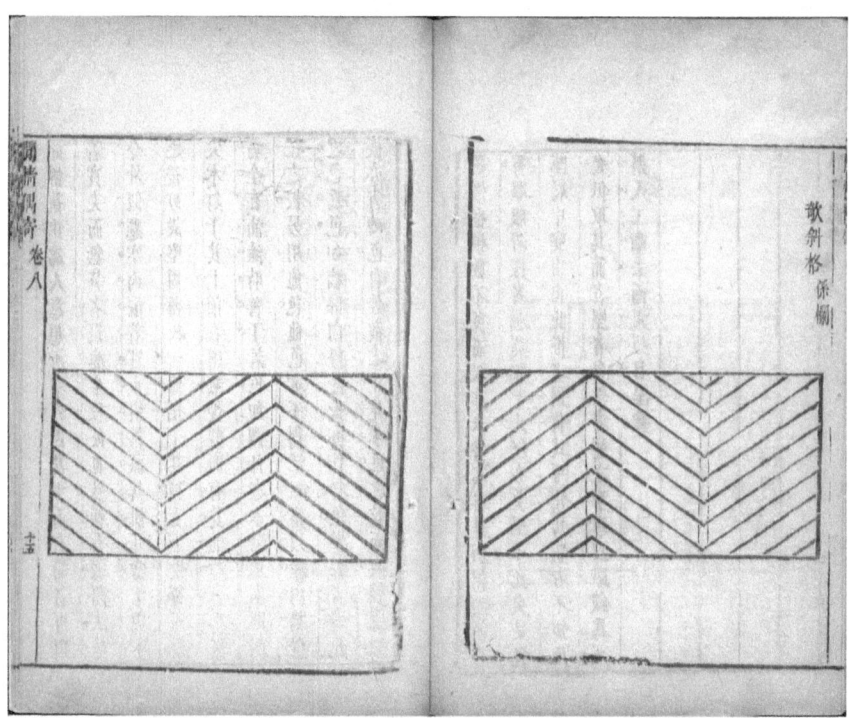

FIGURE 4.1 Illustrations of the "Elusive Technique" window lattice design. (Li Yu. *Xianqing ouji*. Yishengtang, 1671, 8:14b–15a.) Harvard-Yenching Library.

180 *Part II: Spatial Media*

throws the window design itself into relief, in a technique we might analogize to the intrusive narrator's voice in his fiction.

Li Yu's designs invite visitors to scrutinize the frame, and perhaps to walk around it to examine the other side. His garden designs thereby exploit alternative three-dimensional possibilities, adding a narrative element by encouraging movement from one side to the other: rather than imagining a stroll among the framed miniature landscape, they invite inspection from multiple vantage points. One of his windows, for example, has two different names, "Peach Blossom Waves" (Taohua lang 桃花浪) and "Plum Blossoms Amidst the Waves" (Langli mei 浪裏梅)—one for each side (figure 4.2).[52] Ji Cheng's rhetoric suggests that the real miniature landscape is a copy (or perhaps a sculpture) of a painted one. While Li Yu's rhetoric embraces the considerable continuities between the

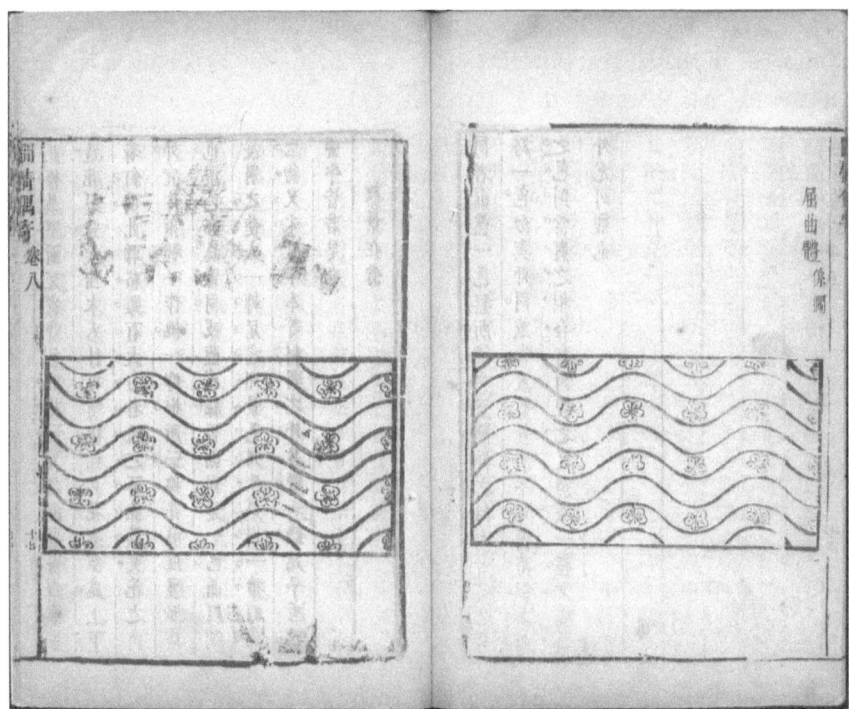

FIGURE 4.2 Illustrations of "Peach Blossom Waves" and "Plum Blossoms Amidst the Waves" window lattice designs. (Li Yu. *Xianqing ouji*. Yishengtang, 1671, 8:17b–18a.) Harvard-Yenching Library.

Garden Space in Leisure Notes 181

garden's scenes and the tradition of literati painting, he does not participate in this connective agenda to elevate garden design by association. Instead of solely emphasizing the similarities between the framed garden and an imagined painting, he adds a quality of life (*huo* 活) that, while associated with literati painting, is specific to the three-dimensional space of the garden: the objects he designs appear to float in midair, suggesting incipient movement. In addition, the two-sided quality of the design directs a visitor to Li Yu's garden to move back and forth within that space, in a process not so different from turning to a new chapter of a story: "as soon as a person turns around, the entire scene has already changed."[53]

Li Yu also literalizes the interplay between *xu* and *shi* across his fiction and garden design, as we see by comparing the transformative effects of a building's naming with his design for a building's name placard. In the *Twelve Towers* story "Return-to-Right Tower," the trickster protagonist Bei Qurong fools his prospective benefactors into believing that he possesses supernatural powers. He does so in one instance by using turtle urine, "a substance that penetrates through wood and resists all efforts to scrub or plane it off," to leave a message on an official's gate.[54] The official called "a carpenter to shave the characters off with his plane, but, incredibly, the message was still there after the carpenter had planed off the top layer of wood. And it was still there when he took the next layer off. Even when he got right through to the other side, it was still visible. At that stage [the official] began to believe just a little."[55] This fabulous plot twist parallels a sign-making method that Li Yu advocates in *Leisure Notes*. In a section devoted to inscribed placards, Li Yu describes several new designs he installed in his own garden residence, some of which featured the calligraphy of famous men of his day. The designs manipulate medium, shape, and color to achieve novel effects, such as boards in the shape of plantain or maple leaves. Two other designs in this section, named "Empty White Board" (Xubai bian 虛白匾) and "Gleaming Rock Board" (Shiguang bian 石光匾) use another innovative method: the board is painted black, while the characters of the inscription are carved out completely (figure 4.3).[56] A thin white cloth is then affixed to the back of the board, so that light will shine through and the characters will glow—a sort of premodern version of a neon sign. In the absence of electricity, placement is crucial: the viewer needs to stand in a place

FIGURE 4.3 Illustration of the "Empty White Board," depicting the characters carved out of the base. (Li Yu. *Xianqing ouji*. Yishengtang, 1671, 9:15b.) Harvard-Yenching Library.

relatively darker than the back of the board—inside a rockery cave, for example—so that light can shine through.

By removing the characters from these placards, Li Yu inverts the usual relationship between canvas and content. At the start of the essay he declares that "there is nothing more marvelous than emptiness [*xu*]; substance [*shi*] is just so wooden [*ban* 板] by comparison,"[57] thus literalizing "wooden" as the opposite of "marvelous." In the story "Return-to-Right Tower," the characters etched out with turtle urine allow a man to successfully impersonate a god; here, these glowing, carved-out characters invite readers to scrutinize and marvel at the novel design.

For Li Yu, the transformative potential of illusion in the garden derives from the fictional realm of "that which is within the range of the eyes and ears," rather than the lyric ideal of a far-off paradise of immortals. This key element of Li Yu's garden design seems to emerge through his fiction, and we see it clearly when we move from Li Yu's sign for his rockery cave to examine Ji Cheng's design for a rockery cave instead. Ji Cheng's description included a number of design options, including paths and stepping stones on water, which would evoke the sense of being transported to another realm. Looking up from within his cave, he writes, "moonlight will seep in and clouds gather," leading to the sense that "this very place is the Yinghu Island of Immortals."[58] In contrast, when Li Yu sought to transport visitors with marvelous visual effects, he transformed a usually empty surface of a wall into a journey of perspective and illusion within the actual space, inspiring a new relationship to the space of the garden rather than a journey to distant islands.

This interest in the transformation of immanent material surroundings is evident in Li Yu's suggestion to render the inside of a study like the interior of a teapot by papering the walls to resemble patterned ceramic:

> Pasting walls with paper is something that is done everywhere, and yet people always make the whole room monochrome white. I take issue with its being a "thing" but not "changing" [as things naturally should], and I want to make it new. In the process of endlessly making it new, I change bits of paper into pottery, and transform my secluded studio into earthenware. Although I dwell within a room, it is as if I am inside of a teapot: this is yet another thing that can refresh people's senses.[59]

In this design, pasting green paper of varying sizes on top of reddish-brown wallpaper results in an imaginary journey of scale, shrinking the room and its inhabitant to fit inside a teapot. Journeys through scale had long been part of the Chinese literary tradition, and they were central to the imagination of what a garden should do.[60] A world in miniature, capable of containing the whole of nature within a small, walled-off space, was supposed to achieve the effect that bodhisattvas had with Mount Sumeru and the mustard seed (*jiezi na xumi* 芥子納須彌): to contain the very large within the very small without changing either one. By Li Yu's time, however, this expression had transformed: whereas in early

Buddhist texts it served as a diatribe against form and femininity, by the late Ming it was seen as an aesthetic principle describing the transformative power of garden design.

Just as the "Elusive Technique" for latticework windows invited a visitor to move back and forth between the front and back of a window, this imaginative journey offers the viewer a transformative experience that nevertheless remains within the confines of the preexisting space—a journey into the garden residence rather than beyond it. The experience is intended to be transformative for viewers, but it is not intended to transport them elsewhere. While the transcendent approach was already common in garden designs that focused on manipulating a distant scene, Li Yu's emphasis on proximate transformations expanded the "empty" (*xu*) space *within* the garden. It seems fitting that the author who relied on the chemical properties of turtle urine to create the appearance of supernatural intervention in his fiction would resist referring to magical fairylands in his garden design. Less obvious, perhaps, is the way that the medium of print and the social practice of *shenjiao* it facilitated likewise replace the transcendental in Li Yu's garden design: this is, after all, the book that carries us into our own teapot.

BORROWING SCENES FROM FICTION AND DRAMA

The intermediation of Li Yu's garden design by his theater practice is most evident in his treatment of the well-known garden design practice of "borrowing scenes" (*jiejing*): that is, framing distant views to incorporate them into the experience of a garden. Whereas Ji Cheng's account ties borrowed scenes to the more established rhythm of the garden in seasonal, or natural, time, I argue that Li Yu's offers strategies for speeding up and altering that time, based on personal preference. The framed and orchestrated "borrowed scenes" that feature prominently in *Leisure Notes* might be productively compared, I suggest, to theatrical scenes that were performed within gardens. Like garden windows, dramatic scenes offered an alternative temporality, opening onto fictional worlds that could be adjusted at will. Li Yu applied that sensibility to Ji Cheng's garden design concept of "borrowing scenes," inviting various material elements in the garden to step onto the stage.

Ji Cheng's essay "Borrowing Scenes" (Jiejing) presents the first extended discussion of this practice, but it contains almost no design suggestions.[61] It offers instead a lyrical account of the aesthetic effects a garden should achieve as it moves through the seasons of the year, with allusions to historical men of leisure like Tao Hongjing 陶弘景 (456–536) and Pan Yue 潘岳 (247–300, the Western Jin poet who wrote *The Rhapsody on Dwelling in Leisure* [*Xianju fu* 閒居賦]).[62] Ji Cheng enumerates seasonal scenes as just one of five sorts of scene one can borrow, but his description of all the scenes borrowed—which include high, low, near, and far—is wedded to seasonal time.

Li Yu's essay "Finding Scenes Is in the Borrowing" (Qujing zai jie) reworks Ji Cheng's concept of borrowed scenes by proposing alternative aesthetic possibilities for harnessing the potential of empty space (*xu*) in gardens. This approach is epitomized in Li Yu's "empty landscape painting," which is simply an empty scroll fitted around an open window.[63] Much like the fan-shaped window discussed in chapter 1, which substituted a fan-shaped aperture for a canvas and paintwork, this empty landscape painting frames an existing view rather than painting one onto a surface. In his first textual attempt to depict this innovation, Li Yu included an illustration of such an "Empty Landscape Painting" (figure 4.4, left). The scene represented in the center is not a painted scene, but a vista of the garden through the window. Purportedly because of the difficulty of representing empty space (*xu*) in woodblock print, the text was supplemented after production with an additional page (numbered "additional 29" *you nianjiu* 又廿九) to its right (figure 4.4, right). The supplemental illustration depicts a painting being fitted over the "Empty Landscape Painting" opening. In an attempt to make this emptiness visible, the painted scene and the garden scene are visible simultaneously.

Ji Cheng's seasonal scenes, framed through his design practice, as well as Li Yu's empty-scroll window, which makes the exterior scene appear to be a landscape painting, are examples of the aesthetic principle of borrowing scenes. Their implications, however, are quite distinct. I propose that Ji Cheng's design prompts reminiscences of old poems and lyrical moments inspired by seasonal change: slow, cyclical, predictable.

FIGURE 4.4 Illustrations of the "Empty Landscape Painting" window design. A garden vista is pictured on the left, while the right pane depicts a landscape painting mounted on a hanging scroll. The illustration on the right offers an alternative perspective: the interior wall is depicted at a diagonal, revealing the scene from the left-hand page as the garden beyond the window rather than a painting. (Li Yu. *Xianqing ouji*. Yishengtang, 1671, 8:*you* 又29b and 29a.) Harvard-Yenching Library.

In contrast, Li Yu's design borrows the rhythm and resources of vernacular narrative to offer a contemporary, forward-looking aesthetic experience, albeit under the same name. Li Yu celebrates seasonal blossoming throughout *Leisure Notes*, but he detaches garden scenes from seasonal time, locating them instead in temporality that is associated with the viewer. His method here again resembles his design for a "fan window painting." In that design, the empty space offers the viewer a continuous reel of moving picture entertainment: "In a single day, one hundred, a thousand, ten thousand pictures of fine mountains and waters will appear, and they will all be taken in [*shou* 收] by the fan."[64]

Li Yu's designs for windows in the home evince further strategies for harnessing time in service of innovative design. His designs for bird and flower windows show how he accelerates a viewer's sense of time (figure 4.5). In 1669, a flood had destroyed several trees on Li Yu's property. Repurposing some dead branches, he created a small diorama outside a window. He fashioned artificial flowers out of ribbon and attached them to the branches, so that "it was just like a living plum tree at first bloom."⁶⁵ Once the artifice of flowers blooming has been achieved, he explained, the display could be changed constantly. The desired effect is what he describes in *Leisure Notes* as the "Technique of the Daily Updates" (Yitian huanri zhi fa 移天換日之法), a reiterative practice by which "yesterday can be made into today and the wooden transformed into the living, making it so that everything before your eyes and ears will constantly be alive and dancing!"⁶⁶

Through this shift in emphasis away from seasonal time, the reader comes to play the protagonist in this narrative garden of Li Yu's design,

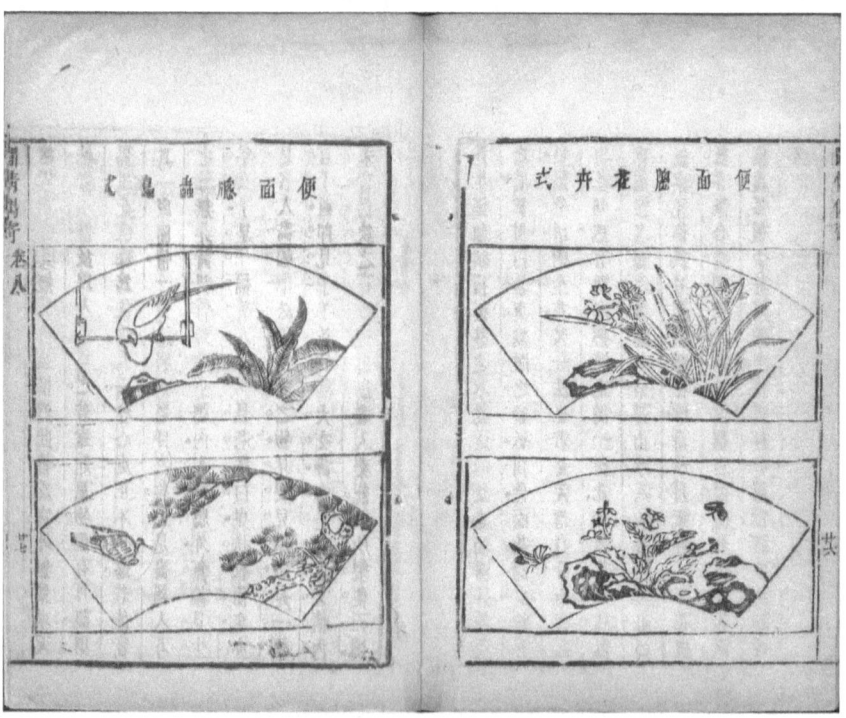

FIGURE 4.5 Illustration of bird and flower fan window designs. (Li Yu. *Xianqing ouji*. Yishengtang, 1671, 8:26b–27a.) Harvard-Yenching Library.

overriding seasonal time by participating in the acceleration of borrowed garden scenes. Li Yu explains how to repurpose the empty space of a window, capturing scenes by borrowing both the time and vision of his readers:

> If you can truly manage to get hold of a quantity of spare time and a pair of eyes possessed of discernment, then everything that passes before your eyes will be a picture, and every sound that enters your ears will be the stuff of poetry. Consider, for example, if I were to sit just inside a window, and people were walking along outside of it. Not only would a young woman I saw become a "beautiful woman" picture, but even if I saw an old lady and a white-haired old man coming along leaning on walking sticks, they are also things that the paintings of famous men cannot do without. Were I to see a group of children at play, it would be a "hundred children" picture, and even if I were to see cattle and sheep being herded along or dogs and chickens yapping and squawking at one another—none of this material has ever been absent from the literary sentiments of poets.[67]

Unlike his other designs for updatable picture windows, this one exists only in analogy: this is a window design that requires no construction, for it is a readymade concept that is already available in the readers' own homes—a way of seeing that Li Yu seeks to install directly into their newly discerning eyes. Transforming every lived moment into a painting, Li Yu might seem here to be drawing on the discourse that derived garden design as an art from painting. But after his initial use of the compound *huatu* 畫圖, which translates easily as "painting," he refers to *tu* "pictures" rather than *hua* "paintings." Although the referent is probably a painted image, I suggest that he is drawing attention exclusively to the framing of a scene, the making of an image, in the manner of modern photography. Neither the emphatically nonmimetic brushstrokes of literati painters nor the technical skill of professionals make an appearance here. Li Yu claims to be teaching readers to see paintings and hear poetry, and in the process his designs further put readers (and garden visitors) in a new position. Rather than a quiet stroll with a likeminded friend through the seasons, Li Yu's garden visitors move through rowdy scenes of everyday life, expanding the range of subject matter appropriate for borrowed scenes by imagining a window as they walk.

The new flexibility of individualized time in Li Yu's garden is likely related to his involvement with the market and to the dynastic transition from Ming to Qing. It fundamentally transforms his intermedial understanding of garden design, for the temporal connection that he proposed between writing and garden design—both guiding readers along lively paths full of surprises—was one that he did not find between garden design and painting. In Li Yu's designs, pictures become moments of aesthetic delight, quickly snapped by the eye as it shifts to the next frame of the narrative. Ji Cheng's garden designs, in contrast, looked backwards, aiming to recreate earlier experiences of garden space described in classical poetry through the compositional tools of painting. While these designs too required the cultivation of empty spaces (*xu*), Li Yu's development of emptiness (*xu*) in garden aesthetics was distinctively oriented toward novelty, enabling him to update garden aesthetics for the early Qing. Although Chinese painting frequently had a narrative logic, Ji Cheng's deployment of painting principles embraced the emphasis on moments found in poetry: while the spatial nature of the garden necessarily involved a temporal dimension of the visitor's experience, that experience was valorized in terms that minimized the individual's experience of time, emphasizing seasonal time instead.[68] In Li Yu's garden design, in contrast, the garden visitor's experience of time is central, creating an account—and a practice—of garden design that unfolds according to the principles of narrative. Whereas Ji Cheng's proposed garden targets wealthy literati, promising an experience of one's own future garden in keeping with the established aesthetic principles of landscape painting and classical poetry, Li Yu's garden design describes how a single window in a home, or even in one's eyes, can create marvelous new stories out of everyday space. In the process, the garden itself becomes a kind of narrative: a story composed of *shi* and *xu*, that is, from rocks, plants, buildings, and placards, and from their necessary companion, empty space.

We might approach Li Yu's designs for borrowed scenes from a broader perspective. In the Chinese context, the term *jing* ("scene") originally meant "sun" or "sunlight," and it came to be associated with natural scenes through association with wind, as in the common compound *fengjing* 風景.[69] As a dominant term in Chinese aesthetics, *jing* were explored largely in the genres of poetry and painting, with the ideal being harmonious balance between the depicted scene and human emotion (*qing*), and, albeit occasionally and often loosely, the objective and subjective.[70] The expression *chujing shengqing* 觸景生情 was used to describe the poetic disposition, found in an emotive response to a particular scene, and it began to be used as well for adaptability: *jing* indicated a particular situation, while *qing* suggested one's plans.

Li Yu juxtaposes that expression with the related expression *fengchang zuoxi* 逢場作戲. Originally meaning "to take part in festivities as the occasion demanded," the expression dates at least to the Song, and it literally means "to encounter a stage and put on a play." Although in the Song the *xi* implied was likely some sort of performed entertainment other than a play, it retained and developed the sense of "a play" performed on the occasion of an encountered stage. By Li Yu's time it was used to indicate creatively working with whatever situation and resources are available. By pairing this phrase with *chujing shengqing*, he implies that "scene" is to "stage" as "emotion" is to "play." Li Yu took these two expressions—one with roots in poetry composition, and the other in personal enjoyment—as directives in his creative process. Whereas a *jing* was a source of inspiration, a stage (*chang*) is an empty container awaiting content inspired from elsewhere. In this sense, the play as a work of art served to further detach art from seasonal time and the physical environment.

In *Leisure Notes,* the relatively new notion of *jing* being "borrowed" in garden design meant that one could understand pictured scenes as segments of the natural world that could be incorporated into one's garden. Ji Cheng's notion of borrowed scenes does not aim to frame them in any literal sense, whereas Li Yu is obsessed with physical frames, writing repeatedly of windows that direct the gaze and ensure that the view be acknowledged as a scene. Even without considering that gardens frequently functioned as theaters in this period, the way Li Yu directs the gaze of spectators in a newly individualized time, detached from seasons to tell new stories, lends a specifically theatrical quality, bringing *jing* closer to *chang.*

THE PLACE OF MUSTARD SEED GARDEN IN *LEISURE NOTES*

Mustard Seed Garden had been built by at least 1668; *Leisure Notes* was first published in 1671.[71] We do not have many details about how Li Yu's patrons supported him, but records of his patronage trips suggest that during his travels to Shaanxi in 1666 he was able to raise enough capital to purchase a small garden estate, located near the southern city wall in Nanjing. Many of the ideas featured in *Leisure Notes* derive from his experience designing that small garden residence—and yet, Mustard Seed Garden is mostly absent from *Leisure Notes*. It is explicitly named only thrice: once as a place that readers may visit to purchase stationary, and twice in a discussion of the pomegranate tree on the property. Elsewhere, the name is invoked to describe the limitations caused by its extremely small size. In those expressions the *effect* of Mustard Seed Garden is emphasized: that is, the very large Mount Sumeru fitting into a tiny mustard seed.

I began this chapter by noting the relatively limited nature of Li Yu's actual garden design practice. Unlike Ji Cheng and other professional garden designers who designed hundreds of gardens in their lifetimes, most of Li Yu's designs are based on his Mustard Seed Garden. Li Yu's legacy as a garden designer, however, was created by his decision, first, to design an actual garden—Mustard Seed Garden—and second, to provide only a notional sense of that garden in *Leisure Notes*. He thus made his garden design reproducible through print in a new way. Rather than representing an absent garden on paper or explaining exactly how to build your own, Li Yu connected Mustard Seed Garden to the reader of *Leisure Notes* by making present in print just a few key aspects that were, in the garden itself, already reproductions: that is, he printed the garden's placards.

Li Yu had already experimented in his fiction with rendering his own garden generic so that others, whether his fictional characters or his readers, could occupy it. As we have seen, in the final story of the *Twelve Towers* collection, Li Yu directly incorporated a series of eight poems on his garden at Yi Hill Estate. But although he explicitly claimed authorship of the poems in the story, he nevertheless revised them to be less specific to his personal experience: he changed the title, removed the reference to Yi Hill, and omitted the last two poems, one of which referred specifically to a local legendary immortal. The remaining poems lack any elements that would tie them to a particular place.

Since Mustard Seed Garden is mentioned explicitly only a few times throughout *Leisure Notes,* the text could never be termed a record (*ji*) of an absent garden. Nor does *Leisure Notes* claim, as did other contemporary texts, that the represented garden was the real one, and that any built garden would only cheapen the beauty of pure representation, which was most itself on the page, shorn of the dross of material substance.[72] Instead, Mustard Seed Garden emerges obliquely yet repeatedly in *Leisure Notes,* visited by the reader but without the representation of an absent object. The effect of this representational practice is enhanced because the form of *Leisure Notes* is itself modeled on a garden, equipped with many entry points and paths for readers with varying aims and interests.

Li Yu accomplishes this nonrepresentational inclusion in part through his innovative use of illustrations. Eight of the text's twenty-three illustrations depict Li Yu's original designs for placards, all of which were displayed in Mustard Seed Garden. He suggests that designs for placards should be associated with writing, and he proposes new designs for surfaces like plantain leaves, bamboo, stone steles, and handscrolls, complete with detailed instructions. The illustrations to these placards are accompanied by a disclaimer: we are warned that their necessarily small size means that the calligraphy of some of the most famous men of the day cannot be perfectly reproduced.[73]

The relationship between these illustrations and their captions is unusual. The text and captions describe the medium of the placard in detail, noting its shape, its color, and its carving and mounting techniques.[74] Each illustration is thus presented as a design that is both distinct and reproducible, which in turn offers new possibilities for placards as representational media. But only by examining the inscriptions on the illustrated placards can readers discover that these illustrations depict placards actually displayed at Mustard Seed Garden. Nor is any additional explanation offered for the eminent figures of the early Qing, such as Bao Xuan, Gong Dingzi, Zhou Lianggong, He Cai 何采 (*jinshi* 1649), and Fang Hengxian 方亨咸 (1620–1679), whose calligraphy is featured on the placards in the illustrations. The illustrations thus omit information that would almost surely been of interest to the text's readers: for instance, an illustration of a placard that names the garden

Garden Space in Leisure Notes   193

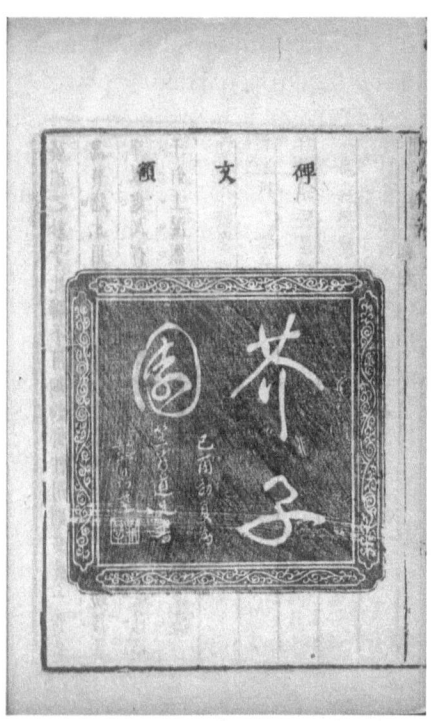

FIGURE 4.6 Illustration of the "Inscribed Stele Placard" (Beiwen e 碑文額) design. This placard, with calligraphy by Gong Dingzi, illustrates the "stele" design. It appears to be carved on stone but is in fact on painted wood. This inscription reads, "Jieziyuan" (Mustard Seed Garden) and is dated 1669. (Li Yu. *Xianqing ouji*. Yishengtang, 1671, 9:13b.) Harvard-Yenching Library.

residence Mustard Seed Garden, dated 1669 and signed by Gong Dingzi (figure 4.6); one that features a couplet from one of Li Yu's poems on his garden residence (figure 4.7); or another that contains a line by Bao Xuan that was matched by Li Yu (figure 4.8).

The illustrated couplet written by Li Yu reads, "As if the boat were moving through the Three Gorges; as though one were in the midst of myriad mountains" 彷彿舟行三峽裏, 儼然身在萬山中.[75] This line is reminiscent of descriptions elsewhere in *Leisure Notes*: a window onto the garden appears is *"as if [yanran* 儼然] it were a scroll painting in a main hall,"[76] or "*just like* [*yanran*] a living plum tree at first bloom."[77] In the former, the scroll painting simulacrum is in fact an empty window; in the latter, it is a dead branch fitted with ribbons as fake flowers. Importantly,

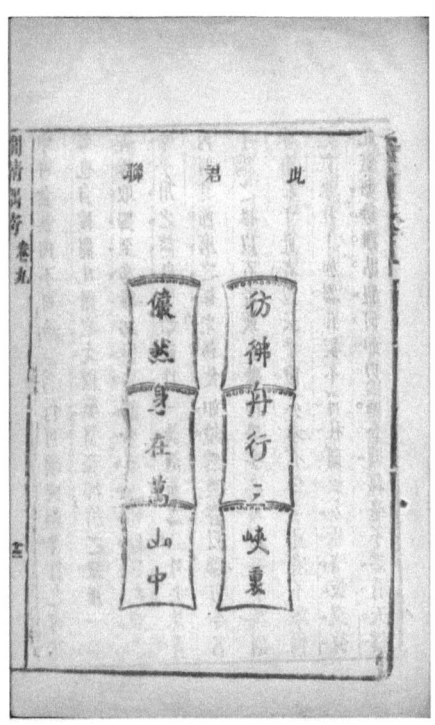

FIGURE 4.7 Illustration of "Bamboo Couplet" (Cijun lian 此君聯) placards. This illustration features the bamboo design, which features couplets carved on vertical curved boards, suitable for hanging on round pillars. It features two lines from Li Yu's poem about a site in his Mustard Seed Garden, Cloud-Dwelling Grotto (*Qiyun gu* 棲雲谷). (Li Yu. *Xianqing ouji*. Yishengtang, 1671, 9:12a.) Harvard-Yenching Library.

whether as garden visitor or reader, one is never in fact in the midst of myriad mountains: imagination is always required for the phrase to apply. As a consequence, the effect of including such language on a placard in a garden, and on an illustration of the same placard in a book, is arguably the same. Because the reader is not reading an *account* of Mustard Seed Garden but is instead encountering the garden's placards—and its sites (*jing*), famous visitors, and ethos—through these illustrations, the text can offer an experience of Mustard Seed Garden that is relatively uncompromised by the intrusion of mechanical reproduction and the printed page.

Finally, in reproducing a placard in something close to the calligraphy of its ostensible original, Li Yu makes a case for the validity of prints. These illustrations of garden placards appear without explanation in the main text: even their location within the Mustard Seed Garden must be

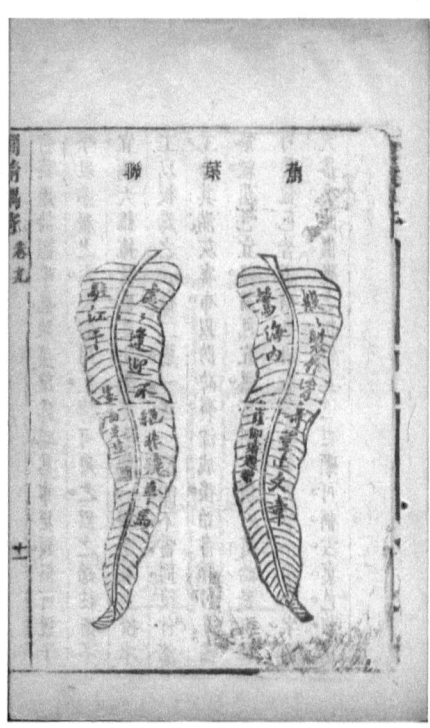

FIGURE 4.8 Illustration of "Plantain Leaf Couplet" (Jiaoye lian 蕉葉聯) placards. These placards illustrate the plantain leaf design, which features couplets carved on vertical boards hewn in the shape of plantain leaves. The first line is by Bao Xuan, and the second is Li Yu's matching line. (Li Yu. *Xianqing ouji*. Yishengtang, 1671, 9:11a.) Harvard-Yenching Library.

gleaned from the illustrations themselves. Even before the moment of print reproduction, however, these placards were already reproductions of the original brushstrokes of the calligraphy, for the men who offered these lines to Li Yu did not do the carving themselves. In this sense, any given placard, no matter how original in its calligraphy, lacks the direct impress of these men's calligraphic style—much as Li Yu's print illustrations necessarily do. The placard in its printed form thus transmits the garden experience, emphasizing these singular originals (calligraphed by famous men!) while implicitly accepting their already-reproduced nature (carved by unknown men). Through this canny use of the medium of print, Li Yu's *Leisure Notes* thus renders a garden reproducible and transmittable, in ways that sidestep the absence-presence dichotomy of conventional representation.

PART III
Corporeal Media

CHAPTER FIVE

Remodeling Fictional Bodies

The human body is central to Li Yu's experiments at the intersection of multiple media forms in the early Qing. This interest may be motivated in part by his historical and cultural circumstances: the Qing conquest and its concomitant dress and grooming requirements inspired renewed examination of the body at a time when experimentation with gender was the prerogative of elite men.[1] As they explored the signifying power of clothing, many extended these explorations to consider the dermal and subdermal layers.[2] Li Yu's interest in the body reflects longer term cultural factors as well: the increasing commoditization of everyday life, especially in the realm of printed books, and the lingering influence of the teachings of Wang Yangming and Li Zhi, who valorized the exploration and expression of individual subjectivities.

After the fall of the Ming, explorations of radical subjectivity were frequently charged with indulgence and blamed for the fall of the Ming—even as many writers looked back to the lost dynasty with nostalgia. Li Yu responded to these combined trends by remodeling the late-Ming investment in the illusory, reframing it as a demonstration of the powers of human ingenuity. Rather than denouncing the illusory, he orchestrated technological effects so marvelous that they seemed supernatural. Li Yu thereby continued to engage with the power made available to dreamers and dramatists in the late Ming, even as he dismissed the power of transformative emotions, illusions, ghosts, gods, or religious transcendence; he thereby profited from widespread nostalgia without embracing it himself. Skepticism about grand narratives pervades Li Yu's writing, and he frequently claims that he assists the Creator (*zaowu zhe* 造物者) in manipulating the natural world. By narrating supernatural-seeming effects that could be rationally explained by mundane reality (*zhen* 真, *shi*), Li Yu claims credit for himself as an ingenious author who could outdo the Creator. His religious skepticism started early. Upon the death of his father, the nineteen-year-old Li Yu refused to participate in the customary evacuation of the home for the "soul's return" (*huisha* 回煞), reasoning, "If my father does not have a soul, there is no need to avoid it; if he actually does have a soul, then it is likewise inappropriate to avoid it."[3] Some scholars have associated Li Yu's attitude with the modern refusal of superstition, but it seems to me that it could just as easily refer to the Confucian imperative to focus on the living.[4]

I posit that Li Yu's manipulation of the material and fictional worlds to reflect his subjective vision is best understood as a new association of the term *shen* 神 (magical) with the technological, as well as an integration of the notion of *xu*—now understood as the *seemingly* illusory—into the realm of everyday life. As Du Jun explains in his commentary at the end of a long story in *Priceless Jade* (the title under which the *Silent Operas* stories were reissued):

> The marvel of *Silent Operas* is that every chapter tells of people, not once being willing to speak of ghosts or spirits. What is even more marvelous is that even when it seems to suddenly speak of spirits or of ghosts, if you read on to what comes after, it will actually have been speaking of humans all along, not, in fact, having spoken of spirits or ghosts. To achieve truth in the midst of illusion, presence in the midst of absence: this, truly, is a book that has rarely been seen.[5]

Du Jun is writing of the story, "A Woman Preserving Her Virtue Meets Strange Slander; A Gang of Guys Joking Around Leads to a Bizarre Injustice" 貞女守貞來異謗, 朋儕相謔致奇冤, in which a young man fabricates an account of an affair with his friend's wife and maid. Relying on his keen observational skills, the man provides highly detailed, persuasive, and individualized descriptions of their alleged sexual encounters; enraged, the friend forces him to drink cold liquor, and the man dies. The supernatural enters this story when the resulting court case is resolved through a signed confession by the deceased man purportedly delivered from the underworld. We then learn that the magistrate investigating the case has relied on what amounts to forensic graphology, forging the literary style and handwriting of the deceased with fake (*huan* 幻) evidence so that real (*zhen*) justice may be served. This story shows how the skills of the clever magistrate are the very skills of perception that enabled the deceased friend's ill-fated prank, revealing the supernatural itself as a cosmic prank of sorts.

Li Yu's manipulation of the categories of the real and the illusory (whether *kong, xu, huan,* or *jia*) in his fiction reworks the late-Ming obsession with love (*qing*) as the ultimate form of subjective expression. The period witnessed, as Wai-yee Li has argued, both a "fascination with dreams and illusions" and the "celebration of the intensity and autonomy of subjective projection."[6] Late-Ming literary and theatrical culture was defined by complex negotiations between the celebration of such illusions and the reality of social responsibilities, epitomized in the *chuanqi* play *The Peony Pavilion*, in which the protagonist Du Liniang is resurrected by the power of her love for a man she encountered in a dream. Death is, in a sense, the ultimate embodied experience, but a Li Yu "Du Liniang" would likely have found a clever way to fake her death instead. We find, perhaps counterintuitively, more direct inspiration for Li Yu's writing about bodies in the great Ming novel *The Journey to the West*, which was filled with fantastic elements and supernatural abilities. *The Journey to the West* contains many instances of features that extend the body's capacity much as technology does—such as the "bodies-beyond-body" (*shenwai shen* 身外身) technique, by which the monkey protagonist can produce hundreds of duplicate monkeys from a single strand of his fur.[7] Li Yu builds on this widespread interest in bodily transformation, but he does so in a manner that inverts established readerly expectations.

Many of the stories in Li Yu's first collection of *huaben* vernacular fiction, *Silent Operas*, feature extensive descriptions of unusual bodies. He writes at length of arresting bodily modifications, including castration, simulated menstruation, intentional genital disfiguration, and penile enhancement. Some of these were possible at the time, and others were not, but almost all are described in physical or surgical, rather than magical or imaginary, terms. In this chapter, I examine the distinctive critical vocabulary that Li Yu developed for representing fictional bodies: printing (*yinxialai* 印下來), bestowing form (*fuxing* 賦形), and remodeling (*gaizao*). I discussed *gaizao* in relation to the fan window in chapter 1 and to building remodeling in chapter 3; in this chapter, I show how Li Yu uses *gaizao* to liken bodies to buildings, constructed and remodeled according to human plans. The other two terms perform some of the functions we saw around writing in chapter 2 and garden design in chapter 4: print as metaphor likens the reproduction of flesh with that of text, complementing Li Yu's use of printed texts to render gardens reproducible, while "bestowing" denaturalizes the creation of human bodies, rendering the Creator an artisan, in a reprise of the move through which Li Yu likened the writer to a builder.

In his fiction, discussed in this chapter, Li Yu works on the surface and the interior of the physical body; this dynamic is particularly evident when contrasted with the less graphic approach to bodies he takes in his *chuanqi*. In his nonfiction essays in *Leisure Notes* (discussed in chapter 6) he is primarily concerned with modulating the physical body from the skin to its conceptual exterior. The divergence results from what each genre affords: as I have discussed elsewhere, the fictionality of his plays enabled Li Yu to experiment with gender through his training and presentation of the performers in his theater troupe, who were usually people he had purchased.[8] In this chapter, we see how fiction enables Li Yu to play with the most invasive of procedures on imaginary human bodies, before learning, in the following chapter, how the body remains a key site of play and innovation in *Leisure Notes* even as its experimentations with the body are less invasive. Li Yu thus engages three kinds of human bodies through his work in three different genres: the bodies of purchased persons, in his dramatic practice; of imaginary characters, in his fiction writing; and of his readers, in his nonfiction prose.

In all three instances, Li Yu's treatment of the relationship between the body and its possible technological modifications resembles Marshall McLuhan's claim that all technologies should be understood as "extensions of man." We can approach Li Yu's engagement with media in early modern China as a useful comparative case for considering the universal applicability of McLuhan's sweeping claims. The human body drives all media experimentation—through what W. J. T. Mitchell characterizes as its "capacity for relationality"[9]—and Li Yu, like McLuhan three centuries later, highlights how technologies transform those bodies. McLuhan's insights were prompted by a revolution in technology, Li Yu's by a dynastic transition: both men saw the represented world as disconnected from lived reality.

Though much media theory seems entirely Western in its focus, Lydia Liu has shown how Western media theorists have drawn on early Chinese sources to argue for the universality of their claims, for both traditions have long privileged the work of the mind over that of the hands, disparaging manual labor along with the physical body.[10] In bridging these long-established yet misleading dichotomies, I have found useful Bernard Stiegler's notion of "originary technicity," wherein any understanding of the human experience must account for its tools and material supports. In my analysis, I use "technicity" to refer to the coconstitutive relationship between humans and technology that I argue is fundamental to Li Yu's project.

PRINTING BODIES

As we saw in the previous chapters, Li Yu's innovative use of print for reproducing his ideas relied, in part, on its widespread operation as a well-established technology. With several late-Ming technological advances that made print more efficient (such as cheaper paper production and easier-to-carve fonts), print was also a key site of creative experimentation: late-Ming printers produced the most technically and semantically complex illustrations in woodblock publishing history, and *dibao* 邸報 (gazettes) carried news swiftly across long distances.[11] Li Yu understood that print played a foundational role in shaping his world, and his use of print as a metaphor for embodied human experience reflects his understanding of that experience as technologically mediated.

The changing significance of print in the early modern period can be glimpsed in its changing usage as a metaphor, primarily in dramatic works, prior to Li Yu's time.[12] In the *zaju* plays of the Yuan dynasty, various characters invoke woodblock printing to lend weight to their promises, a pattern found across various editions of early plays and right up through the 1615/1616 publication of *Selected Yuan Plays* (*Yuanqu xuan* 元曲選), Zang Maoxun's 臧懋循 (1550–1620) heavily edited but highly influential late-Ming compilation of *zaju* plays.[13] For example, in *Zhang Liang Fetches a Shoe from Beneath the Bridge* 張子房圯橋進履, Zhang Liang promises the Duke of Yellowstone that "after you leave, Master, I will remember your words as if they had been printed on my heart [似印板兒記在心上一般]."[14] Another *zaju*, *Wang Dingchen, the Woodcutter, and the Fisherman on a Snowy Eve* 王鼎臣風雪漁樵記 employs the metaphor of woodblock printing on the heart-mind in a marital spat: "I've taken to heart the words you just spoke, saying you will seek divorce, recording them upon my heart, as if they were printed on it with a woodblock [似印板兒一般記在我這心上]."[15] A third *zaju* that uses this metaphor, *To Repay a Kindness, Three Tigers Go Down the Mountain* 爭報恩三虎下山, dramatizes an incident from *The Water Margin* (*Shuihu zhuan* 水滸傳). In this last instance, people, rather than words, are said to be printed on the heart, but the implication remains a sincere and serious commitment: "I will imprint on my heart your husband, Magistrate Zhao, you, Li Qianjiao, your two children, Jinlang and Yujie, as if printed with a woodblock [印板兒也似印在我這心上]." [16] As these instances of the woodblock printing metaphor show, the technology was often invoked to suggest the permanence of speech, whether as a promise or a threat. The metaphor thus harnesses the power of technology to enhance the semantic weight of language, as if those words had been memorialized rather than merely spoken.

In these early examples, the woodblock indicates information stamped onto the heart-mind; it never indicates the pattern that we will find in Li Yu, where something is stamped onto the faces or forms of individual persons. In *zaju*, the woodblock metaphor serves to emphasize a character's oath to commit something to memory: characters declare that they will either "print" (*yin* 印) or "record" (*ji* 記) it "on the heart," vouching for the persistence of the information with their very physicality. More than simply contrast the written word to the spoken one, this use of the print metaphor raises the question of what the technology of printing promises that the older technology of writing did not. First, a print on the heart brings to mind the seal that would, with a single stamp and a singular impression, indicate and verify one's identity. Second, whereas writing proceeds incrementally and at a pace slower than that of reading, stamping a print is much faster than reading, and the process has the technological efficiency of transferring a substantial amount of information in a single action. Finally, by describing human memory as a woodblock print, *zaju* writers imply the existence of an original block that also carries the information in question, lending the metaphor greater weight than a single printed item might imply. That notion of an extant master woodblock grounds (and reiterates) the information it bears, much like a photographic negative.

The printing metaphor was crucially linked to the specificity of woodblock printing, not the far more widely theorized technology of moveable type. The difference between woodblock and moveable type is both conceptually and aesthetically significant: whereas movable type printing facilitates the reuse of carved or cast characters, which are arranged temporarily in a regular and standardized fashion on a tray, woodblock printing prioritizes detail and singularity. This means that the mechanical reproduction of text in various calligraphic styles is on a continuum with the reproduction of illustrations, thanks to the flexibility of the surface of the woodblock and its similarity to paper as a medium for inscription.[17]

In analyzing print as a metaphor for human experience, I challenge the emphasis on moveable type technology in most global studies of print, emphasizing instead the affordances of woodblock printing (xylography). Studies of European modernity (including McLuhan's) have often emphasized the efficiency of combining moveable type printing with the alphabet. But xylography also has its advantages: it is a more adaptable technology, requiring a smaller initial investment than moveable type and featuring a more flexible page design. To use a contemporary analogy, documents produced using xylography have the aesthetic flexibility of a tablet and a stylus, whereas those created with movable type have creative options similar to those of modern word-processing software. Given that word processing emerged conceptually from the world of moveable type, the ongoing desire for tablet and stylus forms of digital inscription may indicate xylography's unique affordances.

In the late Ming, the implications of the woodblock printing metaphor shifted: instead of indicating permanence, it came to denote the speedy and exact reproduction of a likeness. The earliest instance of this transformation that I have found is in the *chuanqi* plays of Ruan Dacheng

阮大鋮 (1587–1646). His *Swallow's Letter* (*Yanzi jian* 燕子箋) centers on two identical heroines from different social backgrounds.[18] Woodblock printing features prominently as a recurrent metaphor as the play proceeds through misrecognitions, chance meetings, and the composition of a portrait. When the two women and the painting finally end up in the same place, the male protagonist exclaims: "The two of you, plus the person in the painting—the three of you were printed from a single woodblock!" 你兩個與畫上的人兒，一印板凑成三个了."[19] Here, the metaphor of woodblock printing renders a person interchangeable with a painting, even as it proposes the possibility of making an exact copy of a human being: individuals, we are encouraged to imagine, might be mere reproductions of one another. The metaphor of print also rehearses a theme famously found in *The Peony Pavilion*, where a stylized painting of Du Liniang cannot be recognized as her representation, showing that "beauty portraits" could be as generic as woodblock prints.[20]

This pattern of theatrical reference to woodblock printing is, in one sense, not surprising: the interchangeability of woodblock-printed people and woodblock-printed paintings is an apt metaphor for dramatic performance, and particularly for romantic comedy, with its showcasing of misrecognitions, imposture, and role-playing.[21] What is important for my argument, however, is the fact that the concerns of theater came to be articulated in terms of print only during the heyday of late-Ming publishing, when plays became the finest imprints produced. This historical coincidence suggests that it was the circulation of plays *as printed books* that inspired the analogies, not their circulation in theatrical performance. Acting, and especially the role-type system, lent an identical actor's face to multiple characters across multiple plays, and woodblock-printed illustrations enhanced that effect, offering contour illustrations of indistinguishable young women and indicating their lines in the text through the generic role-type rather than a character's name.[22]

Li Yu likely read Ruan's plays, and they may have influenced his use of woodblock printing as metaphor in the context of the growing popularity of the theater in the late Ming. He explored the dramatic potential inherent in a pair of lookalikes marrying a single man, exploiting the potential for confusion in the generic "beautiful woman" (*meiren* 美人 or *jiaren* 佳人) portrayed onstage by *dan*-role actors. Like Ruan's *Swallow's Letter*, Li Yu's *chuanqi* play, *The Jade Hairpin* (*Yu saotou* 玉搔頭, ca. 1655), features two lookalike heroines who end up married to the same man (in this case, the emperor). The play likewise brings its two heroines together with a painting that is completed under strict instructions to make it as realistic as possible, rather than generically attractive.[23]

Li Yu did not, however, use the metaphor of woodblock printing to describe those heroines. Instead, references to woodblock-printed lookalikes occur in several of Li Yu's *huaben* stories, including "Tower of Shared Reflections" and "With the Loss Of A Thousand Taels of Silver, Good Luck Results from Calamity" (失千金福因禍至, hereafter "Calamity"). Both describe two fictional characters as appearing as though they were "printed from the same woodblock." In both cases they correlate to decidedly nontheatrical twists: in place of the dramatic doubling of heroines onstage, Li Yu's stories dig into the significance of this metaphor for human reproduction, love, and physiognomy. This suggests an interest in woodblock-printing's implications for human physicality, identity, and relationships that goes beyond questions of theatricality. By considering the medium of print as a metaphor for human resemblance, Li Yu reevaluated bodies, identity, and the human condition in an age of print.

The metaphorical deployment of print in the late imperial period resonates with a concept proposed over a millennium earlier by Liu Xie, in an essay titled "The Sensuous Colors of Physical Things" (Wuse 物色) from his treatise *The Literary Mind and the Carving of Dragons*.[24] Writing before the invention of woodblock printing, Liu described writing as a literary technique that could perfectly capture the contours of the physical world: "[Writers of recent times] consider the highest excellence to be getting the forms of things [*tiwu* 體物], and the greatest accomplishment to reside in close adherence [to the original]. Their artful language catches the manner of things like a seal pressed in paste [巧言切狀如印之印泥], minutely delineating the finest details, with no need of further embellishment. Thus by looking at the language we see the appearance; and through words, we know the moment."[25] Liu Xie deploys the seal as a metaphor to encapsulate the means by which language can capture and preserve the physical world. Earlier in the same chapter, Liu Xie discusses descriptive terms from the *Classic of Poetry* (*Shijing* 詩經) that were able, in Stephen Owen's translation, to "use little to comprehend much, with nothing omitted of circumstance [*qing*] or appearance" 並以少總多, 情貌無遺矣.[26] While *qing* here might be better rendered "substance," Owen's phrasing captures how the role of language has undergone a more fundamental transformation: from a representational system that necessarily relies on a few words to capture something much larger, to a process that creates a true and exact copy. In this metaphor, the exact likeness of the stamp is reproduced, doubled by the material substance of paste that is molded to its form, and the writer, as paste, seeks to coat every crevice of the object. The conventional contrast between "much" (reality) and "little" (its representation) is replaced by "artful language capturing the exact form of things" (*qiaoyan qiezhuang* 巧言切狀) as the physical world and the symbolic writing system merge.[27]

Whereas the earlier image from *zaju* plays of the woodblock stamping words onto the heart suggests that the physical body would reincorporate words, bonding together name and substance, Ruan Dacheng's late-Ming image renders the human body the metaphoric object of the printing process. Not only does this move propose print as a powerful technology that forms physical bodies, but the "little"—that is, the world as rendered in the symbolic system of language—becomes prior to and constitutive of people. A millennium later, in the first story of Li Yu's *Twelve Towers* collection, "Tower of Shared Reflections," we find a similar understanding that print revises the physical world, with organic things produced from textual impressions. He uses print to reconceive a context in which similar features are commonplace: among blood relations. I discussed this story in chapter 3 for its narrative use of a building; here I focus on its metaphorical use of woodblock printing. The protagonists of that story are cousins born around the same time, who look so similar that "their two faces actually looked as though they had been printed from a single woodblock [竟像一副印板印下來的]."[28] These cousins' mothers are very similar-looking sisters, and we are told that each baby has inherited its mother's good looks. What might be a passing simile between printing and biological reproduction, however, develops into a sustained analogy. The narrator brings their relationship closer by suggesting facsimile likeness after birth: because their mothers couldn't tell them apart, each would breastfeed the other's baby, such that "after a while it became the norm that the two mothers simply both breastfed both babies together" (10). Declaring that "children's faces have always resembled their wet-nurses' because their blood and pulses become embedded in one another [*xiangyin* 相蔭]" (10), the narrator suggests that as they suckle the same proportion of milk from both mothers, the children become ever more interchangeable, approaching facsimile status.[29]

When their images appear on the water between their homes (see figure 3.1), the narrative transformation of their physical selves into perfect copies is complete, as their "woodblock printed" faces are once again rendered in a two-dimensional form. In the process, the "shared reflections" referred to in the story's title comes to signal not the usual glimpse of a beautiful stranger, but the experience of finding that oneself and another have been printed from the same woodblock. By gathering together the only two copies in the world and displaying them next to each other in two dimensions, Li Yu's text further invites us to consider the relationship between two printed copies of a page. Instead of suggesting a fated connection resulting from events of previous life, Li Yu transforms "destiny" into two prints of the same page intended to commune forever after. This is a strange proposal: it considers each page as somehow incomplete without a second copy of itself and of true love in terms of a return to an original woodblock. There is, as in woodblock printing, no original print: merely an original woodblock and the many copies that it can create.

The woodblock print metaphor also enables Li Yu to obscure the primary distinctive feature usually noted about babies: their sex. Such an emphasis is evident elsewhere in Li Yu's fiction,[30] yet in this story sexual difference is subsumed by a quality peculiar to both printing and to the refraction of light: the inversion of the image from its original. When the female protagonist Yujuan first sees her cousin's reflection, "she is startled, and wonders, 'Why is my reflection over on their side [爲甚麼我的影子倒去在他家]? For a body and its reflection to be separated is surely a bad omen'" (16). After a moment, she realizes that it is actually the reflection of her male cousin, Zhensheng: "Because he was sitting there bareheaded, without his scholar's hat, he looked just like us women. Because he also looks like me, I mistook him for myself" (16–17). Here, the standard characterization in scholar-beauty romances—of young scholars as feminine—is taken in a different direction: Zhensheng is neither given general feminine attributes nor compared to well-known male beauties such as Pan An. Nor is the feminine image compared to Guanyin or Chang'e, as is common in encounters with an alluring image. Rather, Yujuan mistakes his reflection for her own image, and when Zhensheng realizes that he can also see her reflection, he says, "Are you Cousin Yujuan? What a face! It really is exactly the same as mine, so why don't we get together in one place [*he zai yichu* 合在一處] as husband and wife?" (17–18).

The love of one's own image causes the love of another's: in both cases, though, the love is for the same, in what we might playfully call a "mimeosexual" desire. Moreover, when they fall in love, the male appears as though female, with the famously visible difference of male sex obscured. Just as the printed copy seems to erase evidence of maleness in the couple, moreover, so too does the description of the mothers erase any evidence of their fathers' reproductive contributions. Zhensheng's and Yujuan's fleshly bodies strive to attain "true copy" status through organic means—like the breastmilk and blood that flowed between them as babies—in a series of exchanges that prefigure both sexual intercourse (understood as a coalescence of blood and semen) and a new sort of perfectly matched love, with two identical pages in one place (*he zai yichu*). Keith McMahon has proposed that the ideal types in the vernacular beauty-scholar romances of the early Qing are defined by a "formulaic symmetry" and "mirror opposition," "sometimes neutralizing sexual differences and at other times creating an outright exchange of masculine and feminine characteristics."[31] He identifies writing, or the exchange of matching verses, as the key site of symmetrical exchange between such couples. The print metaphor enhances this sense of symmetry, and in the process it takes away the agency generally associated with poetic composition: the figure of the sensitive and talented poet is replaced with that of an easily reproducible print.[32]

Li Yu also presents people as woodblock copies without the linkages of blood or breastfeeding. In the fourth story in *Silent Operas*, "Calamity," a poor man named Qin Shiliang learns of a local money lender, "Millionaire" Yang (Yang Baiwan), who makes loans based solely on the borrower's facial physiognomy. This story hinges on the physiognomist's ability to perceive qualities in the face that are invisible to the untrained eye but correctly predict business behavior.

When Shiliang requests a loan from "Millionaire" Yang, he is surprised to catch sight of a man who looks exactly like him, whom we later learn is named Qin Shifang. The story describes this likeness in terms of woodblock printing: the other man's "face and physique were exactly the same as his—it seemed just as though they had been printed from a single woodblock [竟像一副印板印下來的]."[33] When Shifang is denied a loan, Shiliang assumes he'll also be denied. To his surprise, however, he is granted a sizeable sum—five hundred taels of silver—followed by another five hundred after he loses the first. The analogy to identical woodblock prints is described from Shiliang's perspective; the ensuing divergence in their fortunes accentuates the divide between Shiliang's mundane vision and "Millionaire" Yang's extraordinary visual acuity. That the object Shiliang fails to discern correctly is his own face lends humor, and existential unease, to the situation: in the fast-paced mercantile economy, it suggests, even one's own face is rendered unfamiliar.

When Shifang's silver goes missing, Shiliang falls under suspicion and ends up handing over his last two hundred taels. Shifang has exceptional luck with Shiliang's silver, ultimately amassing thirty thousand taels, a 150-fold profit. Shifang then discovers that he had left his packet of silver at home and must have wrongly taken Shiliang's, so he returns Shiliang's silver along with all his profits. Convinced that Shifang's recent windfall profits prove that "Millionaire" Yang had misjudged him, Shifang and Shiliang return to test him. This time, however, Yang grants Shifang as large a loan as he would like, saying: "Not only is there no longer any stagnant *qi* on your face, but you have acquired many marks of good deeds done quietly [*yinzhi wen* 陰騭紋]. You must have done a sky-sized good deed to get a complexion like this. In the future you will surely make a fortune."[34] Whereas the initial encounter had underlined for the reader the distinction between Shiliang's ordinary perception and "Millionaire" Yang's specialized face-reading skill, here the reader is alerted to the instability—or, more to the point, the pliability—of the facial surface: not only is there invisible information awaiting retrieval, but it is constantly being updated through one's actions. The face thus functions in this story as a living ledger of merit and demerit (*gongguo ge* 功過格), a medium precisely etched to reflect one's current fortune.[35] Shiliang and Shifang, ignorant of the secrets printed on their own faces, can see only similarity and temporal continuity. Through the eyes of "Millionaire" Yang, however, these two prints of a woodblock are revealed as anything but identical: he identifies fundamental differences from the start, and he is able to trace changes as well. If these faces are woodblock prints, Yang is the only one who knows how to read. In contrast to its usual usage as metaphor, the woodblock copies here invoked are updatable.[36] As such, this instance of the woodblock printing metaphor showcases a meeting, on the one hand, of Li Yu as an editor and publisher with experience altering woodblocks, and, on the other hand, Li Yu as an author of fiction with experience altering characters' fates.

In this respect, his treatment of doubles departs from what we find elsewhere in *huaben* fiction, which tended to explore the narrative potential of two unrelated people bearing an obvious resemblance to one other. For example, the second story in Ling Mengchu's first collection *Slapping the Table in Amazement,* "Yao Dizhu Flees from Disgrace Only to Incur More Disgrace; Zheng Yue'e Uses a Mistake to Advance Her Own Interests" 姚滴珠避羞惹羞 鄭月娥將錯就錯, begins by highlighting the implausibility of the story that follows: "Being born to different parents from different family lines, how in the world could [two people] look exactly the same [*yimu yiyang* 一模一樣]? . . . And yet, strange as it may sound, two entirely unrelated people may just happen to look exactly alike [*yiban wu'er* 一般無二] and can easily pass themselves off as each other."[37] Responding to the platitude that "the greatest difference among people is their looks," the narrator first proposes the language of perfect identity (*yimu yiyang,* "of one and the same appearance") as an impossibility, only to reverse this claim a few lines later: "Two entirely unrelated people may just happen to look exactly alike" (*yiban wu'er,* "one of a kind, without a second"). The strangeness is located here in the separation of human resemblance from sanguinary ties. Although Ling's story questions the relationship of appearance to physiognomy, his narrator is more interested in a similarity of appearance that is clearly apparent to anyone. He cites the historical example of the sage Confucius being mistaken for the belligerent rebel Yang Hu 陽虎.[38] This account of ancient resemblance is alluded to in the *Zihan* 子罕 chapter of the *Analects,* but a full account can be found only in Sima Qian's 司馬遷 (c. 100 BCE) *Records of the Grand Historian* (*Shiji* 史記).[39] In Sima Qian's description, Confucius is initially suspected because of his driver and disciple; the similarity (*zhuanglei* 狀類) in their appearance is incidental. In Ling Mengchu's late-Ming reworking, however, Confucius and Yang Hu look exactly alike, calling into question physiognomic beliefs in which the face reflects character.

The pliability of fate in Li Yu's "Calamity" was not itself without precedent. The prologue of an earlier story by Feng Menglong, "Duke Pei of Jin Returns a Concubine to Her Rightful Husband" 裴晉公義還原配, recounts how Pei Du 裴度 (765–839) initially receives a negative physiognomic reading but his face changes physically as he does good deeds and receives good fortune. The narrator mentions earlier accounts in which physiognomy correctly predicted the unlikely downfall of powerful men, but nonetheless concludes:

> However that may be, there is also the argument that physiognomy [*mianxiang* 面相] is less important than personal character [*xinxiang* 心相]. Among those with the most propitious physiognomic features, some lost their moral credit in the otherworld by committing evil deeds and were, therefore, condemned to a miserable end. By the same token, among those with features that portend calamity, some have turned doom into bliss by grace of their personal integrity and good deeds that earned them merit in the underworld. I am not saying that physiognomy is unreliable, but that human effort can indeed prevail over predestined fate.[40]

The notion of "turning misfortune into good fortune" proposed in Feng's story is developed in Li Yu's fiction in two opposing directions. In a pair of stories in *Silent Operas*, he provides an account of a facial record of good deeds that changes fate ("Calamity") as well as one in which a man's luck proves easily changeable by a fortuneteller ("With the Change of Eight Characters, Trouble Ends and Good Luck Begins" 改八字苦盡甘來), albeit through this-worldly means. In both cases, fate proves amenable to being edited by human effort, whether through good deeds or through the very real (*shi*) way writing signifies in the world. The exploration of changing fortunes in *huaben* fiction was bound up from the start in the way that language and writing produce stories that can themselves alter fate. Li Yu adds the woodblock-printing metaphor to his exploration of the tropes of lookalike strangers, physiognomy, and destiny in *huaben*, even as he also overturns received ideas about woodblock printing as a metaphor.

The use of woodblock printing as a metaphor to describe similar human faces and bodies is provocative, for it invokes fears of unnatural reproduction or loss of individual identity. But the evolution of the metaphor suggests that its significance varied dramatically over time. The earliest example of stamping as a literary metaphor in *The Literary Mind and the Carving of Dragons* posits writing as a seal pressed from the paste of the existing world, offering a perfect rendition. Later, the metaphor of woodblock printing in early *zaju* proposes the stamping of words on the heart to verify or reinforce its message, whereas by the late-Ming and early-Qing examples, the metaphor describes identical bodies and faces. Over the course of this metaphor's transformation, the human is incrementally decentered: in the earliest instance, the task for this metaphor is to capture the world in all its complexity with the technology of writing, which is, it is claimed, uniquely suited to capture the large with the small. Then, after the advent of print, printing wedges itself between people, extending their capacity to record and transmit their writing, but distancing them from their own heart-minds in the process. As a consequence, print becomes a guarantor of people's spoken promises. The stamping metaphor thus becomes ever more deterministic of the human: the woodblock begins as a replacement for human handwriting, then inscribes the human body with language, until finally, the human being itself is rendered a printed thing. In this reformulation, the Creator is reconceptualized as a printer, modeling his creative process on available technologies to economize his production of the ten thousand things. Printed from the same block, but then ferried off on their own unconnected journeys, duplicate people were understood to operate like printed pages, alternately untethered from fate or destined to find their true copy.

BESTOWING BODIES

By using doubles printed from the same woodblock as a metaphor for human likeness, Li Yu implicitly asks us to consider the relationship between human reproduction and technological reproduction. Li Yu continually returns to the question of what bodies are for, pondering the extent to which we can control and modify them. In keeping with the dominance of romantic comedy in his oeuvre, his fictional treatment of the technicity of bodies is gender-specific. Li Yu's heroic male protagonists are mostly interested in obtaining beautiful women, while his valiant women characters are generally preoccupied with preserving their chastity. His stories straddle the boundary between the mundane world and the supernatural. They cannot be called realist depictions, as their aim is to recount the strange. And yet, his desire to keep his fiction plausible (*qingli zhi zhong* 情理之中) means that technological realities, such as the reproducibility of woodblocks, are frequently mobilized in the service of otherwise implausible plots.[41] Consequently, these stories generally propose the sort of bodily alterations that remain right on the edge of the technologically possible, in idea-driven fiction that depicts unprecedented and often futuristic experiments. In this sense, they are akin to the genre of speculative fiction today.

One of Li Yu's recurring ideas is that the Creator, whom he represents as an unmistakably anthropomorphic author of the physical world, is a fallible being whose work should be critically evaluated and possibly corrected by humans—especially by Li Yu himself. This idea manifests explicitly in his repeated use of the term *fuxing*, and it also surfaces symptomatically in his fiction's focus upon the place of human origins: that is, the genitals. Whether in response to his failure at the exams, or the failure of the Ming government, or the new hairstyle required for men under the Qing dynasty,[42] the penis is the primary "tool" (*qixie* 器械) that Li Yu submits to what he terms a "method of remodeling" (*gaizao zhi fa* 改造之法)—a phrase that invokes the *gaizao* he used for buildings.[43] In a memorable early scene in Li Yu's novel *The Fleshy Prayer Mat* (*Rou putuan*), the protagonist Weiyang "Wee One" Sheng 未央生 confesses that he does not know how his penis compares to others.[44] Sai Kunlun—the All-Seeing Thief—inspects it for him in a long set piece that describes its color and shape before a jarring rhetorical deflation:

> Its body glistens white,
> Its head bright red,
> Beside its root, fine hairs cover,
> Under the skin, veins faintly visible.
> Measuring—could it be?—just under two inches,
> It weighs in at just three mace [ten grams].
> A virgin of thirteen would have no trouble;
> A boy of fourteen most delighted.
> When at its business, its body's hard as iron: a very sizeable dried-out razor clam.

When it's done, its body bends like a bow: a seriously thick shrimpy little shrimp.[45]

The initially positive descriptions of color and physical components shift midway through this passage when the measurements are revealed: his "tool" is relegated more appropriate for dalliances with teenage boys than for starring as the romantic hero in this story. The final lines mock him through the juxtaposition of adjectives suggesting large size with tiny sea creatures. Sai Kunlun responds, "Please do put it away," and bursts into laughter at the incongruity between the diminutive size of his friend's "fleshy hairpin" and his confidence that he is entitled to any woman he wants (102).

What I find most fascinating about this deflation of a playboy's ego is its reframing of the human body:

> He grew furious, wanting nothing more than to take a sharp knife and cut it off at once so he wouldn't have to have the thing in name either [having already been denied the value of its substance; *youming wushi* 有名無實] and could put it by his side. He grumbled to himself, "This is all the fault of the Lord of Heaven. If you wanted to take pride in pampering me back then, you should have indulged me all the way. Why did you have to leave these defects? In the matters of looks and smarts—aspects that are well and good, but of no real use—you managed to create me to completion [*sheng fu de wanbei* 生賦得完備]. It's just this one essential thing that you begrudged me. Would it have cost you so dearly to make it a few inches longer or a couple more inches around? Why couldn't you have lent me a little of what others have in excess [*youyu* 有餘] to make up for my deficiency [*buzu* 不足]? Or if each individual's form is predetermined and can't be changed, it would have been sufficient for you to take some of the flesh from my own leg, and the life-force from the rest of my body, and spread some of it on top. Why did you take the stuff that was meant to go on top of it and spread it elsewhere instead? You've made it so I can't use the very thing I want to use, while plenty of that which I don't have any use for is just sitting there. Is this not a mistake on the part of the Lord of Heaven?" (115)

This lament about what Weiyang "Wee One" Sheng perceives as his own physiological inadequacy moves quickly from thoughts of self-castration to thoughts of blaming others—specifically, blaming the "Lord of Heaven"—for failing to "create" him "to completion" (*sheng fu de wanbei*). In advancing this theme, Li Yu criticizes the process of creation and the Confucian tradition of inquiring into that creation as a basis for knowledge. This subversive tendency manifests grammatically in the strange phrasing that Weiyang Sheng uses for the part of himself with which he *is* satisfied: *sheng fu de wanbei*. This expression, "create me to completion," evinces an intentional clumsiness in his description of perfection. Li Yu positions Weiyang Sheng as an interlocutor with the Creator, proposing alternatives to him. Notably, while he starts with an abstract request—"bigger, please"—he then proposes specific methods that the Creator might use to increase the size of his penis. His first idea is to use the flesh of others, a proposal that requires intervening early in the creation process, before flesh has congealed or been claimed for a particular body. He ends by referencing what would have been best known to Li Yu's readers as a supremely filial act: cutting the flesh of one's own thigh to heal one's parents (*gegu* 割股). In this reference, however, Li Yu's protagonist renders this rite self-serving.

Li Yu's usage here of the language of excess (*youyu*) and deficiency (*buzu*) is distinctly gendered, and it is indicated as well in Weiyang Sheng's name, which can be glossed as "not quite masculine" (*weiyang* 未陽). In asking for the flesh of others to cure his deficiency, Weiyang Sheng echoes the pun. This conception of sexual difference is echoed elsewhere in Li Yu's corpus, and it indicates a shift to a purely physical—even structural—notion of sexual difference. Divorced from Confucian gender-based moral responsibilities, gender difference becomes instead a matter of a little extra flesh.

Li Yu graphically develops this notion of gender difference as excess and deficiency of flesh in his *Silent Operas* story "A Male Mencius's Mother Raises Her Son Properly By Moving House Three Times" 男孟母教合三遷. There, his narrator says: "Just look at where a piece juts out [*tuchu* 凸出] on men's bodies, and a piece is hollowed out [*aojin* 凹進] of women's bodies: this bodily form was not created without reason. Male and female bodies embody the intention of Heaven and Earth in granting them form [*fuxing*]: what is in excess [*youyu*] in the one supplements that which is deficient [*buzu*] in the other."⁴⁶ In the juxtaposition of these two passages, we find that Li Yu's narrator has argued for the naturalness of heteronormative gender difference in at least three graphic forms: male/female (*nannü* 男女), surplus/deficiency (*youyu/buzu*) and concave/convex (*aotu* 凹凸). The combination *nannü* serves as the key concept for Li Yu's body remodeling in another story, "A Daughter Is Transformed into a Son by the Bodhisattva's Ingenuity" 變女為兒菩薩巧, which I discuss in the next section, while *youyu/buzu*, as we saw, was central to the remodeling and bestowing envisioned by Weiyang Sheng. The final concept Li Yu introduces for the language of gender difference is also the most innovative: 凹凸, which comes close to the Imagist dream of transparently signifying ideographs.⁴⁷

In "A Tower for the Summer Heat," Li Yu forges a similar sort of graphic connection between written characters and the human body. There, the two eyes at the top of Qu Jiren's surname, 瞿, foreshadow and reduplicate his telescopic experiments.⁴⁸ A rare character that occurs in the *Book of Rites* (*Liji*), where it means "to be startled," 瞿 was used most frequently as a surname. This graphic technique differs from usual puns in fictional names, which tend to play with homophonic rather than visual synonymy, and it is more in keeping with the practice in riddles and fortune-telling of dismantling characters into their component parts (*chaizi* 拆字). Although radicals make such associations fundamental to the form of many characters (眼 and 目, after all, also feature pictogrammic representations of the eye), the meaning of the radical tends to be deflated through familiarity.

Using this visual rhetorical technique that has no alphabetic counterpart, Li Yu's mapping of sex difference onto the characters 凹 and 凸 in "Male Mencius's Mother" refocuses the locus of sexual difference. We might frame this shifting focus in cinematic terms: Li Yu's choice of characters zooms in on the naked body and provides a close-up of the genitals, whereas 男女 suggests a long shot of whole bodies, whether at work in the fields or sitting demurely indoors. Moreover, while 凸 could be visualized from several different angles, 凹 requires lateral bisection to be rendered visible. This transposition of sex from the respectable distance of *nannü* 男女 to the uncomfortable proximity of *aotu* 凹凸 shifts our focus from gendered social roles to physical bodies, separated from their familiar activities.⁴⁹ This is obscene—surely, it is obscene—but it is also rhetorically effective: it is a mode of obscenity that interrupts our absorption in the narrative and pulls us to the surface of the text, only to conjure genitals protruding from and intruding into bodies.

These are graphic representations of a newly visceral process of the Creator bestowing form on human beings, and they reproduce surpluses and deficiencies of flesh in the form of written characters, as if writing itself could provide the missing flesh. The bestowal of form (*fuxing*) I am discussing here was also part of Confucian discourse: for example, Zhu Xi 朱熹 (1130–1200) commented on the *Doctrine of the Mean* (*Zhongyong* 中庸), writing, "The nature of people and things is also my nature, but the form and material substance bestowed on each [*suo fu xing qi* 所賦形氣] are different."[50] But the shared language of the "bestowing of form" belies a crucial distinction. Confucian conceptions of nature and creation understood humans as part of an ongoing cycle: the term *hua* 化 ("transformation") denotes an ongoing process, and it consequently resists anthropomorphization. It forms part of the compound *wuhua* 物化 ("the transformation of things"), which tended to be used euphemistically for death, and also the compound *zaohua* ("creation and transformation"), often used in Ming fiction to mean "luck" or "fate." In the Confucian context, "nature" or "creation" was usually invoked in an impersonal sense. One of Li Yu's preferred combinations, *zaowu zhe*, was less common, and in that term *wu* ("things") are prioritized over the process of *hua* ("transformation"). His inclusion of a nominalizing particle, *zhe*, renders his Creator more human-like, and in the process, "bestowing form" acquires a person-like agent. Finally, the centrality of writing to Li Yu's depictions of the bestowing of form suggests that this Creator is a *writing* person, a *wenren*, or an author.

REMODELING BODIES

In Li Yu's fiction, bodies are bestowed (*fuxing*) by an anthropomorphic and fallible Creator, but they are also remodeled (*gaizao*) through human agency. This combination is evident in *The Fleshy Prayer Mat* through the narrative of a penile implant as a "method for remodeling" (*gaizao zhi fa*) the body. As soon as the protagonist, Weiyang Sheng, finishes his lament, he walks outside and encounters a sign that promises to "transform a micropenis" (微陽)—pronounced "weiyang," like his name—"into a massive member" (*juwu* 巨物).⁵¹ Committed to his goal of bedding the most beautiful woman in the world, he is willing to undergo gruesome surgery, transplanting strips of a dog's penis into incisions in his own. The procedure is described in graphic detail:

> And at that moment [when two dogs are copulating], first use a sharp knife to cut them apart, then cut open the female dog's vagina, take out the male dog's penis, and cut it into four strips. Quickly numb the man's penis with anesthetic so that he won't feel pain, and then cut deep incisions on the top, bottom, and each side and stuff each strip of the hot canine penis into the incisions. Following that, immediately apply some medication to close the wounds. . . . The insides should mix together like water and milk, so that there's no longer any distinction between dog's penis and man's. . . . If you look at it on the outside, it will already be several times bigger than before you had the surgery; once it's inside the vagina, it will grow several times bigger again than that. It's just as if a single penis were turned into several dozen—you tell me: Will the inside of that vagina be happy or what? (119–120)

The reactions that this passage elicits have surely changed over time: plastic surgery is now commonplace, while castration is no longer necessary to further a career or avocation, even as penis enhancement remains associated with scammers rather than physicians. But the visceral effect of the passage remains: How can we not both recoil in disgust and marvel in amazement at the lengths to which this author will go to shock us? Slice by slice, stitch by stitch, Li Yu demonstrates his thorough consideration of numbing medications, surgical skill, and recovery time. In a dramatic departure from the bodily transformations of earlier texts like *The Journey to the West*, here no magical potions or supernatural interventions are necessary.

Li Yu's grotesque use of the term *gaizao* marks a significant departure from its established usage. The term has an old pedigree, dating back to the *Classic of Poetry*, where it was associated with sewing and signified "to make anew:" "How good on you are the black robes! / When worn out, we will make others [*gaizao*] for you" 緇衣之好兮 敝予又改造兮.⁵² *Gaizao* thus began as a term associated with sewing. By the late Ming the term had come to be used most frequently with building construction, where it could mean anything from remodeling to rebuilding, as I discussed in chapter 3. Li Yu's work, however, extends *gaizao* to human bodies. In fiction like *Silent Operas* and *The Fleshy Prayer Mat*, this results in graphic accounts of surgical intervention or bodily experimentation, while in the nonfiction of *Leisure Notes* he highlights technical extensions of the body.

The bodily application of *gaizao* enabled a rhetorical emphasis on the body's malleability, as we see in Wang Jide's *zaju* play *The Male Queen* (*Nan wanghou* 男王后). In that late-Ming text, *gaizao* is used to indicate a change in gender presentation, and the Queen is described as a "remodeled boy" 是箇孩子家改造的哩.[53] This description of a boy remade (*gaizao*) as an imperial concubine leaves ambiguous both the agency and the direction of the remaking process. That is, the conversation does not clarify whether the boy has "remade" himself into a princess, or whether the princess has "been remade" from the boy. The transitional process of the body remade means that neither instance can be easily named as subject to this process, but that one must nonetheless choose a subject for the verb. The ambiguity of the subject of the transformation, as Wang Jide renders it, captures the multivalent energies of an ostensibly two-gender system. Li Yu's description of Weiyang Sheng, through the homophonic pun of *weiyang* (both 微陽 "small penis" and 未陽 "not yet male"), similarly presents him as not yet produced as male, even though Weiyang Sheng expresses a consistent masculine gender identity. Rather than sex difference manifesting as a simple dyad across which bodies oscillate, here the physicality of gender identity is emphasized. With no "other" sex as a destination, this *gaizao* is a visceral transformation rather than an identarian one.

In Li Yu's work, the remodeling of the male body prioritizes its ability to attract beautiful women; the body serves, in effect, as an extension of the phallus. In "A Daughter Transformed," however, the emphasis is on reproduction rather than copulation, for the dismayed male ego in that story wishes to secure his patriline for future generations. The story centers on a wealthy salt worker, Shi Daqing, who is childless and approaching sixty. For twenty years, he has remained devoted to the bodhisattva Cundi, praying that she will grant him a son. In most Li Yu stories, gods turn out to be human characters in disguise: typically conmen committed to convincing other characters, and sometimes readers, of their superhuman powers. In "A Daughter Transformed," however, the bodhisattva is real—and really calculating. She agrees to grant him a son if he donates between 70 and 80 percent of his wealth to charity. A year later, when he has dispensed with 20 percent of his savings, he learns that one of his concubines is pregnant. Daqing prepares himself for the baby's arrival by slowing his donations. According to his calculations, he will end up either with one son or "half a son" (*banzi* 半子)—a son-in-law—but in either instance, he wants to provide dowry or inheritance.[54] Once Daqing's child is born, however, his calculations prove false. The narrator describes the baby's body in vivid terms:

> Below the navel,
> Between the thighs,
> A clove in seed, lacking form, a mere trace;
> A nutmeg in bud, open outside, closed within.
> Neither concave, nor convex, [凹不凹, 凸不凸] but like a wonton rolled out flat.
> Round it was, yet incomplete, [圓又圓, 缺又缺] like a [meat] dumpling newly made.
> It fled the bounds of *yin* and *yang*,
> And fell between male and female.[55]

Twenty percent of Daqing's wealth has purchased him a living baby, but not a sex for that baby. Readers would most likely have assumed the same two possibilities that Daqing did after reading the story's title—"a *daughter* is transformed into a son"—and hence share the surprise that Daqing experiences. Reduplicated here, the graphic characters 凹 and 凸 display visually the opposing poles of sexual difference that the midwife seeks between the baby's legs. But in place of either excess or lack, we are given the metaphors of clove, nutmeg, wonton, and meat dumpling. Although these edible organics all have skin-like wrappers that partially hide them from view, they are otherwise marked by significant differences. As a result, providing these images in quick succession offers a powerful sense of what is *not* there, opening up a palpable space between *nan* 男 and *nü* 女. Once convexity and concavity are dismissed as insufficient, the waxing ("round" *yuan* 圓) and waning ("incomplete" *que* 缺) of the moon offers a spectrum more amenable to in-betweenness than 凹凸.

With this story, Li Yu bestows new meaning on the very common expression "between male and female" *nannü zhi jian* 男女之間. In "Tower of Shared Reflections," which we discussed in chapter 3, *nannü zhi jian* served as the location of a dividing wall; in this story, it names a body, one crowned with a fleshy bud of nutmeg. In this fictional construction, a body that would usually be medically dismissed as neither male nor female, and thus useless, is offered a place and a narrative in between. As Charlotte Furth has shown, medical treatises had proposed particular constructions of anomalous bodies—the nonmale and nonfemale (*feinan feinü* 非男非女)—as dysfunctional.[56] I would argue that this does not apply in the realm of fiction writing, where "between male and female" (*nannü zhi jian*) almost always means nothing anomalous at all. That is, as in "Tower of Shared Reflections," it describes restrictions on interactions between boys and girls, warns of the adverse consequences of intermingling men and women, and draws categorical distinctions between males and females.

After examining of the baby's genitals, the narrator declares: "The baby was a half-female, non-male stone girl."[57] The construction *ban* 半 / *bu* 不 (half/non) usually means neither/nor: the "half" is not meant to be taken literally, and "neither male nor female" would suffice as a translation. But since this child is declared a "stone girl" directly following, I retain the specific difference between "half-" and "non-." "Half a daughter," however, is apparently where Daqing draws the line, and he rejects the child at birth. The narrative has already made clear that, for him, a girl is worth only half a boy: when Daqing hears that the child is female, his "heart grew half-cold."[58] Here the "half" precisely matches the value he had placed on a daughter when he declared that if the baby were a girl, at least he would have a son-in-law—literally, *banzi* ("half a son"). Li Yu's play with the numbers is worth noting: Daqing had paid precisely one quarter of the requested amount before the child's birth.

The equation of a son with the amount of silver Daqing has donated only intensifies as the narrative moves forward. Daqing initially berates the bodhisattva: "If you took everything I've donated to a silversmith, he could make several silver children out of it."[59] The bodhisattva replies that if he simply upholds their agreement, she will happily grant him a son.

Daqing continues to dole out contributions until half his wealth is gone, expecting another of his concubines to become pregnant.[60]

Half a year has gone by when a maid, rushing to the toilet, thrusts the baby into Daqing's arms. Daqing notices its fine features, and implores it, "What evil did you do in your past life that you've been turned into this thing [*dongxi* 東西] as a punishment?"[61] Checking between the child's legs, he discovers a change. A few months later, once he has completed donating the 70 or 80 percent of his wealth the bodhisattva had demanded, the space between male and female has disappeared: the child now has an unambiguous penis, scrotum, and testes. The critique at the end of the story uses this sequence of events to reinterpret the significance of *nannü zhi jian*:

> Shi Daqing was a very calculating person. . . . If he had simply donated all he was to donate and had a son as he had been promised, the outcome would have been predictable and insipid, and he would not have ended up with such a story to perpetuate his name for generations to come. Now, every one of you who does good deeds without seeing them through can be remembered through the ages, provided that you help the author come up with an interesting conclusion![62]

This story may engage the supernatural in the figure of the bodhisattva, but it does so only to desacralize the human body, presenting it as a fungible commodity. It espouses the sexist ideology that values (quite literally, in this instance) male bodies over female ones, yet it does so only to expand and emphasize the continuum between male and female. It signals the importance of finishing one's charitable commitments, yet it does so only by emphasizing how boring it would be to do so. These ironies complicate an otherwise straightforward tale of a benevolent bodhisattva, for here the bodhisattva takes the place of the Creator as the malevolent force behind an undesired body, and the *gaizao* takes place through a monetary transaction rather than a surgical or rhetorical one. Although the workings of *gaizao* in the main story are attributed to supernatural (*shen*) intervention, the more mundane form of flesh remodeling surfaces when we read this story against its prologue tale.

In the prologue, a poor leather worker (*pijiang* 皮匠) prayed that he might find some buried treasure. One night, he receives treasure-finding instructions in a dream. He asks how much he will find only to be told, "Don't ask about the quantity. You certainly won't use it up in a lifetime."[63] Once he finds the spot, he grows concerned to unearth only a single small package buried there, and "half of his excitement was already swept away."[64] The package turns out to be filled with enough pig bristles to last him the rest of his life, which he can use in his work of sewing animal skins. The narrator follows this account with two interpretations: either the dream had no divine involvement, or the gods were playing a joke on the leather worker. Reading backward from the end of the main story, the answer becomes clear: the author is playing with gods and men alike. In the context of this story of a remodeled body—especially given the origins of *gaizao* in sewing—it would be appropriate to translate this *pijiang* more literally, as a "skinsmith." We can then read the pig bristles as tools in the bodhisattva's toolbox as well, linking the *pijiang*'s manipulations of dead skin in the prologue story to the bodhisattva's transformations of living flesh in the main story.

The technicity of the female body in Li Yu's fiction is usually depicted as simultaneously a retraction of the body and a social extension of the person. For example, in "A Female Chen Ping Saves Her Life with Seven Ruses" 女陳平計生七出, the female protagonist Geng Erniang uses several ploys to preserve her chastity when captured by bandits. She prepares by collecting menstrual rags and sewing croton beans into her clothes. Upon capture, she first fakes menstruation while convincing her captor of her affection for him—he sniffs the rags to confirm her story, smells blood, and desists from immediate sexual intercourse. When menstruation no longer seems plausible, she rubs the oil from the croton beans on her genitals. The result is a "swelling the size of a bowl," the description of which is narrated through the eyes of the bandit captor:

> Jade-white flesh that has risen high,
> Held in a purple glow.
> Deep cleft swollen to a shallow slit,
> With no gate to enter.
> Two parts forming a single whole,

> With a crack that is hard to open.
> Like a bun left steaming three whole nights,
> Or a dried mussel soaked for ten days.[65]

In this description, Geng Erniang's genitals can no longer be read as female, but this is not a transformation of her gender. Rather, it is a temporary solution to the threat of sexual violence: an emergency remodeling of 凹 into 凸. The narrator explains that, as a result, her kidnapper must resort to "do[ing] it eunuch-fashion"—that is, conducting intercourse with her as if she were other than female.[66] Her last resort is to slip one of the croton beans into his food, causing him repeated bouts of diarrhea.

With the first of these three ploys, Geng Erniang buys time by exploiting the process of menstruation and the taboo against sex with a menstruating woman. With the second and third ploys she uses her knowledge of the properties of croton oil to enact two bodily transformations: she effectively rids her body of its female vulnerability for a time; and then demolishes the usual vigor of her captor, making him vulnerable to the needs of his ailing body. She has, in effect, taken charge of the "gate" to his body while denying the control he expected over hers.

As these stories indicate, Li Yu's fiction has a consistent interest in the ambiguously sexed body, which, as Furth notes, was usually assigned female.[67] In the *Twelve Towers* story, "Tower of Ten Nuptial Cups," that ambiguity is narrated from the perspective of a young man encountering his bride. Unlike the baby in "A Daughter Transformed," whose gender is determined solely by its genitals, the woman in "Ten Nuptial Cups" is first judged by her feminine external appearance. Yao Zigu cannot wait to get his beautiful wife into bed, but as soon as he does, he sees that there is "no gate for him to enter" (*wumen keru* 無門可入).[68] He describes her body as a mountainous wilderness:

> Gazing out at Wu Mountain, path lost too soon,
> Searching everywhere, finding no place to enter the clouds.
> The jade peak is too tall, the jade gulley lacks depth,
> Five strong men sadly driven back after an attempt.
> What a surprise—the millstone seems fine, why is there no
>   indentation?[69]

The description here is far less graphic: her genitals are not compared to edibles like meat dumplings or dried seafood. Instead, the extended metaphor of a mountain without a path glosses over the physicality of the body, describing what is missing rather than what is there. The question is no longer whether a body is male or female, but whether it is functionally female.

In a marked departure from the previous stories, where a "useless" (*wuyong* 無用) body was never allowed to speak, Zigu's bride then pleads with him to acquire concubines and not send her back to her family. The couple expresses their mutual desire and frustration, which they resolve by having anal sex. But when Zigu tells his parents about his bride's unusual anatomy, they exchange her for one of her sisters. After nine failed attempts to marry other women, including two of her sisters, he ends up remarried to his original wife. Because she is vaginally impenetrable, she has also passed through ten or twenty households since leaving his. He is happy to see his old bride, but still dismayed that she cannot fulfill the proper duty (*zhengshi* 正事) of a woman (524). At the story's end, however, her genitals emerge from beneath her skin. As the narrator explains, her tribulations were due to karmic retribution for past sins. The Creator had "tried to be clever by emptying out her insides [*xu qi zhong*], while solidifying her outside [*shi qi wai* 實其外], concealing that most wondrous thing within her flesh, without letting it make an appearance [lit. "show its face," *chutou lumian* 出頭露面]" (528). Now that her karmic debt was paid, the Creator, playing the role of a skinsmith, "removed the flesh covering [*jiequ fengpi* 揭去封皮], and revealed that most valuable treasure" (528–529).

In this story, through a more subtle approach to remodeling (*gaizao*), Li Yu teases apart the various aspects of what men look for in a wife, inviting readers to reconsider what they see in other people. He uses a plastic body—a beautiful woman who apparently lacks a vagina is revealed to have one—to deconstruct the significance of female beauty, and in doing so he suggests that behind all descriptions of beautiful women lurks the expectation that they will be sexually available to men. This theme is attributed to the narrator at the end of the first chapter, where he implies that by telling the story of a man who is dissatisfied with an extremely beautiful woman simply because she lacks a vagina, he has shown that those men who claim to have tender feelings toward women are actually motivated by lust and not beauty.⁷⁰ At the same time, Li Yu tells a story in which a man slowly realizes that compared with the many imperfect women in the world, a beautiful woman—even one without a vagina—may be the best option.

Whereas "Ten Nuptial Cups" showed that a woman who lacks the capacity for vaginal intercourse and reproduction can be a good wife, "Male Mencius's Mother" asks whether a castrated male body wearing women's garb can be a virtuous woman.⁷¹ In that story, a beautiful male teenage protagonist, You Ruilang, creates a vagina to assuage the fears of his older male lover, Xu Jifang, who worries that when Ruilang's body fully develops the younger man will no longer be content to play the passive sexual role: "This thing of yours is growing longer one day after another [*riri* 日日], and my luck is getting shorter one day after another [*riri*]. Your semen is increasing day by day [*riri*], and my pleasure is decreasing day by day [*riri*]."⁷² Repeating the character *ri* 日 (day) eight times in just a few lines, Jifang drives home the urgency of his prediction.

Ruilang's active and successful assertion of his desire to play a passive role permanently forms an instructive contrast to the role reversal in "A Female Chen Ping." Such a clever and palpable preservation of female chastity was certainly new and entertaining, but Geng Erniang's story can nevertheless be read in a long tradition of heroic and virtuous women. The changes she made to her body were temporary, and upon returning home, her body resumed functioning as before. In contrast, the modifications to create Ruilang's vagina render his body permanently incapable of reproduction, even as they display his ability to manipulate his body for his own ends. The surgical operation here is simple and successful: "Ruilang's wound, as if by divine help [*shenzhu* 神助], closed up in less than a month. Even more remarkably, the resulting scar resembled a vagina."⁷³ The process of castration is described in mild terms, but we nevertheless get a graphic hint of it in the opening lines of the story: "Just look at the places where the male anatomy protrudes and the female recedes."⁷⁴ The story's solution to the problem of physical correspondence is again a graphic one: 凸凸 to 凹凸, which to an extent appears to rely (like the functional but nonprocreative penis) on tinkering with the surfaces of the body. If two woodblock prints in "Tower of Shared Reflections" produced mimeosexual love, then here, a graphic adjustment produces complementary body surfaces: a kind of heterographic stability.

The patterns of sex-specific body remodeling at work in Li Yu's fiction are also evident in his drama. In his *chuanqi* play *As Heaven Would Have It* (*Naihe tian*) adapted from the first story in *Silent Operas*, "A Hideous Fellow Who Is Timid with Pretty Women Ends Up with Gorgeous Wives," for instance, he focuses on the remodeling of a male body by a supernatural character who calls himself a "humansmith" (*renjiang* 人匠).[75] That term resonates with the notion of a "skinsmith" as an alternative translation of "leather worker" in the prologue story to "A Daughter Transformed." In the story version, a grotesque man, Que Lihou, whose nickname is "Not-Quite" Que, marries one beautiful woman after another: one of the women is exceptionally intelligent, one particularly beautiful, and the third is both gifted and gorgeous—and all of them are shocked to have such a hideous husband.

The play rescues all of the characters from the physically prescribed fates of the story version. Looking first at Que's predicament, celestial officials recognize his significant contribution (100,000 taels of silver) to border defense and deem him worthy of "remodeling" (*gaizao*). In scene 27, "Blessings Conferred" (Xiqi 錫祺), we read of a conversation among three Daoist deities that results in one of them offering to facilitate this transformation: "I see. That won't be a problem. Just let me submit a petition to the [Jade] Emperor, asking him to send a Transformer [*bianxing shizhe* 變形使者] to remodel [*gaizao*] the limbs and trunk on his body from scratch, and change him into a handsome man. He'll re-thatch [*qi* 葺] his brows and rebuild [*xiu* 修] his eyes. He'll whittle [*xue* 削] his body and polish [*mo* 磨] his skin. He'll wash away the dirt and get rid of the stink."[76] This Transformer is an emissary sent to earth to change form (*xing*), which is precisely that basic shape of the human body that we saw being bestowed (*fu*) upon characters in the previous section. The work the Transformer is sent to do is thus precisely the sort of operation that Weiyang Sheng had begged the Creator to perform. In "A Daughter Transformed" and in this play, too, supernatural forces exist within the diegetic frame and a supernatural being physically modifies a human body.

In "A Daughter Transformed," however, such modification was quantified ad absurdum, whereas here it is depicted entirely in terms of carpentry and construction: thatching, building, whittling, and polishing. These are unusual combinations of words that marry supernatural intervention with mundane human tools, and in so doing they open new possibilities for imagining bodily transformation. The phrase "polishing the skin" (*mofu* 磨膚), for example, was recently revived to describe the modern technology of microdermabrasion, and the eyes can now be "polished" as well with laser vision correction surgery. Supernatural transformations are usually instantaneous, but these changes are slow and surgical: despite the divine messenger, they require human effort (*renli* 人力), as opposed to "heavenly work" (*tiangong* 天工).

In a feature specific to the medium of the theater, the remodeling planned by these three Daoist deities requires the onstage deployment of unusual props. Subsequently, scene 28, "The Transformation" (Bianxing 變形), opens with the following stage direction: "(JING, dressed as Transformer, enters, carrying a hatchet, a chisel, a carpenter's plane, pronounced bào, and other tools)."[77] Although these are all tools associated with woodworking, the first two items have a rich history as metaphors for literary creation; even before Li Yu's extended analogies, authors had long been likened to carpenters. The third tool, by contrast, has no history of use as a metaphor. As such, it retains a more explicit indication of the physical object and its carpentry function: in English terms, this might be analogous to the difference between "a chiseled brow" and "a forehead worked with a smoothing plane." The novelty of this usage is corroborated in the play's technical details: "carpenter's plane" is one of just ten rare characters glossed for pronunciation in the playscript. Li Yu also features it in another of his stories, where it is used to plane a wooden sign. With no previous literary career, the presence of this carpenter's plane hints at the conversion of the stage into a carpenter's shop, where real planing would be undertaken.

The slowness, and the strangeness, of a god reliant on carpentry tools is drawn out onstage to comic effect:

JING *as* TRANSFORMER *as* MAID *first ladles some water into his mouth.*
CHOU *as* QUE LIHOU [*speaks*]: Why are you pouring water into my mouth? Ah! I bet you want to help me clean out my insides—I'll drink it right down.
[QUE LIHOU *sings*]:
   To the tune of "Changpai"
   Wash out my guts!

Wash out my guts!

Clean out my organs!

Why not take a gulp of this perfumed water?

TRANSFORMER *ladles water onto his hair, and then uses something to spray his eyes.*

QUE LIHOU [*speaks*]: Ai ya! What's gotten into my eyes? Quick! Rub them for me.

TRANSFORMER *acts out rubbing his eyes.*

QUE LIHOU [*sings*]:

A breeze by my brow,

something's gotten into my eyes,

after I roll them around a bit,

I can finally open them again.

QUE LIHOU [*speaks*]: The face is of utmost importance, scrub it extra.

TRANSFORMER *uses a wet hand to wipe the marks and powder off of his face.*

QUE LIHOU [*sings*]:

She's not only cleaning off the dirt,

but she's trying to get rid of the rest of my pock marks too.

TRANSFORMER *uses a carpenter's plane to scrape him from head to toe.*

QUE LIHOU [*speaks*]: Scraping my skin clean vigorously—though it hurts, I happily endure.

TRANSFORMER *puts one hand on his chest and another on his back, and presses hard.*

QUE LIHOU [*sings*]:

She's stuffing in the skin on my back and chest!

TRANSFORMER *tugs at his feet, stretching them out and back.*

QUE LIHOU [*sings*]:

She's even rubbing my joints and pressing my bones,

stretching them this way and that.[78]

This scene must have been hilarious in performance: a *chou* 丑 (clown) performer seated in a tub, singing happily as he is worked over with tools. Once the Transformer (played by the *jing* 淨 or "painted-face" performer) takes form as a maid, that character does not speak to Que at all. Instead, the audience gets to watch the slow remodeling of the unwitting Que: Que thinking he's having a regular bath with his maid, while we know

Remodeling Fictional Bodies 231

that he is being transformed much more fundamentally; the surprising first move of pouring water down his throat, in a bathing action that confounds the distinction between inside and out; the moment when the *jing* actor uses an actually wet hand to wipe the makeup off of the *chou* actor; and the continued good humor with which Que endures even a carpenter's plane.

The scene also features a distinctive juxtaposition of Que's slow transformation with the much quicker transformation of the Transformer. Before Que's operation begins, the Transformer undergoes a change of his own when he takes on the form of a maid to interact with Que. His transformation takes place by means of a stage direction: "He heads toward the stage door, and acts out [*jie* 介] changing into a woman."[79] This theatrical context, the speed and ease of that change, makes the slow, laborious, and painful transformation of Que (the *chou* role-type) all the more striking. It is unclear what this "acting out" even means. The stage direction does not indicate that he changes clothes or that he is replaced by another actor. Instead, the transformation seems to rely primarily on the fact that he has stated that he will first change his own form: "Just wait while I first change myself." That such a performative statement would suffice to "change form" in this theatrical context perhaps suggests a distinction between the transformations of gods and those of humans; here, however, the juxtaposition of the two transformations seems intended to enhance the theatrical effect. If one character can change instantly, how does it affect the status of theatrical performance that the other is depicted as changing slowly, and surgically, rather than taking advantage of the tools already offered by the theater, like words, movement, costume, makeup—in a word, performance?

Although not so blatantly as *A Couple of Soles*, Li Yu's *As Heaven Would Have It* also depicts the inner workings of a theater troupe; the play has become central to current scholarly interest in the significatory potential of theatricality in the seventeenth century. Sophie Volpp has noted that by having an actor who usually plays clown (*chou*) roles perform as the male protagonist, only to transform the character into a person who looks like a *sheng* (young male lead) role-type, Li Yu "underscores the distinction between the nouveaux riches' lack of cultivation and their social status."[80] The Transformer's own transformation, she argues, ruptures both "the illusory self-sufficiency of the theatrical realm" and the social realm at once.⁸¹ These theatrical experiments depart from conventions to challenge social roles and are made explicit by the characters themselves, in a self-referential fashion that had long been part of theatrical performance.⁸²

The mode through which this theatricality and social imposture operates is that of role-playing, in which actors, and sometimes the characters played by those actors, "stand in for" someone else. When the character described as a *sheng* actor (played, in turn, by a *sheng* actor) is hired in to "stand in" (*tidai* 替代) for Que, it reminds us that Que himself is standing in for (*tidai*) a male lead by taking his place as the male protagonist.⁸³ In addition, in place of a troupe name in the playscript, there are two blank spaces, ostensibly so that the actor can replace them with the name of their own troupe. Although this role-playing is sometimes called out as imposture, proving that it is possible to distinguish an actor's role-playing from a person's legitimate identity, instances of performance proliferate throughout the play, highlighting the ease with which actors perform roles and move between them. As the *sheng* who plays Que in scene 9 explains, whatever the situation may mean to Que, for him it is a performance: "You may be arranging a marriage, but from my perspective, it's all simply a show."⁸⁴ As we know from theories of theatricality, when actors perform actors and spectators onstage, a new early modern spectatorial position comes into being, characterized by the displacement of the self.⁸⁵

Alongside such easy role-switching and performance, with its emphatic self-referential theatricality, we find the antitheatricality, if you will, of physical contact getting under the skin in the Transformer's *gaizao* remodeling of Que's body: water, guts, tools, scraping. This scene presents the physical body of the character, and of the actor, being cleansed of its role-type, and it is theatricality itself that is being washed off. In the terms that I have been developing across this chapter, what we are witnessing here is not *tidai*, "standing in for," but *gaizao*.

As Heaven Would Have It breaks new ground for its cross-casting of a *chou* actor in the place of a *sheng*, whether as celebration of the comic potential of staged mismatches or as social critique of the nouveaux riches. It also challenges the current tendency to approach cross-gender performance as always more significant—as more of a crossing—than the crossing of role-types or social roles with a consistent gender. At the most basic level, this play dramatizes the fundamental physical transformation that official success entails. In the process, Li Yu suggests that the transformation from male to female can sometimes prove easier than transforming across the normative categories of male. We thus see the Transformer, played by the *jing*, transform instantly into the likeness of a maid, here played by a *fujing*, while moving from *sheng* to *chou* is presented as a more challenging shift. To recognize these possibilities, we must think in terms of the construction of physical and social bodies (*fuxing, gaizao*), rather than in terms of a bipolar sexual dimorphism with anomalous bodies in between.

But what is a role-type that is not itself? For an actor trained so intensively as to overcome even the difference of biological sex, becoming a role-type is truly transformative—indeed, it is the very transformation that constitutes a person as an actor. Considered as a form of *gaizao* (remodeling), this play invites us to recall the problem of describing such transformations: after all, the young man who sets out on a *chuanqi* journey is never the same man who concludes it. Marvelous transformation is at the heart of the always-complex *chuanqi* plots, but I would argue that when the main male character is consistently played by a *sheng*, transformative potential is partially foreclosed: after all, to use the woodblock-printing metaphor discussed earlier in this chapter, heroism is stamped onto the *sheng* role-type's face, body, and name through the process of role-type training that makes ordinary bodies into actors' bodies. This play, in contrast, invites us to consider a world of greater possibilities, in which we are not simply in the business of becoming what we have always been. A real transformation (*gaizao*), after all, has to start from somewhere else: the role-type, too, and not just the character, are here transformed. This slow process of transformation is the theatrical equivalent of the graphic 凹凸: a reminder of the physical body, both that of the *chou* actor being transformed and possibly also those of the spectators who witness the slow remodeling carried out onstage. After the transformation, the *chou* role-type actor realizes that the physical transformation is all-encompassing: as suits his attractively remodeled body, he is suddenly able to read, his wives come out of hiding, and everything goes his way.

This difference is particularly striking if we compare it to an earlier, late-Ming account of physical transformation. The final novella in the late-Ming erotic collection *Fragrant Forms Fit for Spring* (*Yichun xiangzhi* 宜春香質) is a story about an ugly young man named Niu Jun.[86] In a parody of the notion that good looks and intelligence (*caimao* 才貌) come as a set, he faults Heaven for granting him intelligence but making him ugly, when having both or neither would be more appropriate. He phrases his complaint as directed to Heaven (*tian* 天) about the way he was "born" or "made" (*sheng* 生).[87] In this fantastic plot, which is ultimately revealed to have been a dream, a chariot appears instantly to convey him to the Kingdom of As-You-Wish. Buddhist rhetoric pervades his transformation: he passes through a wheel of fire—a figure of samsara, the Buddhist cycle of rebirth—and then bathes in the Cleansing Passions Pond (Zhuoqing chi 濯情池), where he discovers a corpse (11a). When he sees his reflection, he realizes that his body has been transformed in the process, which he describes as "peeling off the skin and replacing the bones" (*tuopi huangu* 脫皮換骨) (13b). This text may have inspired Li Yu in his descriptions of physical transformation, as it shares some concepts and the notion of a cleansing bath. But it further shows just what was novel about Li Yu's way of describing physical transformation. The admittedly visceral description of "peeling off" skin and "replacing" bones is deflated substantially by the Buddhist discourse in which it is lodged here: anyone moving through the wheel of samsara would acquire a new body of some sort, for that is the basis of transmigration.[88] By contrast, we can see how Li Yu's development of *gaizao*, involving a carpenter's toolbox and humansmith emissary, has reimagined physical transformation for this world.

Li Yu's interest in the remodeling of the body embraces technologies that were brand-new in his day. For instance, the telescope in "A Tower for the Summer Heat" is described as a "thousand-league eye" (*qianli yan* 千里眼), rather than the more conventional phrasing of a "thousand-league lens" (*qianli jing* 千里鏡). By incorporating the telescope as a prosthetic eye, the protagonist Qu Jiren invokes a familiar character—the Guardian General of Sea Goddess Ma Zu, Thousand-League Eyes, who is well-known from *Journey to the West*. In both of those contexts, Thousand-League Eyes appears always with Down-the-Wind Ears (*Shunfeng er* 順風耳).[89] Li Yu's rhetorical move here is once again to transform a magical ability into a technological one, so that his protagonist can successfully impersonate an immortal. By deploying tools as though they could remodel bodies, Li Yu's story suggests that human bodies could be remodeled as easily as buildings are.

In this chapter I have discussed a pattern of printing, bestowing, and remodeling of bodies that can elucidate the normative gendering of the body in late-Ming and early-Qing China. I am convinced by Furth's description of a "relative and flexible bipolarity" between yin and yang in philosophical and medical approaches to the body, yet something rather different seems to have been taking place in literature. I propose that in fiction, expressions like *nannü zhi jian* effectively established and divided the sexes into two socially salient categories of men and women. When this boundary was transgressed, a story ensued. Li Yu's stories open up an interstitial space between the embodied categories of male and female, and this space operates in surprising and unpredictable ways. Rather than, for instance, ferrying an indeterminate body over to the side of a (deficient) female, I show that Li Yu uses this unusual body to conceptualize any human body as a medium, one that can be remodeled for many different ends. When we read Li Yu's many stories of remodeling and remodeled bodies as a composite corpus, sexual reproduction is revealed as a particular desire modeled onto bodies, but not the crucial one.

In conceiving of the human body as a medium, I approach the human as constituted together with tools, and the sorts of extensions that tools allow. In this framing, two ideas are crucial: first, that tools—including that of woodblock print—be considered in light of their function to extend the capacity of the person in some way, and second, that the body be considered a pliable thing that can be altered by human actions, whether of the self or of others, not as a preformed entity coexistent with an abstract self or mind (*xin*). This is not a primarily discursive or performative body, but rather an interactive one, in which the body and the social are mutually constituted through constrained interactions. In Li Yu's fiction, these interactions are frequently shaped around extreme versions of gendered norms. The result is a gendering of bodily mediation in which the technological extension functions as a mediator or matchmaker (*meiren* 媒人) between people. When Li Yu leaves the realm of fiction, he takes with him these ideas about the body's capacity for remodeling, and its fundamental technicity, offering readers tools to remodel their own bodies. Carpenter's plane, anyone?

CHAPTER SIX

Remodeling Real Bodies in *Leisure Notes*

The genres of fiction and drama that I discuss in chapter 5 allowed Li Yu to speculate about the design possibilities of the human body with exuberance, and the results made for good entertainment—they shocked readers with extreme but plausible revisions. In this chapter I explore Li Yu's nonfiction design possibilities for flesh. These emerge primarily in his magnum opus *Leisure Notes*, where he conceives of real bodies as sharing with his fictional bodies a fundamentally mediated quality. In Li Yu's nonfiction writing, the technicity of the body manifests as a rethinking of how bodies have incorporated technologies, and of what the relationship is between the body and the material world; it also works in the other direction, considering how the body is figured through analogy to other media. Many of his proposals denaturalize ingrained functions and habits. Some suggested techniques and modifications propose further developing the body to render it more efficient or aesthetically pleasing, while others draw attention to prior modifications that have caused us to neglect the body's capacities.

The rhetorical connections we find in Li Yu's nonfiction are somewhat anticipated by the metaphors of bestowing (*fuxing*), remodeling (*gaizao*), and printing (*yinxialai*) that likened the Creator to an artisan and likened the human body to a printed page in his fiction. Silk—a humanmade textile—appears as an extended metaphor for the design possibilities of human skin, whereas images of fetters and extensions propose that the body should be conceived as an ever-modifiable machine. My approach reevaluates the relationship between Li Yu's writing and his world by showing how his conception of the body as a medium—one that can be manipulated through metaphor, fictional techniques, and technological interventions—traveled across his fiction and his nonfiction to get under his readers' skin.

In *Leisure Notes*, even when Li Yu is making a nonfictional point about nonfictional bodies, his imaginative phrasing reorders the discursive constitution of the human body, thus intervening in the Creator's imperfect design. *Leisure Notes* includes instances where he revises the Creator's work outside of the bodily realm, as for instance his suggestion that summer be removed from the line-up of seasons.[1] His most outrageous proposals to rewrite the creative processes of nature, however, tend to center on human bodies. For instance, a reader of *Leisure Notes* would reach the end of the book on interior decorating, "Furnishings and Fine Things" (Qiwan bu)—which culminates in an essay titled "Prioritize Lively Change" (Gui huobian 器玩部) on how to enliven the space within one's home by rearranging everything but the walls—and turn the page to find a tongue-in-cheek questioning of the very structure of the human body. That essay becomes effective through juxtaposition, for its placement links the remodeling of the human body to the common practice of moving vases and paintings around inside the home. It opens the book "Food and Drink" (Yinzhuan bu), and begins:

> When I observe the human body, it seems that each part—eyes and ears, nose and tongue, hands and feet, and the skeletal frame—is indispensable. That which it could absolutely have done without, but which nevertheless was bestowed [*fu*] on it, and which subsequently became the burden of living people throughout the ages, is none other than the mouth and the belly [*koufu* 口腹]. Once possessed of mouth and belly, stratagems for making a living multiplied; when stratagems for living multiplied, swindles, forgeries, malice, and danger appeared. When swindles, forgeries, malice, and danger appeared, the Five Punishments had to be used [by the state]. That a sovereign cannot care for and nurture [the people], that parents cannot dote on [their children], that the Creator [*zaowu*] loves life and yet cannot help but go against his own will, are all because when

he bestowed form on humankind, he did not do so perfectly, adding superfluously the burden of these two things. (650)

In this passage, Li Yu asks us to consider the most absurd of possibilities under the ruse of practicality and social harmony: a body shorn of its mouth and digestive system, yet somehow still possessing a tongue. As we begin reading this section, he marshals us through a predictable list of body parts, oscillating outward to encompass the entire body, and he offers the familiar Confucian observation that each of these parts is natural, even "indispensable." A long sentence then describes how the body would have been better off without the "mouth and belly" (*koufu*). The Confucian tradition is well known for its denigration of the digestive system. The status of the appetite, denoted by "mouth and belly," features prominently in Confucian discussions of human nature. In a well-known passage from Mencius's debate with Gaozi, Mencius proposes that the appetite can be accommodated, so long as it is maintained in its properly subordinate place. Zhu Xi's influential commentary to that text leaves no room for ambiguity: "The "base and inferior parts are the mouth and stomach; the lofty and superior parts are the heart-mind and will."[2] Given this common denigration of mouth and belly in Neo-Confucian thought, we can read Li Yu's strategy here as building on Confucian claims, exaggerating them to the point at which they become ridiculous.

Whereas the logical direction of Li Yu's passage is indebted to Confucian reasoning, his radical revision of possibilities links it to classical Daoist texts: we hear, for instance, echoes of Zhuangzi's dream conversation with a skull in his use of the expression "the burden of living people" (*shengren zhi lei* 生人之累).[3] Li Yu borrows from Zhuangzi an audacious willingness to imagine human bodies in radically altered forms. In drawing these connections, I do not mean to propose Li Yu as a philosopher, whether in a syncretist mode or in any particular tradition. Rather, I suggest that he is activating and then undermining certain associations in the minds of his readers, who would surely have been familiar with classical texts.

Li Yu's proposal distances his work from late-Ming casual essays (*xiaopin*), for those texts celebrate a pleasurable, sensuous experience of delicate flavors. In contrast to these contemporaneous works, Li Yu's food and drink essay begins by dismissing the tasting of food. Instead, he proposes a body entirely dedicated to the pursuit of other aesthetic pleasures. He develops this proposal through analogies that parody the familiar tropes of Confucianism:

> Grass and trees have no mouth or belly, and yet they live. Mountains and stones, and the soil of the earth do not eat or drink, yet I have not heard of them not coming into being. Why single out the bodies of people to be different, and bestow on them a mouth and a belly? And even if they did need a mouth and belly, it could have been like the fishes and shrimp that drink water or cicadas that imbibe dew: this supplies them with ample energy, and they are able to dive, jump, fly, and sing. Were it like this for people, we would want for nothing from the world, and our troubles would come to an end. However, since we are born with a mouth and a stomach, and with a large appetite to boot, it is like a big pit that cannot be filled.... This is the extent of it: peoples' entire lives are spent exhausting the strength of their vital organs and bones to provide for the consumption of this one thing, and it is still not enough! (650)

These references to grass, shrimp, and cicadas are obviously in jest, for naturalist study was already highly developed, and it echoes common expressions of the time like "People are not so much grass and trees, how could they be without knowledge?"[4] Li Yu concludes with an unambiguous assignation of fault: "I cannot but place the blame squarely on the Creator. I also know that the Creator has most likely regretted his error in this, but because that which is completed is difficult to change, he simply had to let his mistake continue on to the end" (650).

The voice and argument we encounter here echoes Li Yu's fictional characters, narrators, and commentators. Yet whereas Li Yu's fictional narrator often seems larger than life, fully in control of his creations and chiding the Creator (*zaohua*) for his failures, the Li Yu of *Leisure Notes* frequently refers to his own labor: the fact that he has had to "plow with his brush" (*bigeng* 筆耕) or "smear some sustenance on his mouth" (*hukou* 糊口) to make a living. Excoriating the Creator for the difficulty of living, in *Leisure Notes* he prioritizes finding cheap alternatives, frequently advocating the superiority of frugality even for people of means. In a rhythm similar to that in his fiction, in which the narrator's or commentator's protests serve primarily as a contrast to the main story's claims, Li Yu draws out his arguments at length, rendering them ever more ludicrous. By faulting the Creator for giving us a digestive system, Li Yu translates the kinds of conceits he often deploys in his fiction into a text that nevertheless also shares practical advice regarding food.

Outrageous proposals are not the norm in *Leisure Notes*, yet the *gaizao* mode from Li Yu's fiction surfaces throughout, manifesting in proposals for at-home, do-it-yourself body design. In this chapter I analyze how he applies *gaizao* to two different types of bodies: those of women purchased as concubines, wherein aesthetics are emphasized; and those of the primarily male readers of *Leisure Notes*, wherein Li Yu emphasizes efficiency instead. These dichotomously gendered concerns are reunited at the end of the second section; there we see how Li Yu related the limits of innovation to the interplay between aesthetics and functionality.

REMODELING WOMEN

Li Yu's iconoclast opinions and penchant for rationality have been interpreted as harbingers of a modernity that was interrupted by subsequent political and social developments in the Qing state; the way he depicts competent and interesting women in his fiction, especially in his plays, has been marshalled as evidence in favor of such an interpretation.[5] His essays in *Leisure Notes* likewise differ from late-Ming connoisseurship manuals in their inclusion of essays on objects long dismissed as "things of the women's quarters," such as parrots and low-backed armchairs.[6] During his lifetime, Li Yu was frequently criticized by his contemporaries for his relationships with women: his concubines performed his plays and sometimes traveled with him, which violated norms of concealing women in the inner chambers, and his writing flagrantly flouted Confucian values. His rebellion against those values led to some arguably protofeminist positions, like promoting women's literacy. And yet, as I show in this chapter, he was just as comfortable with the literal objectification of women, discussing them at length as bodies for sale.

The connections I draw across the different essays of *Leisure Notes* complicate our understanding of Li Yu's potential protofeminism, even as they reveal his interest in rethinking the possibility for bodily optimization across the gender spectrum. The bodies that receive the most systematic evaluation in *Leisure Notes* are those of prospective concubines. The third book of *Leisure Notes* is intended to guide gentlemen in their purchase and training of women based on his own training of his concubines to perform his plays; he titled it "Exquisite Ingénues" (Shengrong bu), a euphemism for courtesans or concubines composed of characters that denote "voice" and "appearance." Li Yu wrote to several prospective readers of *Leisure Notes* that they should skip the first two books on playwriting and performance and begin with this book. Yet it has received comparatively little attention in the modern period, likely because of its explicit commodification of women and its open promotion of colorism, favoring lighter skin to darker.[7] I situate his unabashed advocacy of a more commodified and plastic female body alongside his discussion of other bodies, arguing that by using the conception of *gaizao* from his fiction and by likening bodies to buildings and cloth, Li Yu encouraged men and women alike to understand all bodies differently.

In "Exquisite Ingénues," Li Yu explains that by training purchased women to be tastefully dressed, exquisitely made-up, literate, and conversationally engaging, the reader can enjoy constantly varied entertainment. It opens with a section titled "Selecting Features" (Xuanzi 選姿), which discusses those parts of the body that are usually thought to be unchangeable: skin, eyes, hands and feet, and bearing. From there, the discussion moves outward: we read essays in "Modifying Appearance" (Xiurong 修容) on hygiene, hairstyles, fragrance, and make-up, and in "Managing Attire" (Zhifu 治服) on accessories, clothing, shoes, and socks. The final section, "Developing Skills" (Xiji 習技), moves inward, emphasizing the value of learned pursuits, from reading and playing musical instruments to singing and dancing. Across these essays, the operative metaphor that emerges for the material of the human is that of cloth.

Li Yu's conception of skin as fabric draws on existing conventions: the definitions of skin in the Eastern Han dictionary *Shiming* 釋名, for instance, are a "quilt covering the body," a "cloth spread on the exterior surface," and a "sturdy curtain."[8] Li Yu's extensive discussion of this metaphor also builds on his fictional and dramatic examples of the "skinsmith" and "humansmith" discussed in chapter 5, which raised the possibility of "skin stitching." Across the essays, the notion of skin-as-cloth solidifies as Li Yu layers upon it skin care, then make-up, and finally clothing. This layering produces a particular resonance between skin care—discussed in terms of cloth-dyeing—and clothing, which was actually made of dyed cloth.

This conception of skin as cloth also resonates with Angela Zito's discussion of conceptions of the body in the context of imperial sacrifice. An emphasis on "the body as boundary maker focuses us firmly in the realm of culturally constructive practices like dress and gesture," she suggests, with a body that demarcates its own inside and outside rather than possessing in advance a "secret, hidden interiority."[9] This perspective comes from a slightly later period and a very different context, yet it shows how a focus on skin can make and remake the body. Whether in imperial sacrifice or in Li Yu's writings, skin's operation as a boundary marker can demonstrate the body as remodelable, in a way that is as thoroughgoing as the washed-out guts of Que Lihou in *As Heaven Would Have It*.

In Li Yu's fiction, *gaizao* constructed extensive points of resonance between bodies and architectural design; in the realm of real bodies for sale, it proposes remodeling the human body through the metaphor of cloth-dyeing. In contrast to the extreme accounts in his fiction, his designs for real bodies develop these productive analogies into an aesthetic principle that I call "resonant innovation." I name it in these terms to indicate how Li Yu's advocacy of novelty nonetheless harnessed the cultural energies of the influential idea of correlative resonance (*ganying* 感應), which he then applied to his own ends. The opening essay on women's beauty, "Skin" (Jifu 肌膚), begins by reworking the conventional metaphoric usage of silk fabric: "Many indeed are the charms of a woman, but chief among them is her complexion (*se* 色). Does the *Poems* not say: 'Plain silk (*su*) to paint on' [素以爲絢兮]? 'Plain,' here means 'white (*bai*).'"[10] This passage references the *Classic of Poetry*, but the line mentioned did not appear in any canonical versions of that text. Instead, this line was known through its metaphorical usage in the *Analects*, where it likened the plain silk canvas of a painting—necessary before any painting can be undertaken—to the preparations required before the rites can be practiced: "Zixia asked, '[A poem says:] Clever smile all adimple, pretty eyes darkly sharp. Plain silk to paint on. [巧笑倩兮, 美目盼兮, 素以爲絢兮。]' What is it about? The Master answered, 'Painting takes place after the [plain] silk [*su* 素] is there.' Zixia said, 'Do the rites come after?' The Master answered, 'It is you, Shang, who inspire me. At last I can speak with you about the *Poems*.'"[11] By tacitly inserting the *Analects* between the *Leisure Notes*' citation and what remained of the original poem, Li Yu invokes the *Analects* only to overturn its interpretation, and the format of a rhetorical question prompts the reader's hesitation. The *Analects* passage, moreover, writes of smiles and eyes before moving to silk. Li Yu's citation, however, bypasses the *Analects* and points to a lacuna in the *Classic of Poetry*, and in the process, it returns the silk metaphor to what was ostensibly its original significance: the skin of the face as a canvas that sets off the darker eyes and lips. We might read Li Yu's citation, then, as his response to Zixia's request for interpretation. In a narrowing of the distance between words and meaning, Li Yu's resonant innovation returns the metaphor to its original referent.

Following the quotation, Li Yu provides an unnecessary gloss of a common word—"'plain' [*su*] here means 'white'"—yet he does not gloss the final character, *xuan* 絢; in contrast, the *Annotated Analects* (*Lunyu zhushu*) glosses *xuan* but not *su*.[12] I suggest that Li Yu's gloss provides emphasis rather than clarification, making whiteness—its attainment, variations, and origins—the central concern. He proclaims: "As to women's intrinsic endowments [*benzhi* 本質], whiteness is the most difficult to attain.... Could it be that the Creator, for all his skill in making people, could not do as cloth-dyers do, but rather hastily added patterns and colors before he had finished bleaching [*piao* 漂] and scouring [*lian* 練] the silk? No, that's not right. White is difficult to attain, whereas colors are easy."[13]

Li Yu's fiction improved upon the Creator's work on behalf of his characters; here he raises the possibility that the Creator is inferior to a common cloth-dyeing artisan, only to refute it. Instead, he declares that whiteness is intrinsically difficult.[14] To support this claim, he moves from an aesthetic realm to a scientific one. Li Yu proposes that human complexions are determined from the moment of conception, yet he deduces this theory from the cloth-dyeing process, rather than from the medical knowledge of his time. Following the common belief that the human body is formed from a coalescence of semen and blood, he claims that a person's complexion is determined by their proportions, much as dye colors are extracted from natural objects:

When things come into being, they do so according to their essences. Whatever color they are originally will be the color of their later developments. What is the essence of people? Semen and blood. The color of semen is white, while the color of blood is purplish red. If a fetus receives proportionally more of its father's semen, then when the person is born, they'll necessarily be whiter. If there happens to be a greater proportion of blood and a smaller proportion of semen when the father's semen and the mother's blood coalesce to form a fetus, the person who is produced will surely have a complexion between light and dark.[15]

Li Yu's linking of the colors of blood and semen with that of skin color is decidedly unusual. Li Yu is the only person I know of to propose that semen and blood, as the yin- and yang-endowed "essences" of humanity, be analyzed primarily for their pigments.[16] His account accords with a complementary rather than dichotomous understanding of yin and yang: each parent contributes a variable amount to the fetus, which leads to different complexions for the people they produce. This idea links skin to the multi-ingredient dyes used for cloth, where "light red" (*xiaohong* 小紅) dye might be created by mixing, say, four *liang* of sappanwood (*sumu* 蘇木) with one *liang* of red lead (*huangdan* 黃丹, lead oxide), according to a recipe in the Ming encyclopedia for daily use, *No Matter Too Small: A Multi-Functional Reference Book*.[17] This equation, notably, has gendered implications, since Li Yu valorizes whiteness as most attractive. In Li Yu's fiction, both male and female offspring are described as exceptionally good-looking precisely because of the higher proportion of influence from their mothers, and several stories' happy resolutions are crucially dependent on an exclusively maternal resemblance. In *Leisure Notes*, in contrast, a greater paternal influence, via a higher proportion of white semen, produces a lighter-skinned and thus ostensibly more attractive child.

By conceiving of reproduction as dyeing rather than as printing, Li Yu opens up a spectrum of infinite variation. Much as his focus on the space between buildings or between genders had enabled many of his short stories, in *Leisure Notes* he focuses on the space between light and dark complexions (*heibai zhi jian* 黑白之間) to concoct ever finer points of distinction. He introduces gradations, characteristics, and hence categorizations for in-between cases, drawing on the variable color of blood:

> If the color of the blood that forms the fetus is light red, although her complexion will be somewhere between light and dark, if, after birth, you feed her the finest foods and keep her in a secluded room, it is still possible for her to grow lighter by the day, as she is not completely black to the core. Those who are darker when young and grow lighter as they age are of this type. As for fetuses produced by those whose blood is deep purple, they are dark to their very core, and there is no way to bleach them. Once such a child is born, even she is given decoctions of crystal and mica and housed in a jade mansion, it would still be extremely difficult to change her complexion from dark to light. At best, one could try to preserve [her complexion] as it is, and count oneself lucky if it doesn't grow even darker with age. Those from well-to-do families who are not light-skinned at birth, and who remain that way as they grow older, are of this type.[18]

Through gradations of color—like "light red" (*qianhong* 淺紅), "purplish red" (*hong er zi* 紅而紫), and "deep purple" (*shenzi* 深紫), which produce bodies that are "white/light," "black/dark," or somewhere in between (*heibai zhi jian*)—we move from variations in blood to those of life outcomes. The difficulty of this intervention is articulated as the impossibility of changing the deep (*shen* 深) to the shallow (*qian* 淺), adding depth to the depiction of human skin, again based on knowledge of cloth dyeing.

It is important to note that Li Yu's strong preference for lighter skin is not linked to ideas of racial or ethnic difference. Instead, his colorism is most obviously motivated by class. Only the wealthy can cultivate light skin tones in their children, though only in some instances, and not through the consumption of expensive medicines like mica (*yunmu* 雲母) and crystal (*shuijing* 水精). Li Yu's selection of these two materials is curious: both are classified as medicines in Li Shizhen's 李時珍 (1518–1593) *Materia medica* (*Bencao gangmu* 本草綱目), but not for their skin-lightening effects. Rather, crystal is mainly used to treat the eyes, while mica is described as a panacea that can expel heteropathic *qi* (*xiaqi* 邪氣),

clear the eyes (*mingmu* 明目), increase semen production (*yi zijing* 益子精), and prolong life (*yannian* 延年).[19] Here Li Yu may be repurposing the transparent properties of crystal and mica that associated them with improved vision, to claim that they can "brighten" the skin.

In proposing a range of natural possibilities for complexion, Li Yu also adds gradations to the established moral imagery of black and white. In *Analects* 17.7, for instance, Confucius uses a metaphor of dyeing—or rather, of *resisting* dye—to describe how he will not be negatively influenced by the company of inferior men: "Is it not said, that, if a thing be really white, it may be steeped in a dark fluid without being made black?"[20] This association of white with purity, and especially with the resistance to dyeing, became a common reference, as in Meng Jiao's 孟郊 Tang-dynasty poem "Exhorting a Friend" (*Quanyou* 勸友): "Truest white turns not black tho' it be immersed in dark dye" 至白涅不緇.[21] Although Li Yu's aim is to attain whiteness, his valorization of whiteness does not claim its inherent superiority and impermeability. Instead, his entire essay on skin hovers in the space between light and dark. Given that Li Yu refers to these middling shades of skin as less desirable yet devotes the whole essay to them, I argue that he is less interested in attaining whiteness as such than in the capacity of skin for transformation.

Li Yu describes black as a highly desirable shade for hair and eyes, and we can link his championing of light skin to his general advocacy of high contrast coloring. Contrast is one of the most sustained recommendations in his later discussion of fashion:

> The color of socks and shoes should contrast [*xiangfan* 相反]. Socks should be very light in color, and shoes very dark. Only when they contrast [*xiangxing* 相形] with one another are the colors finally revealed. Women these days all prefer white socks and wear dark red or dark blue shoes: this can truly be called the ultimate design. But now that every single household is wearing this style, it is necessary to avoid exact replication. I would like to switch the placement of these colors, darkening the sock and lightening the shoe, so that the smallness of the shoe will be even more pronounced. That said, the color of the shoe should not be exactly the same as that of the ground. . . . Those with large feet should do the opposite, matching the color of the ground with their shoes as a way to

disguise their inadequacies. They need not rely only on high heels for that.²²

Using the operative language of contrasting colors (*xiangfan, xiangxing*), Li Yu commends the current trend of high contrast between shoes and socks and suggests a novel revision, reversing the colors and adding a second contrast between the shoes and the ground. Color is significant for its ability to create optical illusions, such as diminishing the apparent size of a foot. Although high heels depend on partly visual perception to yield their efficacy, they also change the actual position of the foot. Color, however, engages vision alone. This combination of visual and material effects shows Li Yu attending to the interplay between *xu* and *shi* in the realm of fashion, designing a scene in a similar manner to those in his garden.

As these instructions on footwear indicate, contrasting colors are compelling because they create an illusion of depth. The association of shallowness with a lighter complexion foregrounds the skin as a surface—prepared silk—inviting embellishment. Li Yu also draws on the concept of a "deep hue" in cloth-dyeing, which ties darkness to depth even as it works entirely at the surface:

> Once you understand this, you'll know that the correct method for selecting material [*xuancai* 選材; here, a concubine's skin] is to follow the example of a dyer accepting clothing. If someone wants him to clean white clothes, he will accept them as it requires little effort on his part. If someone wants him to clean slightly soiled white clothes, he will likewise accept them. . . . However, if someone asks him to strip the color from cloth that has already been dyed a deep hue, and to clean it until it is white, even if they were to pay him ten or one hundred times his usual rate, he would still certainly refuse to accept it. That is because although his human effort is skillfully deployed, it is difficult to undo Heaven's handiwork, and he cannot force that which exists [*you* 有] to disappear into thin air [*wu* 無]. (566)

Darker skin becomes here, in its potential and possibilities, like silk deeply dyed. Light skin, by contrast, is proposed as scoured and bleached, but *not* dyed: a blank canvas made by processing animal parts. The language of substance and immateriality (here *you* and *wu* rather than *shi* and *xu*) thus associates lighter skin with absence.

Li Yu proposes three additional criteria that will determine whether skin will be receptive to lightening. First, if the face is darker than the body, the face can be lightened by shielding it from the sun and wind, because this is a contrast between the interior and exterior: "The face is on the outside, while the body is on the inside" (566). Second, soft skin is easier to change: "Skin that is delicate and soft like silk gauze [*lingluo shajuan* 綾羅紗絹] will be smooth in form, so it will take color easily, and it will likewise lose color easily. With a light breeze or sunshine, the dark colors will fade. Coarse skin, however, is like hemp cloth [*bu* 布] or felt [*tan* 毯]: its difficulty in taking color is ten times that of silk gauze, and removing color is even more than ten times as difficult" (566). Finally, skin that is loose (*kuan* 寬) is easier to lighten than skin that is tight (*jin* 緊) (566). Both terms are more common in discussing the fit of clothing; skin today is more often described as *songchi* 鬆弛 (flabby) than as *kuan*.

By connecting skin with fabric and then, via fabric, with clothing, Li Yu further develops his suggestion that skin too can be modified: "Skin that is dark and loose is like silk or satin that has not yet been pressed, or boots or shoes that have not yet been shaped with a wooden form. Because it is wrinkled and not taut, the light seems dark and the thin seems thick. Once it is pressed and shaped with a wooden form, its composition will change radically, and she will no longer bear the same appearance as in the past" (566). These three properties—interiority, softness, and looseness—each develop the analogy of skin to fabric in different ways. Although the analogy to footwear references the iron and the wooden form, the problem is nonetheless diagnosed as a *lack* of "flesh and blood" (*xuerou* 血肉). Once the flesh and blood are increased so as to "fill out" (*chongman* 充滿) the skin, the depth-creating folds disappear and the skin appears lighter as a result. In a deft inversion, this metaphor of skin as cloth proposes "ironing" from the inside, by increasing the supporting "flesh and blood" (566).

Through this analogy of skin with silk, Li Yu thus shifts the human body from the realm of *tiangong* (heaven-made) to *rengong* (human-made). The fact that the analogy is elaborated in multiple—and sometimes conflicting—directions only strengthens the association, as skin and silk come to share many properties rather than a single one. Importantly, most of the work of the analogy takes place once the initial step of weaving strands into fabric has already been completed, but before the silk has been fully prepared for dyeing. The opening line of the silk metaphor discussed earlier accuses the Creator of moving ahead with dyeing before two requisite earlier steps had been completed, namely scouring and bleaching. This first significant comparison draws on silk's animal residues: sericin, a crucial bonding fiber of the silkworm's cocoon, is undesirable for silk fabric production, which substitutes weaving for its glue function. By drawing an analogy between these natural byproducts of silk cocoons and natural imperfections in the human complexion, Li Yu highlights the way in which both are transformed through human effort to suit human desires. This reasoning also echoes his general emphasis on a flexible interplay between the natural and the artificial, for silk processing and dyeing are both examples of how artificial processing can improve natural materials.[23]

While women's skin is likened most extensively to cloth and the dyeing process in *Leisure Notes*, it is also connected to whitewashed walls and to writing. Each of these examples relates women's bodies to arenas shaped by human action: the production of clothing, of buildings, and of literature. By likening women's bodies to these human-made objects, Li Yu at once heightens women's objectification and, paradoxically, their agency, for by framing bodies as canvases for human intervention, and spending most of his time on average-looking women, Li Yu involves women more than usual in the production of their own beauty. For instance, Li Yu's essay on makeup develops the notion that most women have complexions "between black and white" (*heibai zhi jian*). Unlike the "Skin" essay, which is outlandish but consistent in its claims, the essay on makeup is full of contradictions. It begins by declaring that only the most beautiful women can wear makeup: "Cosmetics are in fact quite worldly in the way they align themselves with the powerful. As such, when beauties use them, they enhance their beauty; however, when the ugly use them, they only enhance their ugliness."[24] This claim of a sympathetic logic suggests a prioritization of the base material: the cloth-like skin beneath, whose quality determines whether it can be embellished.

Yet Li Yu then proposes a universally applicable method for makeup, requiring only that one apply it in very thin layers: "Continuing with this line of reasoning [that thin layers be applied subsequently], two applications can be expanded to three, and deep black can be made no different from light, and in the entire human world, there will be no woman who cannot lighten her complexion with powder applied evenly" (577). This more egalitarian approach gives more credit to makeup's powers, and the argument for its universal applicability underlines its efficacy precisely by contradicting the earlier claim. Li Yu himself notes the anticipated rhetorical effect on his readers: "When I first discussed complexion, I was rather too strict in establishing a theory. But it is only because I was strict in the beginning that it became clear how severe the illness was, and then a kind-hearted doctor was able to rescue you from the very brink of death" (577). Dramatically characterizing himself as a "kind-hearted doctor," Li Yu equates face powder with a treatment for an acute illness, veering from the how-to genre into that of advertising. In the how-to manuals popular in the late Ming, contradictions occurred frequently, whether because sections had been carelessly cut and pasted from different sources, or because sections were written by different people. Li Yu, however, purposefully builds in this contradiction: in fact, he builds the essay around it. Creating an account of skin color as a tension to be resolved, he guides us from "most cannot be helped" to "anyone in the world can do it."

With this transition, we move from considering skin as a particular kind of fabric to focusing on the makeup applied to skin, only to learn that skin is like silk only as long as one does not consider the material that acts upon it. Li Yu invokes the stuff from which paint is made, lamenting that because the skin is *not* silk or paper, the usual methods cannot be used: "When painters apply colors, gelatin must be added to achieve evenness; without it, it cannot be ground into an even mixture. People's faces are not the same as paper or silk, and it certainly does not make sense to use gelatin—this is why it does not end up evenly applied" (576).

Having reached the limits of his silk analogy, Li Yu resorts to another: how masons whitewash walls. The title of the makeup essay hints at whitewashing, writing, and painting alike through his use of the term *dianran* 點染, "to touch up," which is most familiar from the realm of painting. Skin resembles walls, he suggests, because it is less porous than silk and is best treated through multiple applications. Fabric dyes, moreover, are ill-suited to changing colors from dark to light; the powdered lime of whitewash, in contrast, allows for a different argument and a new vocabulary as well. In whitewashing, for the first time, "white" (*bai*) is able to achieve "deep" (*shen* 深) status (for clarity, I have usually translated *shen* as "dark," as in "dark red"). Whereas "white" in the silk metaphor referred to bleached silk, suggesting an originary state of pale skin, the analogy to whitewashing transforms white into a color that must be applied like any other. White is now a substance: "If a woman's face is somewhat dark, and you wish to make it white at once, that would be truly difficult. But now, if you first spread a thin, even layer, the color of her face will already be between light and dark—different from earlier when it was pure black. Add another application, and light white will become deep white" (577). In this proposal, any surface could be transformed through steady application of thin layers of white, rendering the original material virtually insignificant.

By opening his discussion with a description of women's skin as a canvas, Li Yu distinguishes himself from contemporaneous trends of describing women's beauty. For instance, in a frequently anthologized piece (a "*Lianzhu* in the amorous style" "Yanti lianzhu" 艷體連珠), a teen-aged Ye Xiaoluan 葉小鸞 (1616–1632) focused in turn on hair, eyebrows, eyes, lips, hands, waist, feet, and the entire body.[25] Ye's exquisite lyrical skill and early death catapulted her to fame in the late Ming as an ethereal embodiment of the *qing* ideal, and Dorothy Ko has pointed out the youthful sensuousness in these lines, as Ye delights in her own beauty.[26] Although Ye's focus on discrete body parts is unusual, in Li Yu's terms, her categories nevertheless still present a verbal portrait of a beautiful woman that largely ignores its "canvas": the skin. Like many contemporaneous descriptions of beauty, she draws attention to the naturalness of her youthful charm, emphasizing her lack of makeup. Whereas Ye's *lianzhu* isolates and praises particular elements of a naturally beautiful young woman, Li Yu's essays propose any woman's body as a canvas, elaborating specific parts that can be made beautiful. Although women were frequently valued in this period for their talent and virtue as well as their beauty, Li Yu's propositions are striking in their efforts to render beauty accessible, for he designs techniques that anyone could use. This broadening of access is made possible by his emphasis on skin, for the cloth-like skin then appears as a blank canvas, and the body that it enfolds accordingly becomes a medium like any other.

The emphasis on human agency enabled by Li Yu's skin metaphors is particularly apparent when we compare it to the more conventional analogy of women with flowers. After all, flowers were frequently arranged in Li Yu's time, but they were not scoured, dyed, and bleached as silk routinely was. That established metaphor idealizes women as both beautiful and eminently perishable, as for example in the Zhejiang writer and failed scholar Xu Zhen's 徐震 (fl. 1659–1711) "Manual of Beautiful Women" (Meiren pu 美人譜, completed ca. 1659):[27] "It is just like when flowers first open, and their fragrance is enchanting. After this, like flowers at their height, they are all used up, and they will soon wither and die. There are, in this world, people who appreciate beauties though they be middle-aged. . . . But once the fragrance has dissipated and the blush faded from their cheeks, they are in the end like flowers after wilting, eliciting a pity of sorts and nothing more."[28] As the title *Manual of Beautiful Women* suggests, idealized female beauty became an object of connoisseurship in similar terms to luxury goods. The manual consists of eclectic lists of elegant qualities, images, and activities that characterize beauty: from "willowy waist" to "shadow behind a curtain," from "rain on plantain leaves" to "ivory comb." As with other manuals of connoisseurship, the listed items could only be emulated by an already beautiful woman and even then, only briefly. Wei Yong 衛泳 (fl. 1643–54), writing in "Delight in Adornment" (Yuerong bian 悅容編), proposes that beauty might last until twenty-five: "Rosy cheeks are soon to fade: from a virgin of fifteen to the age of twenty-five, how many years of beauty can one enjoy? Like flowers: the time from first bloom to their full glory passes by in the twinkling of an eye: then, worn out and withered, they can never be admired again."[29] Through this floral analogy, self-appointed connoisseurs imposed a strict temporal constraint on women's desirability. The cult of *qing* during this period frequently manifested through an obsession with the early deaths of teenage girls like Ye Xiaoluan, who were understood as ill-fated real-life Du Liniangs.

In contrast to the late-Ming consensus idealizing the flower-like woman who dies young, Li Yu's references to flowers in his essays on beauty are mostly references to actual flowers. For example, in his essay "Accessories" (Shoushi 首飾) he praises seasonal flowers: "Not only are they much more elegant than pearls or jade, but they also differ radically in being alive."[30] He rejected the circular logic frequently at play in analogies of women to flowers, as in a line of Li Bai's 李白 (701–762) poetry: "Renowned flowers and state-toppling beauties delight the one in the other" 名花傾國兩相歡.[31] In his exposition of this line, Li Yu comments: "National beauties are 'flowers among people;' Renowned flowers are 'people among flowers.'"[32] Although the logic here appears parallel to earlier formulations, Li Yu's new coinage of the phrase "people among flowers," to parallel "flowers among people" effectively disrupts the equation between the two: rather than equivalents, people and flowers are two variable categories that have an affinity for each other. Following this logic, Li Yu uses people to explain what flowers are like—rather than, as in the examples above, using flowers to explain women's beauty.

Li Yu also deconstructs existing analogies in the service of his general engagement with the conceptual dynamic of *xu* and *shi*. For instance, Wei Yong wrote: "The way that a beautiful woman cannot be without a maid is similar to the way that flowers are unable to be without leaves."[33] In this established analogy, the natural object is used as a prescriptive metaphor for a relationship between women. By contrast, Li Yu reflects on the relationship between a flower and its leaves in order to make flowers available to all. His proposal is at once practical and subversive: he suggests that the flower can be replaced by cheaper and more durable materials like paper and silk but that the leaves must be real in order for the result to be credible.[34] In so doing, he at once prioritizes the leaves over the usually more valued flowers and also makes the resulting flower available to those who were described as mere leaves. By literalizing the interplay between artificial and real, Li once again demonstrates his flexible approach to aesthetics, one that offers inexpensive alternatives to elite aesthetic practices.

Leisure Notes thus performs two processes at once: even as the use of the extended metaphor to cloth-dyeing opens up new possibilities for evaluating and altering skin, it also wrests the woman's body from its stereotyped role. The effect of this transformation is similarly twofold: first, it means greater critical attention paid to gradations of difference among female bodies, bringing to mind connoisseurship of other "things."[35] Second, it proposes, in fairly neutral terms, the fact that beauty is created, not born. As such, it shifts the beautiful woman from a rapidly wilting otherworldly flower to a malleable body rife with possibilities, a canvas that can be transformed. There is a level of interaction here that is absent in the one-way appreciation of flowers found in earlier accounts, and also a durability and a resilience that flowers definitively lack.

How much transformation is too much? Even as Li Yu proposes that through incremental application contrasting colors can be transformed into each other, he also encourages limits, decrying what he perceives as random variations. Throughout *Leisure Notes*, Li Yu criticizes the proliferation of new designs—the "daily [*riri*] changing fashions" to which "everyone" (*renren* 人人) is attuned.[36] Instead, he emphasizes that subset of possible designs which heighten the resonance between a medium and its thematic message. This mode of design, which I call "resonant innovation" and which Patrick Hanan has described as "an associative logic of design and function,"[37] requires the designer to seek an underlying connecting principle (*li* 理), ensuring that similar things are grouped together (*xianglei tongju* 相類同居).[38] By requiring that designs create resonance between the material substance and its aesthetic formation, Li Yu champions an aesthetic that enhances the material presence of the medium. This resonant innovation forms an interesting counterpoint to the contemporaneous experimentation with disguising materials discussed by Jonathan Hay, who notes that the late sixteenth century was when the practice of disguising more valuable media as less valuable first became widespread: jade, for instance, might be treated to look like bamboo.[39]

We can see how resonant innovation functions in Li Yu's extended discussion of hair, for hairstyles were often modeled after particular objects. Li Yu writes:

> But the forms into which hairstyles have changed pursue novelty alone, not reason; people are interested only in changing their look, caring not if they distort their hairstyle beyond recognition. Whenever you try to design something after something else, you must choose something appropriate to model it after, something that it should be modeled after, something with a similar appearance to

it. By no means should you fabricate something out of thin air, or make arbitrary choices without due consideration. The ancients called hair "raven-black clouds" and buns "coiled dragons," as both of these arise in the sky and are thus suitable for adorning the head. Hair hovers like clouds and twists up like dragons; and there are black clouds and black dragons. In color, shape, sentiment, and sense: in all aspects these correspond, and that is how it is named.[40]

In *Leisure Notes* as a whole, Li Yu invokes ancient practices much more often than he explicitly champions novelty, and here he reaches back to an ancient naming practice. Inserting a temporal element into Li Yu's class-based distinctions reveals one way he was able to carve out a space between *ya* and *su*, by constructing a textual network of traditional writings and their associated modes of reasoning.

In his argument for hairstyles, for instance, Li Yu engaged literary commentary while activating ancient tropes. The correlation of dragons and clouds (but not blackness) was pointed out in the commentary to the first hexagram in the *Classic of Changes* (*Yijing* 易經), which models the kind of analogical reasoning Li Yu promotes in his analysis of hair. The four characteristics Li Yu mentions here are color (*se* 色), shape (*xiang* 相), sentiment (*qing*), and sense (*li*), all of which are operative in the *Changes* as well. Wang Bi's 王弼 (226–249) commentary to the first hexagram reads:

"When a flying dragon is in the sky, it is fitting to see the great man." What does this mean? The Master says: "Things with the same tonality resonate together; things with the same material force seek out one another. Water flows to where it is wet; fire goes toward where it is dry. Clouds follow the dragon; wind follows the tiger. What is rooted in Heaven draws close to what is above; what is rooted in Earth draws close to what is below. Thus each thing follows its own kind."[41]

In the *Changes*, the category of "what is above" connects clouds to dragons; in *Leisure Notes*, what is black, curling like dragons or clouds, and "on top" is suited to black hair atop the head. This is the novelty with which Li Yu is usually associated, but it is novelty with an ancient pedigree. *Changes* used a logic of resonant transformation—prioritizing layering like upon like—to explain the operations of the cosmos. Li Yu, however, shifts this logic away from the metaphysical. Instead, "things with the same tonality resonate together" or "things with the same material force seek out one another" because this produces appropriately novel yet pleasing designs. Such resonant innovation further evokes the "liveliness" (*huo*) that was achieved elsewhere in *Leisure Notes* by changing displays (such as dioramas, paintings, and flower arrangements) to displace "woodenness" (*ban*). Li Yu's resonant innovation thus invites us to play with the material world within limits, just as the *Changes* deploys its series of hexagrams through their associative interpretation.

Li Yu also imbricates an intertextual network of classical studies to address clothing, expounding the relationship between houses and bodies as media and metaphors through an analysis of a sentence from the *Great Learning* (*Daxue* 大學). In the third paragraph of the *Great Learning*, amid an explanation of how to "make thoughts sincere," we find the statement that "riches adorn a house and virtue adorns the person" 富潤屋, 德潤身.[42] The first clause of this sentence offers a tangible general example—that riches adorn the homes of the wealthy—which then serves to illustrate the abstract point: that a person's inner virtue (*de*), when properly cultivated, will manifest visibly on that person. Li Yu singles out this line for a twofold reinterpretation, both in the essay titled "Managing Attire" in *Leisure Notes* and through the narrator in his short story "Tower of My Birth," and he emphasizes the overlap by mentioning the story in the essay. In the story, he refuses the established reading of the first clause as a metaphor for the second, insisting on the materiality of both the house and the body. He then denies that wealth necessarily denotes extravagance, proposing instead that "riches adorn the house" indicates that the owners' wealth will lend its aura (*qi*) to their home. Finally he takes his proposal to its logical limit: if wealth is manifest only through extravagance, such that the wealthy *must* buy and decorate new houses, then virtue can be manifest in people only if they "change out their heads and swap their faces [*gaitou huanmian* 改頭換面], making a completely different body [*ling zao yifu xinghai* 另造一副形骸] before they can be said to have 'adorned themselves'—taking the tasks of 'rectifying the heart' and 'making thoughts sincere' to be instead the study of 'boring eye-holes' and 'carving eyebrows.'"[43] In *Leisure Notes*, similarly, he asks: "would virtuous people also need to cast aside their old bodies and exchange them for new ones before it could be said that their 'minds are expanded and their bodies at ease?'"[44]

Li Yu's refusal here to let the richly adorned house serve as the concrete example for virtuous self-cultivation is a familiar rhetorical move in *Leisure Notes*: rather than accepting that there might be a natural association between riches and adornment, he shifts agency to the person, suggesting that there is no automatic manifestation of wealth in houses. In a fictional illustration of this point, Li Yu's protagonist in "Tower of My Birth," Mr. Little Tower, manifests his wealth by the "impressive air" (*qigai* 氣概) of his modest residence. With this revision, Li Yu connects the step of "making thoughts sincere" to the sequence of self-cultivation detailed in the *Great Learning*. But in the *Great Learning* this point in the self-cultivation process is supposed to be focused on cultivating thoughts and thereby transforming a person. It has not yet reached the step at which this cultivation will be transferred to the family and home. The term *run*, here translated as "adorn," carries a primary sense of moistening: of the nourishment that rain provides to seeds. Consequently, *run* is much more fundamental and life-giving than "adorn" or "embellish" would suggest, and it was frequently invoked to indicate putting the finishing touches on a piece of writing or a painting.

In *Leisure Notes*, this discussion of *run* and the cultivation of virtue is included in an essay on clothing. Li Yu posits that people have associated auras (*qixiang* 氣象) that will "leap right past" (*yuechu* 躍出) whatever they are wearing, revealing their true nature.[45] He then develops another analogy: much as a person needs to wear familiar clothes or adjust to a new kind of outfit, so too will a person feel comfortable in a familiar locale but like a stranger when in a new place.

> "Clothing reveals a person [*yi yi zhang shen* 衣以章身]."[46] Please let me explain this: "to reveal" [*zhang*] means "to clearly indicate" [*zhu* 著]; it does not mean "conspicuous" as in "conspicuously displaying bright colors." Nor does "person" indicate the physical body, but rather the way in which intelligence or stupidity, worthiness or unworthiness manifest in a person, as in the "person" [described] in [the line in the *Great Learning*], "Riches adorn a house, and virtue adorns the person." The very same clothing, if a rich man wears

it, will make known his wealth. If a poor man wears it, it will make his poverty all the more manifest.⁴⁷

Here clothing itself seems to be governed by the rules of a kind of resonant innovation: while suggesting that a self emanates from within, he locates it in a person's heart-mind, which can nonetheless be transformed through inner cultivation at the level of thoughts (*yi* 意). The transformed identity can then "leap beyond" any clothing, costume, or disguise. Rather than situating identity at the surface, at the level of makeup, accessories, and clothing (as in a fully performative theory of social identities), Li Yu intensifies the theatrical through the possibilities of *gaizao*. The person is constructed (*zao*) through this process in which thoughts (*yi*) add luster (*run*) to the body (*shen*). The constructed self then extends outward, resonating or clashing with one's clothing and residence according to their suitability. Yet again, Li Yu's proposal emphasizes human agency: once wealth is detached from possessions to desires, poverty can be overcome from the inside out.

This creative aura (*qigai*) manifests materially through clothing, houses, and writing, but it does so by resonating through these objects, not by means of these objects' metonymic role. According to Li Yu, "the relationship of clothes to the body is like that of human bodies [*renshen* 人身] to a particular locale [*di* 地]. People [*renshen*] develop customs according to their location, and only after a long time do they finally dwell comfortably in accord with the place" (578). The analogy here repeats *renshen* (person-body) in opposite positions: first as the influenced, and then as the influencer. Much as clothes adjust to the human body that wears them, so too human' bodies adjust to the place that houses them, and in all cases, time and repetition (*xi* 習) are required to make this adjustment. In Li Yu's plays, countless characters slip into costumes to try out alternate roles, usually with modest success in their deceptions. In several instances, his characters devise elaborate tests in order to discover whether persons are who they claim to be. The discussion of clothing here invokes those tests indirectly, by focusing on the very first step in trying out a new role.

Immediately following the Manchu conquest of the Ming, at a time when Wang Fuzhi 王夫之 (1619–1692) was theorizing essential and inalterable connections between locales and those who inhabit them, Li Yu was envisioning clothing slowly growing accustomed to a person. His theory of what we might call acclimatization or acculturation championed habituation rather than adaption, once again prioritizing slow transformation over performance as such. Through this intervention, Li Yu is corroborating and further developing claims about self-cultivation found in the classics while also maintaining the possibility of adaptation: a stranger in a strange land, after all, will not remain so indefinitely, as long as that person is willing to stay a while.

Whereas performativity renders the constitution of identity a matter of consistent demonstration over time, habituation offers a meandering path towards becoming a different self. This process of transformation is stated most forcefully in Li Yu's discussion of the expression "a macaque in a hat [is still a macaque]" (*muhou er guan* 沐猴而冠) (578). The locus classicus of this expression is in the biography of the Hegemon King, Xiang Yu 項羽 (ca. 232–202 BCE), in the *History of the Han* (*Hanshu* 漢書), where an advisor criticized him, and all people from Chu, by saying: "People say that the people of Chu are just macaques in hats. I now see that they are right." Xiang Yu immediately had him killed. This earliest recorded usage was thus a dehumanizing slur with regionally specific implications, and it was then glossed in ways that reinforced this pejorative tendency.[48] The phrase occurs in general use today without any indication of these associations, and Li Yu's discussion of this expression is similarly devoid of its original anti-Chu sentiment. Instead, he explains the expression through a sober literalism: "The reason people make fun of 'a macaque in a hat' is not because a macaque cannot [*buke* 不可] wear a hat, but rather that he is not accustomed to wearing it [*zhuozhi buguan* 著之不慣], and his head and the hat thus don't match [*bu xiangchen* 不相稱]."[49] Rather than disparage the macaque, Li Yu proposes that even a monkey could adapt to hat-wearing. The reciprocity indicated in both of these instances refers in the first place to people and their environments, and in the second to monkeys' heads and their hats. In deploying regional difference as metaphor, Li Yu gestured toward the shifting notions of place and regional belonging in the early Qing, even as he diverged dramatically from the regional determinism of many of his contemporaries.

MANAGING YOUR MEDIUM

Li Yu's conception of the human body involves not only a modifiable, layered surface—silk-like skin, paint-like face powder, habit-forming clothing—but also a fundamentally mediated substance. As I show in this section, Li Yu offers a number of designs that are best understood as technological extensions of the body—or, alternatively, he identifies particular extensions of the body as suboptimal, in which case he recommends returning to the body's original capacity. Thus far we have discussed bodies belonging to fictional characters or to commodified persons; here, we examine Li Yu's detailed comments on a new category of bodies: those belonging to his intended readers.

With the bodies of others, Li Yu focused on beauty; in discussing readers' bodies, the critical term is *yong*, meaning "use" or "utility." Li Yu's thinking across media is frequently informed by his desire to make use of everything: he writes of his desire to never throw anything away, and he advocates storage designs as a result. We have seen Li Yu draw on a wide range of imaginative metaphors to goad readers into imagining the human body as a little more malleable than they thought; the gentle extrapolations of his approach are demonstrated by the overlap between his proposals and the surgical interventions we know today. Functionality, too, is a primary factor in his consideration of bodies more generally, whether in the final book of *Leisure Notes*, "Care of the Self" (Yiyang bu 頤養部),[50] or in "Food and Drink."

"Care of the Self" opens with an essay titled "Enjoying Oneself" (Xingle 行樂) that starts with a meditation on the inevitable demise of the body and the Creator's "inhumanity" (*buren* 不仁), a concept derived from the *Daode jing* 道德經:[51]

> How injurious that when the Creator made people, he limited their lifespans to less than a hundred years. To say nothing of those who die prematurely, even those who spend all of the years of a long life—thirty-six thousand days—pursuing happiness and taking pleasure do not have an infinite amount of time, and eventually the day will come when they are sent away. But what is more, over the course of those hundred years, there are countless troubles and

worries, sickness and hardship, the reins of fame and the fetters of wealth, frightening winds and fearsome waves that prevent people from enjoying themselves and make it so they have a hundred years in name only.... Alas! What sort of a thing is death that it can know such violent misery and not avoid it, causing us, who cannot avoid death, to be frightened by the sight of it and distressed by reports of it, day after day? So it would seem that of all the inhumanity of the ages, none surpasses that of the Creator. Although that is the case, there is surely an explanation. The inhumane is the pinnacle of humaneness. To know that we cannot avoid death, and yet to report to us daily regarding death, is to frighten us. And being frightened makes us want to seize the day and make merry—we should consider this as a lesson learned from those who have gone before us.[52]

If we are familiar with Li Yu's characters blaming the Creator for their physical shortcomings in other genres, here we see that sentiment expanded to encompass the entire human condition. Fame and wealth become reins and fetters that prevent the pursuit of enjoyment in life. There are marked similarities between this essay and Yang Zhu's 楊朱 egoist or hedonist philosophy (especially as represented in the seventh chapter of the *Liezi* 列子).[53] Both begin with the eminently countable number of years in a human lifespan and then describe all the lamentable ways that life's circumstances chip away at enjoyment. But Yang's essay describes this predicament as yielding a "harsh clarity" that grasps at any sensual pleasures (clothing, sex, music) within reach, while Li Yu wrings from it an equalizing optimism. For Li Yu, this practice of viewing life from a meditation on death, alternately called "the method of taking a step back" (*tui yibu fa* 退一步法), foregrounds a universally shared concern, enabling him to see all lives differently (696). Yang Zhu's plaint in the *Liezi*, "How are we different from prisoners weighted with chains and fetters?" becomes, in Li Yu, "Now, in discoursing on nourishing life, I begin with 'Finding Happiness,' and to encourage people to enjoy themselves, I frighten them with death."[54]

We can discern Li Yu's divergence from the established discourse of hedonism by focusing on a specific trope in his writing on the body: that of fetters. In *Leisure Notes* Li Yu first uses fetters as an image in his essay on clothing, where he argues: "If you were to take luxurious clothing and suddenly put it on the body [*qu* 軀] of a simple and frugal man, it would render him akin to a stranger in a strange land.... He would want to stick out his hands, but his sleeves would keep them hidden; he would wish to extend his neck, but his collar would keep it bent. These things, then, would not follow the person's instructions, but would be like fetters [*zhigu* 桎梏] on his body instead."[55] Li Yu is writing against the common assumption that poverty is always limiting: following that logic, everybody would find luxurious, expensive clothing desirable. Instead, Li Yu argues, the empowerment ostensibly promised by wealth is undone by the power of habituation: luxurious clothes on a "simple and frugal man" would refuse his instructions and commandeer his body to their ends instead. To support this surprising claim, Li Yu offers multiple examples of how clothing might constrain a person: a long skirt without pleats might hinder movement of the legs, an excessive amount of jewelry might weigh one down, any amount of clothing in the Nanjing summer heat is a burden. Li Yu is not proposing that poverty is a virtue; he is instead encouraging readers to foster an awareness of the materials that envelop them and to optimize them in both functional and aesthetic terms. By using "fetters" (*zhigu*) as metaphor, Li Yu submits all materials that come in contact with the body to a test: Do they enhance? Or do they limit?

In the essay "The Poor Man's Guide to Happiness" (Pinjian xingle zhi fa 貧賤行樂之法), Li Yu uses the idea of the fettered body to elaborate his method of "taking a step back." He writes of two men spending the night in a mosquito-infested postal station: the rich man rues his ineffective mosquito netting, while the station head is sleeping out in the open, flailing about to avoid being bitten, in good spirits nonetheless. Confused, the rich man asks for an explanation, and the station head replies:

> I remember [*yi* 憶] one year when I was captured by the enemy and imprisoned. It was also summer then, and to prevent my escape the prison guards would shackle my hands and feet every night so I could not move them. At that time, there were twice as many mosquitoes and black flies as there are here tonight. They were free to gnaw at me, and I couldn't move to avoid them in the slightest. Consider my running around tonight with four limbs able to move

freely [*siti deyi ziru* 四體得以自如] from that perspective: Is the difference not equal to that between gods and mortals? (697)

The fetters of an earlier year's imprisonment prove liberatory in the present moment, transforming an otherwise pitiful body into a blissful one. What would normally go unremarked—the "four limbs able to move freely"—is refigured as a precious ability: once shackled, now liberated. In a different essay in *Leisure Notes*, the transition from summer to autumn has a similar effect: "the four limbs are able to move freely, with clothing no longer functioning as shackles" (701). Through such examples, Li Yu proposes that all experience is bound up with memories (*yi*) through one's perspective, which emanates from the place (*di*), both spatial and temporal, that any particular individual inhabits (*chu*). The previous two essays, "The Official's Guide to Happiness" (Guiren xingle zhi fa 貴人行樂之法) and "The Rich Man's Guide to Happiness" (Furen xingle zhi fa 富人行樂之法) advise officials and rich men to consider their situation from the perspective of others, yet without any such anecdotes: the mass position of commoners is simply assumed. For the poor man to use this shift in perspective, Li Yu suggests, he must mobilize not a common viewpoint but instead narrate a distraction: his memory of being fettered is transformed into a story that can serve, in turn, as a "memory" for readers.

Li Yu explains that all fetters are a matter of perspective: "Just as calculated above, if you measure your situation against someone who is better off than you, you will not find a moment's peace: instead all sorts of fetters and imprisonments will appear" (696). This process of *gaizao* begins by transforming perception, invoking its shaping by memories and stories, and then proposing that stories can similarly transform experience in what Li Yu calls a "secret formula" (*mijue* 秘訣) (697). This secret formula had already appeared in Li Yu's short story "Tower of Returning as an Immortal Crane," discussed in chapter 3, whose protagonist shared his "secret formula" for married life: "be prudent with blessings, and content with hardship."[56] To the overall message of being "content with one's lot" (*zhizu shoufen* 知足守分), which is also the theme stated at the story's beginning, is added a stranger prospect: finding not just contentment, but "joy" (*le*) in separation (*bieli* 別離).[57] That story, moreover, doubly suggests the value of positions generally imagined as inferior. To understand her husband's true intentions, his wife must place herself *below* the poem and read it backward, that is, from the bottom upward rather than from the top down. Once she does so, we find that this seemingly unloved woman was better off than the one who was explicitly loved (and died from her own longings), in another championing of the seemingly lower position.

To understand how this anecdote in Leisure Notes is intended to work, we might look at a variation of the story of the mosquito-plagued postal station that Li Yu included in the prologue story to "Immortal Crane." In that version, the poor man relies upon his imagination rather than his memory, having already mastered this "secret formula." As he explains to the rich man, "I, too, resented my suffering at first, then I suddenly thought of someplace [*huran xiangdao yichu* 忽然想到一處], and before I knew it, I was delighted."⁵⁸ The awkwardness of this syntax, which I have indicated in the translation as "thought of someplace," indicates imagination rather than memory—and, sure enough, he had thought of prisoners who were shackled to a bed (*xiachuang* 柙牀).⁵⁹ By contrast, in "The Poor Man's Guide to Happiness" in Leisure Notes, the poor man in the story becomes "station head," and he is not showing off his imagination, but positively deploying a negative personal experience. Whereas in the story the voice of Li Yu the author threatens to overshadow that of the character, in the essay in Leisure Notes Li Yu puts more distance between himself and the characters. As a consequence of this distancing, the anecdote becomes more easily assimilable for readers who might wish to "take a step back" and deploy this secret formula.

Li Yu further develops his argument that stories and imagination can transform human embodiment in his essay titled "Winter," where he details and quantifies how stories can transport, and thus sustain, people in extreme temperatures. He proposes using a visual aid:

> Enjoying oneself in the winter requires "imagining oneself in the place of another [*sheshen chudi*]." Imagine that you are a traveler on the road, and fully prepare yourself to be subjected to the hardships of wind and snow. After that, recall that you are at home, whether it is cold or warm, night or day, and you'll be one hundred times happier than others.
>
> I once had a landscape painting that depicted a snowy scene. Someone was carrying a tattered umbrella, or else goading a lame

donkey, traveling alone along an old path, passing under steep cliffs with forbidding rocks jutting up all around, such that he looked as though he would plunge down [into the depths]. This is just the sort of rugged painting that should be centrally displayed in the main hall in the dead of winter.

When the master faces it, it is both a screen to block the wind and snow, and a restorative to warm the belly and calm the heart. Yang Guozhong's Row of Plump Women [in the Tang dynasty], or Commander-in-Chief Dang [Jin]'s mutton and wine [in the Song], might warm one at first, but if you pause for even a moment, the extreme cold will reach you. One who excels at enjoying himself must first look at things in this way, and only then carry on with his enjoyment.[60]

The journey here is a mental one: the term *huan* (imaginary, illusory) invites readers to imagine themselves as the traveler on the road. Nevertheless, a narrative trajectory guides the proposed imagination, in an operation not unlike that in the story of the man who pursues a beautiful woman into a painting in the story "The Painted Wall" (Huabi 畫壁) in *Liaozhai zhiyi*.[61]

Li Yu also quantifies the effectiveness of his method of "imagining oneself in the place of another" (*sheshen chudi*)—in this case, a tiny painted figure in a winter mountain scene. His numerical pronouncements reinforce the affordability found throughout his suggestions in *Leisure Notes*:

> In this way, one portion of happiness can come to equal two or three; five or seven portions can come to equal ten or twelve. But once happiness reaches its maximum level and you have forgotten your cares, it will gradually decrease, so that ten portions will become only five or seven, and two or three portions will become just a single portion. You need then to think of all of those difficulties from the beginning again, and your happiness will gradually increase to the same height as before. This is the best method for getting ahead on the cheap (701).

The inclusion of specific quantifications ("portions") for this journey may invite laughter, yet they also lend the recommended journey the substance of a dye recipe or a medical prescription. The multiplicative nature of the quantification also connects the painting of a snowy scene and the reader's body in a process of repetitive modification, for the narrated sequence can unfold any number of times via recollection. Because one cannot simply hop into the painting and never feel cold again, the effectiveness of viewing one's situation from the perspective of a worse-off traveler will inevitably peak and then decline, at which point one must begin the mental exercise again. This gradual build-up and dissipation of heat is suggestive of the heat sources of the period, such as the charcoal brazier. It is, in this sense, reminiscent of the temporal aspect of bodily mediation that we saw in his discussion of clothing, region, and habituation.

In addition to encouraging his readers to modify their bodies through clothing, habit, and memory, Li Yu further improves the literatus body by modifying the home, especially the study. His discussions focus on servants, whom he tacitly considers extensions of the body of the master, and his designs frequently redistribute tasks between servants and the newly modified home. For instance, in "Furnishings and Fine Things," Li Yu proposes that drawers installed in desks would serve as efficient extensions of literati arms:

> The first [design I've made for tables and desks] is drawers. Drawers have long existed, but they have often been overlooked, with some people installing them and some not. People do not know that with this single thing comes great ease, and in its absence, much trouble. What's more, it can be used as a place to store your laziness and hide your inadequacies. None of the necessities of a man of culture, such as letter paper, knives and awls, ink and glue, can be done without. Although you may say that someone [a servant] is in charge of them, and that they store them elsewhere, in the end you are not able to obtain them as you wish and use them as if they were your left or right hand. (628)

Drawers function as a place (*di*) that transforms the necessities of a man of culture into the extensions of his very body. By storing letter paper, knives, and ink, drawers make these tools instantly available, enabling him to record and transmit his art. He no longer depends on others' services; instead, he can use these tools autonomously and immediately, as he might his hands. Li Yu's drawer design not only renders the literatus body more capable and efficient, but it also makes the bodies of servants superfluous:

> I am by nature rather impatient. Often, when I call for a servant and he doesn't come, I just handle the task myself. When it comes to the study, it does not matter whether it is near or far, [connected by a path] that is direct or circuitous, it is a bother to walk to and from it. Once drawers are installed, anything you may need can be kept inside them. Not only are you able to get them instantaneously, but it even seems like there is a god [*shenwu* 神物] inside awaiting the commands of its master. (628)

The reference to the "god inside" links this design and its efficiency to the way in which his fiction confers supernatural status on certain people and things. In the story "A Tower for the Summer Heat," for example, the telescope was revered as a god (*shenwu*) after it successfully served as matchmaker. There, it is not only the thing that would be promoted to god status, but the literatus himself would be as well, just as the protagonist Qu Jiren who used the telescope was called a "fake god" (*jia shenxian* 假神仙) in that story. Here, Li Yu imagines the speediest of servants—a god—assisting him in the drawer. In a seeming contradiction, Li Yu also used this term in *Leisure Notes* to describe lamps installed with pulleys, even though his design in that instance renders servants crucial rather than irrelevant, for they operate the pulleys that raise and lower the lamps. Yet this apparatus too has a similar effect, for it enlarges the literatus's apparent powers: because the servants are unseen, the lamps seem to move as though at the literatus's will.

In all of the modifications of the literatus body suggested in this book of *Leisure Notes*, Li Yu aims to accelerate literary production. He considers even the most mundane of needs, as for instance in his invention of a bamboo urinal for one's study:

> A place to collect excreta is even more indispensable. Everyone drinks and must, therefore, urinate. Because defecation is infrequent, there's no need to find an alternative to the latrine. But because urination happens frequently—who knows how many times a day

people go?—if you don't select a place for it, then your "Pureland" will turn into a cesspit. If you avoid clean areas and go to the lavatory, you will exhaust yourself running back and forth.... As for a literatus who is controlling his wrist [to wield the brush], whenever he is in the midst of happily writing swiftly, as soon as his agile thoughts are disturbed, they'll be cut off with no hope of returning. Now one can do without sleeping and eating, but urinating cannot be avoided.... Often I'll have a sentence and be about to write it but be stopped by the need to urinate. After I have gone, I look for the sentence, but it's nowhere to be found. I experience this frequently, so I was especially pressed to set this up. Next to the study, you should bore a hole into the wall, and insert a small section of bamboo, so that if one urinates on the inside, it flows to the outside. You'll smell no stench—it will be as if you have not urinated. (603)

Whereas the essay with which this chapter began, "Food and Drink," embraces a fantasy of a body without a mouth or a stomach, this passage addresses the other end of the digestive tract, and it does so through a technological renovation. Rather than reproaching the Creator or advocating for surgical intervention, Li Yu provides a detailed design that makes it "as if" (*ruo* 若) one has not urinated. In the process, he effectively produces a body that has overcome its most basic needs, through his reliance on technological mediation—and one which, in keeping with his priorities, can be a more efficient producer of texts.

In remodeling the literati body to produce texts more effectively, Li Yu nonetheless insists on the integrity of that body even as he prioritizes its literary function above all others. His design for a Warming Chair, for instance, insists that the entire body need be warmed appropriately for writing to be possible:

When I write in the winter months, my body balks at the cold and my inkstone freezes. I want to set up extra braziers to warm the whole room, but not only would the cost be outrageous, but my desk would also become covered in dust, and before the day's end, it would turn to a world of ashes. If I just set up a large and a small stove to warm my hands and feet, that would suffice for my limbs but neglect the rest of my body, dividing a single body between winter and summer, and my ears and eyes and thoughts might as well style themselves disgraced ministers or sons of disfavored concubines. I have considered this from all angles in planning a solution to warm the entire body, and that is the origin of this design for a Warming Chair. (629)

When the literatus body is disjointed by hot and cold, it is divided between seasons and transformed, as it were, into the bodies of others—specifically, less prestigious others like "disgraced ministers or sons of disfavored concubines." Li Yu salvages the literatus body from this dire fate, restoring its integrity through a design for a chair:

The wondrous effect of this chair lies entirely in the installation of a drawer under the foot slats. This single thing can ward off the bitterest cold, and the five sense organs and four limbs all benefit without even being aware of it.... Make the drawer out of wood, and lay thin bricks on the bottom, with copper on all four sides. The ashes that you put inside should be very fine, like those used for burning incense in a censer. When you place coal inside, cover it with ashes so that the heat won't be too intense and warm the whole room. This is another world in the midst of winter. (630)

This "warming chair" can reunite a disjointed body, bringing the "five sense organs" and "four limbs" back into one place even as its work goes unnoticed. This widespread benefit of which one is not even aware, combined with the creation of "another world" mentioned at the end of the passage, is distinctly reminiscent of the "god" in the drawer that Li Yu had proposed with that earlier furniture design.

As we have seen, *Leisure Notes* features two fundamentally different kinds of bodies, bodies of readers and bodies for sale, a division that loosely correlates to but is not synonymous with that between male and female. The widespread appreciation of young male bodies in this period has been well studied, and Li Yu's short stories treat male same-sex attraction with a mixture of ambivalence and sympathy.[62] The proposals just discussed, which aid the literati in their compositions, are aimed primarily at male readers, yet their function as bodily modifications connects these literati bodies with the female ones discussed earlier, which were described mostly in terms of skin and clothing. We can understand the connection between these different sections of *Leisure Notes*, and, consequently, very differently valued bodies, through Li Yu's discussion of feet. This idea is an example of his paring the body down to what he sees as its most basic functions. In contrast to most of his contemporaries, Li Yu embraces what Dorothy Ko has called an "aesthetic of function," prioritizing the use of women's bound feet in addition to their size.[63]

Confucian norms regarding gender segregation in his day and the modern tendency to dismiss footbinding as uniquely cruel make it difficult for Li Yu's contemporaries and our own—though for different reasons—to see past the gendered quality of bound feet to think about what they do. Yet we find such a consideration in Li Yu's description of women's feet:

> Someone once said to me, "Zhou Xiangguo of Yixing purchased a beautiful woman for a thousand taels of silver. Her name was 'Miss Carry,' which she was called because her feet were so small that she could not take even a small step unassisted, so that whenever she went anywhere, someone would have to carry her." I replied, "In that case, she's no more than a clay statue of a beautiful woman, which could be acquired for a few cash—how could he have spent one thousand taels?" When the Creator made people with feet, he intended that they would walk. In the past when people described women's beauty, did they not say, "every step a lotus" and "each step graceful as smooth jade?" Both expressions indicate that their feet were small and that they could walk—even walk into a pretty picture. This is the reason that they were cherished. If they had been small but unable to walk, how is that any different from amputating the feet [*yue* 刖]?[64]

For Li Yu, the commodified body must also be a functional body. Asserting that feet are made for walking, he conveniently literalizes expressions like "every step a lotus" as proof. The ancient punishment of "cutting off the feet" through a single character, *yue* 刖, which translates graphically to "knife flesh," and the visceral presentation of his argument is reminiscent of his description of a disjointed *chuanqi* play as a body cut up and then sutured back together.

Although the above passage discusses the body of a woman who has been purchased, Li Yu uses the same language of footlessness to disparage the bodies of the rich and sedentary. Echoing his ongoing interest in technological innovations that make servants unnecessary, he uses a reference to footless people to disparage wealthy people's reliance on servants for their mobility:

> When rich people go out, they always ride in a carriage or on a horse. Although this may be relaxing, it doesn't quite conform with the Creator's intention in bestowing this form on us. If people have legs but don't use them, they may as well have no legs at all. How much better to be among those who are content to stroll along rather than ride in a carriage, and are thus able to make use of all of their organs and limbs? Such are the words of a poor man trying to impress.... As for the poor scholar's superiority, it is not just that he can use his feet for walking, but that he can leave quickly or slowly as necessary. If he has only a few leisurely errands, he can stroll instead of riding; if he has urgent matters to attend to, he can stride quickly rather than ride a horse. He can leave whether people are there to attend to him or not. He can walk with a friend or alone.... How different is his situation from that of the wealthy who must wait for others to bring them feet: if no one shows up, and the wealthy person consequently cannot go out, this is indeed a case of a man being as if with no feet, despite having a pair. What an absurd offense against the Creator who endowed us with these bodies! (704)

Triangulating among women, rich people, and poor scholars, Li Yu uses feet to connect the modifications of bodies across distinctions of gender, class, and occupation. In all instances, he encourages people to avoid the kind of technology that reduces one's functionality: that is, to avoid letting things that should serve as extensions and amplifications of the body (like horses, carriages, bindings, or servants) operate as amputations instead. Such modulation echoes the existing discourse on how to be content in poverty, but such inadvisable luxuries had not been previously described in such a technological way.

This pairing of extensions with amputations reminds readers to periodically reevaluate the stories we tell ourselves about our bodies, as some of their basic functions may have been lost in the pursuit of luxurious advancement. Li Yu seeks to reintegrate bodies that were at risk of separating between the climatic extremes of summer and winter, or of coming apart because of overly contrasting clothing, or of losing their feet by failing to use them. All of these proposals invite participation on the part of the reader, encouraging a reacquaintance with the body and with its possibly atrophied functions. In doing so, Li Yu underscores how even our bodily existence is mediated by things—and he renders the human body, as a result, a place for human agency and mediation.

Li Yu's mediations and modifications of the literati body invariably culminate in writing. Writing, was, after all, the most durable way to extend the reach of a literati body, and that reach could be best substantiated through the construction of durable textual creations, conceived of in terms of buildings. But, as we saw in chapter 2, the transmission (*chuan*) of literati creations in *Leisure Notes* also required the remodeling (*gaizao*) of nonliterati bodies in order to communicate universally. At this point, we have come full circle, working through the significance of buildings and bodies to return to the productive power of writing, substantiated through its impact on other media. At one end of a spectrum of possibilities for text, Li Yu has optimized language for oral communication, making everyday language into a condensed and literarized form; at the other end, he has imagined new possibilities for print to bring people together. But, although his work across media always intersects with text, it continually gestures outward to the world beyond. *Leisure Notes* offers details on how people might most effectively master their media—from their own bodies to their homes, and to texts circulating beyond their gates—encouraging them to empty and remake the content usually associated with a particular medium. The media themselves are redesigned in the process and marked with Li Yu's brand; as a consequence, your play, your flower arrangement, your retractable eaves, or even your sock choices are recognizably informed by Li Yu's designs. It is in this way that *Leisure Notes* prescribes modes of being in the world, always advocating modes in which Li Yu is present, through media that might carry him into our homes and our very flesh, remodeling our spaces and our bodies in the process.

Epilogue

The letter was the social medium of Li Yu's day, and he revolutionized it. One of Li Yu's designs for Mustard Seed Garden letter paper resembled the cover and pages of a woodblock-printed book. At the top of the center column of each folio, along which the page would normally be folded in half during the binding process, we find a book title; and at the bottom of that center column, where the name of the publisher is sometimes printed, are two columns of smaller text:

芥子園藏版　Blocks held by Mustard Seed Garden
竊刻者必究　Anyone who furtively engraves them will necessarily be investigated[1]

This letter paper design depicts a three-dimensional book on the two-dimensional space of the page: to the right of the open folio, we see another page that appears to be folded in half, with half of the copyright notice visible. By distilling into the space of a single woodblock-printed page an image depicting several woodblock-printed pages, each with exactly the same warning against reproduction, Li Yu calls attention to woodblock reproducibility, even as he forbids readers from reproducing the letter paper that depicts it. This product emblematizes Li Yu's marketing strategies as a cultural entrepreneur: capitalizing on the affordances of woodblock print to create an easily reproducible product that allows him a mediating role in the social worlds of the people around him. By emptying out just the text from the pages of a printed book (*xu qi zhong*), he offers readers a chance to see their handwritten letters filling the columns of a virtual printed book, even as he retains the copyright to that book based on his design of the paper.

Li Yu mastered social media through his creative approach to woodblock print. In his later projects like letter collections and stationery, he spurred a new market for collections from each major urban center, developed a page-numbered index to quickly link readers to the content they desired, and, in this example, offered a proprietary writing surface on which those letters might be written in the first place. Respectively, these moves transformed the social world by printing and making public the private exchanges of individuals; accelerating the functionality of the printed book; and offering individuals the prestige of print for their private correspondence. Had he produced more collections of letters as he hoped to do, his design for a social networking platform would have come full circle, with him profiting both from offering a place for users to write, and then from printing and circulating those private messages to a broader public. That entrepreneurial endeavor seems to share a conception—if not a digital platform—with the way that social media sites operate and profit today. Consequently, Li Yu's endeavors beg the question of how and to what extent early modern text-based media share aims and outcomes with our contemporary media.

I have focused *Towers in the Void* on the moment of rupture following the dynastic transition from the Ming to the Qing, when old media became new for a pressing political reason: they had to be rebuilt. My book stands in productive contrast, consequently, to studies of media history that explore moments when old media became new as a result of technological development or cultural exchange.[2] Yet even in this different causality of newness, I have found that the novelty of media forms as used by Li Yu reflects the dynamic of our digital media age, in which new media capture our attention, as Jay Bolter and Richard Grusin have argued, by "presenting themselves as refashioned and improved versions of other media." Their novelty "comes from the particular ways in which they refashion older media and the ways in which older media refashion themselves" in response.[3] To use a term that surfaces in discussion throughout this book, we might say that new media *gaizao* old media:

they remodel existing media forms and create novelty in the process. The massive political upheavals of Li Yu's day destroyed and rendered unrecognizable familiar media, whether books, buildings, or bodies. Li Yu and his contemporaries were involved in rebuilding infrastructure and homes, producing new bodies to replace the old, commemorating the lost world in writing and in print: in short, rebuilding the material edifices of culture itself.[4] In those early years of the Qing, these old media shimmered with communicative and ontological potential, offering the tools not only to rebuild a culture, but to remodel the media in which it was lodged.

Li Yu took advantage of this disruption to reimagine not only those media that take the material form of paper and print, such as letters and books, but also the even older media of buildings and bodies. The indiscriminate destruction of the dynastic transition, which did not pause to distinguish between media forms, ended up "emptying out the middle" (*xu qi zhong*) of them all by exposing fissures between form and content. In a culture steeped in the written and printed word, that great equalizing of material media forms offered Li Yu a chance to reimagine the containers and connectors of culture.

The complementary pair of terms *xu/shi* that I have been developing throughout this book indicates how the relationship between the material world and its simulacra was up for remodeling in this moment as well. Li Yu's experiments with how buildings could change fiction, and with how writing could transform the home and garden, seem to presage virtual reality experiences: he insists on giving the fictional structure and substance, even as the code of language is used to revise design possibilities for the built environment. Because Li Yu envisioned books, bodies, and buildings as new at the same time, he had little patience for the immateriality of a purely literary, and hence fully virtual, world: his complex, structured textual worlds led back to his social space (*shi*). This intermedial quality of Li Yu's work underscores the value of approaching virtuality itself as part of a bidirectional creative process. In the escapist writings of the early Qing and in traditional aesthetics, *xu*'s affective significance lay in its ability to denote something beyond, usually via the imagination of the reader. Li Yu's work refutes these fantasies, using *xu* and *shi* to build connections across different media forms. As this study has shown, his use of familiar aesthetic terms like *xu/shi* can mask the novelty of his designs, in which buildings morph into stories and stories into buildings, bodies into stories and buildings, and stories into bodies.

Live theater coalesces Li Yu's experiments in architectural design, social networking, storytelling, and the possibilities of the human body, each contributing elements of *xu* and *shi* to an evening-length multimedia experience. With his fast-paced, funny, and plot-driven comedies, he offered social experiences in his garden residence that combined his interest in books, buildings, and bodies. Li Yu printed not only his plays, but also a comprehensive guide to performing them, or simply writing your own. He thereby used the technologies available to him to transport this multimedia experience far beyond his immediate social circle.

In approaching Li Yu's cultural production as mediation, I have intentionally invoked associations with the related term that Li Yu himself would have known: the go-betweens (*meipo* 媒婆) ubiquitous in Ming fiction. It is unlikely that Li Yu thought himself similar to these elderly women, yet as an author, publisher, theater director, and home garden designer, he was in charge of mediating between large numbers of real and fictional people. He expanded this role beyond that of a client-focused go-between much as he expanded the role of the garden designer or the painter: by using the reproducible media of writing and of print. To do so, he developed the notion of *shen*, usually denoting "spiritual," "transcendent," or "god-like," to resemble what we think of as the "technological." His use of this term can help us apprehend what made him, in our terms, media savvy. Throughout this book, I have translated *shen* in the standard way as "spiritual," with some variation for context, as in a "spiritual social exchange" (*shenjiao*) or a "spiritual journey" (*shenwang*), to indicate a meeting or a journey that took place virtually rather than face-to-face. Many of Li Yu's rhetorical strategies and literary innovations were designed to enhance this technological relationship, transmitting (*chuan*) him wherever his books traveled. He uses *shen* elsewhere in a compound with "speed" to mean "at the speed of the gods" (*shensu* 神速), and usually used to describe the speed of galloping horses, military operations (or, today, modern trains and internet service): the "Liweng Incense Chop" he designed, for instance, will tidy your incense marvelously fast. Although he did not consistently articulate his work with media in terms of *shen*, it seems to me to epitomize the way he transformed mediation through his emphasis on god-like effects. When conceived as *shen*, this early modern idea of the technological bumps up against the older idea of spirits. Consequently, Li Yu had to slow down this speedy, technologically enhanced journey to explain that his "gods" were products of human ingenuity, for instance, by explaining the telescope-tower function at the end of "A Tower for the Summer Heat."[5]

War and the Qing dynasty's visceral regulations had rendered bodies new as well, and Li Yu refigured them as a physical medium open to many kinds of human intervention. As Angela Zito has argued, Li Yu "queered filiality" by reconceptualizing the body's function beyond of Confucian discourse.[6] I demonstrate in this book that his interventions bore even further into the flesh, reimagining the body in ways that prefigured, frequently both in concept and terminology, our contemporary surgical procedures like microdermabrasion, vulvoplasty, penile transplant, and phalloplasty. He did so, I have suggested, by approaching bodies as analogous to the other—also recently new—media of his moment: books and buildings.

"Since people disregard the old and ordinary for the new and different," Li Yu wrote in *Leisure Notes*, it is likely that "they will also find the physical body that they have had since birth to grow stale and off-putting, and want to exchange it for a new one." He explains:

> Today your soul would adhere to one body, and tomorrow to another: would you find it more lovely the more you changed it and made it new? The reason it cannot be changed and updated is that it is fixed from birth. But if you want to change and update it, there is a way. Change your cap and robe frequently, change the bed curtains and seat covers often, then look at all of these in a mirror and it will seem that you have changed the whole place.[7]

This description of fast-paced sartorial turnover culminates in its capture on the flat, reflective surface of a mirror, in the process creating a scene (*jing*) using the body much as we might, using other natural materials, in the garden. From our contemporary vantage point, Li Yu's description evokes a thumb moving on the screen of a smartphone, whether to scroll, or to refresh, or to click on a hyperlink—all actions that will transport us instantly to a new two-dimensional scene. In this passage, he dials back his most outrageous proposals for fictional body remodeling, suggesting accommodation and compromise, and demonstrating his pragmatic side.[8] But as with the unreliability of Li Yu's fictional narrators, this passage underscores that the human body is not fixed from birth. Rather than discourage readers from pursuing body modifications, it emphasizes that the early modern body is no traditional body, nor even a Ming body. Instead, it is a bounded entity capable of *gaizao*—just like a building or a book.

Because Li Yu's remodeling of all of these media takes place through reference to the others, my account of media history in *Towers in the Void* is tethered to social and political rupture. I have reenvisioned Li Yu as a cultural mediator: his much-discussed cultural entrepreneurship, I argue, operated by fundamentally expanding and changing processes of mediation. In the process, I have attempted to offer a model for media history of the global early modern period. In its expansion of the study of early modern media beyond the rubric of print, I hope that this book will encourage us to situate print and books within a larger mediascape in historically informed terms, as we grapple with the persistence of all of Li Yu's media—books, buildings, and bodies—in the renovated novelties of our time.

Appendix: Li Yu's Oeuvre

This appendix includes information on Li Yu's works, organized according to the logic of a recently discovered document from 1674. While traveling to Beijing in 1674, Li Yu wrote several letters to an acquaintance, Yan Guangmin 顏光敏 (1640–1686), in which he urged him to purchase some of his books so that he would not have to carry them back home to Nanjing—and he attached a catalogue of his works.

Only rediscovered by scholars in 2006, the catalogue is revelatory for the study of Li Yu.[1] First, because it lists the works Li Yu was selling just six years before his death, it resolves some longstanding issues regarding the extent of his oeuvre. Second, it displays several aspects of Li Yu's thinking, for he organized the list to appeal to potential buyers' tastes. In addition, these facsimile reprints of his letters offer a rare glimpse of the stationery he designed and sold at Mustard Seed Garden.

Rather than proceeding chronologically or by genre, this appendix follows the order in which Li Yu chose to list his fourteen works for sale. Those fourteen items are followed by notes on works that he excluded or wrote after 1674. Because in many cases library catalogues do not include information that would distinguish the earliest editions from later editions, I provide information for those I have confirmed as early editions and list facsimile or digitized reproductions where available. I also provide each item's location in the typeset *Li Yu quanji* (*LYQJ*, Zhejiang) and suggest select modern annotated editions and English translations. This list is not exhaustive, and it focuses mainly on editions published during Li Yu's lifetime. I provide further information on editions at liyu-resource.org.

LI YU'S BOOK CATALOGUE, CIRCA 1674

1. *A New Aid to Administration, First Collection* (*Zizhi xinshu chuji* 資治新書初集), in eight books.

Preface dated 1663. Administrative documents solicited from individuals serving in the Qing government. Contains Li Yu's essays on governance and critical commentary.

First edition by Yishengtang, held at Bayerische Staatsbibliothek. Title page of original edition reads only *Zizhi xinshu*. Fine later edition by Jieziyuan, held at Peking University Library. Jieziyuan edition has main title page that reads *Xinzeng zizhi xinshu quanji* 新增資治新書全集, and a second title page that reads *Xinzeng zizhi xinshu chuji*. Included in complete collection (see item 2). *LYQJ* 16.

2. *A New Aid to Administration, Second Collection* (*Zizhi xinshu erji* 資治新書二集), in twelve books.

Preface dated 1667. Second solicitation of contemporary administrative documents. Extant as part of combined edition and in later editions.

Fine Qing edition by Jingyetang 敬業堂 with some Jieziyuan blocks, held at Harvard-Yenching Library (http://id.lib.harvard.edu/alma/990080401170203941/catalog). *LYQJ* 17.

The first and second collections were later combined to form a "complete collection," not mentioned in Li Yu's catalogue. Early complete edition, *Xinzeng zizhi xinshu quanji*, by Daiyuelou, held at University of California, Los Angeles, Library. Large number of later complete editions suggest broad popularity throughout the Qing.

3. *A First Solicitation of Parallel Prose* (*Siliu chuzheng* 四六初徵), in sixteen books.

Preface dated 1671. Parallel prose solicited from more than one hundred individuals, with instructional annotations.

First edition by Yishengtang, held at Nanjing Library, at National Library of China, at Shanghai Library (reproduced in *Siku jinhui shu congkan*, Jibu, 135:1–514) and at Harvard-Yenching Library (http://id.lib.harvard.edu/alma/990080701820203941/catalog). Title page has "new" (*xin* 新) before the title; perhaps there was an earlier imprint without that designation.

4. *A First Solicitation of Letters* (*Chidu chuzheng* 尺牘初徵), in six books.

Preface dated 1660. Includes letters by 178 individuals, mostly Li Yu's contemporaries, with page-numbered index.

Earliest extant edition by Baobianzhai 豹變齋, held at Chinese Academy of Social Sciences (reproduced in *Siku jinhui shu congkan*, Jibu, 153:499–704) and at Library of Congress (https://lccn.loc.gov/2014514084).

5. *Leisure Notes* (*Xianqing ouji* 閒情偶寄), in eight books.

Preface dated 1671. Idiosyncratic guide to the good life, with commentary by Li Yu's friends.

First edition by Yishengtang, held at Jilin University Library (reproduced in *Xuxiu siku quanshu*, Jibu, 1186:485–722) and at Harvard-Yenching Library (http://id.lib.harvard.edu/alma/990080074400203941/catalog). Versions held at Academia Sinica (reproduced in *Guoxue zhenji huibian* [Taipei: Guangwen shuju, 1977]) and at National Library of China (http://read.nlc.cn/allSearch/searchDetail?searchType=all&showType=1&indexName=data_892&fid=411999028376) contain preface by You Tong, excluded from most extant editions. *LYQJ* 3.

For modern annotated editions, see: Chen Duo, ed., *Li Liweng quhua* (Changsha: Hunan renmin chubanshe, 1980); and Du Shuying, ed., *Xianqing ouji*, 2 vols., *Zhonghua jingdian mingzhu quanben quanzhu quanyi congshu* (Beijing: Zhonghua shuju, 2014).

Select essays from *Xianqing ouji* have been translated into English, primarily from the first three books on playwriting, performance, and women. See Faye Chunfang Fei, trans., "From Li Liweng on Theater," in *Chinese Theories of Theater and Performance from Confucius to the Present* (Ann Arbor, MI: University of Michigan Press, 1999), 77–88; David Pollard, trans., "Li Yu on the Theatre: Excerpts from *Pleasant Diversions*," *Renditions* 72 (Autumn 2009): 30–70; David Pollard, trans., "*Pleasant Diversions*: Voice and Looks; Accomplishments; Literacy; Clothes," *Renditions* 51 (Spring 1999): 21–28; and David Pollard, trans., *The Chinese Essay* (New York: Columbia University Press, 2000), 110–115. For selections from later books, see Lin Yutang, trans., "The Arts of Sleeping,

Walking, Sitting, and Standing," in *The Columbia Anthology of Traditional Chinese Literature*, ed. Victor H. Mair (New York: Columbia University Press, 1994), 602–606; and David Pollard, trans. "Snippets from Li Yu's *Pleasant Diversions*," *Renditions* 73 (Spring 2010): 78–94. See also translated selections here and in monographs cited in the introduction, notes 26 and 54. The most substantial translation into a European language to date is Jacques Dars, *Au gré d'humeurs oisives: Les carnets secrets de Li Yu* (Arles: Editions Philippe Picquier, 2003).

6. *Independent Words* (*Yijia yan* 一家言), in six books.

Preface dated 1672. First installment of Li Yu's poetry (eight volumes) and prose (four volumes), with commentary by his friends.

First edition by Yishengtang, full title *Liweng's Independent Words, First Collection* (*Liweng yijia yan chuji* 笠翁一家言初集), held at Palace Museum Library (reproduced in *Siku jinhui shu congkan bubian*, 85:1–185) and at Anhui Normal University.

See item 18 for the second and complete collections.

7. *Outline of History* (*Gujin shilüe* 古今史略), in six books.

Preface dated 1659. A digest of Chinese history from ancient times to Ming with commentary by Li Yu; almost half devoted to Ming history.

Early Qing edition, no named publisher, held at Northeast Normal University Library (reproduced in *Siku jinhui shu congkan bubian*, 16: 1–206). *LYQJ* 15:1–424.

8. *Discourses on the Past* (*Lungu* 論古), in four books.

Preface dated 1661. Series of essays on history, largely taking issue with existing historiography. Not extant but survives in revised form in later editions.

Revised edition preface dated 1664, published under the title *Expanded and Corrected Liweng's Discourses on the Past* (*Zengding Liweng lungu* 增定笠翁論古). Held at Sonkeikaku bunko 尊經閣文庫. (See Wang Dingyong and Chen Anmei, "Riben Zunjingge wenku cang *Zengding Liweng lungu* de wenxian jiazhi," *Wenxian* 4 [July 2017]: 165–173.)

Revised edition included in 1678 edition of *Liweng's Independent Words* as "separate collection" (*bieji* 別集) titled *Judgements on History* (*Shiduan* 史斷). See item 18.

Revised version closest to original version exists in the 1730 edition of *Liweng yijia yan quanji* (see item 18). *LYQJ* 1:205–527.

9. *Expanded Collection of Characters* (*Guang zihui* 廣字彙), in twelve books.

Not extant. Unknown before the rediscovery of Li Yu's book catalogue, this was likely an expanded version of the largest dictionary at the time, the *Collection of Characters* (*Zihui*) published by Mei Yingzuo 梅膺祚 in 1615. First edition of *Zihui* held at Harvard-Yenching Library (http://id.lib.harvard.edu/alma/990080980970203941/catalog).

The following three items are collections of Li Yu's chuanqi *plays. The plays are extant, but not in this configuration. Written beginning in the early 1650s, they were first published individually before being issued in sets (see note after item 12). The several extant individual plays with fine round illustrations (no publisher listed) are likely first editions, and most sets during Li Yu's lifetime were likely printed with these same blocks.*

10. *Earlier Four Plays* (*Chuanqi qian sizhong* 傳奇前四種), in eight books.

    Likely included Li Yu's first four *chuanqi* plays:

The Fragrant Companions (*Lianxiang ban* 憐香伴)
    Published ca. 1653.
    For an English translation, see Stephen Roddy and Ying Wang, trans., *The Fragrant Companions: A Play About Love Between Women* (New York: Columbia University Press, 2022).

Mistake with a Kite (*Fengzheng wu* 風箏誤)
    Published shortly thereafter; these first two plays were frequently mentioned together.
    No publisher listed, held at Chinese National Academy of Arts (reproduced in *Xuxiu siku quanshi*, Jibu, 1775:505–576), and at Peking University Library (includes first illustration missing from reproduced copy).

A Much-Desired Match (*Yizhong yuan* 意中緣)
    Huang Yuanjie's 黃媛介 preface likely mid-1650s. Fan Xiang's 范驤 preface dated 1659. Later editions exclude Fan's preface.
    No publisher listed, held at National Library of China (reproduced in *Zheng Zhenduo cang zhenben xiqu wenxian congkan*, 29:1–331)

Tower in a Mirage (*Shenzhong lou* 蜃中樓)
    Sun Zhi's preface written in Hangzhou, ca. late 1650s

11. *Later Four Plays* (*Chuanqi hou sizhong* 傳奇後四種), in eight books. Would likely have included Li Yu's next four *chuanqi* plays:

As Heaven Would Have It (*Naihe tian* 奈何天)
    Hu Jie's 胡介 undated preface, ca. late 1650s
    No publisher listed, held at Peking University Library.

The Jade Hairpin (*Yu saotou* 玉搔頭)
    Lu Mengxiong's 陸夢熊 preface dated 1658.

A Couple of Soles (*Bimu yu* 比目魚)
    Wang Duanshu's 王端淑 preface dated 1661.
    For an English translation, see Jing Shen and Robert E. Hegel, trans., *A Couple of Soles: A Comic Play from Seventeenth-Century China* (New York: Columbia University Press, 2020).

Woman in Pursuit of Man (*Huang qiu feng* 凰求鳳)
    Published before 1666.

12. *Inner Two Plays* (*Chuanqi nei erzhong* 傳奇內二種), in four books. Likely included Li Yu's last two *chuanqi* plays:

Be Careful About Love (*Shen luanjiao* 慎鸞交)
    Guo Chuanfang's 郭傳芳 preface dated 1667.
    No publisher listed, held at the National Palace Museum Library.

The Ingenious Finale (*Qiao tuanyuan* 巧團圓)
    Preface dated 1668.

There exists a preface by Sun Zhi to a collection of the first five plays, likely written before Li Yu moved to Nanjing; no copy of the collection is extant. Qian Qianyi wrote a preface to a collection of eight dated 1661; such a collection is also not extant.

Liweng chuanqi shizhong 笠翁傳奇十種

The ten extant *chuanqi* were published probably in the 1670s as a set titled *Liweng chuanqi shizhong*.

First edition by Yishengtang, held at Zhejiang Library and at Capital Library of China. I believe that the facsimile copies of individual plays described above are identical to those included in this collection, with fine round illustrations for the first eight plays (with calligraphied lines on the reverse) and rectangular embellished frames with rounded corners on the last two. No facsimile or digitized version of the collection is available, but some of the illustrations are reproduced in Zhou Xinhui, ed., *Zhongguo gudai xiqu banhua ji* (Beijing: Xueyuan chubanshe, 2000), 618–636.

Please note that three recent collections erroneously state that they reproduce Yishengtang editions of Li Yu's *chuanqi* plays. The collections are *Zhongguo zaizao shanben Qingdai bian,* Jibu, vol. 42, 2002; *GBXQCK,* ser. 6, vols. 1–2, 2016; *Zheng Zhenduo cang zhenben xiqu wenxian congkan,* vols. 23–28. All three actually reproduce the mid- or late-Qing Dazhitang 大知堂 edition held in the National Library of China. That edition is smaller, has no illustrations or commentary, and was likely printed with movable type. It is digitized here (http://read.nlc.cn /allSearch/searchDetail?searchType=all&showType=1&indexName =data_892&fid=412000013556).

In the absence of an accessible version of the Yishengtang edition, the best option is the fine early Qing Shidetang 世德堂 edition. It features rectangular illustrations based on the original round ones but of a slightly inferior quality, with a standardized style across the ten plays. Held at Sun Yat-sen University and at Stanford University. Reproduced in Helmut Martin, comp., *Li Yu quanji,* vols. 7–11. *LYQJ* 4–5. For a modern annotated edition, see Wang Xueqi, Huo Xianjun, and Wu Xiuhua, eds., *Liweng chuanqi shizhong jiaozhu,* 2 vols. (Tianjin: Tianjin guji chubanshe, 2009).

13. *Twelve Towers* (*Shi'er lou* 十二樓), in six books.

The earliest extant edition of *Shi'er lou* is the fine illustrated Xiaoxianju edition held at Peking University Library, at the Chinese Academy of Social Sciences, and at Tenri Library (reproduced in *Guben xiaoshuo jicheng* 4; title page missing in that copy is reproduced at the beginning of *LYQJ* 9). Xiaoxianju edition has an undated preface by Du Jun. Most other extant editions carry the longer title, *Famous Words to Awaken the World: Twelve Towers* (*Jueshi mingyan Shi'er lou*). Those editions carry a date of 1658 at the end of Du Jun's preface, contain no illustrations, and lack a list describing lenses in the fourth story. These editions are generally thought to be based on a lost first edition, which had been published before Xiaoxianju. I argue that they are revisions of Xiaoxianju, and that Xiaoxianju, if not the earliest edition, is at least printed from revised original blocks. I explain my argument below. Here, I first point researchers to the excellent imprint of an early *Jueshi mingyan* edition held at National Library of China (http://read.nlc.cn/allSearch /searchDetail?searchType=all&showType=1&indexName=data_892

&fid=412000001068), hereafter Guotu copy. This edition, while lacking the list of lenses in story 4, includes many upper-margin comments that are not found in the Xiaoxianju edition. It is also an extremely clear imprint, so many characters that are illegible in earlier reproductions can easily be read. A less clear copy of a similar edition held at Academia Sinica is reproduced in Helmut Martin, comp., *Li Yu quanji* 12–13. It is also held at Peking University (SB/813.35/4037.1) and at Zhejiang University. No publisher is listed for these editions; later editions of *Jueshi mingyan Shi'er lou*, such as the Baoningtang 寶寧堂 and Wenbaotang 文寶堂 editions held at Peking University, were printed with new blocks based on this edition.

The most compelling evidence for Xiaoxianju coming first is the fact that the pages in story 4 that describe various lenses have clearly been removed from the text of Xiaoxianju rather than added to the Guotu text. The Xiaoxianju edition and the Guotu copy were printed from the same blocks, which were carefully revised to fit in the available space on each page. After pages were removed, the old pagination was retained, so that the later imprints skip from page 15a to page 18b, acknowledging this lacuna with the word *zhi* 至 ("to") before "18." Elsewhere, the blocks are virtually identical, suggesting small changes to the blocks rather than newly carved ones. Later editions fixed the page number issue by renumbering.

Second, the first editions of Li Yu's other fiction and plays were illustrated, like Xiaoxianju. The illustration to "Fuyun lou" also bears the signature of its creator, Hu Nianyi 胡念翌, the artist who also painted the illustrations for the *Wusheng xi heji*, *Bimu yu*, and *Huang qiu feng*, all produced in the late 1650s or early 1660s, suggesting an early date for this edition and Li Yu's hand in it.

Third, Guotu contains more upper-margin comments than Xiaoxianju, suggesting that they were added later.

Fourth, Xiaoxianju's title suggests an early date. Its table of contents opens with "Table of contents for the work of fiction *Twelve Towers*" (*Shi'er lou xiaoshuo muci* 十二樓小說目次). This word choice matches that of the original collection of *Wusheng xi*: "Table of contents for the work of fiction *Silent Operas*" (*Wusheng xi xiaoshuo muci* 無聲戲小說目次). In later editions of *Wusheng xi*, the word *xiaoshuo* was removed. In the Guotu copy, Du Jun's preface remains exactly the same with the exception of a changed signature line that adds a date and the replacement of four references to *xiaoshuo* with the term *baishi* 稗史 ("unofficial history"). Although these terms have similar meanings, I propose that the term *xiaoshuo* had become problematic in the 1660s, and the Guotu text applied a quick fix. This means that the dated preface was written after the nondated preface, which diverges from the usual interpretation.

The early *Jueshi mingyan* edition uses *Jueshi mingyan* before the title of *Shi'er lou* on the title page and as a standalone title throughout the body of the text (the title page is missing in the Guotu copy of this edition). Scholars have wondered if *Jueshi mingyan* was the original title, and *Shi'er lou* a later one. I resolve this issue through reference to the "E edition" of *Liancheng bi* (described in item 14), which is called *Jueshi mingyan Liancheng bi* on its title page. Both the early *Jueshi mingyan* edition of *Shi'er lou* and the E edition of *Liancheng bi* were issued without illustrations, and their title pages are designed in the same format, style, and font: large, bold characters reading *Jueshi mingyan* on the right and the books' respective title on the left. No other words appear on the title page of *Shi'er lou*, whereas "Inner and Outer Totaling Eighteen" (*neiwai ji shiba ji* 內外計十八集) appears in smaller characters following the title in *Liancheng bi*, and "Lingering Sounds of a Bell" (Muduo yuyin 木鐸餘音) appears across the top. Both the Xiaoxianju edition of *Shi'er lou* and the first *Wusheng xi* edition, then, use *xiaoshuo*, whereas the later edition is called *jueshi mingyan*, just as *Liancheng bi* was, when the term *xiaoshuo* came under attack. This indicates that the Xiaoxianju edition with the title *Shi'er lou* was earlier than the Guotu and other *Jueshi mingyan* editions, and the "alternate title *Twelve Towers*" (*yiming* Shi'er lou 一名十二樓), which appears on the first page of each story in the Guotu copy, can be interpreted as referring to an earlier title rather than a secondary one.

To determine the date of the Xiaoxianju edition, it is crucial to consider the textual history of the catalogue from which the inserted material on lenses to story 4 was adapted. That list of lenses was advertised in a catalogue, *A History of Lenses* (*Jingshi* 鏡史, preface dated 1681), by a lens crafter, Sun Yunqiu 孫雲球, with whom Li Yu shared a mutual friend, Zhu Sheng 諸昇 (1617–1690). Scholars offer different dates for Sun: some suggest, based on dates in his catalogue, that he was born around 1650, while others suggest the 1620s. No one has offered conclusive evidence. It is possible that Zhu saw Sun's catalogue only when he visited Suzhou in 1672 and brought a copy to Li Yu. The textual history of *Shi'er lou* editions, however, suggests that Li Yu had access to some version of the catalogue more than a decade earlier.

For full English translations of six of the twelve *Shi'er lou* stories (stories 4–7, 9, and 11), see Patrick Hanan, trans., *A Tower for the Summer Heat* (New York: Columbia University Press, 1998; [New York, Ballantine Books, 1992]). Sir John Francis Davis's translations of the first three *Shi'er lou* stories, excluding prologue stories, poetry, and other parts of the text, were among the earliest Chinese stories translated into English. An English translation of the third story was originally published in 1815 in Canton and then in *Asiatic Journal* 1 (January–June 1916): 37–41, 132–234, 243–249, 338–342. All three are available in Sir John Francis Davis, trans., *Chinese Novels: Translated from the Originals:* The Shadow in the Water, The Twin Sisters, The Three Dedicated Chambers, *with observations on the language and literature of China* (London: J. Murray, 1822 and 1843). On these early translations, see Chun-shu Chang and Shelley Hsueh-lun Chang, *Crisis and Transformation in Seventeenth-Century China: Society, Culture, and Modernity in Li Yü's World* (Ann Arbor: University of Michigan Press, 1992), 34n23–24. For a study of the subsequent multiple translations of story 1 in Europe, see Yunfei Bai, "Translingual Adaptations: Asian Works in Late Nineteenth- and Early Twentieth-Century French Literature" (PhD diss, University of Toronto, 2018), chap. 1. Nathan Mao's renditions of all twelve of the stories are aptly characterized by him as "retellings" rather than translations, as his versions correspond quite loosely to the original text: see Nathan Mao, *Twelve Towers: Short Stories by Li Yü*, retold by Nathan Mao (Hong Kong: Chinese University Press, 1979, 2nd ed.).

14. *Priceless Jade* (*Liancheng bi* 連城璧), in six books [original title: *Silent Operas* (*Wusheng xi* 無聲戲)].

Priceless Jade is the later name of Li Yu's earliest short stories, which were first published in the mid-1650s in *Silent Operas* (*Wusheng xi*, A), an illustrated collection of twelve stories, and in *Silent Operas, A Second Collection* (*Wusheng xi erji*, B), of six stories. With Du Jun's help, Li Yu then published a combined selection called *Silent Operas, A Combined Collection* (*Wusheng xi heji*, C), which included seven stories from the first collection and five from the second, all under new titles. After around 1660, he published *Priceless Jade* (*Liancheng bi*, E), a combined collection of twelve stories with an additional six "outer" stories (*waibian* 外編). Another early edition with nine of twelve stories extant (a different selection of six from the first collection and three from the second) exists under the title *Silent Operas, A Combined Selection* (*Wusheng xi hexuan*, D). Only one copy of each of the four extant printed versions exists (B is not extant).

The best and earliest versions of these stories are A and E. The first collection of twelve stories (A) is extant in an illustrated edition held at Sonkeikaku bunko (reproduced in Helmut Martin, comp., *Li Yu quanji*, vols. 12–13). The second collection (B) is not extant, but its six stories can be found in the combined eighteen-story version of *Liancheng bi* (E) held at Saeki Municipal Library (reproduced in *Guben xiaoshuo congkan* 20, vols. 1–3): they are stories 1, 3, 6, 9, 12, and *waibian* 3. The *Liancheng bi* eighteen-story version contains all the known *Wusheng xi* stories under their new titles. *LYQJ* 8.

Heji (C) exists only in a fragmentary copy featuring twelve new illustrations but only two stories: it is held at Peking University. *Heji* contained twelve new and stylistically very different illustrations, which I believe provide important clues about this work's history. The illustrations to the original *Wusheng xi* collection (A), with their exaggerated features and empty backgrounds, are easily recognizable as the style of Chen Hongshou. See Sun Kaidi, *Riben Dongjing suojian Zhongguo xiaoshuo shumu tiyao* (Beijing: Guoli Beiping tushuguan, 1931), 23. That set of illustrations credits only a carver, a Hangzhou resident named Cai Sihuang 蔡思璜 (ca. 1620–1670). Cai also carved the illustrations for at least four of Li Yu's early plays (*Fengzheng wu, Shenzhong lou, Yizhong yuan,* and *Yu saotou*): see Zhou Xinhui, *Zhongguo gu banhua tongshi* (Beijing: Xueyuan chubanshe, 2000), 236. The *heji* (C) has a new set of twelve illustrations in a more standard style for fiction illustration with elaborate backgrounds, natural features, and buildings (both sets are juxtaposed with calligraphic couplets; although not identical, the *heji* calligraphy was clearly influenced by the original). Cai Sihuang is identified as the carver of the new illustrations as well, and Hu Nianyi is credited with the painting (Hu also painted *Shi'er lou* illustrations, see above). That the same carver is credited with both sets of illustrations suggests that the *heji* is also the work of Li Yu. He may have commissioned new illustrations because he had to sell the original blocks or because there was demand for more elaborate scene composition. All twenty-four existing illustrations are reprinted in *LYQJ* 8.

Itoh Sohei has suggested that the pirated version of *Wusheng xi* that might have caused Li Yu to move to Nanjing was likely the *hexuan* (D), published by Sanjintang 三近堂 and lacking illustrations. It is owned by Kong Xianyi 孔憲易; see Liu Yeqiu et al., eds., *Zhongguo gudian xiaoshuo da cidian* (Shijiazhuang: Hebei renmin chubanshe, 1998), 591. Whereas *heji* (C) reordered and renamed the stories, *hexuan* (D) offered a different selection of twelve while preserving the original story titles. I have not seen this edition.

A scholarly consensus regarding the above editions has been reached, thanks to the many meticulous investigations undertaken over the past century, the most important of which are referenced at the end of this note. Questions remain about how, when, and why the title of *Silent Operas* was changed to *Priceless Jade*, and exactly how Zhang Jinyan was involved with the two collections of *Silent Operas*. Because the seal used in the preface points to Zhang, I suspect that Zhang wrote the preface to the first collection, sponsored the publication of both collections (A and B), and possibly also the illustrated combined edition (C) (see the introduction in this book, n. 45). After his exile, *Silent Operas* was not issued again. The stories were rearranged and reissued as *Priceless Jade*, by which title they were still known in 1674, when this book catalogue was written. The book catalogue thus proves that Li Yu was involved in publishing *Priceless Jade* and that he was not selling the collection as *Silent Operas*. But it is not clear whether this version contained twelve or eighteen stories, since "six books," which is the same as *Twelve Towers*, could contain either number of stories.

After 1660, the collection seems to have circulated freely as *Liancheng bi*, rearranged and with new titles. Because *Shi'er lou* is such a coherent and distinctive collection, I do not believe that some of its stories were originally part of the second collection of *Wusheng xi*, or that one of the stories in the complete *Liancheng bi* collection was written later, simply because a comment references its title—*Liancheng bi waibian*—at the end of its fifth story, "With Ghostly Words She Aims to Trick the Living; In

A Display of Magic She Recovers Lost Property" (說鬼話計賺生人 顯神通智恢舊業), as has been suggested by Itoh Sohei and Xiao Xinqiao. See Itoh Sohei, "Ri Gyo no shōsetsu no hampon to sono ryuden—Museigeki wo chushin shite," *Chūgoku gaku kaihō* 36 (1984): 191–206, 199; Xiao Xinqiao, "Li Yu *Wusheng xi, Liancheng bi* banben shanbian kaosuo," *Wenxian*, no. 1 (1987): 64–80, 78–79. Such metafictional references are frequent throughout Li Yu's fiction and could easily have been recarved from *Wusheng xi erji* to *Liancheng bi waibian*. Until further evidence of the *erji* emerges, I remain convinced that the *Liancheng bi* collection simply rearranges and retitles existing *Wusheng xi* stories; a comparison of the same story in the two versions shows identical format and almost no textual variations.

The information provided in this note is based on the following studies: Sun Kaidi, "Li Liweng zhu *Wusheng xi* ji *Liancheng bi* jieti," *Guoli Beiping tushuguan guankan* 6, no. 1 (1932): 9–25; Itoh Sohei, "Ri Gyo no shōsetsu no hampon to sono ryuden—Museigeki wo chushin shite," *Chūgoku gaku kaihō* 36 (1984): 191–206; Itoh Sohei, "Ri Gyo no shōsetsu 'Museigeki' no hampon ni tsuite," *Chū tetsubun gakkaihō* 9 (June 1984): 126–133; Xiao Xinqiao, "Li Yu *Wusheng xi, Liancheng bi* banben shanbian kaosuo," *Wenxian*, no. 1 (1987): 64–80; Huang Qiang, *Li Yu yanjiu* (Hangzhou: Zhejiang guji chubanshe, 1996), 371–383; Zhu Ping, "Zhang Jinyan yu *Wusheng xi* banben de guanxi zhi wojian," *Jianghuai luntan* 203, no. 1 (2004): 145–149.

English translations exist for six of the original twelve *Wusheng xi* stories and two of the six from the second series that are extant in *Liancheng bi*. Patrick Hanan, trans., *Silent Operas* (Hong Kong: Renditions, 1990) includes *Wusheng xi* stories 1–2, 3–4, 9; and *Liancheng bi* story 1. Commentary for this last story can be found in Maria Franca Sibau and Patrick Hanan, trans. "Tan Chuyu Declares his Love while Performing a Play; Liu Miaogu Dies to Preserve her Chastity at the End of the Aria" (with commentary). *Renditions* 81–82 (Spring–Fall 2014): 231–78. For *Wusheng xi* story 12, see Paul Or, trans., "Wife and Concubine Remarry, Maid-concubine Remains Constant" (*Renditions* 49 [Spring 1998]: 86–114). For *Liancheng bi* story 7, see Yenna Wu, trans., "A Jealous Wife Becomes a Widow While Her Husband is Still Alive," in *The Lioness Roars: Shrew Stories from Late Imperial China* (Ithaca, NY: Cornell University Press, 1995), 11–56.

WORKS BEFORE 1674 NOT LISTED IN BOOK CATALOGUE

15. *Juvenilia* (*Tiaoling ji* 髫齡集).

Not extant. Li Yu mentions that this published collection of writing from his youth was lost in the war.

16. *The Fleshy Prayer Mat* (*Rou putuan* 肉蒲團).

Preface dated 1657. Humorous erotic novel in twenty chapters. Li Yu wrote it under a new pseudonym, "Man of the [Buddhist] Way Who, After Being Crazed with Passion, Returned to the True Path" (*Qingchi fanzheng daoren* 情癡反正道人). See Patrick Hanan, "Introduction," in Patrick Hanan, trans., Li Yu, *The Carnal Prayer Mat* (Honolulu: University of Hawai'i Press, 1990), xii. Huang Qiang has pointed out that the first four characters of this pseudonym amount to a definition of *jue* 覺, "enlightened," slyly linking it to one of his usual pseudonyms, "Enlightened Man of the Way" (Jue daoren). See Huang Qiang, "*Rou putuan* zuozhe yu xunian zai kaobian," *Jiangnan daxue xuebao* (*renwen shehui kexue ban*) 18, no. 1 (2019): 82.

Hanan proposed that a manuscript copy at the Institute of Oriental Culture, Tokyo University, is the most complete extant version. He suggested that it was likely copied from a manuscript of the original edition because it includes upper-margin commentary; it has the same number of columns and rows per page as Li Yu's other first editions; and it lacks the many errors that exist in other versions. This manuscript also solves a thorny question in the scholarship regarding Li Yu's authorship of this text: though it is undeniably written in the style of Li Yu's fiction, the only date previously associated with the text was *guiyou* 癸酉 in some prefaces—1633 or 1693—and both dates are unlikely given Li Yu's chronology. The date in the manuscript has an alternate first character—*ding* 丁—which dates the text to 1657, placing the novel right in the middle of Li Yu's short-lived burst of creativity as a fiction writer in the second half of the 1650s. This manuscript copy can be accessed from a list found at (http://hong.ioc.u-tokyo.ac.jp/list.php?p=5&order=si_no&jump_data=2). Hanan also identified the best extant print edition of the novel, distinguished by pages containing ten columns of twenty-five characters, two copies of which are held at Harvard-Yenching Library. A 1705 Japanese print edition by Seishinkaku 青心閣 is available online at Harvard-Yenching Library (http://id.lib.harvard.edu/alma/99008836083

0203941/catalog). See Patrick Hanan, *Han Nan Zhongguo xiaoshuo lunji*, trans. Wang Qiugui et al. (Beijing: Beijing daxue chubanshe, 2008), 312–320.

Rou putuan was censored from the *LYQJ*. Without a good early print edition, it is helpful to consult modern editions which have been edited with reference to multiple source texts. For one that consulted multiple early versions, see Huang Qiang and Guo Di, eds., *Rou putuan jiaozheng* (Taipei: Guojia chubanshe, 2019). For an English translation, see Patrick Hanan, trans., Li Yu, *The Carnal Prayer Mat*. Previously, Richard Martin had translated Franz Kuhn's German version into English: see Richard Martin and Franz Kuhn, trans., *Jou Pu Tuan: The Prayer Mat of Flesh* (New York: Grove Press, 1963).

WORKS PUBLISHED AFTER 1674

17. *Singable Lyrics* (*Naige ci* 耐歌詞), in four volumes; with "A Humble Look at the Lyric" (*Kui ci guanjian* 窺詞管見), in one volume; and *A Rhymebook for Lyrics* (*Ciyun* 詞韻) in four volumes.

Preface dated 1678. A collection of Li Yu's *ci* 詞 lyrics with commentary by his friends; an essay on lyric composition; and a reference book of rhymes appropriate for lyric composition.

First edition has no named publisher. Two copies are held at Capital Library of China, and one at National Library of China (http://read.nlc.cn/allSearch/searchDetail?searchType=all&showType=1&indexName=data_892&fid=411999028464). *Naige ci*: *LYQJ* 2:374–505; *Kui ci guanjian*: *LYQJ* 2:505–518; *Ciyun*: *LYQJ* 18:359–440.

18. *Independent Words, Second Collection* (*Yijia yan erji* 一家言二集), in twelve volumes.

Preface dated 1678. The second collection is not extant, but it is included in its original format in the earliest combined collection.

A combined collection of *Liweng yijia yan*, called *Liweng yijia yan quanji* in twenty-eight volumes, published later (most likely after Li Yu's death), added twelve volumes of the second collection (*erji*), five of poetry and seven of prose. It also added a "separate collection" (*bieji*) in four volumes that contained an abridged version of *Liweng lungu*, a previously published collection of essays on history.

First edition of the combined collection by Yishengtang uses the original blocks from the first two collections. Held in two copies at Peking University Library, at People's University Library, at Huadong Normal University, and at Library of Congress (https://lccn.loc.gov/2014514395). The term *quanji* is only included on the title page of one of the Peking University copies.

Some extant versions of the combined edition include a larger number of works, like *Naige ci*, its rhymebook, and *Xianqing ouji*, but Huang Qiang has shown that such editions (like one in the Shanghai Library) were simply gathered at a later date. See Huang Qiang, *Li Yu yanjiu*, 425–437. The preface to the 1730 edition, described below, notes that it combines Li Yu's four most popular works—*Yijia yan*, *Naige ci*, *Lungu*, and *Xianqing ouji*—which suggests that *Naige ci* was circulating primarily as a separate collection. See Huang Qiang, "*Liweng yijia yan chuji* kaoshu," *Wenxian* 4 (2006): 51–60.

In 1730 the contents of this work were reordered and supplemented, resulting in a sixteen-volume work issued under the same title, *Liweng yijia yan quanji*. It contains four volumes of prose, three of poetry, a single volume of his *Naige ci*, called a "leftover" collection (*yuji* 餘集, *ci* lyrics were known as *shiyu* 詩餘), essays on history in two volumes, and *Xianqing ouji* in six volumes. This sixteen-volume work, published in at least four different editions by Jieziyuan and Shidetang, is the most widely available version today. The original Jieziyuan edition says *Jieziyuan cangban* 芥子園藏版 on the title page, and the first page of the text proper ends on *xi* 兮. One copy is held at Beijing Normal University (847.2/292-03, 1–8). Kyoto University version reproduced in Helmut Martin, comp., *Li Yu quanji*, vols. 1–6. *LYQJ* 1–2.

19. *Liweng's Rhymebook for Poetry* (*Liweng shiyun* 笠翁詩韻).

Undated preface by Li Yu; suggests that he prioritizes current pronunciations.

First edition by Yishengtang. One copy held at University of California, Berkeley, Library. *LYQJ* 18: 205–358.

20. *A Choice of Famous Lyrics* (*Mingci xuansheng* 名詞選勝).

Not extant. A selection of contemporary *ci* lyrics that Li Yu compiled. Extant prefaces by You Tong and Li Yu. See You Tong, *You Xitang quanji* (Shanghai: Wenrui lou, Republican period), 8:10a–b; *LYQJ* 1:34–35.

21. *Marvelous Tales from History* (*Qiangu qiwen* 千古奇聞), in eight volumes.

Preface dated 1679. An account of the achievements of historical women with Li Yu's commentary. Adapted from a now-lost work called *Women's History* (*Nüshi* 女史) by Chen Baifeng 陳百峰.

First edition held at the Capital Library of China and the Chinese Academy of Social Sciences (reproduced in *Beijing shi guji shanben jicui*, Xueyuan chubanshe, 2010). *LYQJ* 15:429–873.

Notes

INTRODUCTION

1. The name "Mr. Nonexistent" connects Li Yu's design to a reference to the same imaginary figure *Wuyou xiansheng* in Sima Xiangru's 司馬相如 (179–117 BCE) *"Fu on the Excursion Hunt of the Son of Heaven"* (Tianzi youlie fu 天子游獵賦). Tamara Chin has noted that *Wuyou xiansheng* is featured in the least extravagant section of this *fu*, making it less illustrative of the aesthetic contradiction between the attested value of thrift and the usual extravagance of the *fu*. Because of Li Yu's abiding interest in the power of *xu* to create value, in his hands, Mr. Nonexistent takes on a role more similar to the *fu*'s other two interlocuters. Tamara T. Chin, *Savage Exchange: Han Imperialism, Chinese Literary Style, and the Economic Imagination* (Cambridge, MA: Harvard University Asia Center, 2014), 71–96.
2. *Yijia yan chuji*, 34.
3. The play between these two terms is fundamental to traditional aesthetic criticism. As David Rolston has argued, the distinction between them is "somewhat similar to Plato's between diegesis and mimesis": in prose criticism, *xu* was "argument" (*yilun* 議論) to *shi*'s "straight narration" (*xushi* 敘事); for examination essays, *xu* connoted indirect argument, and *shi* direct; and in painting, *shi* refers to more detailed elements, and *xu* the sparser. David L. Rolston, *Traditional Chinese Fiction and Fiction Commentary: Reading and Writing Between the Lines* (Stanford, CA: Stanford University Press, 1997), 182.
4. Patrick Hanan, *The Invention of Li Yu* (Cambridge, MA: Harvard University Press, 1988), viii.

5. See Wai-yee Li, *Enchantment and Disenchantment: Love and Illusion in Chinese Literature* (Princeton, NJ: Princeton University Press, 1993), 47–64.
6. Marshall McLuhan, *Understanding Media: The Extensions of Man*, ed. W. Terrance Gordon (Corte Madera, CA: Gingko Press, 2003), 5.
7. See Shen Xinlin, *Li Yu xinlun* (Suzhou: Suzhou daxue chubanshe, 1997), 189–203.
8. See Marshall McLuhan, *Understanding Media*, 63–70.
9. *Yijia yan chuji*, 3.
10. See, for example, Cynthia Brokaw and Kai-wing Chow, eds., *Printing and Book Culture in Late Imperial China* (Berkeley: University of California Press, 2005); Cynthia Brokaw, "Book History in Premodern China: The State of the Discipline I," *Book History* 10, no. 1 (2007): 253–290; Tobie Meyer-Fong, "The Printed World: Books, Publishing Culture, and Society in Late Imperial China," *The Journal of Asian Studies* 66, no. 3 (August 2007): 787–817.
11. See especially Robert E. Hegel, *Reading Illustrated Fiction in Late Imperial China* (Stanford, CA: Stanford University Press, 1998); Yuming He, *Home and the World: Editing the "Glorious Ming" in Woodblock-Printed Books of the Sixteenth and Seventeenth Centuries* (Cambridge, MA: Harvard University Asia Center, 2013); Paize Keulemans, *Sound Rising from the Paper: Nineteenth-Century Martial Arts Fiction and the Chinese Acoustic Imagination* (Cambridge, MA: Harvard University Asia Center, 2014); Suyoung Son, *Writing for Print: Publishing and the Making of Textual Authority in Late Imperial China* (Cambridge, MA: Harvard University Asia Center, 2018).
12. See, for instance, Elizabeth Eisenstein, *The Printing Press as an Agent of Change: Communications and Cultural Transformations in Early-Modern Europe* (London: Cambridge University Press, 1979); Kai-wing Chow, *Publishing, Culture, and Power in Early Modern China* (Stanford, CA: Stanford University Press, 2007), 1.
13. Francesca Bray, *Technology, Gender and History in Imperial China: Great Transformations Reconsidered* (London: Routledge, 2013), 5.
14. Christopher M. B. Nugent, "Literary Media: Writing and Orality," in *The Oxford Handbook of Classical Chinese Literature*, ed. Wiebke Denecke, Wai-yee Li, and Xiaofei Tian (Oxford: Oxford University Press, 2017), 46–60; Christopher M. B. Nugent, "Manuscript Culture," in *The Oxford Handbook*, 61–75.
15. See the essays in Judith T. Zeitlin, Lydia H. Liu, and Ellen Widmer, eds., *Writing and Materiality in China: Essays in Honor of Patrick Hanan* (Cambridge, MA: Harvard University Asia Center, 2003).
16. Patrick Hanan, *Invention*, 199.
17. The plays are: *Dongting hu Liu Yi chuan shu* 洞庭湖柳毅傳書 and *Shamen dao Zhangsheng zhuhai* 沙門島張生煮海. See Huang Lizhen, *Li Yu yanjiu* (Taipei: Chun wenxue chubanshe, 1974), 157. For an English translation of the first, see David Hawkes, trans., *Liu Yi and the Dragon Princess: A Thirteenth-Century Zaju Play by Shang Zhongxian* (Hong Kong: The Chinese University of Hong Kong, 2003). For the second, see Allen A. Zimmerman, trans., "Scholar Zhang Boils the Sea," in *The Columbia*

Anthology of Yuan Drama, ed. C. T. Hsia et al. (New York: Columbia University Press, 2014), 371–402.

18. As *shen* came to indicate "mirage" over time, it was paired with the term *haishi* 海市 (sea market). An early description appears in the account of the Feng and Shan sacrifices in the *Records of the Grand Historian* (*Shiji* 28). Burton Watson, trans., Sima Qian, *Records of the Grand Historian of China* (New York: Columbia University Press, 1961), 2:26. By the Jin dynasty (266–420), this "sea market" was clearly defined: see Fu Chen, *Sanqi lüeji*, in Chen Menglei and Jiang Tingxi, eds., *Gujin tushu jicheng* (Shanghai: Zhonghua shuju, 1934), 527:38b.

19. The Royal Lord of the East, the directional counterpart to the Queen Mother of the West, was the "Director of Destinies" (Siming 司命), which explains his matchmaking role here. See Paul W. Kroll, "A Poetry Debate of the Perfected Highest Clarity," *Journal of the American Oriental Society* 132, no. 4 (October–December 2012): 579n6.

20. *Chuanqi shizhong*, 8:3682.

21. David L. Rolston, *Traditional Chinese Fiction*, 177, 179.

22. For the relationship between the two worlds in this play, see Lee Chia-lian, "Liangge shijie de yuhe—chongdu Li Yu *Shenzhong lou*," *Donghai Zhongwen xuekan* 32 (December 2016): 81–124.

23. Patrick Hanan, *Invention*, chap. 4.

24. See, for example, Huang Guoquan, *Yasu zhi jian: Li Yu de wenhua renge yu wenxue sixiang yanjiu* (Beijing: Zhongguo shehui kexue chubanshe, 2004). Li Yu frequently uses the terms *ya* and *su*; he talks about the middle ground between *fengliu* and *daoxue* in "Heying lou," which features two characters who adhere to each extreme described as a "Mr. *Daoxue*" and a "Mr. *Fengliu*." *Shi'er lou*, 7.

25. See introductions in Robert E. Hegel, trans., Aina the Layman, *Idle Talk Under the Bean Arbor* (Seattle: University of Washington Press, 2017); Qiancheng Li and Robert E. Hegel, trans., Master of Silent Whistle Studio, *Further Adventures on the Journey to the West* (Seattle: University of Washington Press, 2020); Judith T. Zeitlin, *Historian of the Strange: Pu Songling and the Chinese Classical Tale* (Stanford, CA: Stanford University Press, 1993).

26. For a general introduction in English to Li Yu's life and works, see Patrick Hanan, *Invention*; Nathan K. Mao and Cunren Liu, *Li Yü* (Boston: Twayne Publishers, 1977). For Li Yu in historical context, see Chun-shu Chang and Shelley Hsueh-lun Chang, *Crisis and Transformation in Seventeenth-Century China: Society, Culture, and Modernity in Li Yü's World* (Ann Arbor: University of Michigan Press, 1992). There are many critical biographies in Chinese: see especially Sun Kaidi, "Li Liweng yu *Shi'er lou*," *Guoxue jikan* 9, no. 43 (1935): 379–441; Huang Lizhen, *Li Yu* (Taibei: Guojia chubanshe, 1982); Shen Xinlin, *Li Yu pingzhuan* (Nanjing: Nanjing shifan daxue chubanshe, 1998). For a chronological account, see Shan Jinheng, "Li Yu nianpu," in *LYQJ* 19:1–130.

27. Shan Jinheng, "Li Yu nianpu," 15.

28. See *Yijia yan chuji*, 113–114.
29. Tobie S. Meyer-Fong, *Building Culture in Early Qing Yangzhou* (Stanford, CA: Stanford University Press, 2003), 102.
30. Li Yu moved to Hangzhou around 1651. For a synopsis of evidence regarding his moves among Lanxi, Hangzhou, and Nanjing after the fall of the Ming, see Patrick Hanan, *Invention*, 216n37; Chun-shu Chang and Shelley Hsueh-lun Chang, *Crisis and Transformation*, 115n78; Huang Qiang, *Li Yu yanjiu* (Hangzhou: Zhejiang guji chubanshe, 1996), 262–272.
31. For a translation, see Stephen Roddy and Ying Wang, trans., Li Yu, *The Fragrant Companions: A Play about Love between Women* (New York: Columbia University Press, 2022).
32. For a divergent interpretation, see Patrick Hanan, *Invention*, 15–16.
33. *Yijia yan chuji*, 33.
34. Stephen Owen, *The End of the Chinese "Middle Ages": Essays in Mid-Tang Literary Culture* (Stanford, CA: Stanford University Press, 1996), 33; Xiaoshan Yang, *Metamorphosis of the Private Sphere: Gardens and Objects in Tang-Song Poetry* (Cambridge, MA: Harvard University Asia Center, 2003), 21–36.
35. *Yijia yan chuji*, 33.
36. In comparing his mark on the mountain to the name and date inscribed on objects, Li Yu is participating in a culture of marking objects that was new in the Ming dynasty. As calligraphy and painting had long been tightly bound up with the signature of their author, so now were objects marked with a signature that would guarantee their quality and value. See Craig Clunas, *Empire of Great Brightness: Visual and Material Cultures of Ming China* (Honolulu: University of Hawai'i Press, 2007), 22, 50–51.
37. See Judith T. Zeitlin, "Disappearing Verses: Writing on Walls and Anxieties of Loss in Late Imperial China," in *Writing and Materiality in China: Essays in Honor of Patrick Hanan*, ed. Judith T. Zeitlin, Lydia H. Liu, and Ellen Widmer (Cambridge, MA: Harvard University Asia Center, 2003), 73–79.
38. Cynthia Brokaw, *Commerce in Culture: The Sibao Book Trade in the Qing and Republican Periods* (Cambridge, MA: Harvard University Asia Center, 2007), 9–10 and 10n26. Brokaw draws these estimates from the work of Zhang Xiumin, *Zhongguo yinshua shi* (Shanghai: Shanghai renmin chubanshe, 1989), 343–348, 365–372, 550–551, and 553–554.
39. See Lucille Chia, *Printing for Profit: The Commercial Publishers of Jianyang, Fujian (11th–17th centuries)* (Cambridge, MA: Harvard University Asia Center, 2002), 247–249.
40. For Li Yu's literary production during this period, see Patrick Hanan, *Invention*, 15–23. For an introduction to his short stories and plays, see Patrick Hanan, *Invention*, 76–110, 138–84; Mao and Liu, *Li Yü*, 31–112. For detailed analysis of four of his plays, see Eric Henry, *Chinese Amusements: The Lively Plays of Li Yü* (Hamden, CT: Archon Books, 1980).

41. See Patricia Sieber, *Theaters of Desire: Authors, Readers, and the Reproduction of Chinese Song-Drama, 1300–2000* (New York: Palgrave, 2003), xvi.
42. There has long been speculation that Li Yu wrote more than ten plays, based on his claim in *Xianqing ouji* to have the "eight earlier and later plays" in print and the "eight inner and outer plays" written but not yet printed (514). This account of sixteen plays was echoed in the preface to his ninth play, *Be Careful About Love* (*Shen luanjiao* 慎鸞交), by Guo Chuanfang, as that play would have been first of the second eight. This plan was likely never realized: in 1674, Li Yu was selling his plays in three sets: "earlier four," "later four," and "inner two." The "inner two" do feature a distinctive style of illustration—rectangular with a decorative border—that sets them apart from his earlier plays (see the appendix). Nevertheless, elsewhere in *Xianqing ouji* he refers to his "ten plays" (526), and in 1678, his plays were still known collectively as *Liweng shizhong*, as is mentioned in Huang Zhouxing's "Zhiqu zhiyu 製曲枝語," appended to *Rentian le*. Huang Zhouxing, *Xiaweitang Rentian le chuanqi*, GBXQCK, ser. 3, box 12, vols. 7–8 (Beijing: Wenxue guji kanxingshe, 1957), 7:3b; cited in Patrick Hanan, *Invention*, 220n74. Huang Qiang is convinced, following Sun Kaidi's suggestion, that Li Yu wrote but did not publish these plays. Huang Qiang, *Li Yu yanjiu*, 322–330. Without further evidence, I do not think Li Yu's comments warrant this conclusion, as he often spoke of or advertised forthcoming works that he seems to have never written.
43. "Yu Chen Ruixian 與陳藎仙," in *Yijia yan chuji*, 58.
44. Huang Qiang, "*Rou putuan* zuozhe yu xunian zai kaobian," *Jiangnan daxue xuebao* 18, no. 1 (2019): 74–83, esp. 75–79.
45. See Zhang's biography in *Qingshi liezhuan*, ed. Guoshiguan (Taipei: Taiwan Zhonghua shuju, 1983), 10:79:63b. First noted in Sun Kaidi, "Li Liweng yu Shi'er lou," 414–415. Some have attributed the preface to the first edition to Zhang Jinyan, based on a seal that reads "Leading the Army at Mount Huayang" (*Zhang Huayang bing* 掌華陽兵). See Ding Xigen, "Jiaodian houji," in *Wusheng xi* (Beijing: Renmin wenxue chubanshe, 1989), 212–213, 219–220. It is possible that further incriminating evidence was in the now-lost second collection.
46. Many literati opposed this change, which required less rhetorical competence and classical training. The Kangxi emperor restored the eight-legged essay and emphasis on the classics in 1667. See Benjamin A. Elman, *A Cultural History of Civil Examinations in Late Imperial China* (Berkeley: University of California Press, 2000), 530–533.
47. Cited in Wang Dingyong and Chen Anmei, "Riben Zunjingge wenku cang *Zengding Liweng lungu* de wenxian jiazhi," *Wenxian* 4 (July 2017): 169.
48. Patrick Hanan translates it as *Casual Expressions of Idle Thoughts* in *Invention*.
49. Andrew Plaks, "Terminology and Central Concepts," in *How to Read the Chinese Novel*, ed. David L. Rolston (Princeton, NJ: Princeton University Press, 1990), 121.
50. *Xianqing ouji*, 543.

51. For a reprint of the original, see Wang Gai, Wang Shi, and Wang Nie, *Jieziyuan huazhuan*, ed. Shang Zuowen, Shen Leping, and Qian Weiqiang, 10 vols. (Shanghai: Shanghai shuhua chubanshe, 2012). For a translation, see Mai-mai Sze, trans., Wang Gai, *The Mustard Seed Garden Manual of Painting: Chieh Tzǔ Yüan Hua Chuan, 1679–1701* (Princeton, NJ: Princeton University Press, 1992).
52. Patrick Hanan, *Invention*, 195.
53. *Xianqing ouji*, 600.
54. Craig Clunas, *Chinese Furniture* (London: Bamboo Publishing, 1988); Francesca Bray, *Technology and Gender: Fabrics of Power in Late Imperial China* (Berkeley: University of California Press, 1997), 59–90; Dorothy Ko, *Cinderella's Sisters: A Revisionist History of Footbinding* (Berkeley: University of California Press, 2005), 152–156; Susan E. Wright, "Chinese Decorated Letter Paper," in *A History of Chinese Letters and Epistolary Culture*, ed. Antje Richter (Leiden: Brill, 2015), 97–134; Jonathan Hay, *Sensuous Surfaces: The Decorative Object in Early Modern China* (Honolulu: University of Hawai'i Press, 2010), discussed throughout, see especially 23, 306–307.
55. *Yijia yan, erji*, 12:11a.

1. CULTURAL ENTREPRENEURSHIP AND WOODBLOCK PRINT

1. *Yijia yan, erji*, 7:9a–b.
2. For a detailed study of this process, see chapters 1 and 2 in Joseph McDermott, *A Social History of the Chinese Book: Books and Literati Culture in Late Imperial China* (Hong Kong: Hong Kong University Press, 2006).
3. See, for example, Yu Huai 余懷, "Yu Gong Xiaosheng sandu 與龔孝升三牘," in *Chidu*, 669–670.
4. In her study of the apparent rapid rise and sharp decline of commercial publishing between the Ming and the Qing in Nanjing, Lucille Chia has suggested that Nanjing publishers did cater to lower end of the market as well, but without attaching their names to the publications. Lucille Chia, "Of Three Mountains Street: The Commercial Publishers of Ming Nanjing," in *Printing and Book Culture in Late Imperial China*, ed. Cynthia J. Brokaw and Kai-wing Chow (Berkeley: University of California Press, 2005), 140–141. For a study of the new reading publics of the late Ming, see Anne E. McLaren, "Constructing New Reading Publics in Late Ming China," in *Printing and Book Culture*, 152–183.
5. See the appendix and Huang Qiang, *Li Yu yanjiu* (Hangzhou: Zhejiang guji chubanshe, 1996), 295–302; Huang Qiang, "Li Yu wei Jinling Yishengtang shufang zhuren kaobian—yu 'Li Yu yu Yishengtang, Jieziyuan shufang guanxi kaobian' yiwen zuozhe kaobian," *Chongqing shifan daxue xuebao*, no. 5 (2012): 5–10.
6. Huang Guoquan, *Yasu zhi jian: Li Yu de wenhua renge yu wenxue sixiang yanjiu* (Beijing: Zhongguo shehui kexue chubanshe, 2004), 46–47.

7. For an example of the former practice, see Wen Gehong, *Qingdai qianqi tongsu xiaoshuo kanke kaolun* (Nanchang: Jiangxi renmin chubanshe, 2008), 326. For arguments that government or literati publications often served commercial ends as well, see Lucille Chia, "Of Three Mountains Street," 120; Cynthia Brokaw, "On the History of the Book in China," in *Printing and Book Culture*, 17. For more on Wang Qi, see Ellen Widmer, "The Huanduzhai of Hangzhou and Suzhou: A Study in Seventeenth-Century Publishing," *HJAS* 56, no. 1 (June 1996): 77–122.
8. Wen Gehong, *Qingdai qianqi tongsu xiaoshuo*, 427.
9. Wang Qi and Xu Shijun, *Chidu xinyu guangbian*, 1668 edition, 24 vol. (Microfilm, Cambridge, MA: General Microfilm Co., ca. 1970), 18:8a, cited and trans. in Ellen Widmer, "Huanduzhai," 89.
10. For more on advertising in book production of the Ming and early Qing, see Yuming He, *Home and the World: Editing the "Glorious Ming" in Woodblock-Printed Books of the Sixteenth and Seventeenth Centuries* (Cambridge, MA: Harvard University Asia Center, 2013); Suyoung Son, *Writing for Print: Publishing and the Making of Textual Authority in Late Imperial China* (Cambridge, MA: Harvard University Asia Center, 2018).
11. See Kai-wing Chow, *Publishing, Culture, and Power in Early Modern China* (Stanford, CA: Stanford University Press, 2007), 1–3.
12. See Zheng Yuanxun's 鄭元勳 preface to Ji Cheng's *Yuanye*, where print divides the body into parts so that it can reach everywhere in the land. In Ji Cheng, *Yuanye zhushi*, ed. Chen Zhi (Beijing: Zhongguo jianzhu gongye chubanshe, 1981), 32.
13. On the range of new organizational systems in late Ming publications, see Uluğ Kuzuoğlu, "Indexing Systems," in *Literary Information in China: A History*, ed. Jack W. Chen et al. (New York: Columbia University Press, 2021), 25–35.
14. See, generally, Timothy Brook, *The Confusions of Pleasure: Commerce and Culture in Ming China* (Berkeley: University of California Press, 1999).
15. See James Cahill, *The Painter's Practice* (New York: Columbia University Press, 1994); Jonathan Hay, *Shitao: Painting and Modernity in Early Qing China* (New York: Cambridge University Press, 2001).
16. See, for example, Yulian Wu, *Luxurious Networks: Salt Merchants, Status, and Statecraft in Eighteenth-Century China* (Stanford, CA: Stanford University Press, 2017).
17. Cynthia Brokaw, "Commercial Publishing in Late Imperial China: The Zou and Ma Family Businesses of Sibao, Fujian," *LIC* 16, no. 1 (June 1996): 49–92, 64.
18. Kai-wing Chow, *Publishing, Culture, and Power*, chap. 3.
19. Keming Yang, *Entrepreneurship in China* (Abingdon: Ashgate, 2012), 8.
20. *Xianqing ouji*, 637, 722. Song Danxian 宋澹仙 comments that Li Yu's warming chair should be named after him as well: "Liweng Warming Chair" (631).
21. Li Yu's interior design proposals were part of the period's exploration of the aesthetic possibilities of the "literal realization of metaphor." See Judith T. Zeitlin, *Historian of the Strange: Pu Songling and the Chinese Classical Tale* (Stanford, CA: Stanford University Press, 1993), 199.

22. On the tradition of ghostpainting, see James Cahill, *The Painter's Practice*, 113–148; Wen Fong, "The Problem of Forgeries in Chinese Painting Part One," *Artibus Asiae* 25, no. 2/3 (1962): 95–119, 121–140.
23. Greenbaum defines Chen Jiru's celebrity by his collaboration in the commodification of a self that circulates to its audience, as well as his independence from earlier forms of fame (such as aristocracy). Jamie Greenbaum, *Chen Jiru (1558–1639): The Background to, Development and Subsequent Uses of Literary Personae* (Leiden: Brill, 2007), xxviii–xxix, n1, n4.
24. *Xianqing ouji*, 658.
25. Jamie Greenbaum, *Chen Jiru*, 143, 195–202.
26. From "Wu dai renhao" 物帶人號 in "Wanju" 玩具, Shen Defu, *Wanli yehuo bian* (Beijing: Zhonghua shuju, 1959), 663–664. Greenbaum suggests that Chen may not have been involved in the production of such goods, but even if the practice of adding his name to products were more widespread, the language here suggests that he started the trend himself. Jamie Greenbaum, *Chen Jiru*, xxxiv, 203.
27. Qian Qianyi, *Liechao shiji xiaozhuan* (Shanghai: Gudian wenxue chubanshe, 1957), *xia* 637. Cited in Jamie Greenbaum, *Chen Jiru*, 203.
28. See Judith T. Zeitlin, *Historian*, 6. Qianshen Bai, *Fu Shan's World: The Transformation of Chinese Calligraphy in the Seventeenth Century* (Cambridge, MA: Harvard University Asia Center, 2003), 13.
29. For an introduction to this play, see Patrick Hanan, *The Invention of Li Yu* (Cambridge, MA: Harvard University Press, 1988), 50–55, 69–75; S. E. Kile, "A Much-Desired Match: Playwriting, Stagecraft, and Entrepreneurship," in *How to Read Chinese Drama*, ed. Patricia Sieber and Regina Llamas (New York: Columbia University Press, 2022), 257–284. Some of my observations here are also included in that essay (275, 279–281).
30. All four of the play's protagonists were historical late-Ming artists. While acquaintances, they did not marry (though Li Yu's play led many to assume that they had). See Chen Yinke, *Liu Rushi biezhuan* (Shanghai: Shanghai guji chubanshe, 1980), 371. The two historical women were often considered together, as for instance in Wang Duan's 汪端 (1793–1839) poem "At Zhiguo Temple, Mourning the Tomb of the Ming Woman Yang Yunyou" 智果寺弔明女士楊雲友墓. See Kang-i Sun Chang, Haun Saussy, and Charles Kwong, eds., *Women Writers of Traditional China: An Anthology of Poetry and Criticism* (Stanford, CA: Stanford University Press, 1999), 578–579. The preface to this play was written by a well-educated woman poet and painter, Huang Yuanjie. For more on her, see Dorothy Ko, *Teachers of the Inner Chambers: Women and Culture in Seventeenth-Century China* (Stanford, CA: Stanford University Press, 1994), 117–123.
31. The historical Dong Qichang was known to have depended on other painters to keep up with demand: see Wen Fong, "The Problem of Forgeries in Chinese Painting Part One," 101n25.
32. *Yizhong yuan*, 327–328.

33. Richard Mather, trans., Liu I-ch'ing, *Shih-shuo Hsin-yü: A New Account of Tales of the World* (Ann Arbor: University of Michigan Press, 2002), 330.
34. Li Yu has been characterized as a *shanren* since the Qing. See, for example, Huang Guoquan, who posits that Li Yu shifted from literatus to disparaged "literati-merchant sycophant" or "mountain man" during his Nanjing years. Huang Guoquan, *Yasu zhi jian*, 10. Wai-yee Li has suggested that these terms convey both participation in and transcendence of "the social relations of life . . . through the connoisseurly enjoyment of things." Wai-yee Li, "The Collector, the Connoisseur, and Late-Ming Sensibility," *T'oung Pao*, Second Series 81, no. 4/5 (1995): 284.
35. *Yizhong yuan*, 37.
36. Richard Mather, trans., Liu I-ch'ing, *Shih-shuo Hsin-yü*, 149.
37. Jing Shen, *Playwrights and Literary Games in Seventeenth-Century China: Plays by Tang Xianzu, Mei Dingzuo, Wu Bing, Li Yu, and Kong Shangren* (Plymouth, MA: Lexington Books, 2010), 123–150.
38. Wu Bing, *Lü mudan chuanqi*, GBXQCK, ser. 3, box 2, vol. 18 (Beijing: Wenxue guji kanxingshe, 1957), *xia* 25b.
39. For the distinctiveness of Li Yu's approach to forgery, see Wai-yee Li, *The Promise and Peril of Things: Literature and Material Culture in Late Imperial China* (New York: Columbia University Press, 2022), 209.
40. *Chuanqi shizhong*, 9:3931.
41. *Yizhong yuan*, 41.
42. For this trope, see Robert Hymes, "Truth, Falsity, and Pretense in Song China: An Approach through the Anecdotes of Hong Mai," *Chūgoku shigaku* 15, no. 1 (2005): 1–26.
43. Wang Gai, *Jieziyuan huazhuan*, 5 vols., early Qing edition, 1679, "Preface," 2a.
44. For this genre, see J. P. Park, *Art by the Book: Painting Manuals and the Leisure Life in Late Ming China* (Seattle: University of Washington Press, 2012).
45. See Craig Clunas, *Superfluous Things: Material Culture and Social Status in Early Modern China* (Honolulu: University of Hawai'i Press, 1991).
46. *Xianqing ouji*, 607.
47. *Xianqing ouji*, 607.
48. *Xianqing ouji*, 607.
49. *Xianqing ouji*, 609.
50. Xiaolin Duan, "The Ten Views of West Lake," in *Visual and Material Cultures in Middle Period China*, ed. Patricia Buckley Ebrey and Susan Shih-Shan Huang (Leiden: Brill, 2017), 151–190.
51. The Old Man of West Lake had already in the Southern Song dynasty referred to the scenery at West Lake as "fan paintings," though referring to round fans rather than folding fans. Xihu laoren, *Xihu laoren Fansheng lu*, ca. 1250, in *Dongjing menghua lu wai sizhong*, 111–128 (Shanghai: Zhonghua shuju, 1962), 122–123. Cited in Hui-shu Lee, *Exquisite Moments: West Lake and Southern Song Art* (New York: China Institute Gallery, 2001), 19.

52. We can situate this play with paintings alongside Pu Songling's 蒲松齡 (1640–1715) contemporary experiments with the borders between paintings and the physical world. See Judith T. Zeitlin, *Historian*, 183–193. Li Yu is also participating in a contemporary interest in illusion and role reversal epitomized in Zhang Dai's 張岱 (1597–1684) writing. See Wai-yee Li, *Enchantment and Disenchantment: Love and Illusion in Chinese Literature* (Princeton, NJ: Princeton University Press, 1993), 48–49.
53. See, for example, Patrick Hanan, *Invention*, 21.
54. See, for example, the copy held in the Shandong Provincial Library. On installment printing in this period, see Suyoung Son, *Writing for Print*, chap. 4.
55. On the lack of legal protection for intellectual property in imperial China, see William P. Alford, *To Steal a Book Is an Elegant Offense: Intellectual Property Law in Chinese Civilization* (Stanford, CA: Stanford University Press, 1995).
56. "Yu Zhao Shengbo wenxue 與趙聲伯文學," *Yijia yan chuji*, 52. For Hanan's translation of the latter part of this passage, see Patrick Hanan, *Invention*, 12–13.
57. *Xianqing ouji*, 646. On decorated letter paper in this period, see Susan E. Wright, "Chinese Decorated Letter Paper," in *A History of Chinese Letters and Epistolary Culture*, ed. Antje Richter (Leiden: Brill, 2015), 97–134.
58. *Xianqing ouji*, 645.
59. *Xianqing ouji*, 646. For a translation of the latter part of this passage, see Hanan, *Invention*, 14.
60. The Wolf of Zhongshan refers to a fable, set in the Spring and Autumn period, about a wolf who tried to eat a Mohist scholar who had rescued him from hunters.
61. *Xianqing ouji*, 646, trans. in Patrick Hanan, *Invention*, 14–15.
62. Li Yu may have published a second collection of contemporary letters (*erzheng*), but no copies are extant. A publisher's note on *Gujin chidu daquan* indicates that a second collection of letters was completed and was about to be published by the time that text was completed (see Peking University copy). Huang Qiang suggests that Li Yu was collecting letters for a second collection, based on requested letters that do not appear in the first collection. Huang Qiang, *Li Yu yanjiu*, 424–425. Li Yu may also have been involved with the publication of a historical letter collection that included letters from the Ming dynasty and earlier, called *Gujin chidu daquan*. Liang Yu has argued that Li Yu was working on the collection with his son-in-law, Shen Xinyou, who was the "Master of Baoqingge" (抱青閣主人) referred to on the title page. Liang Yu, "Liweng zhushu sanzhong kaoshu," MA thesis, Yangzhou, Yangzhou University, 2013, 23–30. David Pattinson has proposed that this work was published in the 1660s. David Pattinson, "The Market for Letter Collections in Seventeenth-Century China," *Chinese Literature: Essays, Articles, Reviews* 28 (2006): 134.
63. *Yanshi jiacang chidu* (Shanghai: Shanghai kexue jishu wenxian chubanshe, 2006), 5:250–261.
64. David Pattinson, "Market," 137.

65. For excerpts from some of these anthologies, see Xie Zhengguang and She Rufeng, *Qingchu ren xuan Qingchu shi huikao* (Nanjing: Nanjing daxue chubanshe, 1998).
66. Ellen Widmer, "Huanduzhai," 89.
67. Tobie S. Meyer-Fong, *Building Culture in Early Qing Yangzhou* (Stanford, CA: Stanford University Press, 2003), 105.
68. "Fu Wang Zhecun 復王柘邨" in Zhang Chao, ed., *Chidu oucun*, 1780, 11:7b.
69. On collaborative editing projects during this period, see Suyoung Son, *Writing for Print*, 20–42.
70. *Chidu*, 503.
71. See Ellen Widmer, "Huanduzhai," 84.
72. Huang Rong and Wang Weihan, eds., *Chidu lanyan, fanli*, item 2, trans. and cited in David Pattinson, "The Chidu in Late Ming and Early Qing China," PhD diss., Australia National University, 1998, 72. This passage also suggests that Wang Qi's collections did not render Li Yu's obsolete: two of Zhou's installments are grouped together for their Nanjing publication, whereas Wang Qi's are referred to collectively as a counterpart to Li Yu's. This categorization may be helpful in understanding why Li Yu never came out with a second installment. In 1662, shortly after the publication of *Letters*, Li Yu left Hangzhou and moved to Nanjing, which, according to these comments, was already associated with Zhou's collections. It is possible, then, that Li Yu moved on to new endeavors because he did not want to compete with a patron, Zhou Lianggong.
73. For important studies of the letter collections of this period, see Ellen Widmer, "Huanduzhai," 104–105; David Pattinson, "Market," 127; David Pattinson, "Chidu," 56, 59–61. For a new reading public comprising failed examination candidates, see Ōki Yasushi, *Mingmo Jiangnan de chuban wenhua*, trans. Zhou Baoxiong (Shanghai: Shanghai guji chubanshe, 2014), chap. 3.
74. Qian Qianyi, *ECCP* 148–150; Wang Siren, *DMB* 1420–1425; Zhang Fengyi, *DMB* 63–64; Zhong Xing, *DMB* 408–409; Tan Yuanchun, *DMB* 1246–1248; Zhang Pu (and Zhang Cai), *ECCP* 52–53; Chen Zilong, *ECCP* 102–103.
75. *Chidu*, 503.
76. Chih-p'ing Chou, *Yüan Hung-tao and the Kung-an School* (Cambridge: Cambridge University Press, 1988), 27.
77. *Chidu*, 694–695.
78. *Chidu*, 503.
79. Shen did not divide letters into multiple sections as Li Yu would, but he did include the most common types of letters near the beginning of the collection. See David Pattinson, "Market," 133–134. Pattinson suggests that Wang Qi's organization of letter collections was informed by Li Yu's organizing principle, which he adapted to avoid alienating his better educated customers.
80. On these alternate ideas of reading, especially *kan*, see Anne E. McLaren, "Constructing New Reading Publics in Late Ming China."

81. *Chidu*, 504.
82. Compare this with the index of medical prescriptions developed by the publisher Wang Ang 汪昂 (1615–1694). See Nathan Sivin, *Traditional Medicine in Contemporary China* (Ann Arbor: University of Michigan Press, 1987), 197; Ellen Widmer, "Huanduzhai," 114–115.
83. In this version, the date of Wu Weiye's preface has been changed from 1660 to 1684 by altering just three characters (Shunzhi reign period *geng* 順治庚 to Kangxi reign period *jia* 康熙甲). This is curious because by 1684 Wu Weiye had been dead for twelve years.
84. Li Yu, ed., *Xinzeng zizhi xinshu*, Jieziyuan edition, *Zizhi xinshu chuji* preface dated 1663, held at Peking University Library, 13a.
85. Between this collection of administrative documents and the second collection published five years later, he collected documents from more than 180 current and former officials. There is a record of Li Yu having an ongoing relationship with only about a quarter of these men, while the rest seem to have been associated with him only through their submission of documents for publication. The majority of them attained the *jinshi* degree under the Qing. Only three were Ming officials who did not serve under the Qing.
86. Preface to Li Yu, ed. *Zizhi xinshu erji* (1667), trans. and cited in Patrick Hanan, *Invention*, 24.
87. That collection contained contributions by more than 150 individuals, many of whom had also contributed to his *Letters*. Two-thirds of these were people with no other relationship to Li Yu, while the remaining third were longtime friends. Ming loyalists are better represented here (about twenty) than in the previous collections.

2. BUILDING WITH WORDS

1. For comparisons among fiction, drama, and historical narrative in the Ming, see David L. Rolston, *Traditional Chinese Fiction and Fiction Commentary: Reading and Writing Between the Lines* (Stanford, CA: Stanford University Press, 1997), 131–165. For those among fiction, drama, and the human condition, see Patricia Sieber, *Theaters of Desire: Authors, Readers, and the Reproduction of Chinese Song-Drama, 1300–2000* (Basingstoke: Palgrave, 2003), 123–161.
2. Ellen Widmer, *The Margins of Utopia: Shui-hu hou-chuan and the Literature of Ming Loyalism* (Cambridge, MA: Harvard University Press, 1987), chap. 3; Wilt L. Idema, "Drama after the Conquest: An Introduction," in *Trauma and Transcendence in Early Qing Literature*, ed. Wilt L. Idema, Wai-yee Li, and Ellen Widmer (Cambridge, MA: Harvard University Asia Center, 2006), 375–386. For an account that identifies the late Ming as "a time of relative individualism," when "writers generalized less than they would after the Ming collapse," see Robert E. Hegel, *The*

Novel in Seventeenth-Century China (New York: Columbia University Press, 1981), 52, and throughout.
3. See Tina Lu, "The Literary Culture of the Late Ming (1573–1644)," in *The Cambridge History of Chinese Literature* (Cambridge: Cambridge University Press, 2010), 83.
4. For a historical approach attentive to the materiality of poetry collections, see Tobie S. Meyer-Fong, *Building Culture in Early Qing Yangzhou* (Stanford, CA: Stanford University Press, 2003). For a literary approach that focuses on poetic tropes and self-expression, see Wai-yee Li, "Introduction," in *Trauma and Transcendence*, 1–72.
5. *Yijia yan chuji*, 70.
6. Wilt L. Idema, "Drama after the Conquest," 379.
7. The reference is to two men renowned for their devotion to study in poverty. Kuang Heng 匡衡 was a Western Han statesman. When he was young, his family could not afford candles, so he would bore a hole in the wall to borrow light from a neighbor. Sun Kang 孫康 was an imperial censor in the Jin dynasty who devised a way to read by the moonlight reflected off of snow.
8. Yuan Jun 袁峻, an official during the Liang dynasty, was orphaned when young, and he had to copy books by hand because he could not afford them. See his biography in *Liangshu*, Yao Silian, 3 vols. (Beijing: Zhonghua shuju, 1973), 3:688–689.
9. *Yijia yan chuji*, 113.
10. "Bian Shao zhuan" 邊韶傳, in *Hou Hanshu*, Fan Ye (Beijing: Zhonghua shuju, 1965), 9:2623.
11. Fu Sheng managed to preserve the text by hiding the book in the wall of his home. In the early Han, he had the only preserved copy (see *Shiji* 121). Wang Can (177–217) was able to memorize texts after reading them just once. See "Wang Can zhuan" 王粲傳 in *Sanguo zhi*, Chen Shou, commentary by Pei Songzhi (Shanghai: Shangwu yinshuguan, 1944), 9:1a–1b.
12. *Yijia yan chuji*, 113.
13. Dong Sigao, *Lushan ji* (Shanghai: Shangwu yinshuguan, 1935), 3:19.
14. *Yizhong yuan*, 177.
15. *Yijia yan chuji*, 113.
16. See, for example, Shi Mining's (active ca. 1200) heptasyllabic poem, "Green Hill" (Qing shan 青山), which includes the line, "three cups of warm Tao Yuanming [365–427] wine, one clear Xi Kang [ca. 223–ca. 262] tune on the *qin*" 三杯暖熱淵明酒 / 一曲淒清叔夜琴. Shi Mining, *Youlin yigao* (Beijing: Zhongguo shudian, 1994), 1a.
17. Another reference to the Qin emperor's burning of the books.
18. *Yijia yan chuji*, 113.
19. See Richard B. Mather, trans., Liu I-ch'ing, *Shih-shuo Hsin-yü: A New Account of Tales of the World*, 2nd ed. (Ann Arbor: University of Michigan Press, 2002), 486.
20. See, for example, Guo Yingde, *Ming Qing chuanqi shi* (Beijing: Renmin wenxue chubanshe, 2011), 377–378.
21. *Xianqing ouji*, 527.

22. *Xianqing ouji*, 495. This notion of "common possession" can be traced to the Tianyun 天運 chapter of the *Zhuangzi*, which reads, "Fame is a common possession. One cannot arrogate it too much to oneself." Guo Qingfan, ed., *Zhuangzi jishi* (Beijing: Zhonghua shuju, 1961), 517. Wang Heng, in *Yulun pao*, writes, "In my opinion, only literature is the common possession of all under Heaven." See Wang Heng, *Yulun pao*, Sheng Ming zaju (Beijing: Zhongguo shudian, 2012), *chubian, xia*, 671. That line is spoken by a character based on the historical figure Pei Di 裴迪 (b. 716); according to Greenbaum, Wang was a friend of Chen Jiru's, and he based the character on Chen. Jamie Greenbaum, *Chen Jiru (1558–1639): The Background to Development and Subsequent Uses of Literary Personae* (Leiden: Brill, 2007), 184.
23. Although Li Yu catered to a broad audience with his accessible writing style, his plays are not considered part of popular culture. Another group of playwrights, now known as the "Suzhou playwrights," wrote plays that were more didactic than Li Yu's. Li Yu is usually grouped with the *fengliu* artists associated with *wenren* identity. See Wang Ay-ling, "Qingchu Jiang, Zhe diqu wenren 'fengliu juzuo' zhi shenmei zaojing yu qi wenhua yihan," in *Kongjian, diyu yu wenhua—Zhongguo wenhua kongjian de shuxie yu chanshi*, ed. Li Fengmao and Liu Yuanru (Taibei: Zhongyang yanjiu yuan Zhongguo wenzhe yanjiusuo, 2002), 91–210.
24. In his discussion of manuscript culture in middle period China, Christopher Nugent has noted that there *wenli* might mean the correction of perceived errors to the "meaning and order" (*wenli*) of a text. *Wenli* is not a language called "classical Chinese," but an understanding of the norms of expression in particular genres that might take precedent over the written words on a page. Christopher M. B. Nugent, "Manuscript Culture," in *The Oxford Handbook of Classical Chinese Literature*, ed. Wiebke Denecke, Wai-yee Li, and Xiaofei Tian (Oxford: Oxford University Press, 2017), 72.
25. Rivi Handler-Spitz, Pauline C. Lee, and Haun Saussy, ed. and trans., Li Zhi, *A Book to Burn and a Book to Keep (Hidden): Selected Writings of Li Zhi* (New York: Columbia University Press, 2016), 23.
26. For the discursive expansion of readership in the Ming, see Anne E. McLaren, "Constructing New Reading Publics in Late Ming China," in *Printing and Book Culture in Late Imperial China*, ed. Cynthia J. Brokaw and Kai-wing Chow (Berkeley: University of California Press, 2005), 160.
27. *Xianqing ouji*, 589. Hui Shi 惠施, quoted in *Zhuangzi*, is the locus classicus for the allusion in the middle of the paragraph to that which is so large it has no outside. Guo Qingfan, ed., *Zhuangzi jishi*, 1102.
28. *Xianqing ouji*, 589.
29. *Xianqing ouji*, 590.
30. This method of learning to read has some commonalities with the traditional method of memorizing works before learning characters. See Li Yu, "Character Recognition: A New Method of Learning to Read in Late Imperial China," *LIC* 33, no. 2 (2012): 1–39.

31. *Xianqing ouji*, 589.
32. This story is extant in the *Liancheng bi* collection. For a translation with commentary, see Patrick Hanan and Maria Franca Sibau, trans., Li Yu, "Tan Chuyu Declares His Love While Performing a Play; Liu Miaogu Dies to Preserve Her Chastity at the End of the Aria," *Renditions* 81–82 (Spring–Autumn 2014): 231–278. For a translation of the play, see Jing Shen and Robert E. Hegel, trans., Li Yu, *A Couple of Soles: A Comic Play from Seventeenth-Century China* (New York: Columbia University Press, 2020).
33. *Liancheng bi*, 36; *Chuanqi shizhong*, 10:4182.
34. *Liancheng bi*, 36.
35. Patrick Hanan, trans., Li Yu, *Silent Operas* (Hong Kong: Renditions, 1990), 170.
36. *Chuanqi shizhong*, 10:4182.
37. My use of this term differs from Sheldon Pollock's, who uses it to denote the elevation in status of a vernacular language that had previously been used only for documentary purposes. See Sheldon Pollock, *The Language of the Gods in the World of Men: Sanskrit, Culture, and Power in Premodern India* (Berkeley: University of California Press, 2006), 5.
38. *Chuanqi shizhong*, 10:4191–4192.
39. This passage alludes to a romantic couple who flew away with phoenixes. See Stephen H. West and Wilt L. Idema, trans., Wang Shifu, *The Story of the Western Wing* (Berkeley: University of California Press, 1995), 204n8.
40. *Xianqing ouji*, 526.
41. Robert Hymes, "Getting the Words Right: Speech, Vernacular Language, and Classical Language in Song Neo-Confucian 'Records of Words,'" *Journal of Song-Yuan Studies* 36 (2006): 46, 50; Shang Wei, "Writing and Speech: Rethinking the Issue of Vernaculars in Early Modern China," in *Rethinking East Asian Languages, Vernaculars, and Literacies, 1000–1919*, ed. Benjamin A. Elman (Leiden: Brill, 2015), 278.
42. *Xianqing ouji*, 590.
43. *Xianqing ouji*, 525.
44. See, for example, Wang Jide, *Wang Jide Qulü*, ed. Chen Duo and Ye Changhai (Changsha: Hunan renmin chubanshe, 1983), 166, 202.
45. *Xianqing ouji*, 507.
46. See Lu Eting, *Kunju yanchu shigao* (Shanghai: Shanghai wenyi chubanshe, 1980), 156.
47. See Yuan Zongdao, *Bai Su zhai leiji*, ed. Shi Zhecun (Shanghai: Shanghai zazhi gongsi, 1935), 21:271.
48. *Xianqing ouji*, 508.
49. See David L. Rolston, *Traditional Chinese Fiction*, 25–26.
50. Xiaofei Tian, *Beacon Fire and Shooting Star: The Literary Culture of the Liang (502–557)* (Cambridge, MA: Harvard University Asia Center, 2007), chap. 7. Xu Wei, an iconoclast whose conservatism has surprised some commentators, wrote adamantly against what he perceived as the barbaric influence on northern music. Xu

Wei, *Nanci xulu zhushi*, ed. Li Fubo and Xiong Chengyu (Beijing: Zhongguo xiju chubanshe, 1989), 24.
51. *Xianqing ouji*, 528–529.
52. Wai-yee Li, "Introduction," 44.
53. Wai-yee Li, "Introduction," 46–48.
54. *Xianqing ouji*, 524–525. Peng Jian was said to have lived for 800 years. Part of this passage is translated in Patrick Hanan, *The Invention of Li Yu* (Cambridge, MA: Harvard University Press, 1988), 36.
55. Judith T. Zeitlin, *Historian of the Strange: Pu Songling and the Chinese Classical Tale* (Stanford, CA: Stanford University Press, 1993), 166.
56. Zang Maoxun (1550–1620) wrote in the preface to his *Yuanqu xuan* of the difficulty of achieving a tight plot (*Yuanqu xuan, xu er*). Wang Jide, in his *Qulü*, likened the structure of a play to that of a painting: "Take the entire book (play) as the overall structure [*jianjia* 間架], each scene as a particular application of the brush, and the arias and dialogue as the white and vermilion colors." Qi Biaojia 祁彪佳 (1602–1645) went even further by prioritizing structure over aria composition: "Structure is the most difficult [element of playwriting], followed by arias and dialogue" (*Yuanshantang qupin* 遠山堂曲品). Finally, Ling Mengchu, in his *Tanqu zazha* 譚曲雜札, wrote: "A play's structure is also an important element, if it is not properly prepared, the whole thing will be loathsome." These examples are cited in Guo Yingde, *Ming Qing chuanqi shi* (Beijing: Renmin wenxue chubanshe, 2011), 288. Chen Duo points out that it is not until the Wanli period (1572–1620) that structure is described as a separate element from arias and dialogue. Li Yu, *Li Liweng quhua*, ed. Chen Duo (Changsha: Hunan renmin chubanshe, 1980), 8.
57. Andrew Plaks has used this structure-focused criticism to articulate "a poetics of the Chinese novel" (84). See Andrew Plaks, "Terminology and Central Concepts," in David L. Rolston, ed., *How to Read the Chinese Novel* (Princeton, NJ: Princeton University Press, 1990), 75–123.
58. Guo Yingde, *Ming Qing chuanqi shi*, 385. These statistics are based on the extant *chuanqi* delineated in Guo Yingde, *Ming Qing chuanqi zonglu* (Shijiazhuang: Hebei jiaoyu chubanshe, 1997).
59. For James Liu, Li Yu exemplifies "the technical concept of literature, according to which literature is a craft much like other crafts such as carpentry except that it uses language as its material instead of physical substances" and "construes the process of writing not as one of spontaneous expression but as one of deliberate composition." Although Liu identifies some earlier references to tools like the carpenter's square or the compass, he argues that Li Yu sees "the process of creation in Nature, that of artistic creation, and that of mechanical production" as "all basically the same." James J. Y. Liu, *Chinese Theories of Literature* (Chicago: University of Chicago Press, 1979), 88, 91. Using the same classificatory system, Chang and Chang have proposed that Li Yu combined the expressive and technical approaches. Chun-shu Chang and Shelley Hsueh-lun Chang, *Crisis and Transformation in*

Seventeenth-Century China: Society, Culture, and Modernity in Li Yü's World (Ann Arbor: University of Michigan Press, 1992), 189n83.
60. *Xianqing ouji*, 523.
61. David L. Rolston, *Traditional Chinese Fiction*, 12, 17–21.
62. For the influence of literary concepts on architecture, see Jiren Feng, *Chinese Architecture and Metaphor: Song Culture in the* Yingzao Fashi *Building Manual* (Honolulu: University of Hawai'i Press, 2012).
63. *Xianqing ouji*, 496.
64. Stephen Owen, *Readings in Chinese Literary Thought* (Cambridge, MA: Harvard University Asia Center, 1992), 255.
65. Stephen Owen, Chapter 28: "Wind and Bone," in *Readings in Chinese Literary Thought*, 219. Discussing wind and bone in *Wenxin diaolong*, Owen identifies wind as "the affective force of a literary work," after *qi*, which "is what gives the body motion and force." Bone, by contrast, "is an animate integrity in the text, something that holds it together, as the skeleton holds the body together, a structure that allows for motion" (220).
66. Xu Fuzuo, *Qulun* on Liang Chenyu's 梁辰魚 (1521–1594) *Huansha ji*. Cited in Guo Yingde, *Ming Qing chuanqi shi*, 288.
67. *Xianqing ouji*, 506.
68. See Andrew Plaks, "Terminology and Central Concepts," 85–87; David L. Rolston, *Traditional Chinese Fiction*, 257.
69. *Xianqing ouji*, 496.
70. Wang Jide, *Wang Jide* Qulü, 121–122.
71. *Xianqing ouji*, 503.
72. Li Zhi, "On Miscellaneous Matters" (*Zashuo* 雜說), trans. Pauline C. Lee, in Rivi Handler-Spitz, Pauline C. Lee, and Haun Saussy, ed. and trans., *A Book to Burn and A Book to Keep (Hidden): Selected Writings of Li Zhi*, 102–106.

3. FICTIONAL SPACE IN *TWELVE TOWERS*

1. *Xianqing ouji*, 603. I use the British spelling "storey" to differentiate a storey of a building from a fictional story.
2. Sun Kaidi, "Li Liweng yu *Shi'er lou*," *Guoxue jikan* 9, no. 43 (1935): 422.
3. See Hanan's introduction to his translation of six of the *Shi'er lou* stories (SEL3–6, 9, and 11): Patrick Hanan, trans., Li Yu, *A Tower for the Summer Heat* (New York: Columbia University Press, 1992), x. For a discussion of the symbolism of some of the towers, see Patrick Hanan, *The Chinese Vernacular Story* (Cambridge, MA: Harvard University Press, 1981), 176.
4. Chen Jianhua, "'Kongzhong louge' de shili changyu—Li Yu *Shi'er lou* yu xiaoshuo de jindai jinlu," *Dongyue luncong* 40, no. 4 (April 2019): 76–89.
5. Craig Clunas, *Fruitful Sites: Garden Culture in Ming Dynasty China* (Durham, NC: Duke University Press, 1996), 164.

6. *Shi'er lou*, 63–64.
7. "Palaces are built in airy nothingness; manifestations of the mind soar beyond rosy clouds" 空中結樓殿 / 意表出雲霞. Song Zhiwen, "You fahua si," in Peng Dingqiu, ed., *Quan Tang shi* (Beijing: Zhonghua shuju, 1960), 2:652.
8. *Zhuzi yulei* glosses *kongzhong louge* as "all-knowing" (*sitong bada* 四通八達). Zhu Xi, *Zhuzi yulei daquan*, ed. Li Jingde, 1850, 100:2b.
9. The complex relationship of this fictional garden to real spatial arrangement (and representation) has been fruitfully examined by many scholars, including Shang Wei, "Truth Becomes Fiction When the Fiction Is True: *The Story of the Stone* and the Visual Culture of the Manchu Court," *Journal of Chinese Literature and Culture* 2, no. 1 (April 2015): 207–248.
10. For an introduction to literary representations of gardens in the Chinese and Western traditions, as well as instructive observations on the relationship of garden design to other art forms, see Andrew H. Plaks, *Archetype and Allegory in the Dream of the Red Chamber* (Princeton, NJ: Princeton University Press, 1976). C. T. Hsia has argued that in prioritizing the *Yijing* (and *yinyang* 陰陽 and *wuxing* 五行 symbolism), Plaks imposes a structure of analysis on *Honglou meng* that dismisses the mimetic to focus solely on the allegorical. See C. T. Hsia, *C. T. Hsia on Chinese Literature* (New York: Columbia University Press, 2004), 172–187.
11. Keith McMahon, *Causality and Containment in Seventeenth-Century Chinese Fiction* (Leiden: Brill, 1988), 21.
12. On literary representation and place, see Yongqiang Liu, "West Lake Fiction of the Late Ming: Origin, Development, Background and Literary Characteristics," trans. Roland Altenburger, *Asiatische Studien / Études Asiatiques* 63, no. 1 (2009): 135–196; Linda Rui Feng, *City of Marvel and Transformation: Chang'an and Narratives of Experience in Tang Dynasty China* (Honolulu: University of Hawai'i Press, 2015).
13. On mapping narratives in particular genres, see Tina Lu, *Accidental Incest, Filial Cannibalism, & Other Peculiar Encounters in Late Imperial Chinese Literature* (Cambridge, MA: Harvard University Asia Center, 2008), chap. 1.
14. Patrick Hanan, *The Invention of Li Yu* (Cambridge, MA: Harvard University Press, 1988), 50.
15. *Xianqing ouji*, 598.
16. The former is "Zhao the Nun Drugs a Beauty into a Stupor; Jia the Scholar Takes Revenge in a Brilliant Move" 酒下酒趙尼媼迷花　機中機賈秀才抱怨. Ling Mengchu, *Pai'an jingqi* (Shanghai: Shanghai guji chubanshe, 1985), 1:256; Shuhui Yang and Yunqin Yang, trans., Ling Mengchu, *Slapping the Table in Amazement: A Ming Dynasty Story Collection* (Seattle: University of Washington Press, 2018), 125. The latter is: "With His Merciless Heart, Squire Wei Plots to Seize Another Man's Property; With His Clever Plan, Scholar Chen Wins Back His House" 衛朝奉狠心盤貴產　陳秀才巧計賺原房 Ling Mengchu, *Pai'an jingqi*, 1:594–595; Shuhui Yang and Yunqin Yang, *Slapping the Table*, 296.

17. Ling Mengchu, *Pai'an jingqi*, 1:373; Shuhui Yang and Yunqin Yang, *Slapping the Table*, 184. For a well-known earlier example of this trope, see Bai Pu's 白樸 (1226–1306) *zaju*, *On Horseback at the Garden Wall* (*Qiangtou mashang* 牆頭馬上).
18. Although production of *huaben* collections peaked during the seventeenth century, *Shi'er lou* did influence at least one later collection, *Yuhua xiang*, by Shi Chengjin (b. 1659). See Shi Chengjin, *Yuhua xiang* (Shanghai: Shanghai guji chubanshe, 1990). For a brief introduction to this text, see Patrick Hanan, *The Chinese Vernacular Story*, 209–210. The first story in that collection is named after a tower (Jinjue lou 今覺樓, "Studio of Present Enlightenment," in Hanan's translation) and it shares many elements with the third and twelfth stories in Li Yu's collection—the two that feature protagonists that could be most easily identified with Li Yu. Shi also follows his rather uneventful story with a list of ten pleasures, including reading.
19. Earlier examples, such as the stories in the *Qingping shantang huaben* 清平山堂話本 collection, were irregularly titled, with some "records" of buildings included, as in "Xihu santa ji" 西湖三塔記. For a discussion of this practice in Feng Menglong's collections, see Shuhui Yang, "Introduction," in *Stories to Awaken the World: A Ming Dynasty Collection*, vol. 3 (Seattle: Washington University Press, 2009), xxi. See also Cyril Birch, "Feng Meng-lung and the Ku-chin Hsiao-shuo," in *Bulletin of the School of Oriental and African Studies* 18 (1956): 82; and Robert E. Hegel, "Foreword," in Shuhui Yang and Yunqin Yang, trans., Ling Mengchu, *Stories to Awaken the World: A Ming Dynasty Collection*, vol. 3 (Seattle: University of Washington Press, 2009), xvi.
20. For example, the first story in *Wusheng xi*, "A Hideous Fellow Who Is Timid with Pretty Women Ends Up with Gorgeous Wives" 醜郎君怕嬌偏得艷, is paired with the second, "A Handsome Youth Tries to Avoid Suspicion But Arouses It Instead" 美男子避惑反生疑. When *Wusheng xi* was reissued as *Liancheng bi*, Li Yu retitled each story with a complete parallel couplet and reordered the collection. In the *Liancheng bi* collection, the first becomes the fifth story and is renamed the still recognizable "Beautiful Women Together Meet with Injustice in Marriage; A Rustic Fellow Enjoys the Good Fortune of Their Gentle Warmth" 美女同遭花燭冤 村郎偏享溫柔福. The second, however, is moved to the fourth position, and is unrecognizable: "An Incorruptible Official Refutes an Accusation of Incest; A Righteous Scholar Takes Pains to Plead the Injustice of Adultery" 清官不受扒灰謗 義士難伸竊婦冤.
21. There was other experimentation with titling and structure of *huaben* stories and collections during this period. Shorter collections with three-character collection titles were particularly popular, as in the collections *Rocks Nod Their Heads* (*Shidian tou* 石點頭, late Ming) and *Sobering Stone* (*Zuixing shi* 醉醒石, late Ming / early Qing). In his discussion of framing devices in *huaben* collections, Shang Wei discusses the trend toward linking stories thematically or through the use of a frame story. The collection *Guzhang juechen*, for example, includes four long stories divided into ten chapters each, on the themes of wind, flowers, snow, and the moon, respectively—seasonal imagery that, when combined, produces the phrase "romantic

dalliances" (*fenghua xueyue* 風花雪月). See Shang Wei, *Rulin Waishi and Cultural Transformation in Late Imperial China* (Cambridge, MA: Harvard University Press, 2003), 184n12. *Doupeng xianhua* has the most developed frame story of any story collection, as its twelve storytelling sessions are represented as being recounted by various narrators in the setting of a bean arbor. It was likely influenced by *Shi'er lou*. See the introduction to Robert E. Hegel, ed. and trans., Aina the Layman, *Idle Talk Under the Bean Arbor* (Seattle: University of Washington Press, 2017); Zhao Jicheng, "Jiegou duicheng yu yiyi de bu pingheng: *Doupeng xianhua* yishu jiegou xintan," *Jinan zhiye xueyuan xuebao* 2, no. 47 (2005): 28–35.

22. Gerard Genette, *Paratexts: Thresholds of Interpretation*, trans. Jane Lewin (Cambridge: Cambridge University Press, 1997), 65–66.
23. Michel de Certeau, *The Practice of Everyday Life*, trans. Steven Rendall (Berkeley: University of California Press, 1984), 117.
24. *Shi'er lou*, 2: Jibu 輯補, 4–5.
25. *Guzhang juechen*, *Guben xiaoshuo congkan*, ser. 11, ed. Liu Shide, Chen Qinghao, and Shi Changyu, vols. 1–3 (Beijing: Zhonghua shuju, 1990). The delimitation of the collection to just twelve stories, rather than the forty found in the most popular collections, is another significant development. This development is also found in the similarly named collection *Shi'er xiao* 十二笑 (*Twelve Laughs*), as well as *Doupeng xianhua*, in addition to Li Yu's own earlier collections.
26. *Shi'er lou*, 118–119.
27. For example, he believes there are only three things that a person can truly possess: "the rooms one lives in during the day; the bed one sleeps in at night; and the coffin one is stored in after death" (*Shi'er lou*, 119). Other things, he claims, "all belong to other people"—a sentiment Li Yu had expressed in his deed "Selling a Mountain" and in his essay on beds in *Xianqing ouji*, 631.
28. Sun Kaidi, "Li Liweng yu *Shi'er lou*," *Guoxue jikan* 9, no. 43 (1935): 425–426.
29. I follow Burton Watson's translation of these lines in the *Zhuangzi* of a simulated conversation between Confucius and his disciple Yan Hui 顏回: "'Well then, suppose I am inwardly direct, outwardly compliant, and do my work through the examples of antiquity? By being inwardly direct, I can be the companion of Heaven. . . . By being outwardly compliant, I can be a companion of men. . . . By doing my work through the examples of antiquity, I can be the companion of ancient times.'" Burton Watson, trans., *Zhuangzi: Basic Writings* (New York: Columbia University Press, 2003), 52.
30. *Shi'er lou*, 322. This third man is described as a "[Lord] Longyang," an allusion to the male favorite of King Anxi of the Wei (Warring States period, 403–225 BCE).
31. The comment is illegible in this version of *Shi'er lou*. See the Shunzhi period *Jueshi mingyan* edition held at the National Library of China, 3:4a; *LYQJ* 9:130.
32. Patrick Hanan translated the term *lou* (tower) in these titles differently depending on the type of building depicted in each story. Although the buildings in this story

are clearly described as pavilions (*ge* 閣) in keeping with Li Yu's titling practice and my argument in this chapter, I translate every instance of *lou* in a title as "tower." See Patrick Hanan, *A Tower for the Summer Heat*.

33. From Liu Wei 劉威 (early 9th c.), "You Donghu Huang chushi yuanlin" 遊東湖黃處士園林, in Peng Dingqiu, ed., *Quan Tang shi*, 17:6524–6525.
34. The line "the glittering stream between them" is borrowed from the tenth poem of the *Nineteen Old Poems* (*Gushi shijiu shou*), "The Faraway Cowherd" (Tiaotiao qian niuxing 迢迢牽牛星). The poem memorializes the story of the star-crossed lovers, the Cowherd and the Weaving Maiden. These two constellations are usually separated in the sky by the Milky Way, meeting just one night a year. Sui Shusen, ed., *Gushi shijiu shou jishi* (Hong Kong: Zhonghua shuju, 1958), 15–16.
35. *Shi'er lou*, 8–9.
36. *Shi'er lou*, 16. Li Yu has altered the final line, which should be: "The arbors are filled with roses, the whole courtyard perfumed" 滿架薔薇一院香. See Peng Dingqiu, ed., *Quan Tang shi*, 18:6921.
37. See Xiaoshan Yang, *Metamorphosis of the Private Sphere: Gardens and Objects in Tang-Song Poetry* (Cambridge, MA: Harvard University Asia Center, 2003), 61–72.
38. *Shi'er lou*, 64. Lines from *Xixiang ji* adapted from Stephen H. West and Wilt L. Idema, trans. *The Story of the Western Wing* (Berkeley: University of California Press, 1995), 184.
39. I will use Hanan's translations for this story, Patrick Hanan, *A Tower for the Summer Heat*, cited here and elsewhere as *Tower*; *Shi'er lou*, 178; *Tower*, 8.
40. For a longer discussion, see S. E. Kile, "Science Fictions: Early Modern Technological Change and Literary Response," *Journal for Early Modern Cultural Studies* 17, no. 2 (Spring 2017): 111–145.
41. *Shi'er lou*, 500–501.
42. *Shi'er lou*, 578; see also *Tower*, 198.
43. An account of Ding Lingwei is included in *Soushen houji*. Tao Qian and Wang Shaoying, *Soushen houji* (Beijing: Zhonghua shuju, 1981), 1.
44. *Shi'er lou*, 713–715; *Tower*, 245–246.
45. Li Yu's previously composed poetry is used in SEL3, SEL5, SEL6, and SEL12. For an analysis of Li Yu's depiction of himself in his fiction, see Shen Xinlin, *Li Yu xinlun* (Suzhou: Suzhou daxue chubanshe, 1997), 319–332.
46. I attribute this commentary to Li Yu based on its similarity in tone and argument to his main text and on the existence of the supplemental comment to SEL1 that is marked specifically as "Du Jun's comment." Since Du Jun is the "commentator" of the collection, if his comment is distinguished from the usual ones, it follows that Li Yu likely wrote the rest of them.
47. Patrick Hanan, *Vernacular Story*, 176; David L. Rolston, *Traditional Chinese Fiction and Fiction Commentary: Reading and Writing Between the Lines* (Stanford, CA: Stanford University Press, 1997), 293–294.

48. *Shi'er lou*, 109. This *jueju* quatrain is included in *Yijia yan chuji*, 146. The 庵 in the first line here is 齋 in the *Yijia yan* version. Note that the title is included only in the *Yijia yan* version.
49. *Shi'er lou*, 110. This heptasyllabic regulated verse is also included in *Yijia yan chuji*, 112. The 尚 in the second line is 幸 in the *Yijia yan* version.
50. Bai Juyi's 白居易 (772–846) New Music Bureau (*xin yuefu* 新樂府) poem, "With Apricot Wood for Beams" (Xingwei liang 杏為梁) discusses property changing hands (*yizhu* 移主), for example: "Their hearts owned the houses, their bodies were guests" 心是主人身是客. In *Bai Juyi ji jianjiao*, ed. Zhu Jincheng (Shanghai: Shanghai guji chubanshe, 1988), 1:4:243–244), cited and translated in Xiaoshan Yang, *Metamorphosis*, 16–17. This poem is critical of extravagance, but it also emphasizes transitoriness. Li Yu was likely inspired by Bai Juyi's poem lamenting property that belonged to someone else, "Thanking Wang the Eighteenth and Li the First for Inviting Me to Visit the Mountain" (Chou Wang Shiba Li Da jianzhao youshan 酬王十八李大見招遊山) (*Bai Juyi ji jianjiao*, 2:13:744), cited and translated in Xiaoshan Yang, *Metamorphosis*, 29n38. See also Stephen Owen, *The End of the Chinese "Middle Ages": Essays in Mid-Tang Literary Culture* (Stanford, CA: Stanford University Press, 1996), 12–33.
51. *Shi'er lou*, 712. The 地 in the first line is 窟 in the *Yijia yan* version.
52. In post-story comment to SEL2: "As I [*yu*] see it;" in post-story comment to SEL6: "I [*yu*] also scoff at his inability to weigh his options properly;" in post-story comment to SEL9: "I [*yu*] propose." *Shi'er lou*, 106, 379, 619.
53. The two instances are: "As I [*yu*] see it, regardless of whether there is order or disorder, it is always better to stay in the country," and "In my fifty years on this earth, I [*yu*] have served for ten in the deep mountains as Prime Minister of the Mountain, so I am very familiar with the pleasures of country living." *Shi'er lou*, 722–723.
54. Li Yu only uses this term within the narrative of one of his other stories, "His Son and Grandson Abandon His Corpse; His Servant Rushes to Bury His Body" 兒孫棄骸骨僮僕奔喪, whose protagonist, a loyal servant, frequently refers to groups of men as *zhugong*.

4. GARDEN SPACE IN *LEISURE NOTES*

1. See, for example, "Yiyuan zayong" 伊園雜詠, *Yijia yan chuji*, 137.
2. Wai-yee Li argues that "what is new in the late Ming is a more self-conscious discourse on how creators of gardens take their models and inspiration from paintings." Wai-yee Li, "Gardens and Illusions from Late Ming to Early Qing," *HJAS* 72, no. 2 (December 2012): 317.
3. Jay David Bolter and Richard Grusin, *Remediation: Understanding New Media* (Cambridge, MA: MIT Press, 1999), 11.
4. Maggie Keswik, *The Chinese Garden: History, Art, and Architecture* (London: Academy Editions, 1986), 73.

5. Craig Clunas, *Fruitful Sites: Garden Culture in Ming Dynasty China* (Durham, NC: Duke University Press, 1996), 137–138.
6. Stephen H. West, "Body and Imagination in Urban Gardens of Song and Yuan," in *Gardens and Imagination: Cultural History and Agency*, ed. Michael Conan (Washington, DC: Dumbarton Oaks Research Library and Collection, 2008), 42.
7. Wai-yee Li, "Gardens and Illusions," 323.
8. See the discussions in Zhang Jiaji, *Zhongguo zaoyuan lun* (Taiyuan: Shanxi renmin chubanshe, 1991).
9. See, for example, Huang Qiang, *Li Yu yanjiu* (Hangzhou: Zhejiang guji chubanshe, 1996), 206–224. Even then, there is frequent cross-reference to other media to describe the garden: Huang mentions that "'the sentiments of poetry and the mood of painting' are the soul of the art of the Chinese garden" (220).
10. Song Shiyong and Zhang Caixia, "Li Yu *Xianqing ouji* yuanlin meixue yu xiqu lilun de guanxi," *Hengyang shifan xueyuan xuebao* 23, no. 2 (April 2002): 76–80.
11. Jonathan Chaves, "'Meaning Beyond the Painting:' The Chinese Painter as Poet," in *Words and Images: Chinese Poetry, Calligraphy, and Painting*, ed. Alfreda Murck and Wai-Kam Ho (New York and Princeton, NJ: The Metropolitan Museum of Art and Princeton University Press, 1991), 458.
12. For the overlap between landscape painting and literary narrative, see David L. Rolston, *Traditional Chinese Fiction and Fiction Commentary: Reading and Writing Between the Lines* (Stanford, CA: Stanford University Press, 1997), 14.
13. Mary Scott, "The Image of the Garden in *Jin Ping Mei* and *Hongloumeng*," *Chinese Literature: Essays, Articles, Reviews* 8, no. 1/2 (July 1986): 86.
14. This is the Western Garden. There are a number of poems associated with Li Yu's visit to Zhang Yong, but there is no mention in them of his designing a garden. It seems to have been remuneration from Zhang Yong that allowed Li Yu to purchase Mustard Seed Garden. Cao Xun, "Zouchu wuqu, gei Li Yu yige dinglun," *Jianzhu shi* 130, no. 12 (2007): 1–8.
15. Cao Xun, "Zouchu wuqu, gei Li Yu yige dinglun," 7.
16. These also include Goodwill Garden (Hui yuan 惠園) and another Mustard Seed Garden in Beijing. See Qian Yong, *Lüyuan conghua* (Beijing: Zhonghua shuju, 1979), 520; Linqing, *Hongxue yinyuan tuji* (Taipei: Guangwen shuju, 1981), v. 2, n.p. On the Half-Acre Garden, see J. L. Van Hecken and W. A. Grootaers, "The Half Acre Garden, Pan-Mou Yüan," *Monumenta Serica* 18 (1959): 360–387. Hanan mentions his skepticism regarding the attribution of Half-Acre Garden to Li Yu. See Patrick Hanan, *The Invention of Li Yu* (Cambridge, MA: Harvard University Press, 1988), 212n13.
17. "Yu Gong Zhilu Dazongbo" 與龔芝麓大宗伯, *Yijia yan chuji*, 49.
18. *Kongyan* can mean the impoverished mere record of reality, or it can mean the complex synthesis of that reality, and so Burton Watson translates it as "theoretical judgements." *Shiji*, Sima Qian (Beijing: Zhonghua shuju, 1964), 130:3298;

Burton Watson, *Sima Qian, Grand Historian of China* (New York: Columbia University Press, 1958), 51, 211n67.
19. *Yijia yan chuji*, 49.
20. *LYQJ* 3:2. You Tong's preface is included in only a few of the Yishengtang imprints of *Xianqing ouji*. See the appendix for details.
21. See Craig Clunas, *Fruitful Sites*, 69.
22. Huang Zongxi, *Huang Lizhou wenji*, ed. Chen Naiqian (Beijing: Zhonghua shuju, 1959), 85; Xie Guozhen, "Dieshi mingjia Zhang Nanyuan fuzi shiji," *Guoli Beiping tushuguan guankan* 5, no. 6 (1931): 14.
23. Susan Bush, *The Chinese Literati on Painting* (Cambridge, MA: Harvard University Press, 1971), 16, 21, 23.
24. Another famous garden designer was Zhu Sansong 朱三松, who was also a sought-after bamboo carver and painter. See Xie Guozhen, "Dieshi mingjia Zhang Nanyuan fuzi shiji," 14-17.
25. Wu Weiye, *Wu Meicun quanji*, ed. Li Xueying (Shanghai: Shanghai guji chubanshe, 1990), 3:1060. For a translation of this biography, see Alison Hardie, "The Life of a Seventeenth-Century Chinese Garden Designer: 'The Biography of Zhang Nanyuan,' by Wu Weiye (1609–71)," *Garden History* 32, no. 1 (Spring 2004): 137–140.
26. See Xie Guozhen, "Dieshi mingjia Zhang Nanyuan fuzi shiji," 15.
27. For an argument that Ji Cheng's patron, the infamous late-Ming politician and playwright Ruan Dacheng (1587–1646), considered Ji Cheng to be a member of the privileged literati, see Joseph McDermott, "Review of *The Craft of Gardens by Ji Cheng*, trans. Alison Hardie," *Garden History* 18, no. 1 (1990): 72, 74.
28. *Xianqing ouji*, 599.
29. Ji Cheng, *Yuanye zhushi*, ed. Chen Zhi (Beijing: Zhongguo jianzhu gongye chubanshe, 1981), 41.
30. *Xianqing ouji*, 599.
31. Kan Duo, "Yuanye shiyu," in Ji Cheng, *Yuanye zhushi*, 7; *Xianqing ouji*, 615.
32. Ji Cheng, *Yuanye zhushi*, 197. See Philippe Forêt, *Mapping Chengde: The Qing Landscape Enterprise* (Honolulu: University of Hawai'i Press, 2000), 103. See also Stanislaus Fung, "The Interdisciplinary Prospects of *Yuanye*," *Studies in the History of Gardens and Designed Landscapes* 18, no. 3 (1998): 211–231.
33. Ji Cheng, *Yuanye zhushi*, 197.
34. *Xianqing ouji*, 623.
35. *Xianqing ouji*, 624.
36. *Xianqing ouji*, 624.
37. *Xianqing ouji*, 624.
38. *Xianqing ouji*, 624.
39. *Xianqing ouji*, 624.
40. Ji Cheng, *Yuanye zhushi*, 214.

41. See Judith T. Zeitlin, *Historian of the Strange: Pu Songling and the Chinese Classical Tale* (Stanford, CA: Stanford University Press, 1993), 74–87; Xiaoshan Yang, *Metamorphosis of the Private Sphere: Gardens and Objects in Tang-Song Poetry* (Cambridge, MA: Harvard University Asia Center, 2003), chap. 3.
42. Zhang Chao, *Yuchu xinzhi, Xuxiu siku quanshu*, Jibu, vol. 1783 (Shanghai: Shanghai guji chubanshe, 1995), 6:238.
43. See *Wusheng xi*, 5089–5091.
44. *Xianqing ouji*, 603.
45. *Xianqing ouji*, 603.
46. *Xianqing ouji*, 628–636.
47. *Wusheng xi*, 5165–5229.
48. Ji Cheng, *Yuanye zhushi*, 205.
49. Ji Cheng, *Yuanye zhushi*, 219.
50. Ji Cheng, *Yuanye zhushi*, 214.
51. *Xianqing ouji*, 605.
52. *Xianqing ouji*, 606.
53. *Xianqing ouji*, 606.
54. *Shi'er lou*, 310; *Tower*, 79.
55. *Shi'er lou*, 298; *Tower*, 72–73.
56. *Xianqing ouji*, 621–622. Note that the Yishengtang versions of *Xianqing ouji* that I have seen have a caption describing the "Gleaming Rock Board," but only a blank page where the illustration should be. For the illustration of "Gleaming Rock Board" from the later Jieziyuan edition, see *LYQJ* 3:194.
57. *Xianqing ouji*, 622.
58. Ji Cheng, *Yuanye zhushi*, 197, 203.
59. *Xianqing ouji*, 617.
60. Stories involving play with scale are common in the Buddhist canon, and the Daoist tradition was also a rich source for riddles that confounded subjective identification with a particular perspective. See Yinong Xu, "'Mt. Sumeru in a Mustard Seed:' Imagery and Polemics in Wang Shizhen's Garden Essays," in *Gardens and Imagination: Cultural History and Agency*, ed. Michael Conan (China: Dumbarton Oaks Research Library and Collection, 2008).
61. See Wybe Kuitert, "Borrowing Scenery and the Landscape That Lends—The Final Chapter of *Yuanye*," *Journal of Landscape Architecture* 10, no. 2 (2015): 32–43.
62. Ji Cheng, *Yuanye zhushi*, 233–234.
63. *Xianqing ouji*, 612.
64. *Xianqing ouji*, 607.
65. *Xianqing ouji*, 608.
66. *Xianqing ouji*, 608.
67. *Xianqing ouji*, 611.

68. Julia K. Murray, "What Is 'Chinese Narrative Illustration'?," *The Art Bulletin* 80, no. 4 (December 1998): 602–615.
69. My discussion of the notion of *jing* relies on the excellent survey in Jin Feng, "*Jing*, the Concept of Scenery in Texts on the Traditional Chinese Garden: An Initial Exploration," *Studies in the History of Gardens and Designed Landscapes* 18, no. 4 (1998): 339–365.
70. Stephen Owen, *Readings in Chinese Literary Thought* (Cambridge, MA: Harvard University Asia Center, 1992), 585.
71. Huang Qiang, *Li Yu yanjiu*, 289. Huang also notes that Li Yu traveled through western Shaanxi and Gansu to raise money for it.
72. See Ellen Widmer, "Between Worlds: Huang Zhouxing's Imaginary Garden," in *Trauma and Transcendence in Early Qing Literature*, ed. Wilt L. Idema, Wai-yee Li, and Ellen Widmer (Cambridge, MA: Harvard University Asia Center, 2006), 249–281; Wai-yee Li, "Gardens and Illusions."
73. *Xianqing ouji*, 619.
74. On illustrations in *Xianqing ouji*, see Patricia Sieber, "Seeing the World Through *Xianqing ouji* (1671): Visuality, Performance, and Narratives of Modernity," *Modern Chinese Literature and Culture* 12, no. 2 (Autumn 2000): 1–43.
75. *Xianqing ouji*, 620.
76. *Xianqing ouji*, 608.
77. *Xianqing ouji*, 608.

5. REMODELING FICTIONAL BODIES

1. See Wai-yee Li, "The Late Ming Courtesan: Invention of a Cultural Ideal," in *Writing Women in Late Imperial China*, ed. Ellen Widmer and K'ang-i Sun Chang (Stanford, CA: Stanford University Press, 1997), 46–73, 428–434; Sophie Volpp, *Worldly Stage: Theatricality in Seventeenth-Century China* (Cambridge, MA: Harvard University Asia Center, 2011), chaps. 4 and 5; Wai-yee Li, *Women and National Trauma in Late Imperial Chinese Literature* (Cambridge, MA: Harvard University Asia Center, 2014), chaps. 1, 3, and 6; and Guojun Wang, *Staging Personhood: Costuming in Early Qing Drama* (New York: Columbia University Press, 2020), chap. 2.
2. On the effect of the transition on literati conceptions of the body, see Xiaoqiao Ling, *Feeling the Past in Seventeenth-Century China* (Cambridge, MA: Harvard University Asia Center, 2019).
3. *Yijia yan chuji*, 26.
4. For the former position, see Zhong Mingqi, "Li Yu fangqi keju kaoshi chengyin shuobian," *Zhongguo wenxue yanjiu* 4, no. 4 (2010): 13–18.
5. *Liancheng bi*, 2:980.
6. Wai-yee Li, *Enchantment and Disenchantment: Love and Illusion in Chinese Literature* (Princeton, NJ: Princeton University Press, 1993), 46, 50.

7. On *Xiyou ji* as a harbinger of a newly theatrical orientation to emotions, see Ling Hon Lam, *The Spatiality of Emotion in Early Modern China* (New York: Columbia University Press, 2018), 55–68.
8. S. E. Kile, "Transgender Performance in Early Modern China," *differences: A Journal of Feminist Cultural Studies* 24, no. 2 (2013): 130–149. See also Sophie Volpp, "The Literary Circulation of Actors in Seventeenth-Century China," *The Journal of Asian Studies* 61, no. 3 (August 2002): 949–984.
9. W. J. T. Mitchell and Mark B. N. Hansen, eds., *Critical Terms for Media Studies* (Chicago: University of Chicago Press, 2010), xiii.
10. Lydia Liu, *The Freudian Robot: Digital Media and the Future of the Unconscious* (Chicago: University of Chicago Press, 2010), 3–6.
11. See, for example, Yin Yungong, *Zhongguo Mingdai xinwen chuanbo shi* (Chongqing: Chongqing chubanshe, 1990); Cynthia Brokaw and Kai-wing Chow, eds., *Printing and Book Culture in Late Imperial China* (Berkeley: University of California Press, 2005); Kai-wing Chow, *Publishing, Culture, and Power in Early Modern China* (Stanford, CA: Stanford University Press, 2007).
12. For the older metaphorical usage of printing, see T. H. Barrett, "Images of Printing in Seventh Century Chinese Religious Literature," *Chinese Science* 15 (1998): 92.
13. The extant editions of these plays may reflect Ming rather than Yuan period usage. See Zang Maoxun, ed. *Yuanqu xuan*, in *Xuxiu siku quanshu*, Jibu, vols. 1760–1762 (Shanghai: Shanghai guji chubanshe, 1995).
14. Li Wenwei, *Zhang Zifang yiqiao jinlü*, GBXQCK, ser. 4, box 3, vol. 15 (Shanghai: Shangwu yinshuguan, 1958), 28a–b.
15. Yu Tianxi, *Wang Dingchen fengxue yuqiao ji*, GBXQCK, ser. 4, box 12, vol. 6 (Shanghai: Shangwu yinshuguan, 1958), 15a.
16. Zang Maoxun, ed., *Zheng bao'en sanhu xiashan*, in *Xuxiu siku quanshu*, Jibu, vol. 1760 (Shanghai: Shanghai guji chubanshe, 1995), 440.
17. For an analysis of the flexibility of the woodblock medium, see Shang Wei, "*Jin Ping Mei* and Late Ming Print Culture," in *Writing and Materiality in China: Essays in Honor of Patrick Hanan*, ed. Judith T. Zeitlin, Lydia H. Liu, and Ellen Widmer (Cambridge, MA: Harvard University Asia Center, 2003), 193–194.
18. For a discussion of the print metaphor in this play, see Allison E. Bernard, "History as Meta-Theater: Kong Shangren's (1648–1718) *The Peach Blossom Fan*" (PhD diss., New York: Columbia University, 2019), chap. 4.
19. Ruan Dacheng, *Huaiyuantang pidian Yanzi jian*, GBXQCK, ser. 2, box 10, vols. 4–5 (Shanghai: Shangwu yinshuguan, 1955), *xia* 63a; also *shang* 1b and 34b, *xia* 11b. The metaphor recurs less centrally in his *Double Honor Roll* and *Spring Lantern Riddles*; see Ruan Dacheng, *Yonghuaitang xinbian Kan hudie shuang jinbang ji*, GBXQCK, ser. 2, box 10, vols. 8–9 (Shanghai: Shangwu yinshuguan, 1955), *xia* 21b; Ruan Dacheng, *Yonghuaitang xinbian Shi cuoren chundeng mi ji*, GBXQCK, ser. 2, box 10, vols. 6–7 (Shanghai: Shangwu yinshuguan, 1955), *shang* 24b.

20. See Judith T. Zeitlin, "The Life and Death of the Image: Ghosts and Female Portraits in Sixteenth- and Seventeenth-Century Literature," in *Body and Face in Chinese Visual Culture*, ed. Wu Hung and Katherine R. Tsiang (Cambridge, MA: Harvard University Asia Center, 2005), 229–256.
21. For theatricality as a figure for social identity during this period, see Sophie Volpp, *Worldly Stage*.
22. On particular role types playing multiple characters, see Regina Sofia Llamas, "Comic Roles and Performance in the Play 'Zhang Xie Zhuangyuan' with a Complete Translation" (PhD diss., Harvard University, 1998), chap. 2. On the superiority of the medium of print for conveying the effect of a play within a play in *Bimu yu*, see Ling Hon Lam, *The Spatiality of Emotion in Early Modern China*, 106–107.
23. *Chuanqi shizhong*, 10:4462.
24. Chap. 46. This is Stephen Owen's "overelaborate translation for the common term *wuse*, which," he notes, "could be rendered simply 'the appearances of things.'" Stephen Owen, *Readings in Chinese Literary Thought* (Cambridge, MA: Harvard University Asia Center, 1992), 277.
25. Translated in Stephen Owen, *Readings in Chinese Literary Thought*, 282. See Liu Xie, *Wenxin diaolong jiaozhu*, ed. Wang Liqi (Shanghai: Shanghai guji chubanshe,1980), 279.
26. Stephen Owen, *Readings in Chinese Literary Thought*, 281; Liu Xie, *Wenxin diaolong jiaozhu*, 278.
27. Stephen Owen, *Readings in Chinese Literary Thought*, 282.
28. *Shi'er lou*, 9.
29. For the medical discourse on this process, see "Renbao" 人胞 in Li Shizhen, *Bencao gangmu* (Shanghai: Shangwu yinshuguan, 1930), 6:52:106–108.
30. *Wusheng xi*, 13:5609.
31. Keith McMahon, *Misers, Shrews, and Polygamists: Sexuality and Male-Female Relationships in Eighteenth-Century Chinese Fiction* (Durham, NC: Duke University Press, 1995), 103.
32. McMahon notes that despite the apparent symmetry of the relationship, the man's idealization of the woman is also a way to project an image of himself onto her and control her. Keith McMahon, *Misers, Shrews, and Polygamists*, 113, 124.
33. *Wusheng xi*, 12:5274.
34. *Wusheng xi*, 12:5317.
35. See Cynthia Brokaw, *The Ledgers of Merit and Demerit: Social Change and Moral Order in Late Imperial China* (Princeton, NJ: Princeton University Press, 1991).
36. See Xiao Ai, *Zhongguo gudai xiangshu yanjiu yu pipan* (Changsha: Yuelu chubanshe, 1996).
37. Shuhui Yang and Yunqin Yang, trans., Ling Mengchu, *Slapping the Table in Amazement: A Ming Dynasty Story Collection* (Seattle: University of Washington Press, 2018), 37; Ling Mengchu, *Pai'an jingqi* (Shanghai: Shanghai guji chubanshe, 1985), 1:81.

38. Shuhui Yang and Yunqin Yang, trans., Ling Mengchu, *Slapping the Table*, 37; Ling Mengchu, *Pai'an jingqi*, 1:81.
39. *Lunyu zhushu, Shisanjing zhushu*, ed. Li Xueqin (Beijing: Beijing daxue chubanshe, 2000), 23:126–127; Edward Slingerland, trans., *Analects: With Selections from Traditional Commentaries* (New York: Hackett Publishing Company, Inc., 2003), 87–88; "Kongzi shijia" 孔子世家 in *Shiji*, Sima Qian (Beijing: Zhonghua shuju, 1964), 6:1919.
40. Shuhui Yang and Yunqin Yang, trans., Feng Menglong, *Stories Old and New: A Ming Dynasty Collection* (Seattle: University of Washington Press, 2000), 160; Feng Menglong, *Gujin xiaoshuo* (Shanghai: Shanghai guji chubanshe, 1985), 1:363. This passage is from the prologue story; the story proper does not deal with physiognomy, but with a more generalized change of fortune.
41. On Li Yu's development of fictionality as plausibility, see David L. Rolston, *Traditional Chinese Fiction and Fiction Commentary: Reading and Writing Between the Lines* (Stanford, CA: Stanford University Press, 1997), 174–179.
42. See Liangyan Ge, "*Rou putuan*: Voyeurism, Exhibitionism, and the 'Examination Complex,'" *Chinese Literature: Essays, Articles, Reviews* 20 (December 1998): 127–153.
43. See *Rou putuan*, 9, 119. Page references for *Rou putuan* refer to the file numbers of the digitized edition of the manuscript held at the Institute of Oriental Culture, Tokyo University, as the pages themselves are not numbered. Angela Zito reads the "nonidentification of the organ with the speaking subject 'I'" as exposing it as a "mere tool for sex," thereby at once rejecting filial duties and "trash[ing] the institution of marriage." Angela Zito, "Queering Filiality, Raising the Dead," *Journal of the History of Sexuality* 10, no. 2 (April 2001): 198.
44. The name Weiyang Sheng has been variously translated: by Franz Kuhn and Richard Martin as "Before Midnight Scholar"; by Robert E. Hegel as "Not Yet Spent"; and by Patrick Hanan as "Vesperus." As Hegel notes, Kuhn based his translation on an explanation given in the text that it derives from a line in the *Shijing*, "*ye wei yang* 夜未央," which explains that licentious students prefer the first half of the night, when they are "not yet spent." *Rou putuan*, 20. Hegel's "Not Yet Spent" is based on the translation of the poem in Arthur Waley, trans., *The Book of Songs* (New York: Grove Press, 1978), 19. Consider as well that *yang* puns with the masculine principle, *yang* 陽, which can also be glossed as "penis." In addition to "not yet" or "not quite," the homophonous *wei* 微 can indicate "small." To capture more of these layered meanings, I call him Weiyang "Wee One" Sheng. See Patrick Hanan, trans., Li Yu, *The Carnal Prayer Mat* (Honolulu: University of Hawai'i Press, 1990); Robert E. Hegel, *The Novel in Seventeenth-Century China* (New York: Columbia University Press, 1981), 167, 298 n.45; Richard Martin and Franz Kuhn, trans., Li Yu, *Jou Pu Tuan: The Prayer Mat of Flesh* (New York: Grove Press, 1963). I also hew more closely to earlier translations of the title, such as Franz Kuhn and Richard Martin's *The Prayer Mat of Flesh*, as Hanan's *The Carnal Prayer Mat* is

too euphemistic for my purposes. I translate these passages myself for the same reason, despite the existence of Hanan's excellent rendition.

45. *Rou putuan*, 101–102.
46. *Wusheng xi*, 13:5382
47. Haun Saussy, "Fenollosa Compounded: A Discrimination," in Ernest Fenollosa and Ezra Pound, *The Chinese Written Character as a Medium for Poetry: A Critical Edition*, ed. Haun Saussy, Jonathan Stalling, and Lucas Klein (New York: Fordham University Press, 2008), 5–6.
48. Lee Moore, personal communication.
49. The *tanci Tianyuhua* (*The Heavens Rain Flowers*) talks about gender in similar terms. Tao Zhenhuai, *Tianyuhua: 30 hui* (Shaozhou: Xueku shanfang, 1891), held at Harvard-Yenching Library, 5:28a–b. Despite a 1651 preface, this text was likely written closer to its first publication in 1804. See Wilt L. Idema and Beata Grant, *The Red Brush: Writing Women of Imperial China* (Cambridge, MA: Harvard University Asia Center, 2004), 720–721; Maram Epstein, "Patrimonial Bonds: Daughters, Fathers, and Power in *Tianyuhua*," *LIC* 32, no. 2 (December 2011): 3–5.
50. Zhu Xi, *Sishu zhangju jizhu*, ed. Xu Deming (Shanghai: Shanghai guji chubanshe, 2001), 38.
51. *Rou putuan*, 116.
52. James Legge, trans. "Black Robes" (Ziyi 緇衣), *The She King or The Book of Poetry* (Hong Kong: Hong Kong University Press, 1960), 124–125.
53. Wang Jide, *Nan wanghou*, in *Sheng Ming zaju*, ed. Shen Tai (Beijing: Zhongguo shudian, 2012), *chubian xia*, 1042. For a translation of this exchange, see Sophie Volpp, *Worldly Stage*, 292–293. Volpp (chap. 4) emphasizes the power of the boy/Queen in accessing the many possibilities and privileges of both genders.
54. *Wusheng xi*, 13:5606.
55. Patrick Hanan, trans., *Silent Operas* (Hong Kong: Renditions, 1990), 152–153; *Wusheng xi*, 13:5611. I use Patrick Hanan's translation of this story except when my reading of quantification requires a more literal rendition.
56. Charlotte Furth, "Androgynous Males and Deficient Females: Biology and Gender Boundaries in Sixteenth- and Seventeenth-Century China," *LIC* 9, no. 2 (December 1988): 1–31.
57. *Wusheng xi*, 13:5611.
58. *Wusheng xi*, 13:5609.
59. *Wusheng xi*, 13:5613.
60. *Wusheng xi*, 13:5616.
61. *Wusheng xi*, 13:5618; see Patrick Hanan, trans., *Silent Operas*, 155.
62. *Wusheng xi*, 13:5625; see Patrick Hanan, trans., *Silent Operas*, 159.
63. *Wusheng xi*, 13:5581; see Patrick Hanan, trans., *Silent Operas*, 139.
64. *Wusheng xi*, 13:5582; see Patrick Hanan, trans., *Silent Operas*, 139.
65. Patrick Hanan, trans., *Silent Operas*, 88–89; *Wusheng xi*, 12:5365.

66. Patrick Hanan, trans., *Silent Operas*, 89; *Wusheng xi*, 12:5366.
67. See Furth, "Androgynous Males." The sorts of nonmales included in *Bencao gangmu* were all classified by their sexual dysfunction, while the category of nonfemales included all people who were not obviously male. Li Shizhen, *Bencao gangmu* (Shanghai: Shangwu yinshuguan, 1930), 6:52:112–116. Note also that *yinan bannü* was a common way to indicate "a couple of kids."
68. *Shi'er lou*, 505.
79. *Shi'er lou*, 504.
70. *LYQJ* 9:195. (This page is missing in the reproduced version of *Shi'er lou* I am citing.)
71. The protagonist, who transitions over the course of the story from male to female, is initially named Ruilang. When he begins to live as a woman, he changes his name to Ruiniang; *lang* 郎 means "man" and *niang* 娘 means "woman."
72. *Wusheng xi*, 13:5421–5422; see Patrick Hanan, trans., *Silent Operas*, 118.
73. Patrick Hanan, trans., *Silent Operas*, 121; *Wusheng xi*, 13:5428.
74. Patrick Hanan, trans., *Silent Operas*, 100; *Wusheng xi*, 13:5382.
75. *Chuanqi shizhong*, 9:4092.
76. *Chuanqi shizhong*, 9:4089.
77. *Chuanqi shizhong*, 9:4091. The character 鞄 is pronounced *páo*; it means "to work leather." Given the pronunciation gloss of *bào* and the fact that it is combined with *tui* 推, this character likely should be 刨, as in *tuibao* 推刨 (a carpenter's plane), whereas 推鞄 is not a common compound. Nevertheless, given the allusions to skin-working across Li Yu's writings, he may have intentionally opted to use the leather radical 革 here.
78. *Chuanqi shizhong*, 9:4100.
79. *Chuanqi shizhong*, 9:4100.
80. Sophie Volpp, *Worldly Stage*, 29.
81. Sophie Volpp, *Worldly Stage*, 30.
82. Patrick Hanan has noted that Que himself comments on the fact that he, a *chou* role-type, has been cast as the male protagonist. Patrick Hanan, *Invention*, 138–139. For a *chou* cast as a high-status character in an earlier play, see Regina Sofia Llamas, "Comic Roles and Performance in the Play 'Zhang Xie Zhuangyuan' with a Complete Translation," 67–68.
83. *Chuanqi shizhong*, 9:3961.
84. *Chuanqi shizhong*, 9:3965–66.
85. On the centrality of the onstage spectator to the development of theatricality, see Ling Hon Lam, *The Spatiality of Emotion in Early Modern China*, 6–7, and chap. 3.
86. On this collection, see Giovanni Vitiello, "Exemplary Sodomites: Male Homosexuality in Late Ming Fiction" (PhD diss., University of California, Berkeley, 1994), chap. 4. For a translation of chap. 2, see Mark Stevenson and Cuncun Wu, eds.,

Homoeroticism in Imperial China: A Sourcebook (New York: Routledge, 2013), 184–192.

87. *Yichun xiangzhi*, Ming Qing shanben xiaoshuo congkan, ser. 1, no. 4 (Taipei: Tianyi chubanshe, 1993), yueji, 4a.
88. In terms of visceral descriptions of body remodeling, this text describes Niu Jun's corporeal and sartorial journeys between genders in terms of a redistribution of flesh. His physical transformation in the service of accommodating different sexual partners has him making decisions about whether to concentrate his energy in the "front" or in the "back," and when he opts for the "front," an impenetrable patch of skin (*wanrou* 頑肉) covers his anus. *Yichun xiangzhi*, yueji, 35b.
89. Both terms are per Waley's translation of *Xiyou ji*; see Arthur Waley, trans., *Monkey* (New York: Grove Press, 1943), 11.

6. REMODELING REAL BODIES IN *LEISURE NOTES*

1. *Xianqing ouji*, 700.
2. Mencius, "Gaozi zhangju (shang)" 告子章句上, *Mengzi jizhu* 孟子集注 in *Sishu zhangju jizhu*, ed. Xu Deming (Shanghai: Shanghai guji chubanshe, 2001), 394.
3. Zhuangzi, "Zhile" 至樂, in Guo Qingfan, ed., *Zhuangzi jishi* (Beijing: Zhonghua shuju, 1961), 618.
4. See, for example, "With His Merciless Heart, Squire Wei Plots to Seize Another Man's Property; With His Clever Plan, Scholar Chen Wins Back His House," in Ling Mengchu, *Pai'an jingqi* (Shanghai: Shanghai guji chubanshe, 1985), 1:608.
5. For example, this is a central argument in Chun-shu Chang and Shelley Hsueh-lun Chang, *Crisis and Transformation: Society, Culture, and Modernity in Li Yü's World* (Ann Arbor: University of Michigan Press, 1992).
6. Craig Clunas, *Superfluous Things: Material Culture and Social Status in Early Modern China* (Honolulu: University of Hawai'i Press, 1991), 42, 55.
7. Patrick Hanan, *The Invention of Li Yu* (Cambridge, MA: Harvard University Press, 1988), 195.
8. Liu Xi, *Shiming*, Congshu jicheng chubian, vol. 1151 (Changsha: Shangwu yinshuguan, 1939), 27.
9. Angela Zito, "Silk and Skin: Significant Boundaries," in *Body, Subject, and Power in China*, ed. Angela Zito and Tani E. Barlow (Chicago: University of Chicago Press, 1994), 117–118.
10. *Xianqing ouji*, 565.
11. This translation is from Bruce Rusk, *Critics and Commentators: The Book of Poems as Classic and Literature* (Cambridge, MA: Harvard University Asia Center, 2012), 19. *Lunyu zhushu*, Shisanjing zhushu, ed. Li Xueqin (Beijing: Beijing daxue chubanshe, 2000), 35.
12. *Lunyu zhushu*, 35.

13. *Xianqing ouji*, 565–566.
14. The operative terms are *lian* 練, which indicates the compound *jinglian* 精練, to scour silk, and *piao* 漂, which refers to bleaching silk. These crucial initial steps in the dyeing process remove sericin and other colorants from the fibers, after which color is added. See Joseph Needham and Dieter Kuhn, *Science and Civilisation in China: Volume 5, Chemistry and Chemical Technology, Part 9, Textile Technology: Spinning and Reeling* (Cambridge: Cambridge University Press, 1988), 303.
15. *Xianqing ouji*, 566.
16. See Yi-Li Wu, *Reproducing Women: Medicine, Metaphor, and Childbirth in Late Imperial China* (Berkeley: University of California Press, 2010), 87–88.
17. Liu Ji, *Duoneng bishi* (Shanghai: Shanghai guji chubanshe, 1995), 49.
18. *Xianqing ouji*, 566.
19. See Li Shizhen, *Bencao gangmu* (Shanghai: Shangwu yinshuguan, 1930), 3:8:43–46. Li Yu did not reference "White hair" (Fabai 髮白) which offers many options for dyeing hair black; see Li Shizhen, 3:6:81–83.
20. I use Legge's translation because he retains the color reference without abstracting it to "purity." James Legge, trans., *The Chinese Classics: A Translation by James Legge* (New York: J. B. Alden, 1890), 1:95–96. *Lunyu zhushu*, 268.
21. Meng Jiao, "Quanyou," in Peng Dingqiu, ed., *Quan Tang shi* (Beijing: Zhonghua shuju, 1960), 11:4195.
22. *Xianqing ouji*, 587.
23. This resonance is also found in *Xunzi*: "Blue dye is taken from the indigo plant, but it is bluer than the indigo plant." *Xunzi* (Shanghai: Shanghai shudian chubanshe, 1989), 7a.
24. *Xianqing ouji*, 576.
25. *Xiangyan congshu* (Shanghai: Guoxue fulunshe, 1911), 3:4a–6b. "Yanti zhulian" is a type of *zhulian* "linked pearls," a prose form of six- and eight-syllable lines that traces its origins to the Han dynasty. See David R. Knechtges and Taiping Chang, eds., *Ancient and Early Medieval Chinese Literature: A Reference Guide, Part One* (Leiden: Brill, 2010), 508–510.
26. Dorothy Ko, *Teachers of the Inner Chambers: Women and Culture in Seventeenth-Century China* (Stanford, CA: Stanford University Press, 1994), 168. Ko has translated the pieces on feet and on the body.
27. See Wu Hung, "Beyond Stereotypes: The Twelve Beauties in Qing Court Art and the *Dream of the Red Chamber*," in *Writing Women in Late Imperial China*, ed. Ellen Widmer and Kang-i Sun Chang (Stanford, CA: Stanford University Press, 1997), 327.
28. Xu Zhen, "Meiren pu," in Zhang Chao and Wang Zhuo, eds., *Tanji congshu* (Shanghai: Shanghai guji chubanshe, 1992), 140.
28. Wei Yong, "Yuerong bian," in *Xiangyan congshu*, 2:4b.
30. *Xianqing ouji*, 580.

31. This is the first line of the third of Li Bai's poems to the tune "Qingping diao" 清平調, in Peng Dingqiu, ed., *Quan Tang shi* (Beijing: Zhonghua shuju, 1960), 5:1703.
32. *Xianqing ouji*, 580.
33. Wei Yong, "Yuerong bian," *Xiangyan congshu*, 2:2b.
34. *Xianqing ouji*, 580–581.
35. On the connoisseurship of commodities during this period, see Craig Clunas, *Superfluous Things*; Wai-yee Li, "The Collector, the Connoisseur, and Late-Ming Sensibility," *T'oung Pao*, Second Series 81, no. 4/5 (1995): 269–302; Wai-yee Li, *The Promise and Peril of Things: Literature and Material Culture in Late Imperial China* (New York: Columbia University Press, 2022).
36. See, for example, *Xianqing ouji*, 574, 576.
37. Patrick Hanan, *Invention*, 73.
38. *Xianqing ouji*, 576.
39. Jonathan Hay, *Sensuous Surfaces: The Decorative Object in Early Modern China* (Honolulu: University of Hawai'i Press, 2010), 82–83.
40. *Xianqing ouji*, 573.
41. Richard John Lynn, trans., *The Classic of Changes: A New Translation of the "I Ching" as Interpreted by Wang Bi* (New York: Columbia University Press, 1994), 137; *Zhouyi zhengyi*, Shisanjing zhushu, ed. Li Xueqin (Beijing: Beijing daxue chubanshe, 2000), 20–21.
42. *Daxue zhangju* 大學章句, in Zhu Xi, *Sishu zhangju jizhu*, ed. Xu Deming (Shanghai: Shanghai guji chubanshe, 2001), 9. From James Legge, trans., *The Chinese Classics*, 1:116.
43. *Shi'er lou*, 666.
44. *Xianqing ouji*, 579.
45. *Xianqing ouji*, 579.
46. Li Yu interprets this four-character phrase as if it were a line from the classics, but I have not been able to locate a source for it.
47. *Xianqing ouji*, 578–579.
48. In his annotated version of the *Hanshu*, Yan Shigu 顏師古 (581–645) glossed this line as meaning "Although he wears a hat and clothing, his heart is not like a human heart." *Hanshu*, Ban Gu (Beijing: Zhonghua shuju, 1975), 7:31:1808. In his *Explication of Flora, Fauna, Fowl, Beasts, Insects and Fishes in the* Classic of Poetry, Lu Ji (261–303) wrote that *muhou* 沐猴, the term used for "macaque" in this expression, is "what people of Chu call macaques." Lu Ji, *Maoshi caomu niaoshou chongyu shu*, vol. 1346–1347, *Congshu jicheng chubian* (Shanghai: Shangwu yinshuguan, 1936), 51.
49. *Xianqing ouji*, 578.
50. *Yiyang* is a synonym of *yangsheng* 養生 ("nourishing life"). Because this section of *Xianqing ouji* focuses so acutely on individual preferences and experiences, I translate it "Care of the Self."
51. "Heaven and earth are ruthless [*buren*], and treat the myriad creatures as straw dogs." Translation from D. C. Lau, trans., *Lao Tzu Tao Te Ching* (New York: Penguin Classics, 1963), 9.

52. *Xianqing ouji*, 694.
53. See A. C. Graham, trans., *The Book of Lieh-Tzu: A Classic of the Tao*, (New York: Columbia University Press, 1990), 139–140. Yang Zhu has also been proposed as the first Chinese thinker to conceive of the human primarily as a "skin-bound individual." John Emerson, "Yang Chu's Discovery of the Body," *Philosophy East and West* 46, no. 4 (October 1996): 335.
54. For the *Liezi*, see Zhang Zhan, *Liezi zhu*, in *Zengding Zhongguo xueshu mingzhu*, ser. 1, vol. 11 (Taipei: Shijie shuju, 1967), 7:78; A. C. Graham, trans., *The Book of Lieh-Tzu*, 40. For Li Yu, see *Xianqing ouji*, 694.
55. *Xianqing ouji*, 578.
56. *Tower*, 186. *Shi'er lou*, 555.
57. *Shi'er lou*, 533.
58. *Shi'er lou*, 535.
59. There are several closely related terms describing beds used in prison and torture: *xiachuang*, used here, and *xiachuang* 匣牀, *yachuang* 押牀, and *bianchuang* 編牀. They appear to be a bed on which a second board is placed directly on top of a supine prisoner; here *xiachuang* seems to refer to a restraint bed that immobilizes a prisoner's limbs rather than a torture device. For a discussion of *xiachuang*, which he translates as "box-bed," as a torture device, see Timothy Brook, *Death by a Thousand Cuts* (Cambridge, MA: Harvard University Press, 2008), 45.
60. *Xianqing ouji*, 701.
61. Pu Songling, "Huabi," in *Liaozhai zhiyi*, ed. Ren Duxing (Jinan: Qilu shushe, 2000), 1:21–27. See Judith T. Zeitlin, "Conclusion," in *Historian of the Strange: Pu Songling and the Chinese Classical Tale* (Stanford, CA: Stanford University Press, 1993).
62. For a discussion see Sophie Volpp, "The Discourse on Male Marriage: Li Yu's 'A Male Mencius's Mother,'" *positions* 2, no. 1 (1994): 113–132. See also the *Wusheng xi* story, "A Ghost Loses Money, and a Living Person Repays a Gambling Debt" 鬼輸錢活人還賭債, in which a mother assumes that any man in Suzhou would be interested in sex with her son, and the narrator concurs that 99 percent of men are interested in this kind of sex. *Wusheng xi*, 13:5532.
63. Dorothy Ko, *Cinderella's Sisters: A Revisionist History of Footbinding* (Berkeley: University of California Press, 2005), 154.
64. *Xianqing ouji*, 568.

EPILOGUE

1. *Yanshi jiacang chidu*, ed. Shanghai Library, 8 vols. (Shanghai: Shanghai kexue jishu wenxian chubanshe, 2006), 250–251.
2. See, for example, Lisa Gitelman and Geoffrey B. Pingree, *New Media, 1740–1915* (Cambridge, MA: MIT Press, 2003); Shaoling Ma, *The Stone and the Wireless: Mediating China, 1861–1906* (Durham, NC: Duke University Press, 2021).

3. Jay David Bolter and Richard Grusin, *Remediation: Understanding New Media* (Cambridge, MA: MIT Press, 1999), 14–15.
4. Tobie S. Meyer-Fong, *Building Culture in Early Qing Yangzhou* (Stanford, CA: Stanford University Press, 2003).
5. *Shi'er lou*, 231.
6. Angela Zito, "Queering Filiality: Raising the Dead," *Journal of the History of Sexuality* 10, no. 2 (April 2001): 195–201; see esp. 198–201.
7. *Xianqing ouji*, 698.
8. For a discussion of this tendency in Li Yu, see Keith McMahon, *Causality and Containment in Seventeenth-Century Chinese Fiction* (Leiden: Brill, 1988), 129.

APPENDIX: LI YU'S OEUVRE

1. Yan's collection of original versions of more than 700 personal letters was not published until the modern period. Although the letters have been widely available since their reprinting in *Congshu jicheng chubian* in 1935, scholars were not aware of the catalogue until the publication of a facsimile reproduction in 2006. *Yanshi jiacang chidu*, ed. Shanghai Library, 8 vols. (Shanghai: Shanghai kexue jishu wenxian chubanshe, 2006), 5:250–261. See Huang Qiang, "*Yanshi jiacang chidu* zhong de Li Yu zilie *shumu*," *Zhongshan daxue xuebao* 54, no. 1 (2014): 14–24.

Works Cited

Translations of pre-twentieth-century Chinese texts are listed by translator. Dynastic histories and anonymous premodern texts are listed by title; pseudonyms are provided only for modern published translations.

Alford, William P. *To Steal a Book Is an Elegant Offense: Intellectual Property Law in Chinese Civilization.* Stanford, CA: Stanford University Press, 1995.
Bai Juyi 白居易. *Bai Juyi ji jianjiao* 白居易集箋校. Ed. Zhu Jincheng 朱金城. Shanghai: Shanghai guji chubanshe, 1988.
Bai, Qianshen. *Fu Shan's World: The Transformation of Chinese Calligraphy in the Seventeenth Century.* Cambridge, MA: Harvard University Asia Center, 2003.
Barrett, T. H. "Images of Printing in Seventh Century Chinese Religious Literature." *Chinese Science* 15 (1998): 81–93.
Bernard, Allison E. "History as Meta-Theater: Kong Shangren's (1648–1718) *The Peach Blossom Fan*." PhD diss., Columbia University, 2019.
Birch, Cyril, "Feng Meng-lung and the Ku-chin Hsiao-shuo." *Bulletin of the School of Oriental and African Studies* 18 (1956): 64–83.
Bolter, Jay David, and Richard Grusin. *Remediation: Understanding New Media.* Cambridge, MA: MIT Press, 1999.
Bray, Francesca. *Technology and Gender: Fabrics of Power in Late Imperial China.* Berkeley: University of California Press, 1997.
———. *Technology, Gender and History in Imperial China: Great Transformations Reconsidered.* London and New York: Routledge, 2013.
Brokaw, Cynthia. "Book History in Premodern China: The State of the Discipline I." *Book History* 10, no. 1 (2007): 253–290.

———. *Commerce in Culture: The Sibao Book Trade in the Qing and Republican Periods.* Cambridge, MA: Harvard University Asia Center, 2007.

———. "Commercial Publishing in Late Imperial China: The Zou and Ma Family Businesses of Sibao, Fujian." *LIC* 16, no. 1 (June 1996): 49–92.

———. *The Ledgers of Merit and Demerit: Social Change and Moral Order in Late Imperial China.* Princeton, NJ: Princeton University Press, 1991.

———. "On the History of the Book in China." In *Printing and Book Culture in Late Imperial China.* Ed. Cynthia J. Brokaw and Kai-wing Chow, 3-54. Princeton, NJ: Princeton University Press, 2005.

Brokaw, Cynthia, and Kai-wing Chow, eds. *Printing and Book Culture in Late Imperial China.* Berkeley: University of California Press, 2005.

Brook, Timothy. *The Confusions of Pleasure: Commerce and Culture in Ming China.* Berkeley: University of California Press, 1999.

Brook, Timothy, Jérôme Bourgon, and Gregory Blue. *Death by a Thousand Cuts.* Cambridge, MA: Harvard University Press, 2008.

Bush, Susan. *The Chinese Literati on Painting: Su Shih (1037–1101) to Tung Ch'i-ch'ang (1555–1636).* Cambridge, MA: Harvard University Press, 1971.

Cahill, James. *The Painter's Practice: How Artists Lived and Worked in Traditional China.* New York: Columbia University Press, 1994.

Cao Xun 曹汛. "Zouchu wuqu, gei Li Yu yige dinglun" 走出誤區，給李漁一個定論. *Jianzhu shi* 130, no. 12 (2007): 1–8.

Certeau, Michel de. *The Practice of Everyday Life.* Trans. Steven Rendall. Berkeley: University of California Press, 1984.

Chang, Chun-shu, and Shelley Hsueh-lun Chang. *Crisis and Transformation in Seventeenth-Century China: Society, Culture, and Modernity in Li Yü's World.* Ann Arbor: University of Michigan Press, 1992.

Chang, Kang-i Sun, Haun Saussy, and Charles Kwong, eds. *Women Writers of Traditional China: An Anthology of Poetry and Criticism.* Stanford, CA: Stanford University Press, 1999.

Chaves, Jonathan. "'Meaning beyond the Painting:' The Chinese Painter as Poet." In *Words and Images: Chinese Poetry, Calligraphy, and Painting.* Ed. Alfreda Murck and Wai-Kam Ho, 431–458. New York and Princeton, NJ: The Metropolitan Museum of Art and Princeton University Press, 1991.

Chen Jianhua 陳建華. "'Kongzhong louge' de shili changyu—Li Yu *Shi'er lou* yu xiaoshuo de jindai jinlu" "空中樓閣"的勢力場域—李漁《十二樓》與小說的近代進路. *Dongyue luncong* 40, no. 4 (April 2019): 76–89.

Chen Menglei 陳夢雷 and Jiang Tingxi 蔣廷錫, eds. *Qinding gujin tushu jicheng* 欽定古今圖書集成. 1672 vols. Beijing, [1890 reprint of 1725 edition]. Held at C. V. Starr East Asian Library, Columbia University.

Chen Yinke 陳寅恪. *Liu Rushi biezhuan* 柳如是別傳. Shanghai: Shanghai guji chubanshe, 1980.

Chia, Lucille. "Of Three Mountains Street: The Commercial Publishers of Ming Nanjing." In *Printing and Book Culture in Late Imperial China*. Ed. Cynthia J. Brokaw and Kai-wing Chow, 107–151. Princeton, NJ: Princeton University Press, 2005.

——. *Printing for Profit: The Commercial Publishers of Jianyang, Fujian (11th–17th centuries)*. Cambridge, MA: Harvard University Asia Center, 2002.

Chin, Tamara T. *Savage Exchange: Han Imperialism, Chinese Literary Style, and the Economic Imagination*. Cambridge, MA: Harvard University Asia Center, 2014.

Chou, Chih-p'ing. *Yüan Hung-tao and the Kung-an School*. Cambridge: Cambridge University Press, 1988.

Chow, Kai-wing. *Publishing, Culture, and Power in Early Modern China*. Stanford, CA: Stanford University Press, 2007.

Clunas, Craig. *Chinese Furniture*. London: Bamboo Publishing, 1988.

——. *Empire of Great Brightness: Visual and Material Cultures of Ming China*. Honolulu: University of Hawai'i Press, 2007.

——. *Fruitful Sites: Garden Culture in Ming Dynasty China*. Durham, NC: Duke University Press, 1996.

——. *Superfluous Things: Material Culture and Social Status in Early Modern China*. Honolulu: University of Hawai'i Press, 1991.

Ding Xigen 丁錫根. "Jiaodian houji" 校點後記. In *Wusheng xi* 無聲戲, 210–221. Beijing: Renmin wenxue chubanshe, 1989.

Dong Sigao 董嗣杲. *Lushan ji* 廬山集. Shanghai: Shangwu yinshuguan, 1935.

Duan, Xiaolin. "The Ten Views of West Lake." In *Visual and Material Cultures in Middle Period China*. Ed. Patricia Buckley Ebrey and Susan Shih-Shan Huang, 151–190. Leiden: Brill, 2017.

Eisenstein, Elizabeth. *The Printing Press as an Agent of Change: Communications and Cultural Transformations in Early-Modern Europe*. London: Cambridge University Press, 1979.

Elman, Benjamin A. *A Cultural History of Civil Examinations in Late Imperial China*. Berkeley: University of California Press, 2000.

Emerson, John. "Yang Chu's Discovery of the Body." *Philosophy East and West* 46, no. 4 (October 1996): 533–566.

Epstein, Maram. "Patrimonial Bonds: Daughters, Fathers, and Power in *Tianyuhua*." *LIC* 32, no. 2 (December 2011): 1–33.

Feng, Jin. "*Jing*, the Concept of Scenery in Texts on the Traditional Chinese Garden: An Initial Exploration." *Studies in the History of Gardens and Designed Landscapes* 18, no. 4 (1998): 339–365.

Feng, Jiren. *Chinese Architecture and Metaphor: Song Culture in the* Yingzao Fashi *Building Manual*. Honolulu: University of Hawai'i Press, 2012.

Feng, Linda Rui. *City of Marvel and Transformation: Chang'an and Narratives of Experience in Tang Dynasty China*. Honolulu: University of Hawai'i Press, 2015.

Feng Menglong 馮夢龍. *Gujin xiaoshuo* 古今小說. 2 vols. Shanghai: Shanghai guji chubanshe, 1985.

Fenollosa, Ernest, and Ezra Pound. *The Chinese Written Character as a Medium for Poetry: A Critical Edition*. Ed. Haun Saussy, Jonathan Stalling, and Lucas Klein. New York: Fordham University Press, 2008.

Fong, Wen. "The Problem of Forgeries in Chinese Painting Part One." *Artibus Asiae* 25, no. 2/3 (1962): 95–119, 121–140.

Forêt, Philippe. *Mapping Chengde: The Qing Landscape Enterprise*. Honolulu: University of Hawai'i Press, 2000.

Fu Chen 伏琛. *Sanqi lüeji* 三齊略記. In Chen Menglei 陳夢雷 and Jiang Tingxi 蔣廷錫, eds., *Gujin tushu jicheng* 古今圖書集成. Vol. 527. Shanghai: Zhonghua shuju, 1934.

Fung, Stanislaus. "The Interdisciplinary Prospects of *Yuanye*." *Studies in the History of Gardens and Designed Landscapes* 18, no. 3 (1998): 211–231.

Furth, Charlotte. "Androgynous Males and Deficient Females: Biology and Gender Boundaries in Sixteenth- and Seventeenth-Century China." *LIC* 9, no. 2 (December 1988): 1–31.

Ge, Liangyan. "*Rou putuan*: Voyeurism, Exhibitionism, and the 'Examination Complex.'" *Chinese Literature: Essays, Articles, Reviews* 20 (December 1998): 127–153.

Genette, Gerard. *Paratexts: Thresholds of Interpretation*. Trans. Jane Lewin. Cambridge: Cambridge University Press, 1997.

Gitelman, Lisa, and Geoffrey B. Pingree. *New Media, 1740–1915*. Cambridge, MA: MIT Press, 2003.

Goodrich, L. Carrington, with Chaoying Fang, eds. *Dictionary of Ming Biography, 1368–1644*. 2 vols. New York: Columbia University Press (The Ming Biographical History Project of the Association for Asian Studies), 1976.

Graham, A. C., trans. *The Book of Lieh-Tzu: A Classic of the Tao*. New York: Columbia University Press, 1990.

Greenbaum, Jamie. *Chen Jiru (1558–1639): The Background to, Development and Subsequent Uses of Literary Personae*. Leiden: Brill, 2007.

Guo Qingfan 郭慶藩, ed. *Zhuangzi jishi* 莊子集釋. Beijing: Zhonghua shuju, 1961.

Guo Yingde 郭英德. *Ming Qing chuanqi shi* 明清傳奇史. Beijing: Renmin wenxue chubanshe, 2011.

———. *Ming Qing chuanqi zonglu* 明清傳奇綜錄. Shijiazhuang: Hebei jiaoyu chubanshe, 1997.

Guzhang juechen 鼓掌絕塵. *Guben xiaoshuo congkan* 古本小說叢刊, ser. 11. Ed. Liu Shide 劉世德, Chen Qinghao 陳慶浩, Shi Changyu 石昌渝. Vols. 1–3. Beijing: Zhonghua shuju, 1990.

Hanan, Patrick, trans. Li Yu. *The Carnal Prayer Mat*. Honolulu: University of Hawai'i Press, 1990.

———. *The Chinese Vernacular Story*. Cambridge, MA: Harvard University Press, 1981.

———. *Han Nan Zhongguo xiaoshuo lunji* 韓南中國小說論集. Trans. Wang Qiugui 王秋桂 et al. Beijing: Beijing daxue chubanshe, 2008.

———. "Introduction." In Patrick Hanan, trans., Li Yu, *The Carnal Prayer Mat*. Honolulu: University of Hawai'i Press, 1990. v–xiv.

———. *The Invention of Li Yu*. Cambridge, MA: Harvard University Press, 1988.

———, trans. Li Yu. *Silent Operas*. Hong Kong: Renditions, 1990.

———, trans. Li Yu. *A Tower for the Summer Heat*. New York: Columbia University Press, 1992.

Hanan, Patrick, and Maria Franca Sibau, trans. Li Yu. "Tan Chuyu Declares His Love While Performing a Play; Liu Miaogu Dies to Preserve Her Chastity at the End of the Aria." *Renditions* 81–82 (Spring–Autumn 2014): 231–278.

Handler-Spitz, Rivi, Pauline C. Lee, and Haun Saussy, eds. and trans. Li Zhi. *A Book to Burn and A Book to Keep (Hidden): Selected Writings of Li Zhi*. Translations from the Asian Classics. New York: Columbia University Press, 2016.

Hanshu 漢書. Ban Gu 班固. 6 vols. Beijing: Zhonghua shuju, 1975.

Hardie, Alison, trans. Ji Cheng. *The Craft of Gardens*. New Haven: Yale University Press, 1988.

———. "The Life of a Seventeenth-Century Chinese Garden Designer: 'The Biography of Zhang Nanyuan,' by Wu Weiye (1609–71)." *Garden History* 32, no. 1 (Spring 2004): 137–140.

Hawkes, David, trans. *Liu Yi and the Dragon Princess: A Thirteenth-Century Zaju Play by Shang Zhongxian*. Hong Kong: The Chinese University of Hong Kong, 2003.

Hay, Jonathan. *Sensuous Surfaces: The Decorative Object in Early Modern China*. Honolulu: University of Hawai'i Press, 2010.

———. *Shitao: Painting and Modernity in Early Qing China*. New York: Cambridge University Press, 2001.

He, Yuming. *Home and the World: Editing the "Glorious Ming" in Woodblock-Printed Books of the Sixteenth and Seventeenth Centuries*. Cambridge, MA: Harvard University Asia Center, 2013.

Hegel, Robert E. "Foreword." In Shuhui Yang and Yunqin Yang, trans. Ling Mengchu. *Stories to Awaken the World: A Ming Dynasty Collection*. Vol. 3. Seattle: University of Washington Press, 2009. xiii–xviii.

———, ed. and trans. Aina the Layman. *Idle Talk Under the Bean Arbor*. Seattle: University of Washington Press, 2017.

———. *The Novel in Seventeenth-Century China*. New York: Columbia University Press, 1981.

———. *Reading Illustrated Fiction in Late Imperial China*. Stanford, CA: Stanford University Press, 1998.

Henry, Eric. *Chinese Amusements: The Lively Plays of Li Yü*. Hamden, CT: Archon Books, 1980.

Hou Hanshu 後漢書. Fan Ye 范曄. 12 vols. Beijing: Zhonghua shuju, 1965.

Hsia, C. T. *C. T. Hsia on Chinese Literature*. New York: Columbia University Press, 2004.

Huang Guoquan 黃果泉. *Yasu zhi jian: Li Yu de wenhua renge yu wenxue sixiang yanjiu* 雅俗之間: 李漁的文化人格與文學思想研究. Beijing: Zhongguo shehui kexue chubanshe, 2004.

Huang Lizhen 黃麗貞. *Li Yu* 李漁. Taipei: Guojia chubanshe, 1982.

———. *Li Yu yanjiu* 李漁研究. Taipei: Chun wenxue chubanshe, 1974.

Huang Qiang 黃強. "Li Yu wei Jinling Yishengtang shufang zhuren kaobian—yu 'Li Yu yu Yishengtang, Jieziyuan shufang guanxi kaobian' yiwen zuozhe shangque" 李漁為金陵翼聖堂書坊主人考辨, 與《李漁與翼聖堂, 芥子園書坊關係考辨》一文作者商榷. *Chongqing shifan daxue xuebao*, no. 5 (2012): 5–10.

———. *Li Yu yanjiu* 李漁研究. Hangzhou: Zhejiang guji chubanshe, 1996.

———. "*Liweng yijia yan chuji* kaoshu" 笠翁一家言初集考述. *Wenxian* 4 (2006): 51–60.

———. "*Rou putuan* zuozhe yu xunian zai kaobian"《肉蒲團》作者與序年再考辨. *Jiangnan daxue xuebao* 18, no. 1 (2019): 74–83.

———. "*Yanshi jiacang chidu* zhong de Li Yu zilie *shumu*"《顏氏家藏尺牘》中的李漁自列《書目》. *Zhongshan daxue xuebao* 54, no. 1 (2014): 14–24.

Huang Qiang 黃強 and Guo Di 郭迪, eds. Rou putuan *jiaozheng*《肉蒲團》校證. Taipei: Guojia chubanshe, 2019.

Huang Zhouxing 黃周星. *Xiaweitang Rentian le chuanqi* 夏為堂人天樂傳奇. *GBXQCK*, ser. 3, box 12, vols. 7–8. Beijing: Wenxue guji kanxingshe, 1957.

Huang Zongxi 黃宗羲. *Huang Lizhou wenji* 黃梨洲文集. Ed. Chen Naiqian 陳乃乾. Beijing: Zhonghua shuju, 1959.

Hummel, Arthur W., ed. *Eminent Chinese of the Ch'ing Period, 1644-1912*. Washington D. C.: United States Government Printing Office, 1943-1944. Taipei: Literature House, 1964.

Hymes, Robert. "Getting the Words Right: Speech, Vernacular Language, and Classical Language in Song Neo-Confucian 'Records of Words.'" *Journal of Song-Yuan Studies* 36 (2006): 25–55.

———. "Truth, Falsity, and Pretense in Song China: An Approach through the Anecdotes of Hong Mai." *Chūgoku shigaku* 15, no. 1 (2005): 1–26.

Idema, Wilt L. "Drama after the Conquest: An Introduction." In *Trauma and Transcendence in Early Qing Literature*. Ed. Wilt L. Idema, Wai-yee Li, and Ellen Widmer, 375–386. Cambridge, MA: Harvard University Asia Center, 2006.

Idema, Wilt L., and Beata Grant, eds. *The Red Brush: Writing Women of Imperial China*. Cambridge, MA: Harvard University Asia Center, 2004.

Idema, Wilt L., Wai-yee Li, and Ellen Widmer, eds. *Trauma and Transcendence in Early Qing Literature*. Cambridge, MA: Harvard University Asia Center, 2006.

Itoh Sohei 伊藤漱平. "Ri Gyo no shōsetsu 'Museigeki' no hampon ni tsuite" 李漁の小說 '無聲戲'の版本について. *Chū tetsubun gakkaihō* 9 (June 1984): 126–133.

———. "Ri Gyo no shōsetsu no hampon to sono ryuden—Museigeki wo chushin shite" 李漁の小說の版本とその流傳—『無聲戲』を中心として. *Nippon Chūgoku gakkaihō* 36 (1984): 191–206.

Ji Cheng 計成. *Yuanye zhushi* 園冶注釋. Ed. Chen Zhi 陳植. Beijing: Zhongguo jianzhu gongye chubanshe, 1981.
Kan Duo 闞鐸. "Yuanye shiyu" 園冶識語. In Ji Cheng 計成, *Yuanye zhushi* 園冶注釋. Ed. Chen Zhi 陳植. Beijing: Zhongguo jianzhu gongye chubanshe, 1981.
Keswik, Maggie. *The Chinese Garden: History, Art, and Architecture*. London: Academy Editions, 1986.
Keulemans, Paize. *Sound Rising from the Paper: Nineteenth-Century Martial Arts Fiction and the Chinese Acoustic Imagination*. Cambridge, MA: Harvard University Asia Center, 2014.
Kile, S. E. "*A Much-Desired Match*: Playwriting, Stagecraft, and Entrepreneurship." In *How to Read Chinese Drama*. Ed. Patricia Sieber and Regina Llamas, 257–284. New York: Columbia University Press, 2022.
———. "Science Fictions: Early Modern Technological Change and Literary Response." *Journal for Early Modern Cultural Studies* 17, no. 2 (Spring 2017): 111–145.
———. "Transgender Performance in Early Modern China." *differences: A Journal of Feminist Cultural Studies* 24, no. 2 (2013): 130–149.
Knechtges, David R., and Taiping Chang, eds. *Ancient and Early Medieval Chinese Literature: A Reference Guide, Part One*. Leiden: Brill, 2010.
Ko, Dorothy. *Cinderella's Sisters: A Revisionist History of Footbinding*. Berkeley: University of California Press, 2005.
———. *Teachers of the Inner Chambers: Women and Culture in Seventeenth-Century China*. Stanford, CA: Stanford University Press, 1994.
Kroll, Paul W. "A Poetry Debate of the Perfected Highest Clarity." *Journal of the American Oriental Society* 132, no. 4 (October–December 2012): 577–586.
Kuitert, Wybe. "Borrowing Scenery and the Landscape That Lends—The Final Chapter of *Yuanye*." *Journal of Landscape Architecture* 10, no. 2 (2015): 32–43.
Kuzuoğlu, Uluğ. "Indexing Systems." In *Literary Information in China: A History*. Ed. Jack W. Chen et al., 25–35. New York: Columbia University Press, 2021.
Lam, Ling Hon. *The Spatiality of Emotion in Early Modern China: From Dreamscapes to Theatricality*. New York: Columbia University Press, 2018.
Laozi Daode jing 老子道德經. Shanghai: Shanghai shudian, 1989.
Lau, D. C., trans. *Lao Tzu*. New York: Penguin Classics, 1963.
Lee Chia-lian 李佳蓮. "Liangge shijie de yuhe—chongdu Li Yu *Shenzhong lou*" 兩個世界的遇合—重讀李漁《蜃中樓》. *Donghai Zhongwen xuekan* 32 (December 2016): 81–124.
Lee, Hui-shu. *Exquisite Moments: West Lake and Southern Song Art*. New York: China Institute Gallery, 2001.
Legge, James, trans. *The Chinese Classics: A Translation by James Legge*. 2 vols. New York: J. B. Alden, 1890.
———, trans. *The She King or The Book of Poetry*. Hong Kong: Hong Kong University Press, 1960.
Li, Qiancheng, and Robert E. Hegel, trans. *Master of Silent Whistle Studio. Further Adventures on the Journey to the West*. Seattle: University of Washington Press, 2020.

Li Shizhen 李時珍. *Bencao gangmu* 本草綱目. 6 vols. Shanghai: Shangwu yinshuguan, 1930.

Li, Wai-yee. "The Collector, the Connoisseur, and Late-Ming Sensibility." *T'oung Pao*, Second Series 81, no. 4/5 (1995): 269–302.

———. *Enchantment and Disenchantment: Love and Illusion in Chinese Literature*. Princeton, NJ: Princeton University Press, 1993.

———. "Gardens and Illusions from Late Ming to Early Qing." *HJAS* 72, no. 2 (December 2012): 295–336.

———. "Introduction." In *Trauma and Transcendence in Early Qing Literature*. Ed. Wilt L. Idema, Wai-yee Li, and Ellen Widmer, 1–72. Cambridge, MA: Harvard University Asia Center, 2006.

———. "The Late Ming Courtesan: Invention of a Cultural Ideal." In *Writing Women in Late Imperial China*. Ed. Ellen Widmer and K'ang-i Sun Chang, 46–73, 428–434. Stanford, CA: Stanford University Press, 1997.

———. *The Promise and Peril of Things: Literature and Material Culture in Late Imperial China*. New York: Columbia University Press, 2022.

———. *Women and National Trauma in Late Imperial Chinese Literature*. Cambridge, MA: Harvard University Asia Center, 2014.

Li Wenwei 李文蔚. *Zhang Zifang yiqiao jinlü* 張子房圯橋進履. GBXQCK, ser. 4, box 3, vol. 15. Shanghai: Shangwu yinshuguan, 1958.

Li Yu 李漁, ed. *Chidu chuzheng* 尺牘初徵. Baobianzhai 豹變齋 edition, preface dated 1661, held at Chinese Academy of Sciences. Facsimile reprint in *Siku jinhui shu congkan*, Jibu, vol. 153, 499–704. Beijing: Beijing chubanshe, 2000.

———, ed. *Chidu chuzheng* 尺牘初徵. Baobianzhai 豹變齋 edition. Preface dated 1661, held at the Library of Congress (https://lccn.loc.gov/2014514084).

———, ed. *Gujin chidu daquan* 古今尺牘大全. Preface dated 1688, held at Peking University Library.

———. *Li Liweng quhua* 李笠翁曲話. Ed. Chen Duo 陳多. Changsha: Hunan renmin chubanshe, 1980.

———. *Li Yu quanji* 李漁全集. 20 vols. Hangzhou: Zhejiang guji chubanshe, 1991.

———. *Liancheng bi* 連城璧. First edition, early 1660s, sole extant copy held at Saeki Municipal Library, Japan. Facsimile reprint in *Guben xiaoshuo congkan*, ser. 20, vols. 1–3. Ed. Liu Shide 劉世德, Chen Qinghao 陳慶浩, Shi Changyu 石昌渝. Beijing: Zhonghua shuju, 1991.

———. *Liweng chuanqi shizhong* 笠翁傳奇十種. Shidetang 世德堂 edition, published ca. 1670s. Facsimile reprint in Helmut Martin, comp., *Li Yu quanji* 李漁全集. Vols. 7-11. Cheng Wen Publishing Co., 1970.

———. *Liweng chuanqi shizhong jiaozhu* 笠翁傳奇十種校注. Ed. Wang Xueqi 王學奇, Huo Xianjun 霍現俊, and Wu Xiuhua 吳秀華. 2 vols. Tianjin: Tianjin guji chubanshe, 2009.

———. *Liweng yijia yan chuji* 笠翁一家言初集. Yishengtang 翼聖堂 edition, preface dated 1672, held at the Palace Museum Library. Facsimile reprint in *Siku jinhui shu congkan bubian* vol. 85, 1–185. Beijing: Beijing chubanshe, 2005.

———. *Liweng yijia yan: shiji ba juan, erji shi'er juan, wenji si juan, bieji si juan* 笠翁一家言：詩集八卷，二集十二卷，文集四卷，別集四卷. Yishengtang 翼聖堂 edition, preface dated 1678, held at the Library of Congress (https://lccn.loc.gov/2014514395).

———. *Rou putuan xiaoshuo ershi hui* 肉蒲團小說二十回. Early manuscript copy, dated 1657, sole extant copy held in the Shuanghongtang 雙紅堂 collection at the Institute of Oriental Culture, Tokyo University (item 95 at http://hong.ioc.u-tokyo.ac.jp/list.php?p=5&order=si_no&jump_data=2).

———. *Shi'er lou* 十二樓. Xiaoxianju 消閒居 edition, ca. 1658, from the collection of Wu Xiaoling 吳曉鈴. Facsimile reprint in *Guben xiaoshuo jicheng* 古本小說集成, ser. 2. 2 vols. Shanghai: Shanghai guji chubanshe, 1990.

———. *Wusheng xi* 無聲戲. Sole extant copy of first edition, published mid-1650s, held at the Sonkeikaku bunko 尊經閣文庫 in Tokyo. Facsimile reprint in Helmut Martin, comp., *Li Yu quanji* 李漁全集. Vols. 12–13. Cheng Wen Publishing Co., 1970.

———. *Xianqing ouji* 閒情偶寄. Yishengtang 翼聖堂 edition, published 1671, held at Jilin University Library. Facsimile reprint in *Xuxiu siku quanshu*, Zibu, vol. 1186, 485–722. Shanghai: Shanghai guji chubanshe, 1995.

———. *Xianqing ouji* 閒情偶寄. Ed. Du Shuying 杜書瀛. 2 vols. Beijing: Zhonghua shuju, 2014.

———, ed. *Xinzeng zizhi xinshu* 新增資治新書. Jieziyuan 芥子園 edition, *Zizhi xinshu chuji* preface dated 1663, held at Peking University Library.

———. *Yizhong yuan* 意中緣. Shunzhi edition (1650s), held at National Library of China. Facsimile reprint in *Zheng Zhenduo cang zhenben xiqu wenxian congkan* 鄭振鐸藏珍本戲曲文獻叢刊, vol. 29:1–331. Beijing: Guojia tushuguan chubanshe, 2017.

———, ed. *Zizhi xinshu erji* 資治新書二集. Jingyetang 敬業堂 with some Jieziyuan blocks, held at Harvard-Yenching Library (http://id.lib.harvard.edu/alma/990080401170203941/catalog).

Liang Yu 梁喻. "Liweng zhushu sanzhong kaoshu" 笠翁著述三種考述. MA thesis, Yangzhou University, 2013.

Liangshu 梁書. Yao Silian 姚思廉. 3 vols. Beijing: Zhonghua shuju, 1973.

Ling Mengchu 凌濛初. *Pai'an jingqi* 拍案驚奇. 2 vols. Shanghai: Shanghai guji chubanshe, 1985.

Ling, Xiaoqiao. *Feeling the Past in Seventeenth-Century China*. Cambridge, MA: Harvard University Asia Center, 2019.

Linqing 麟慶. *Hongxue yinyuan tuji* 鴻雪因緣圖記. Taipei: Guangwen shuju, 1981.

Liu, James J. Y. *Chinese Theories of Literature*. Chicago: University of Chicago Press, 1979.

Liu Ji 劉基. *Duoneng bishi* 多能鄙事. Shanghai: Shanghai guji chubanshe, 1995.

Liu, Lydia. *The Freudian Robot: Digital Media and the Future of the Unconscious*. Chicago: University of Chicago Press, 2010.

Liu Xi 劉熙. *Shiming* 釋名. *Congshu jicheng chubian*. Vol. 1151. Changsha: Shangwu yinshuguan, 1939.

Liu Xie 劉勰. *Wenxin diaolong jiaozheng* 文心雕龍校證. Ed. Wang Liqi 王利器. Shanghai: Shanghai guji chubanshe, 1980.

Liu Yeqiu 劉葉秋, Zhu Yixuan 朱一玄, Zhang Shouqian 張守謙, and Jiang Dongfu 姜東賦, eds. *Zhongguo gudian xiaoshuo da cidian* 中國古典小說大辭典. Shijiazhuang: Hebei renmin chubanshe, 1998.

Liu, Yongqiang 劉勇強. "West Lake Fiction of the Late Ming: Origin, Development, Background and Literary Characteristics." Trans. Roland Altenburger. *Asiatische Studien / Études Asiatiques* 63, no. 1 (2009): 135–196.

Llamas, Regina Sofia. "Comic Roles and Performance in the Play 'Zhang Xie Zhuangyuan' with a Complete Translation." PhD diss., Harvard University, 1998.

Lu Eting 陸萼庭. *Kunju yanchu shigao* 昆劇演出史稿. Shanghai: Shanghai wenyi chubanshe, 1980.

Lu Ji 陸璣. *Maoshi caomu niaoshou chongyu shu* 毛詩草木鳥獸蟲魚疏. *Congshu jicheng chubian*. Vols. 1346–1347. Shanghai: Shangwu yinshuguan, 1936.

Lu, Tina. *Accidental Incest, Filial Cannibalism, & Other Peculiar Encounters in Late Imperial Chinese Literature*. Cambridge, MA: Harvard University Asia Center, 2008.

———. "The Literary Culture of the Late Ming (1573–1644)." In *The Cambridge History of Chinese Literature*, 63–151. Cambridge: Cambridge University Press, 2010.

Lunyu zhushu 論語注疏. *Shisanjing zhushu* 十三經注疏, ed. Li Xueqin 李學勤. Vol. 24. Beijing: Beijing daxue chubanshe, 2000.

Lynn, Richard John, trans. *The Classic of Changes: A New Translation of the "I Ching" as Interpreted by Wang Bi*. New York: Columbia University Press, 1994.

Ma, Shaoling. *The Stone and the Wireless: Mediating China, 1861–1906*. Durham, NC: Duke University Press, 2021.

Mao, Nathan K., and Cunren Liu. *Li Yü*. Boston: Twayne Publishers, 1977.

Martin, Richard, and Franz Kuhn, trans. Li Yu. *Jou Pu Tuan: The Prayer Mat of Flesh*. New York: Grove Press, 1963.

Mather, Richard B. trans. Liu I-ch'ing. *Shih-shuo Hsin-yü: A New Account of Tales of the World*. 2nd ed. Ann Arbor: University of Michigan Press, 2002.

McDermott, Joseph. "Review of *The Craft of Gardens* by Ji Cheng, Trans. Alison Hardie." *Garden History* 18, no. 1 (1990): 70–74.

———. *A Social History of the Chinese Book: Books and Literati Culture in Late Imperial China*. Hong Kong: Hong Kong University Press, 2006.

McLaren, Anne E. "Constructing New Reading Publics in Late Ming China." In *Printing and Book Culture in Late Imperial China*. Ed. Cynthia J. Brokaw and Kai-wing Chow, 153–183. Princeton, NJ: Princeton University Press, 2005.

McLuhan, Marshall. *Understanding Media: The Extensions of Man*. Ed. W. Terrance Gordon. Corte Madera, CA: Gingko Press, 2003.

McMahon, Keith. *Causality and Containment in Seventeenth-Century Chinese Fiction*. Leiden: Brill, 1988.

———. *Misers, Shrews, and Polygamists: Sexuality and Male-Female Relationships in Eighteenth-Century Chinese Fiction*. Durham, NC: Duke University Press, 1995.

Meyer-Fong, Tobie S. *Building Culture in Early Qing Yangzhou*. Stanford, CA: Stanford University Press, 2003.

———. "The Printed World: Books, Publishing Culture, and Society in Late Imperial China." *The Journal of Asian Studies* 66, no. 3 (August 2007): 787–817.

Mitchell, W. J. T., and Mark B. N. Hansen, eds. *Critical Terms for Media Studies*. Chicago: University of Chicago Press, 2010.

Murray, Julia K. "What Is 'Chinese Narrative Illustration?'" *The Art Bulletin* 80, no. 4 (December 1998): 602–615.

Needham, Joseph, and Dieter Kuhn. *Science and Civilisation in China: Volume 5, Chemistry and Chemical Technology, Part 9, Textile Technology: Spinning and Reeling*. Cambridge: Cambridge University Press, 1988.

Nugent, Christopher M. B. "Literary Media: Writing and Orality." In *The Oxford Handbook of Classical Chinese Literature*. Ed. Wiebke Denecke, Wai-yee Li, and Xiaofei Tian, 46–60. Oxford: Oxford University Press, 2017.

———. "Manuscript Culture." In *The Oxford Handbook of Classical Chinese Literature*, ed. Wiebke Denecke, Wai-yee Li, and Xiaofei Tian, 61–75. Oxford: Oxford University Press, 2017.

Ōki Yasushi 大木康. *Mingmo Jiangnan de chuban wenhua* 明末江南的出版文化. Trans. Zhou Baoxiong 周保雄. Shanghai: Shanghai guji chubanshe, 2014.

Owen, Stephen. *The End of the Chinese "Middle Ages": Essays in Mid-Tang Literary Culture*. Stanford, CA: Stanford University Press, 1996.

———. *Readings in Chinese Literary Thought*. Cambridge, MA: Harvard University Asia Center, 1992.

Park, J. P. *Art by the Book: Painting Manuals and the Leisure Life in Late Ming China*. Seattle: University of Washington Press, 2012.

Pattinson, David. "The Chidu in Late Ming and Early Qing China." PhD diss., Australia National University, 1998.

———. "The Market for Letter Collections in Seventeenth-Century China." *Chinese Literature: Essays, Articles, Reviews* 28 (2006): 125–157.

Peng Dingqiu 彭定求, ed. *Quan Tang shi* 全唐詩. 25 vols. Beijing: Zhonghua shuju, 1960.

Plaks, Andrew H. *Archetype and Allegory in the* Dream of the Red Chamber. Princeton, NJ: Princeton University Press, 1976.

———. "Terminology and Central Concepts." In *How to Read the Chinese Novel*. Ed. David L. Rolston, 75–123. Princeton, NJ: Princeton University Press, 1990.

Pollock, Sheldon. *The Language of the Gods in the World of Men: Sanskrit, Culture, and Power in Premodern India*. Berkeley: University of California Press, 2006.

Pu Songling 蒲松齡. *Liaozhai zhiyi* 聊齋志異. Ed. Ren Duxing 任篤行. 3 vols. Jinan: Qilu shushe, 2000.

Qian Qianyi 錢謙益. *Liechao shiji xiaozhuan* 列朝詩集小傳. Shanghai: Gudian wenxue chubanshe, 1957.

Qian Yong 錢泳. *Lüyuan conghua* 履園叢話. Beijing: Zhonghua shuju, 1979.

Qingshi liezhuan 清史列傳. Ed. Guoshiguan 國史館. 10 vols. Taipei: Taiwan Zhonghua shuju, 1983.

Roddy, Stephen and Ying Wang, trans. Li Yu. *The Fragrant Companions: A Play About Love Between Women*. New York: Columbia University Press, 2022.

Rolston, David L., ed. *How to Read the Chinese Novel*. Princeton, NJ: Princeton University Press, 1990.

———, *Traditional Chinese Fiction and Fiction Commentary: Reading and Writing Between the Lines*. Stanford, CA: Stanford University Press, 1997.

Ruan Dacheng 阮大鋮. *Huaiyuantang pidian Yanzi jian* 懷遠堂批點燕子箋. *GBXQCK*, ser. 2, box 10, vols. 4–5. Shanghai: Shangwu yinshuguan, 1955.

———. *Yonghuaitang xinbian Kan hudie shuang jinbang ji* 詠懷堂新編勘蝴蝶雙金榜記. *GBXQCK*, ser. 2, box 10, vols. 8–9. Shanghai: Shangwu yinshuguan, 1955.

———. *Yonghuaitang xinbian Shi cuoren chundeng mi ji* 詠懷堂新編十錯認春燈謎記, *GBXQCK*, ser. 2, box 10, vols. 6–7. Shanghai: Shangwu yinshuguan, 1955.

Rusk, Bruce. *Critics and Commentators: The* Book of Poems *as Classic and Literature*. Cambridge, MA: Harvard University Asia Center, 2012.

Sanguo zhi 三國志. Chen Shou 陳壽. Commentary by Pei Songzhi 裴松之. 20 vols. Shanghai: Shangwu yinshuguan, 1944.

Saussy, Haun. "Fenollosa Compounded: A Discrimination." In Ernest Fenollosa and Ezra Pound, *The Chinese Written Character as a Medium for Poetry: A Critical Edition*. Ed. Haun Saussy, Jonathan Stalling, and Lucas Klein, 1–40. New York: Fordham University Press, 2008.

Scott, Mary. "The Image of the Garden in *Jin Ping Mei* and *Hongloumeng*." *Chinese Literature: Essays, Articles, Reviews* 8, no. 1/2 (July 1986): 83–94.

Shan Jinheng 單錦珩. "Li Yu nianpu" 李漁年譜. In *Li Yu quanji* 李漁全集, 19: 1–130. Hangzhou: Zhejiang guji chubanshe, 1991.

Shang Wei. "*Jin Ping Mei* and Late Ming Print Culture." In *Writing and Materiality in China: Essays in Honor of Patrick Hanan*. Ed. Judith T. Zeitlin, Lydia H. Liu, and Ellen Widmer, 187–238. Cambridge, MA: Harvard University Asia Center, 2003.

———. Rulin Waishi *and Cultural Transformation in Late Imperial China*. Cambridge, MA: Harvard University Press, 2003.

———. "Truth Becomes Fiction When the Fiction Is True: *The Story of the Stone* and the Visual Culture of the Manchu Court." *Journal of Chinese Literature and Culture* 2, no. 1 (April 2015): 207–48.

———. "Writing and Speech: Rethinking the Issue of Vernaculars in Early Modern China." In *Rethinking East Asian Languages, Vernaculars, and Literacies, 1000–1919*. Ed. Benjamin A. Elman, 254–301. Leiden: Brill, 2015.

Shen Defu 沈德符. *Wanli yehuo bian* 萬曆野獲編. Beijing: Zhonghua shuju, 1959.

Shen, Jing. *Playwrights and Literary Games in Seventeenth-Century China: Plays by Tang Xianzu, Mei Dingzuo, Wu Bing, Li Yu, and Kong Shangren*. Plymouth: Lexington Books, 2010.

Shen, Jing, and Robert E. Hegel, trans. Li Yu. *A Couple of Soles: A Comic Play from Seventeenth-Century China*. New York: Columbia University Press, 2020.
Shen Xinlin 沈新林. *Li Yu pingzhuan* 李漁評傳. Nanjing: Nanjing shifan daxue chubanshe, 1998.
——. *Li Yu xinlun* 李漁新論. Suzhou: Suzhou daxue chubanshe, 1997.
Shi Chengjin 石成金. *Yuhua xiang* 雨花香. Shanghai: Shanghai guji chubanshe, 1990.
Shi Mining 史彌寧. *Youlin yigao* 友林乙稿. Beijing: Zhongguo shudian, 1994.
Shiji 史記. Sima Qian 司馬遷. 10 vols. Beijing: Zhonghua shuju, 1964.
Sieber, Patricia. "Seeing the World Through *Xianqing ouji* (1671): Visuality, Performance, and Narratives of Modernity." *Modern Chinese Literature and Culture* 12, no. 2 (Autumn 2000): 1–43.
——. *Theaters of Desire: Authors, Readers, and the Reproduction of Chinese Song-Drama, 1300–2000*. Basingstoke: Palgrave, 2003.
Sivin, Nathan. *Traditional Medicine in Contemporary China*. Ann Arbor: University of Michigan Press, 1987.
Slingerland, Edward, trans. *Analects: With Selections from Traditional Commentaries*. New York: Hackett, 2003.
Son, Suyoung. *Writing for Print: Publishing and the Making of Textual Authority in Late Imperial China*. Cambridge, MA: Harvard University Asia Center, 2018.
Song Shiyong 宋世勇 and Zhang Caixia 張彩霞. "Li Yu *Xianqing ouji* yuanlin meixue yu xiqu lilun de guanxi" 李漁《閒情偶寄》園林美學與戲曲理論的關係. *Hengyang shifan xueyuan xuebao* 23, no. 2 (April 2002): 76–80.
Stevenson, Mark, and Cuncun Wu, eds. *Homoeroticism in Imperial China: A Sourcebook*. New York: Routledge, 2013.
Sui Shusen 隋樹森, ed. *Gushi shijiu shou jishi* 古詩十九首集釋. Hong Kong: Zhonghua shuju, 1958.
Sun Kaidi 孫楷第. "Li Liweng yu *Shi'er lou*" 李笠翁與《十二樓》. *Guoxue jikan* 9, no. 43 (1935): 379–441.
——. "Li Liweng zhu *Wusheng xi* ji *Liancheng bi* jieti" 李笠翁著《無聲戲》即《連城璧》解題. *Guoli Beiping tushuguan guankan* 6, no. 1 (1932): 9–25.
——. *Riben Dongjing suojian Zhongguo xiaoshuo shumu tiyao* 日本東京所見中國小說書目提要. Beijing: Guoli Beiping tushuguan, 1931.
Sze, Mai-mai, trans. Wang Gai. *The Mustard Seed Garden Manual of Painting: Chieh Tzǔ Yüan Hua Chuan, 1679–1701*. Princeton, NJ: Princeton University Press, 1992.
Tao Qian 陶潛 and Wang Shaoying 汪紹楹. *Soushen houji* 搜神後記. Beijing: Zhonghua shuju, 1981.
Tao Zhenhuai 陶貞懷. *Tianyuhua: 30 hui* 天雨花：三十回. Shaozhou: Xueku shanfang, 1891. Held at Harvard-Yenching Library.
Tian, Xiaofei. *Beacon Fire and Shooting Star: The Literary Culture of the Liang (502–557)*. Cambridge, MA: Harvard University Asia Center, 2007.
Van Hecken, J. L., and W. A. Grootaers. "The Half Acre Garden, Pan-Mou Yüan." *Monumenta Serica* 18 (1959): 360–87.

Vitiello, Giovanni. "Exemplary Sodomites: Male Homosexuality in Late Ming Fiction." PhD diss., University of California, Berkeley, 1994.

Volpp, Sophie. "The Discourse on Male Marriage: Li Yu's 'A Male Mencius's Mother.'" *positions* 2, no. 1 (1994): 113–32.

———. "The Literary Circulation of Actors in Seventeenth-Century China." *The Journal of Asian Studies* 61, no. 3 (August 2002): 949–984.

———. *Worldly Stage: Theatricality in Seventeenth-Century China*. Cambridge, MA: Harvard University Asia Center, 2011.

Waley, Arthur, trans. *The Book of Songs*. New York: Grove Press, 1978.

———, trans. *Monkey*. New York: Grove Press, 1943.

Wang Ay-ling 王璦玲. "Qingchu Jiang, Zhe diqu wenren 'fengliu juzuo' zhi shenmei zaojing yu qi wenhua yihan" 清初江、浙地區文人「風流劇作」之審美造境與其文化意涵. In *Kongjian, diyu yu wenhua—Zhongguo wenhua kongjian de shuxie yu chanshi* 空間、地域與文化—中國文化空間的書寫與闡釋, ed. Li Fengmao 李豐楙 and Liu Yuanru 劉苑如, 91–210. Taipei: Zhongyang yanjiu yuan, 2002.

Wang Dingyong 王定勇 and Chen Anmei 陳安梅. "Riben Zunjingge wenku cang *Zengding Liweng lungu* de wenxian jiazhi" 日本尊經閣文庫藏《增定笠翁論古》的文獻價值. *Wenxian* 4 (July 2017): 165–73.

Wang Gai 王槩. *Jieziyuan huazhuan* 芥子園畫傳. 5 vols. Early Qing edition, 1679.

Wang Gai, Wang Shi 王蓍, and Wang Nie 王臬. *Jieziyuan huazhuan* 芥子園畫傳. Ed. Shang Zuowen 尚佐文, Shen Leping 沈樂平, and Qian Weiqiang 錢偉強. 10 vols. Shanghai: Shanghai shuhua chubanshe, 2012.

Wang, Guojun. *Staging Personhood: Costuming in Early Qing Drama*. New York: Columbia University Press, 2020.

Wang Heng 王衡. *Yulun pao* 鬱輪袍. In *Sheng Ming zaju* 盛明雜劇, ed. Shen Tai 沈泰. 6 vols. *Chubian, xia*. Beijing: Zhongguo shudian, 2012.

Wang Jide 王驥德. *Nan wanghou* 男王后. In *Sheng Ming zaju* 盛明雜劇, ed. Shen Tai 沈泰. 6 vols. *Chubian, xia*. Beijing: Zhongguo shudian, 2012.

———. *Wang Jide* Qulü 王驥德曲律. Ed. Chen Duo 陳多 and Ye Changhai 葉長海. Changsha: Hunan renmin chubanshe, 1983.

Wang Qi 汪淇 and Xu Shijun 徐士俊. *Chidu xinyu guangbian* 尺牘新語廣編. 1668 edition. 24 vol. Microfilm, Cambridge, MA: General Microfilm Co., ca. 1970.

Watson, Burton, trans. Sima Qian. *Records of the Grand Historian of China*. 2 vols. New York: Columbia University Press, 1961.

———. *Sima Qian, Grand Historian of China*. New York: Columbia University Press, 1958.

———, trans. *Zhuangzi: Basic Writings*. New York: Columbia University Press, 2003.

Wen Gehong 文革紅. *Qingdai qianqi tongsu xiaoshuo kanke kaolun* 清代前期通俗小說刊刻考論. Nanchang: Jiangxi renmin chubanshe, 2008.

West, Stephen H. "Body and Imagination in Urban Gardens of Song and Yuan." In *Gardens and Imagination: Cultural History and Agency*, ed. Michael Conan, 41–67. Washington, DC: Dumbarton Oaks Research Library and Collection, 2008.

West, Stephen H., and Wilt L. Idema, trans. Wang Shifu. *The Story of the Western Wing*. Berkeley: University of California Press, 1995.
Widmer, Ellen. "Between Worlds: Huang Zhouxing's Imaginary Garden." In *Trauma and Transcendence in Early Qing Literature*, ed. Wilt L. Idema, Wai-yee Li, and Ellen Widmer, 249–81. Cambridge, MA: Harvard University Asia Center, 2006.
———. "The Huanduzhai of Hangzhou and Suzhou: A Study in Seventeenth-Century Publishing." *HJAS* 56, no. 1 (June 1996): 77–122.
———. *The Margins of Utopia: Shui-hu hou-chuan and the Literature of Ming Loyalism*. Cambridge, MA: Harvard University Press, 1987.
Wright, Susan E. "Chinese Decorated Letter Paper." In *A History of Chinese Letters and Epistolary Culture*, ed. Antje Richter, 97–134. Leiden: Brill, 2015.
Wu Bing 吳炳. *Lü mudan chuanqi* 綠牡丹傳奇. *GBXQCK*, ser. 3, box 2, vol. 18. Beijing: Wenxue guji kanxingshe, 1957.
Wu Hung. "Beyond Stereotypes: The Twelve Beauties in Qing Court Art and the *Dream of the Red Chamber*." In *Writing Women in Late Imperial China*, ed. Ellen Widmer and Kang-i Sun Chang, 306-365. Stanford, CA: Stanford University Press, 1997.
Wu Weiye 吳偉業. *Wu Meicun quanji* 吳梅村全集. Ed. Li Xueying 李學穎. 3 vols. Shanghai: Shanghai guji chubanshe, 1990.
Wu, Yi-Li. *Reproducing Women: Medicine, Metaphor, and Childbirth in Late Imperial China*. Berkeley: University of California Press, 2010.
Wu, Yulian. *Luxurious Networks: Salt Merchants, Status, and Statecraft in Eighteenth-Century China*. Stanford, CA: Stanford University Press, 2017.
Xiangyan congshu 香艷叢書. 20 vols. Shanghai: Guoxue fulunshe, 1911.
Xiao Ai 蕭艾. *Zhongguo gudai xiangshu yanjiu yu pipan* 中國古代相術研究與批判. Changsha: Yuelu chubanshe, 1996.
Xiao Xinqiao 蕭欣橋. "Li Yu *Wusheng xi, Liancheng bi* banben shanbian kaosuo" 李漁《無聲戲》、《連城璧》版本嬗變考索. *Wenxian*, no. 1 (1987): 64–80.
Xie Guozhen 謝國楨. "Dieshi mingjia Zhang Nanyuan fuzi shiji" 疊石名家張南垣父子事輯. *Guoli Beiping tushuguan guankan* 5, no. 6 (1931): 13–23.
Xie Zhengguang 謝正光 and She Rufeng 佘汝豐. *Qingchu ren xuan Qingchu shi huikao* 清初人選清初詩彙考. Nanjing: Nanjing daxue chubanshe, 1998.
Xihu laoren Fansheng lu 西湖老人繁勝錄. Ca. 1250. In *Dongjing menghua lu wai sizhong* 東京夢華錄外四種. Shanghai: Zhonghua shuju, 1962.
Xu Wei 徐渭. *Nanci xulu zhushi* 南詞敘錄注釋. Ed. Li Fubo 李復波 and Xiong Chengyu 熊澄宇. Beijing: Zhongguo xiju chubanshe, 1989.
Xu, Yinong. "'Mt. Sumeru in a Mustard Seed:' Imagery and Polemics in Wang Shizhen's Garden Essays." In *Gardens and Imagination: Cultural History and Agency*, ed. Michael Conan, 207–223. Washington, DC: Dumbarton Oaks Research Library and Collection, 2008.
Xunzi 荀子. Yang Liang 楊倞, ann. *Xunzi* 荀子. Shanghai: Shanghai shudian, 1989.
Yang, Keming. *Entrepreneurship in China*. Abingdon: Ashgate, 2012.

Yang, Shuhui. "Introduction." In Shuhui Yang and Yunqin Yang, trans. Ling Mengchu. *Stories to Awaken the World: A Ming Dynasty Collection.* Vol. 3, xix–xxii. Seattle: Washington University Press, 2009. xix–xxii.

Yang, Shuhui, and Yunqin Yang, trans. Ling Mengchu. *Slapping the Table in Amazement: A Ming Dynasty Story Collection.* Seattle: University of Washington Press, 2018.

——, trans. Feng Menglong. *Stories Old and New: A Ming Dynasty Collection.* Seattle: University of Washington Press, 2000.

Yang, Xiaoshan. *Metamorphosis of the Private Sphere: Gardens and Objects in Tang-Song Poetry.* Cambridge, MA: Harvard University Asia Center, 2003.

Yanshi jiacang chidu 顏氏家藏尺牘. Ed. Shanghai Library. 8 vols. Shanghai: Shanghai kexue jishu wenxian chubanshe, 2006.

Yichun xiangzhi 宜春香質. *Ming Qing shanben xiaoshuo congkan,* ser. 1, no. 4. Taipei: Tianyi chubanshe, 1993.

Yin Yungong 尹韻公. *Zhongguo Mingdai xinwen chuanbo shi* 中國明代新聞傳播史. Chongqing: Chongqing chubanshe, 1990.

You Tong 尤侗. *You Xitang quanji* 尤西堂全集. 24 vols. Shanghai: Wenrui lou, Republican period.

Yu, Li. "Character Recognition: A New Method of Learning to Read in Late Imperial China." *LIC* 33, no. 2 (2012): 1–39.

Yu Tianxi 庾天錫. *Wang Dingchen fengxue yuqiao ji* 王鼎臣風雪漁樵記. *GBXQCK,* ser. 4, box 12, vol. 6. Shanghai: Shangwu yinshuguan, 1958.

Yuan Zongdao 袁宗道. *Bai Su zhai leiji* 白蘇齋類集. Ed. Shi Zhecun 施蟄存. Shanghai: Shanghai zazhi gongsi, 1935.

Zang Maoxun 臧懋循, ed. *Yuanqu xuan* 元曲選. *Xuxiu siku quanshu,* Jibu, vols. 1760–1762. Shanghai: Shanghai guji chubanshe, 1995.

——, ed. *Zheng bao'en sanhu xiashan* 爭報恩三虎下山. *Xuxiu siku quanshu,* Jibu, vol. 1760. Shanghai: Shanghai guji chubanshe, 1995.

Zeitlin, Judith T. "Disappearing Verses: Writing on Walls and Anxieties of Loss in Late Imperial China." In *Writing and Materiality in China: Essays in Honor of Patrick Hanan,* ed. Judith T. Zeitlin, Lydia H. Liu, and Ellen Widmer, 73–125. Cambridge, MA: Harvard University Asia Center, 2003.

——. *Historian of the Strange: Pu Songling and the Chinese Classical Tale.* Stanford, CA: Stanford University Press, 1993.

——. "The Life and Death of the Image: Ghosts and Female Portraits in Sixteenth- and Seventeenth-Century Literature." In *Body and Face in Chinese Visual Culture,* ed. Wu Hung and Katherine R. Tsiang, 229–256. Cambridge, MA: Harvard University Asia Center, 2005.

Zeitlin, Judith T., Lydia H. Liu, and Ellen Widmer, eds. *Writing and Materiality in China: Essays in Honor of Patrick Hanan.* Cambridge, MA: Harvard University Asia Center, 2003.

Zhai Hao 翟灝, et al. *Hushan bianlan* 湖山便覽. Ed. Wang Weihan 王維瀚. 3 vols. Taipei: Cheng Wen Publishing Co., Ltd., 1983.

Zhang Chao 張潮. *Chidu oucun* 尺牘偶存. 9 vols., 1780.

———, ed. *Yuchu xinzhi* 虞初新志. *Xuxiu siku quanshu*, Jibu, vol. 1783. Shanghai: Shanghai guji chubanshe, 1995.

Zhang Chao and Wang Zhuo 王晫, eds. *Tanji congshu* 檀几叢書. Shanghai: Shanghai guji chubanshe, 1992.

Zhang Jiaji 張家驥. *Zhongguo zaoyuan lun* 中國造園論. Taiyuan: Shanxi renmin chubanshe, 1991.

Zhang Xiumin 張秀民. *Zhongguo yinshua shi* 中國印刷史. Shanghai: Shanghai renmin chubanshe, 1989.

Zhang Zhan 張湛. *Liezi zhu* 列子注. In *Zengding Zhongguo xueshu mingzhu*, ser. 1, vol. 11. Taipei: Shijie shuju, 1967.

Zhao Jicheng 趙繼承. "Jiegou duicheng yu yiyi de bu pingheng: *Doupeng xianhua* yishu jiegou xintan" 結構對稱與意義的不平衡：《豆棚閒話》藝術結構新探. *Jinan zhiye xueyuan xuebao* 2, no. 47 (2005): 28–35.

Zhong Mingqi 鍾明奇. "Li Yu fangqi keju kaoshi chengyin shuobian" 李漁放棄科舉考試成因說辨. *Zhongguo wenxue yanjiu* 4, no. 4 (2010): 13–18.

Zhou Xinhui 周心慧. *Zhongguo gu banhua tongshi* 中國古版畫通史. Beijing: Xueyuan chubanshe, 2000.

Zhouyi zhengyi 周易正義. *Shisanjing zhushu* 十三經注疏. Ed. Li Xueqin 李學勤. Vol. 1. Beijing: Beijing daxue chubanshe, 2000.

Zhu Ping 朱萍. "Zhang Jinyan yu *Wusheng xi* banben de guanxi zhi wojian" 張縉彥與《無聲戲》版本的關係之我見. *Jianghuai luntan* 203, no. 1 (2004): 145–149.

Zhu Xi 朱熹. *Sishu zhangju jizhu* 四書章句集注. Ed. Xu Deming 徐德明. Shanghai: Shanghai guji chubanshe, 2001.

———. *Zhuzi yulei daquan* 朱子語類大全. Ed. Li Jingde 黎靖德. 1850.

Zimmerman, Allen A., trans. "Scholar Zhang Boils the Sea." In *The Columbia Anthology of Yuan Drama*. Ed. C. T. Hsia et al., 371–402. New York: Columbia University Press, 2014.

Zito, Angela. "Queering Filiality, Raising the Dead." *Journal of the History of Sexuality* 10, no. 2 (April 2001): 195–201.

———. "Silk and Skin: Significant Boundaries." In *Body, Subject, and Power in China*. Ed. Angela Zito and Tani E. Barlow, 103–130. Chicago: University of Chicago Press, 1994.

Index

actor-network theory, 120
aesthetic ownership, 17
Analects (Confucius), 212, 243–244, 247
architecture. *See* buildings
As Heaven Would Have It (*Naihe tian*) (Li Yu), 45–46, 229–234, 243, 286
autobiography, 78, 310n2

Bai Juyi, "With Apricot Wood for Beams," 320n50
baihua (vernacular Chinese), 92, 94, 96, 97, 104
Bao Xuan, 5, 193, 194, *196*
Be Careful About Love (*Shen luanjiao*) (Li Yu), 286, 303n42
Bian Shao, 84
body: buildings and, 6–7, 142–144, 202; Confucian tradition and, 239–240, 243–244, 278, 330n4; early Qing culture and, 14; fragility of books and, 84; *fuxing* (bestowing form) and, 214–219; garden design and, 163, 176–177; gender and, 214–215, 217–219; intermediality and, 199; mediation and, 4, 237; Ming-Qing dynastic transition and, 14, 85–86, 199, 203, 259–260, 278; playwriting and, 86, 89–90, 97–98, 109, 111, 112–113, 115; print as metaphor and, 206–207, 208–212, 213; reproducibility and, 200, 207, 208–209, 210–212, 267; technologies and, 202–203, 236; theater and, 89–90; writing and, 85, 87–88, 111–112, 218, 219, 273, 315n65. *See also* body remodeling; genitals; print as metaphor
body remodeling, 202, 203, 219–235, 237–273; beauty and, 252–253; body as canvas and, 251–253, 255; classical intertextuality in, 257–260; clothing and, 257–260, 263, 332n48; colorism and, 242, 246–247; Confucian tradition and, 239–240, 243–244, 330n4; Creator and, 217, 229, 238, 240, 244, 250; Daoism and, 239; fashion and, 247–248; feet and,

body remodeling (*continued*) 271–272; fetters and, 262–265, 333n59; flowers and, 253–254; gender and, 218, 221–225, 234–236, 241, 270–271, 328n53, 330n88; grotesque descriptions of, 219–220; habituation and, 260, 332n48; hair and, 255–256; hedonism and, 262, 333n53; human agency and, 253, 258, 259; imagination and, 265–267; interior design and, 238–239, 267–270, 278; Li Yu's protofeminism and, 241–242; makeup and, 250–251; mundane tools for, 229–232, 329n77; natural vs. artificial and, 250, 331n23; as protection, 225–226, 228; reproducibility and, 267; resonant innovation and, 243, 255, 256, 257, 259; same-sex attraction and, 228; skin as fabric and, 242–244, 249–250, 331n14; skin color and, 242, 244–247, 331nn19–20; theater and, 231–234, 259; *xu/shi* interplay and, 254; *yong* (utility) and, 261, 332n50

Bolter, Jay, 275

Book of Rites (*Liji*), 218

books: culture of, 6; fragility of, 13, 79, 81–85, 86–87, 106, 311n11; interactivity and, 1–2; intermediality and, 14; playwriting and, 100–101. *See also* literacy; print; writing

branding practices: Chen Jiru and, 41, 306n26; garden design and, 169; imposture and, 41, 42–44, 45–47; innovation and, 38, 39; intermediality and, 57; "Li Yu fan paintings" and, 50–51, 62; Li Yu's publishing involvement and, 38, 57–58; literary possession and, 39; reproducibility and, 47, 50–51, 60–61; verbal quality of, 41–42

Bray, Francesca, 6

Brokaw, Cynthia, 38

Buddhism, 169, 184–185, 235, 323n60

buildings: body and, 6–7, 142–144, 202; chapter divisions and, 144, 151–152; fate and, 149–150, 152–153; garden design and, 119–120, 125; *huaben* conventions and, 123; interactivity and, 154; intermediality and, 127, 133–134, 139, 141, 148–149; life philosophy and, 128–129; mediation and, 154; Ming-Qing dynastic transition and, 154; names of, 147–150, 152; narrative progression and, 129–133; playwriting and, 11, 97, 109, 110, 113–114, 115; plotting and, 126–127, 128–129, 135–138, 139, 141–146; as property, 155–157, 320n50; reflections and, 136–138, *139*, 139, *140*; sense of self and, 123; set design and, 11–12; stories as, 119–120, 121–122, 125–126; titling conventions and, 121–122, 123–125, 317n19, 318–319n32; *xu/shi* interplay and, 8, 11, 142, 154, 167

Cai Sihuang, 291
Cai Yong, 84
Cao Xun, 165, 169
Certeau, Michel de, 124
Chang, Chun-shu, 314n59
Chang, Shelley Hsueh-lun, 314n59
changtan suyu (*baihua*, vernacular Chinese), 92, 94, 96, 97, 105
Chaves, Jonathan, 164
Chen Duo, 114, 314n56
Chen Hongshou, 20, 291
Chen Jianhua, 119

Chen Jiru: branding practices and, 41, 306n26; as character in *A Much-Desired Match*, 42, 44; cultural entrepreneurship and, 40–41, 306n23; fame of, 5; publishing involvement of, 37; reproducibility and, 36
Chen Zilong, 66, 67, 68
Chia, Lucille, 304n4
Chidu lanyan (Huang Rong and Wang Weihan), 65–66
chidu (letters) genre, 80. *See also* collections
Chidu xinchao (Zhou Lianggong), 65
Chidu xinyu (Wang Qi), 65
Chin, Tamara, 299n1
Choice of Famous Lyrics, A (*Mingci xuansheng*) (Li Yu), 296
Chow, Kai-wing, 35, 38
chuanqi plays, 4, 124, 200, 206. *See also* Li Yu, CHUANQI PLAYS; playwriting; specific works
cinematography, 49
Clapping to Dispel Worldly Dust (*Guzhang juechen*), 126, 317n21, 318n25
Classic of Changes (*Yijing*), 256–257
Classic of Poetry (*Shijing*), 207, 220, 243, 244, 327n44
clothing, 257–260, 263, 332n48. *See also* body
"Cloud-Scraping Tower" (*Fuyun lou*) (Li Yu), 145–146
Clunas, Craig, 120, 163
Collection of Characters (*Zihui*) (Mei Yingzuo), 285
collections, 63–64, 65–66, 74, 309nn72,79. *See also* Li Yu, COLLECTIONS BY
colorism, 242, 246–247
Confucian tradition: body and, 239–240, 243–244, 278, 330n4; Creator and, 217; dyeing and, 247; entrepreneurship and, 37; *fuxing* (bestowing form) in, 219; gender and, 217, 271; Li Yu's religious skepticism and, 200, 241; reproducibility and, 212; scholar-merchants (*shishang*) and, 38. *See also* Neo-Confucianism
connoisseurship manuals, 48
Constant Words to Awaken the World (*Xingshi hengyan*) (Feng Menglong), 21–22
Convenient Guide to the Lake and Hills (*Hushan bianlan*), 51, 54
Couple of Soles, A (*Bimu yu*) (Li Yu), 93–96, 286, 313n38
Creator (*zaowu zhe*): body and, 112–113, 115; body remodeling and, 217, 229, 238, 240, 244, 250; *fuxing* (bestowing form) and, 111, 215, 219; garden design and, 168; genitals and, 215, 217, 219; human condition and, 261–262, 332n51; Li Yu's religious skepticism and, 200; playwriting and, 112–113, 114–115; print as metaphor and, 202, 214; writing and, 219
cultural entrepreneurship: Chen Jiru and, 40–41, 306n23; demand and, 40, 42–43, 48, 306n31; literati and, 37–38, 39; reproducibility and, 40, 45–46; *shanren* (mountain man) and, 43, 307n34. *See also* Li Yu, CULTURAL ENTREPRENEURSHIP

Daode jing, 261–262, 332n51
Daoism, 157, 239, 261–262, 323n60, 332n51
daoxue (moralistic), 13, 170, 301n24, 312n23
"Daughter Is Transformed into a Son by the Bodhisattva's Ingenuity, A" (Li Yu), 218, 221–225, 229–230

"Deed of Sale for a Mountain" (Maishan quan) (Li Yu), 17–18
"Delight in Adornment" (Yuerong bian) (Wei Yong), 253
Deng Hanyi, *Poetry Survey* (*Shiguan*), 63
digital media, 275–276, 278–279
discourse of the strange (*qi*), 42, 108, 215
Discourse on Drama (*Qulun*) (Xu Fuzuo), 112
Doctrine of the Mean (*Zhongyong*), 219
Dong Qichang, 5, 306n31; as character in *A Much-Desired Match*, 42–43, 44, 46, 51, 55
Dong Sigao, "Thinking of Home in the Autumn Chill" (Qiuliang huaigui), 85
Double Honor Roll (*Shuang jinbang*) (Ruan Dacheng), 325n19
doubling. *See* reproducibility
drama. *See* playwriting; theater
Dream of the Red Chamber (*Honglou meng*) (Cao Xueqin), 121
Du Jun, 21, 200, 319n46; preface to *Twelve Towers* by, 22, 119, 125–126, 287, 288–289; *Silent Operas* and, 290
"Duke Pei of Jin Returns a Concubine to Her Rightful Husband" (Feng Menglong), 213, 327n40
dynastic transition. *See* Ming-Qing dynastic transition

early Qing culture: authorship and, 19; autobiography in, 155; collections, 63–64, 65–66, 74, 309nn72,79; fiction in, 14, 155; mediation and, 13–14; publishing industry, 34; regionalism in, 260; same-sex attraction in, 270, 333n62; theater and, 89; *wudi* (no-place) and, 106, 107. *See also* Ming-Qing dynastic transition

emptiness, 2, 120–121. *See also xu/shi* interplay
examination system, 15, 16, 21, 303n46
Expanded Collection of Characters (*Guang zihui*) (Li Yu), 285

fame: imposture and, 42–44; Li Yu's achievement of, 4, 36, 42; *shanren* (mountain man) figure and, 43, 307n34
Famous Words to Awaken the World (*Jueshi mingyan*) (Li Yu), 21–22, 287–290. *See also Silent Operas*
Fan Xiang, 285
Fang Guo'an, 15
Fang Hengxian, 193
Fashioning Gardens (*Yuanye*) (Ji Cheng), 164, 171–173, 175, 177, 179–180, 184, 185, 190, 191
feet, 271–272
"Female Chen Ping Saves Her Life with Seven Ruses, A" (Li Yu), 225–226, 228
Feng Menglong, 19; classical intertextuality and, 155; *Constant Words to Awaken the World* (*Xingshi hengyan*), 21–22; de-emphasis of fiction and, 21–22; "Duke Pei of Jin Returns a Concubine to Her Rightful Husband," 213, 327n40; entrepreneurship and, 37; *huaben* conventions and, 122–123
fengchang zuoxi, 191
fengliu (romantic), 13, 170, 301n24, 312n23
fetters, 262–265, 333n59
fiction: early Qing experiments in, 14, 155; garden design and, 119–120, 125, 162–163, 164–165, 171, 183–184, 192; in late-Ming culture, 78, 122–123, 126; Li Yu on, 102–103; power of,

108; publishing industry and, 35. *See also* Li Yu, FICTION; *specific works*
fictional/real interplay. *See xu/shi* interplay
fictionality, 114
First Solicitation of Letters, A (*Chidu chuzheng*) (Li Yu), 62, 63, 65–75, 69, 72, 283, 309n72, 310n83
First Solicitation of Parallel Prose, A (*Siliu chuzheng*) (Li Yu), 62, 63, 75–76, 282–283, 310n87
Fleshy Prayer Mat, The (*Rou putuan*) (Li Yu), 20, 215–217, 219–220, 221, 294–295, 327–328n44
forgery. *See* imposture
Fragrant Companions, The (*Lianxiang ban*) (Li Yu), 16–17, 19, 285
Fragrant Forms Fit for Spring (*Yichun xiangzhi*), 235, 330n88
"*Fu* on the Excursion Hunt of the Son of Heaven" (Sima Xiangru), 299n1
Fu Sheng, 84, 85, 311n11
Furth, Charlotte, 223, 226, 236
Further Adventures on the Journey to the West (*Xiyou bu*), 14
fuxing (bestowing form), 111, 202, 214–219

gaizao. *See* body remodeling; remodeling
Gao Pian, "A Summer Day at My Mountain Retreat" (*Shanting xiari*), 136–137
garden design, 165–166; body and, 163, 176–177; borrowing scenes (*jiejing*) and, 185–186, 189–191; buildings and, 119–120, 125; clutter and, 177–178; concept pairs in, 164; cultural entrepreneurship and, 173; fiction and, 119–120, 125, 162–163, 164–165, 171, 183–184, 192; history of, 169–171; intermediality and, 163–164, 168–169, 174, 185, 321n9; Ji Cheng on, 164, 171–173, 175, 177, 179–180, 184, 185, 190, 191; in late-Ming culture, 162, 163, 165, 170–171, 184–185, 320n2; by Li Yu, 29, 119–120, 162, 165, 166–169, 172–173, 192, 321n14; literati and, 120, 170, 171–172, 322n27; metafiction and, 178–181, *180*; Ming-Qing dynastic transition and, 162, 165; Mustard Seed Garden and, 192, 193–196, *194*, *195*, *196*; narrative progression and, 171; novelty and, 29, 190; painting and, 162, 169, 173, 179–180, 320n2, 322n24; remediation and, 163; reproducibility and, 196; scale and, 184–185; sewing and, 174; temporality and, 185, 186–190, *187*, *188*; theater and, 163, 164, 185, 191; three-dimensional space and, 181–182, *181*; *Twelve Towers* and, 119, 125–126, 128, 129–130, 158, 161, 192–193; writing and, 166–168, 173–175. *See also xu/shi* interplay in garden design
gender: ambiguity in, 222–223, 226, 228, 329nn67,71; body remodeling and, 218, 221–225, 234–236, 241, 270–271, 328n53, 330n88; Confucian tradition and, 217, 271; genitals and, 217–219, 225–228, 328n49; graphic representation of (凹凸), 217–219, 222–223, 226, 228, 234; in Li Yu's fiction, 214–215, 217–219, 327nn43–44; *nannü zhi jian* and, 223, 224, 236; print as metaphor and, 209–210; symmetry and, 210, 326n32; theater and, 202, 233–234

genitals: ambiguity in, 222–223, 226–228; body remodeling and, 217, 219–220, 225–226, 227; Creator and, 215, 217, 219; deflation of, 215–217, 327n44; filial duties and, 327n43; *fuxing* (bestowing form) and, 219; gender and, 217–219, 225–228, 328n49

genre: choice of, 46, 80, 124. *See also specific genres*

"Ghost Loses Money, and a Living Person Repays a Gambling Debt, A" (Li Yu), 165, 333n62

ghostpainting/ghostwriting. *See* imposture

Gong Dingzi, 167, 193, 194, *194*

Gong'an school of poetry, 68

Goodwill Garden (Hui yuan), 321n16

Great Learning (Daxue), 257, 258

Green Peony, The (Lü mudan) (Wu Bing), 45, 46

Greenbaum, Jamie, 40, 306n23

Grusin, Richard, 275

Gujin chidu daquan, 308n62

Guo Chuanfang, 286, 303n42

Guo Kui, 155

habituation, 260, 332n48

hair, 255–256

Half-Acre Garden (Banmu yuan), 165, 321n16

Han dynasty, 169

Hanan, Patrick, 3, 13, 94, 119, 255, 318–319n32, 321n16, 329n82

"Handsome Youth Tries to Avoid Suspicion But Arouses It Instead, A" (Li Yu), 178

"Hangzhou Ten" (Xiling shizi), 66

Hay, Jonathan, 255

He Cai, 193

Heavens Rain Flowers, The (Tianyuhua) (Tao Zhenhuai), 328n49

hedonism, 262, 333n53

Hegel, Robert E., 327n44

"Hideous Fellow Who Is Timid with Pretty Women Ends Up with Gorgeous Wives, A" (Li Yu), 229

"His Son and Grandson Abandon His Corpse; His Servant Rushes to Bury His Body" (Li Yu), 320n54

History of the Han (Hanshu), 260

Hu Jie, 286

Hu Nianyi, 288, 291

huaben (short story genre): chapter divisions and, 126; collection structure, 317n21; Feng Menglong and, 122–123; garden design and, 119–120, 125; reproducibility in, 212–213; titling in, 317n19; *Twelve Towers* and, 20, 123–124, 132, 133, 147, 163, 317n18. *See also* Feng Menglong; fiction; *Silent Operas*; *Twelve Towers*

Huang Guoquan, 307n34

Huang Qiang, 20, 303n42, 308n62, 321n9

Huang Rong, *Chidu lanyan*, 65–66

Huang Yuanjie, 285, 306n30

Huang Zongxi, 169

"Humble Look at the Lyric, A" (Kui ci guanjian) (Li Yu), 295

Hymes, Robert, 96

Idema, Wilt L., 82

Idle Talk Under the Bean Arbor (Doupeng xianhua), 14, 318n21

illusory, the, 199–200

Imperial Encyclopedia (Qinding gujin tushu jicheng) (Chen Menglei and Jiang Tingxi), 9 imposture: branding practices and, 41, 42–44, 45–47; intellectual property rights and, 60; piracy of Li Yu's works and, 58–59, 61–62, 74; reproducibility and, 45–46; theater and, 232–233, 329n80; value and, 46–47, 58, 61–62; *zhuodao ren* (person who holds the sword) as, 43, 46, 47

Independent Words (*Yijia yan*) (Li Yu). *See Liweng's Independent Words*

indexes, 36, 66, 69–74, 72, 309n82

innovation: branding practices and, 38, 39; garden design and, 29; interactivity and, 57; Li Yu's cultural entrepreneurship and, 24, 25, 38–39; resonant, 243, 255, 256, 257, 259; technologies and, 24; woodblock printing and, 203; writing and, 30

"Inscription on *The Collected Works of Mr. Nonexistent*" (*Wuyou xiansheng ji ming*) (Li Yu), 1–2, 4

interactivity: body remodeling and, 236; buildings and, 154; collections and, 66–67, 75; emptiness and, 2; garden design and, 192; innovation and, 57; Li Yu's cultural entrepreneurship and, 1–3, 39–40, 47, 48–51, 57; in *Twelve Towers*, 154, 159–160, 320n54; *xu/shi* interplay and, 2–3

interior design: body remodeling and, 238–239, 267–270, 278; clutter and, 177–178; interactivity and, 40; literal realization of metaphor and, 40, 305n21; scale and, 184; *xu/shi* interplay and, 184–185

intermediality: body and, 199; branding practices and, 57; buildings and, 127, 133–134, 139, 141, 148–149; garden design and, 163–164, 168–169, 185, 321n9; Li Yu's cultural entrepreneurship and, 5, 24–25; Ming-Qing dynastic transition and, 14–15; novelty and, 276–277; print and, 6, 14, 24–25, 35–36; remodeling and, 50; reproducibility and, 57; theater and, 12, 277; in *Twelve Towers*, 127, 133–135, 139, 141, 148–149, 155, 318n30; writing and, 7; *xu/shi* interplay and, 8

intertextuality, 155, 161, 257–260

Jade Hairpin, The (*Yu saotou*) (Li Yu), 206–207, 286

Ji Cheng: *Fashioning Gardens* (*Yuanye*), 164, 171–173, 175, 177, 179–180, 184, 185, 190, 191; literati and, 322n27

Jiang Yingke, 68

Jiao Hong, 5

jiejing (borrowing scenes), 185–186, 189–191, 278

Jin Shengtan, 102

Journey to the West (*Xiyou ji*), 124, 200, 220, 236

Juvenilia (*Tiaoling ji*) (Li Yu), 294

Ko, Dorothy, 252
Kuang Heng, 311n7
Kuhn, Franz, 327n44

language. *See* writing

late-Ming culture: authorship in, 19; connoisseurship manuals in, 48; discourse of the strange (*qi*) in, 42; fiction in, 78, 122–123, 126; garden design in, 162, 163, 165, 170–171, 184–185, 320n2; illiterate audience and, 101; the illusory and, 199–200; imposture in, 46; individualism and,

Index 359

late-Ming culture (*continued*)
310n2; jocular/pragmatic balance in, 13; literacy and, 91; literary possession and, 302n36; Neo-Confucianism in, 91; nonconformity in, 42; novelty in, 25; playwriting in, 96, 113–115, 206; poetry in, 80; print as metaphor in, 205–206; print in, 5, 35; publishing industry and, 34; Revival Society, 67; romantic comedies, 19–20, 142; scholar-merchants (*shishang*), 37–38; theater and, 89; women as flowers in, 253; woodblock printing in, 203; *xiaopin* genre, 40, 41, 80, 239–240; *xu/shi* interplay in, 3. *See also* Chen Jiru; Li Zhi; Ming-Qing dynastic transition

Legge, James, 331n20

Leisure Notes (*Xianqing ouji*) (Li Yu): advertisements and, 58, 167; branding practices in, 39; on Chen Jiru, 40–41; collaboration in, 76; editions, 63, 283–284; innovation and, 38–39; "Li Yu fan paintings" in, 48–51, 52–53, 56–57, 58, 60, 62; liveliness (*huo*) in, 257; pivotal nature of, 29–30; readerly autonomy and, 28–29, 30; reproducibility and, 48; structure of, 23–24; *Twelve Towers* and, 131; You Tong's preface for, 168, 322n20; *Yuhua xiang* (Shi Chengjin) and, 317n18. *See also* body remodeling; garden design; playwriting; theater

Letters (Li Yu). *See First Solicitation of Letters, A*

Li Bai, 254

Li Shizhen, *Materia medica* (*Bencao gangmu*), 246–247

Li, Wai-yee, 80, 106, 163, 320n2

Li Wenwei, *Zhang Liang Fetches a Shoe from Beneath the Bridge* (*Zhang Zifang yiqiao jinlü*), 204

Li Yu: authorial voice of, 19, 23, 240–241; concubines and, 16–17, 23, 241; as dabbler, 33; early life of, 15–16, 302n30; fame of, 4, 36, 42; financial success of, 5; Hangzhou years (ca. 1651–61), 16, 18, 19, 34, 35; the illusory and, 199–200; jocular/pragmatic balance and, 13, 301n24; literary possession and, 17–18, 39, 155–156; Nanjing years (ca. 1661–77), 22–23, 34, 74; on painting, 44–45, 47; poetry of, 79, 81–85, 86–87, 155, 156–157; protofeminism of, 241; religious skepticism of, 200; as *shanren*, 307n34; sobriquets of, 18, 38; Storied Garden (Cengyuan) residence, 26, 165; theater troupe of, 23, 39, 88, 202, 241; as wordsmith, 34; Yi Hill Estate, 16, 17–18, 39, 162, 165, 166, 192

CHUANQI PLAYS: adaptations of, 25–26; autobiography and, 16–17; body in, 86, 202; body remodeling in, 229–232, 329n77; editions, 285–287; on fame, 42–44; female characters in, 241; garden design and, 165; late-Ming romantic comedies and, 19; on literacy, 93–96; literati identity and, 312n23; print as metaphor in, 206–207; publication of, 19, 303n42; *xu/shi* interplay and, 8, 277. *See also* playwriting; *specific plays*

COLLECTIONS BY: administrative documents, 22, 62, 63, 74–75, 282, 310n85; competitors,

309nn72,79; cultural entrepreneurship and, 62–63, 64–65, 76, 308n62; editions, 282–283; indexes in, 36, 66, 69–74, 72, 309n82, 310n83; L-shaped section separators in, 68–69, 69; Ming-Qing dynastic transition and, 65, 67–68, 76, 310nn85,87; publishing involvement and, 63, 65, 74; social networks and, 65, 66–67, 75, 76, 77, 310n85

CULTURAL ENTREPRENEURSHIP, 4, 14–15; adaptations and, 25–26; advertisements within works and, 58, 76; collaboration and, 36, 63, 76–77, 308n62; collections and, 62–63, 64–65, 76, 308n62; creative ownership and, 59–60; garden design and, 162, 173; innovation and, 24, 25, 38–39; intellectual property rights and, 58–62; interactivity and, 1–3, 39–40, 47, 48–51, 57; intermediality and, 5, 24–25; marketing and, 36, 39, 101; mediation and, 279; novelty and, 25; reproducibility and, 48, 49, 59–62, 274–275; scholar-merchants (*shishang*) and, 38; social networks and, 22, 77, 275; travel in search of patronage and, 22–23. *See also* branding practices; PUBLISHING INVOLVEMENT *below*; reproducibility

FICTION: authorial voice in, 19, 240–241; authorship and, 19, 76; body in, 201–202, 206–207, 208–212, 213, 214–219, 225–228, 327nn43–44; de-emphasis of, 21–22; discourse of the strange (*qi*) and, 215; editions, 20–22, 287–293, 303n45; female characters in, 241; garden design theory and, 162–163, 171, 183–184, 192; gender in, 214–215, 217–219, 327nn43–44; innovation and, 25; interactivity and, 40; on literacy, 93–96; print as metaphor in, 207; publication of, 20–21; reproducibility in, 206–207, 213; titling in, 121–122, 123–124, 317n20. *See also* body; body remodeling; *specific works*

GARDEN DESIGNS BY: branding practices and, 169; cultural entrepreneurship and, 162, 173; fiction and, 119–120; garden design theory and, 165, 167–169; Gong Dingzi and, 167; interactivity and, 192; Ming-Qing dynastic transition and, 162, 165; number of, 165, 169, 192; readerly autonomy and, 29; writing and, 166–168; Zhang Yong and, 165, 321n14

PUBLISHING INVOLVEMENT: branding practices and, 38, 57–58; catalogue and, 63; collections and, 63, 65, 74; financial success of, 5; marketing and, 39; Yishengtang, 5, 23, 34, 282–283, 284, 286, 287, 296 *See also* Mustard Seed Garden

Li Yu, Works: catalogue of, 281–297, 334n1; *Liweng's Independent Words* (*Liweng yijia yan*), 1, 22, 58–59, 76, 284, 295–296; "The Carver" (Jijue

Index   361

Li Yu, Works (continued)
shi), 33; "Deed of Sale for a Mountain" (Maishan quan), 17–18; "Inscription on *The Collected Works of Mr. Nonexistent*" (*Wuyou xiansheng ji* ming), 1–2, 4; *Juvenilia* (*Tiaoling ji*), 294; translations of, 283–284, 285, 286, 290, 293, 295
CHUANQI PLAYS: *As Heaven Would Have It* (*Naihe tian*), 45–46, 229–234, 243, 286; *Be Careful About Love* (*Shen luanjiao*), 286, 303n42; *A Couple of Soles* (*Bimu yu*), 93–96, 286, 313n38; *The Fragrant Companions* (*Lianxiang ban*), 16–17, 19, 285; *The Jade Hairpin* (*Yu saotou*), 206–207, 286; *Liweng's Ten Plays* (*Liweng chuanqi shizhong*), 19, 286–287; *Mistake with a Kite* (*Fengzheng wu*), 19, 46, 285; *Tower in a Mirage* (*Shenzhong lou*), 8, 9, 10, 11–12, 285, 301nn18–19. *See also Much-Desired Match, A*
COLLECTIONS: *A Choice of Famous Lyrics* (*Mingci xuansheng*), 296; *A First Solicitation of Letters* (*Chidu chuzheng*), 62, 63, 65–75, 69, 72, 283, 309n72, 310n83; *A First Solicitation of Parallel Prose* (*Siliu chuzheng*), 62, 63, 75–76, 282–283, 310n87; *A New Aid to Administration* (*Zizhi xinshu*), 22, 62, 63, 74–75, 282, 310n85; *A New Aid to Administration, Second Collection* (*Zizhi xinshu erji*), 22, 62, 282; *A Second Solicitation of Letters* (*Chidu erzheng*), 62

ESSAYS: "A Humble Look at the Lyric" (Kui ci guanjian), 295; *Liweng's Discourses on the Past* (*Liweng lungu*), 21, 22, 76, 284–285. *See also Leisure Notes*
FICTION: "Cloud-Scraping Tower" (Fuyun lou), 145–146; "A Daughter Is Transformed into a Son by the Bodhisattva's Ingenuity," 218, 221–225, 229–230; *Famous Words to Awaken the World* (*Jueshi mingyan*), 21–22; "A Female Chen Ping Saves Her Life with Seven Ruses," 225–226, 228; *The Fleshy Prayer Mat* (*Rou putuan*), 20, 215–217, 219–220, 221, 294–295, 327–328n44; "A Ghost Loses Money, and a Living Person Repays a Gambling Debt," 165, 333n62; "A Handsome Youth Tries to Avoid Suspicion But Arouses It Instead," 178; "A Hideous Fellow Who Is Timid with Pretty Women Ends Up with Gorgeous Wives," 229; "His Son and Grandson Abandon His Corpse; His Servant Rushes to Bury His Body," 320n54; "A Male Mencius's Mother Raises Her Son Properly By Moving House Three Times," 217–218, 228, 329n71; *Priceless Jade* (*Liancheng bi*), 21–22, 200, 290–293, 317n20; "Return-to-Right Tower" (Guizheng lou), 147–149; "Tan Chuyu Expresses His Love in a Play; Liu Miaogu Dies for Honor after a Song," 93–96; "Tower for Hearing My Faults" (Wenguo

lou), 155, 158, 159, 160; "A Tower for the Summer Heat" (Xiayi lou), 142–145, 146, 157, 218, 268, 278; "Tower of Gathered Refinements" (Cuiya lou), 134–135; "Tower of My Birth" (Shengwo lou), 152–154, 257, 258; "Tower of Returning as an Immortal Crane" (Hegui lou), 150–152, 264–265; "Tower of Shared Reflections" (Heying lou), 120, 123, 135–138, 140–142, 207, 208, 223, 228; "Tower of Ten Nuptial Cups" (Shijin lou), 149–150, 226–228; "Tower of Three Companions" (Sanyu lou), 124, 127–134, 155–157, 158; "Tower of Trophies" (Duojin lou), 123–124; "With the Change of Eight Characters, Trouble Ends and Good Luck Begins," 213; "With the Loss Of A Thousand Taels of Silver, Good Luck Results from Calamity," 207, 210–211, 213; "A Woman Preserving Her Virtue Meets Strange Slander; A Gang of Guys Joking Around Leads to a Bizarre Injustice," 200–201. See also Silent Operas; Twelve Towers

POETRY: "Mourning My Books: Four Poems" (Diaoshu sishou), 83–88, 311nn7–8,16; "Recarving the Parasol Tree Poem," 80–81, 83–84; "Seeking Refuge from Turmoil in 1644," 158; "Selling My House," 156–157; "Selling My House and Moving Back To My Old Residence," 156–157; Singable Lyrics (Naige ci), 76, 295

REFERENCE WORKS: *Expanded Collection of Characters* (Guang zihui), 285; *Liweng's Rhymebook for Poetry* (Liweng shiyun), 296; *Marvelous Tales from History* (Qiangu qiwen), 297; *An Outline of History* (Gujin shilüe), 22, 284; *A Rhymebook for Lyrics* (Ciyun), 295

Li Zhi, 5, 25, 42, 115, 170–171, 199
Li Zicheng, 21
Liancheng bi (*Priceless Jade*), 21–22, 200, 290–293, 317n20. See also *Silent Operas*
Liang Yu, 308n62
Liaozhai's Records of the Strange (*Liaozhai zhiyi*), 14
Liezi, 262
Like Talking Face-to-Face (*Ru miantan*), 67
Lin Tiansu, 42
Ling Mengchu, 19, 123, 155, 314n56; *Slapping the Table in Amazement* (*Pai'an jingqi*), 123, 212; "Yao Dizhu Flees from Disgrace Only to Incur More Disgrace; Zheng Yue'e Uses a Mistake to Advance Her Own Interests," 212; "Young Ladies Enjoy a Swing-Set Party," 123
linguistic registers, 92–98, 99–100. See also *changtan suyu*; *wenli*
literacy: late-Ming culture and, 91; learning of, 92–93, 312n30; Li Yu's call for, 7, 90, 91–92, 312n27; Li Yu's downgrading of, 101–102; in Li Yu's fiction and plays, 93–96; Pollock on, 313n37; vs. writing, 92
Literary Mind and the Carving of Dragons, The (*Wenxin diaolong*) (Liu Xie), 112, 207–208, 214, 326n24

literary possession, 17–18, 39, 302n36
literati: cultural entrepreneurship and, 37–38, 39; fiction and, 19, 76, 78; garden design and, 120, 170, 171–172, 322n27; interior design and, 267–270; literacy and, 102; literary possession and, 62; painting and, 169–170; playwriting and, 78, 90, 98, 312n23; publishing industry and, 34–35, 37; theater and, 100. *See also specific people*
literature. *See wenzhang*
Liu, James J. Y., 109, 314n59
Liu, Lydia H., 203
Liu Xie, *The Literary Mind and the Carving of Dragons (Wenxin diaolong)*, 112, 207–208, 214, 326n24
Liweng's Discourses on the Past (Liweng lungu) (Li Yu), 21, 22, 76, 284–285
Liweng's Independent Words (Liweng yijia yan) (Li Yu), 1, 22, 58–59, 76, 284, 295–296
Liweng's Rhymebook for Poetry (Liweng shiyun) (Li Yu), 296
Liweng's Ten Plays (Liweng chuanqi shizhong) (Li Yu), 19, 286–287
Lu Mengxiong, 286
Lu Qi, 66
Lu, Tina, 80

makeup, 250–251
"Male Mencius's Mother Raises Her Son Properly By Moving House Three Times, A" (Li Yu), 217–218, 228, 329n71
Male Queen, The (Nan wanghou) (Wang Jide), 221
"Manual of Beautiful Women" ("Meiren pu") (Xu Zhen), 253
Mao Xianshu, 66

marking objects. *See* literary possession
Martin, Richard, 327n44
Marvelous Tales from History (Qiangu qiwen) (Li Yu), 297
Materia medica (Bencao gangmu) (Li Shizhen), 246–247
McLuhan, Marshall, 4, 202–203, 205
McMahon, Keith, 121, 326n32
media: body as, 89–90; form vs. content and, 3–4; Ming-Qing dynastic transition and, 82, 275–276; modern Chinese terms for, 4–5; remodeling of, 5, 8, 14, 275–276, 279; variety of, 3. *See also* intermediality
media theory, 203
mediation, 3–4; body and, 4, 237; buildings and, 11, 154; early Qing culture and, 13–14; indexes and, 66; Li Yu's cultural entrepreneurship and, 279; *meipo* (go-between) and, 5, 277; *shen* (spiritual) and, 277–278; theater and, 4. *See also xu/shi* interplay
meipo (go-between), 5, 277
memory: body and, 86; fragility of books and, 82, 83–84, 311n11; print as metaphor and, 204–205
Meng Jiao, "Exhorting a Friend" (Quanyou), 247
metacommentary, 139
metafiction: garden design and, 178–181, *180*; *Twelve Towers* and, 128, 154–156, 157–159, 178–179, 318n27, 320nn52–53
Meyer-Fong, Tobie S., 63, 80
Ming-Qing dynastic transition: autobiography and, 78, 310n2; body and, 14, 85–86, 199, 203, 259–260, 278; collections and, 63–64, 65, 67–68, 76, 310nn85,87; fragility of

books and, 13; garden design and, 162, 165; intermediality and, 14–15; Li Yu's life and, 15, 16, 106–107, 158, 162; Li Yu's literary production and, 78–79, 82–83; Li Yu's poetry and, 80; literacy and, 101; media and, 82, 275–276; nostalgia and, 36–37, 199–200; print and, 80; publishing industry and, 18–19; *Silent Operas* and, 21, 303n45; *Twelve Towers* and, 154; *wudi* (no-place) and, 106, 107. *See also* early Qing culture

Mistake with a Kite (*Fengzheng wu*) (Li Yu), 19, 46, 285

Mitchell, W. J. T., 203

"Mourning My Books: Four Poems" (Diaoshu sishou) (Li Yu), 83–88, 311nn7–8,16

Much-Desired Match, A (*Yizhong yuan*) (Li Yu): body in, 86; characters in, 42, 306n30; on demands of painting, 44–45, 47, 50; editions, 285; illusion in, 308n52; imposture in, 42–44, 46–47; intellectual property rights and, 60; "Li Yu fan paintings" and, 50, 51, 55, 56–57; Pu Songling and, 308n52; Zhang Dai, 308n52

multimedia. *See* intermediality

Mustard Seed Garden (Jiezi yuan) (Beijing), 321n16

Mustard Seed Garden (Jiezi yuan) (Nanjing): advertisements and, 76; in *Leisure Notes*, 192, 193–196, *194*, *195*, *196*; Li Yu's departure from, 26; Li Yu's purchase and design of, 22–23, 165, 321n14; Li Yu's theater troupe at, 23, 39, 88, 202, 241; modern reconstruction of, 160; notepaper, 59–61, 274–275; writing and, 167–168

Mustard Seed Garden Painting Manual, The (*Jieziyuan huazhuan*) (Wang Gai), 26, 47, 56–57, *56*

nannü zhi jian (between male and female), 223, 224, 236

Neo-Confucianism, 91, 239. *See also* Confucian tradition

New Account of Tales of the World, A (*Shishuo xinyu*) (Liu Yiqing), 43

New Aid to Administration, A (*Zizhi xinshu*) (Li Yu), 22, 62, 63, 74–75, 282, 310n85

New Aid to Administration, A, Second Collection (*Zizhi xinshu erji*) (Li Yu), 22, 62, 282

Nineteen Old Poems (*Gushi shijiu shou*), 319n34

novelty: body remodeling and, 256–257; garden design and, 29, 190; intermediality and, 276–277; Li Yu's cultural entrepreneurship and, 25–26; media and, 275

Nugent, Christopher, 312n24

orality: destruction of books and, 83; playwriting and, 89; vs. writing, 7. *See also* performance; theater

"Orchid Pavilion" (Wang Xizhi), 43

Outline of History, An (*Gujin shilüe*) (Li Yu), 22, 284

Owen, Stephen, 207–208, 315n65, 326n24

painting: borrowing scenes (*jiejing*) and, 191; demands of, 44–45, 47, 50; garden design and, 162, 169, 173, 179–180, 320n2, 322n24; *The Mustard Seed Garden Painting Manual*, 26, 47, 56–57, *56*

Index 365

Pattinson, David, 66, 308n62, 309n79
Peng Jian, 314n54
Peony Pavilion, The (*Mudan ting*)
   (Tang Xianzu), 124, 200, 206
performance, 4, 86, 97–98, 99, 100–101,
   233. *See also* theater
piracy. *See* imposture
Plaks, Andrew H., 121, 314n57
Plato, 299n3
playwriting, 96–102; body and, 86,
   89–90, 97–98, 109, 111, 112–113, 115;
   buildings and, 11, 97, 109, 110,
   113–114, 115; character in, 107,
   314n54; classics analogy for, 97,
   102–103, 109–110; complexity in,
   108, 314n58; early limits on, 96;
   fictionality and, 114; illiterate
   audiences and, 95, 101–102; in
   late-Ming culture, 96, 113–115, 206;
   Li Yu's metaphors and, 108–109,
   314n59; Li Yu's plays and, 88–89;
   literati and, 78, 90, 98, 312n23;
   performance and, 97–98, 99,
   100–101; print as metaphor and,
   206; structure in, 99, 106, 108–109,
   111, 314nn56–57; titling conventions
   in, 124; *wudi* (no-place) and,
   107–108; *xu/shi* interplay and, 108.
   See also theater
Plum in the Golden Vase, The (*Jin Ping
   Mei*), 124, 165
poetry: borrowing scenes (*jiejing*) and,
   191; garden design and, 190; in
   late-Ming culture, 80; by Li Yu, 79,
   81–85, 86–87, 155, 156–157
Poetry Survey (*Shiguan*) (Deng Hanyi), 63
Pollock, Sheldon, 313n37
Priceless Jade (*Liancheng bi*) (Li Yu),
   21–22, 200, 290–293, 317n20. *See
   also Silent Operas*

print: garden design and, 195–196;
   hypertext and, 36; intermediality
   and, 6, 14, 24–25, 35–36; Ming
   importance of, 5, 35; Ming-Qing
   dynastic transition and, 80;
   nostalgia and, 36–37; reproducibility
   and, 34, 36, 48, 274–275; social
   networks and, 36, 61, 63, 275. *See
   also* woodblock printing
print as metaphor, 202; body and,
   206–207, 208–212, 213; gender and,
   209–210; Liu Xie on writing and,
   207–208; memory and, 204–205;
   reproducibility and, 205–207,
   211–212, 213, 325n19; symmetry and,
   210, 326n32; theater and, 206; in
   zaju, 203–205, 208, 214
Pu Songling, 308n52
publishing industry, 18–19, 35, 304n4.
   See also Li Yu, PUBLISHING
   INVOLVEMENT

qi. *See* discourse of the strange
Qi Biaojia, 314n56
Qian Qianyi, 41, 67, 68, 286
Qiao Fusheng, 23
Qin Shihuang, 84
Qingping shantang huaben, 317n19

reading: late-Ming forms of, 70;
   technologies for, 36, 66, 68–74, 69, 72,
   309nn79,82, 310n83. *See also* literacy
"Recarving the Parasol Tree Poem" (Li
   Yu), 80–81, 83–84
Records of the Grand Historian (*Shiji*)
   (Sima Qian), 212
remodeling (*gaizao*): "Li Yu fan
   paintings" and, 50; media and, 5, 8,
   14, 275–276, 279; sewing and,
   220–221; in *Twelve Towers*, 133, 137;

writing and, 133; *xu/shi* interplay and, 8, 276–277. *See also* body remodeling; reproducibility

reproducibility: acting and, 206; body and, 200, 207, 208–209, 210–212, 267; branding practices and, 47, 50–51, 60–61; Confucian tradition and, 212; cultural entrepreneurship and, 40, 45–46; demand and, 40; emptiness and, 2; garden design and, 196; imposture and, 45–46; intellectual property rights and, 59–62; interactivity and, 49; painting and, 45; print and, 34, 36, 48, 274–275; print as metaphor and, 205–207, 211–212, 213, 325n19; theater and, 206–207; titling conventions and, 124; writing and, 207–208

resonant innovation, 243, 255, 256, 257, 259

"Return-to-Right Tower" (*Guizheng lou*) (Li Yu), 147–149

Revival Society (Fushe), 67

Rhymebook for Lyrics, A (*Ciyun*) (Li Yu), 295

Rocks Nod Their Heads (*Shidian tou*), 317n21

Rolston, David L., 109, 299n3

Ruan Dacheng, 208, 322n27; *Double Honor Roll* (*Shuang jinbang*), 325n19; *Spring Lantern Riddles* (*Chundeng mi*), 325n19; *Swallow's Letter* (*Yanzi jian*), 205–207

Rules of Dramatic Prosody (*Qulü*) (Wang Jide), 113–114

same-sex attraction: body remodeling and, 228; in early Qing culture, 270, 333n62

scalability. *See* reproducibility

scholar-merchants (*shishang*), 37–38

Scott, Mary, 165

Sea of Letters (*Han hai*) (Shen Jiayin), 67, 70, 309n79

Second Solicitation of Letters, A (*Chidu erzheng*) (Li Yu), 62

"Seeking Refuge from Turmoil in 1644" (Li Yu), 158

Selected Yuan Plays (*Yuanqu xuan*) (Zang Maoxun), 204

"Selling My House" (Li Yu), 156–15

"Selling My House and Moving Back To My Old Residence" (Li Yu), 156–157

set design, 11–12

sewing, 174, 220–221

Shang, Wei, 96, 317n21

shanren (mountain man), 43, 307n34

shen (spiritual, magical), 200, 224, 277–278

Shen Defu, 41

Shen Jiayin, *Sea of Letters* (*Han hai*), 67, 70, 309n79

Shen Xinyou, 26, 308n62

shenjiao (spiritual friendship), 61, 64, 77, 185. *See also* social networks

Shi Chengjin, *Yuhua xiang*, 317n18

Shi Mining, "Green Hill" (*Qing shan*), 311n16

signatures. *See* literary possession

Silent Operas (*Wusheng xi*) (Li Yu): body in, 201–202; body remodeling in, 221, 229; editions, 20–22, 290–293, 303n45; *fuxing* (bestowing form) in, 217–218; garden design in, 165; gender ambiguity in, 228; *huaben* conventions and, 122–123; the illusory in, 200; print as metaphor in, 210–211; reproducibility in, 213; titling conventions in, 123, 317n20

Sima Qian, *Records of the Grand Historian* (*Shiji*), 212
Sima Xiangru, "Fu on the Excursion Hunt of the Son of Heaven," 299n1
Singable Lyrics (*Naige ci*) (Li Yu), 76, 295
skin: color of, 242, 244–247, 331nn19–20; as fabric, 237–238, 242–244, 249–250, 331n14
Slapping the Table in Amazement (*Pai'an jingqi*) (Ling Mengchu), 123, 212
Sobering Stone (*Zuixing shi*), 317n21
social media, 275. *See also* social networks
social networks: collections and, 63–64, 65, 66–67, 75, 76, 77, 310n85; fame and, 44; interactivity and, 66–67; Li Yu's cultural entrepreneurship and, 22, 77, 275; print as technology for, 36, 61, 63, 275
Song dynasty, 40, 90, 163, 169, 173, 175, 191
Song Shiyong, 164
Song Zhiwen, "Visiting Lotus Dharma Temple" (You fahua si), 120–121
Spring Lantern Riddles (*Chundeng mi*) (Ruan Dacheng), 325n19
Stiegler, Bernard, 203
Storied Garden (Cengyuan), 26, 165
Story of the Western Wing (*Xixiang ji*), 121, 136, 137, 139, 146, 161
Story of Washing Silk, The (*Huansha ji*), 112
strange (*qi*), discourse of the, 42, 108
Su Shi, 17, 40–41
Sun Kaidi, 119, 127, 155–156, 303n42
Sun Kang, 311n7
Sun Yunqiu, 289

Sun Zhi, 66, 285, 286
Suzhou playwrights, 312n23
Swallow's Letter (*Yanzi jian*) (Ruan Dacheng), 205–207

"Tan Chuyu Expresses His Love in a Play; Liu Miaogu Dies for Honor after a Song" (Li Yu), 93–96
Tan Yuanchun, 67
Tang dynasty, 17, 136, 156, 157, 163, 169, 170, 173
Tang Xianzu, *The Peony Pavilion* (*Mudan ting*), 124, 200, 206
Tao Zhenhuai, *The Heavens Rain Flowers* (*Tianyuhua*), 328n49
technicity, 203, 225. *See also* body; body remodeling
theater: body and, 89–90; body remodeling and, 231–234, 259; dialogue vs. arias in, 95, 96–98, 99–100, 109, 110–111; garden design and, 163, 164, 185, 191; gender and, 202, 233–234; intermediality and, 12, 277; Li Yu's influence on, 4, 89; Li Yu's troupe, 23, 39, 88, 202, 241; linguistic registers in, 93–97, 98, 100; literacy and, 91; novelty and, 25–26; primacy of performance in, 4, 97–98, 99, 100–101; print as metaphor and, 206; regional dialects and, 104, 105, 313n50; reproducibility and, 206–207; role-types in, 232–234, 329nn80,82; social imposture and, 233, 329n80; *xu/shi* interplay and, 11, 12, 277. *See also* playwriting
Tian, Xiaofei, 104
To Repay a Kindness, Three Tigers Go Down the Mountain (*Zheng bao'en sanhu xiashan*), 204

"Tower for Hearing My Faults" (Wenguo lou) (Li Yu), 155, 158, 159, 160
"Tower for the Summer Heat, A" (Xiayi lou) (Li Yu), 142–145, 146, 157, 218, 268, 278
Tower in a Mirage (*Shenzhong lou*) (Li Yu), 8, 9, *10*, 11–12, 285, 301nn18–19
"Tower of Gathered Refinements" (Cuiya lou) (Li Yu), 134–135
"Tower of My Birth" (Shengwo lou) (Li Yu), 152–154, 257, 258
"Tower of Returning as an Immortal Crane" (Hegui lou) (Li Yu), 150–152, 264–265
"Tower of Shared Reflections" (Heying lou) (Li Yu), 120, 123, 135–138, *140*, 141–142, 207, 208, 223, 228
"Tower of Ten Nuptial Cups" (Shijin lou) (Li Yu), 149–150, 226–228
"Tower of Three Companions" (Sanyu lou) (Li Yu), 124, 127–134, 155–157, 158
"Tower of Trophies" (Duojin lou) (Li Yu), 123–124
Twelve Towers (*Shi'er lou*) (Li Yu), 318n25; body remodeling in, 223–225; building names in, 147–150, 152; buildings as body in, 142–144; buildings as property in, 155–157, 320n50; chapter divisions in, 126, 144, 151–152; commentary in, 155, 159, 160, 319n46; Du Jun's preface to, 22, 119, 125–126, 287, 288–289; editions, 287–290; fate in, 149–150, 152–153; garden design and, 119, 125–126, 128, 129–130, 158, 161, 192–193; gender ambiguity in, 226; *huaben* conventions and, 20, 123–124, 132, 133, 147, 163; influence of, 317n18, 318n21; interactivity in, 154, 159–160, 320n54; intermediality in, 127, 133–135, 139, 141, 148–149, 155, 318n30; metafiction in, 128, 154–156, 157–159, 178–179, 318n27, 320nn52–53; Ming-Qing dynastic transition and, 154; narrative progression in, 129–133; *Nineteen Old Poems* and, 319n34; omniscience in, 145–146; plotting in, 126–127, 139, 141–146; print as metaphor in, 207, 208–209; publication of, 20; reflections in, 136–138, 139, *140*; remodeling in, 133, 137; stories as buildings in, 119–120, 121–122, 125–126; *Story of the Western Wing* and, 136, 137, 146, 161; structure of, 161; titling in, 121–122, 123–125, 318–319n32; *xu/shi* interplay in, 134, 141–142, 154, 182; *Yuhua xiang* (Shi Chengjin) and, 317n18; *Zhuangzi* and, 128–129, 131, 318n29

Volpp, Sophie, 232, 329n80

Wang Ang, 309n82
Wang Can, 84, 85, 311n11
Wang Dingchen, the Woodcutter, and the Fisherman on a Snowy Eve (*Yuqiao ji*) (Yu Tianxi), 204
Wang Duanshu, 286
Wang Fuzhi, 259–260
Wang Gai, *The Mustard Seed Garden Painting Manual* (*Jieziyuan huazhuan*), 26, 47, 56–57, *56*
Wang Gen, 91
Wang Jide, 314n56; *The Male Queen* (*Nan wanghou*), 221; *Rules of Dramatic Prosody* (*Qulü*), 113–114

Wang Qi, 35, 63, 65, 74, 309nn72,79; *Chidu xinyu*, 65
Wang Siren, 67, 68
Wang Weihan, *Chidu lanyan*, 65–66
Wang Xizhi, 18; "Orchid Pavilion," 43
Wang Yangming, 25, 199
Wang Zailai, 23
Wang Zuoju, 119
Water Margin (Shuihu zhuan), 204
Watson, Burton, 318n29, 321n18
Wei Yong, 254; "Delight in Adornment" (Yuerong bian), 253
wenli (*wenyan wen*, classical Chinese): vs. *changtan suyu*, 92, 93–94, 97; defined, 90; literacy and, 91–92, 93, 312n27; "meaning and order" of text and, 312n24; particles and, 93–94; regional dialects and, 96, 105; for secret communication, 94–96. *See also* linguistic registers; literacy
wenren: Li Yu's redefinition of, 7, 90. *See also* literati
wenyan wen. *See wenli*
wenzhang (literature), 86, 90, 97, 99, 100, 101, 103; as common possession, 90, 311–312n22
West Lake scenery, 51, 54, 307n51
West, Stephen, 163
Widmer, Ellen, 63, 66
"With the Change of Eight Characters, Trouble Ends and Good Luck Begins" (Li Yu), 213
"With the Loss Of A Thousand Taels of Silver, Good Luck Results from Calamity" (Li Yu), 207, 210–211, 213
Wolf of Zhongshan, 61, 308n60
"Woman Preserving Her Virtue Meets Strange Slander; A Gang of Guys Joking Around Leads to a Bizarre Injustice, A" (Li Yu), 200–201

woodblock printing: innovation in, 203; labor of, 33–34; vs. moveable type, 205; reproducibility and, 34, 274–275. *See also* print; print as metaphor
word processing, 205
writing: body and, 85, 87–88, 111–112, 218, 219, 273, 315n65; choice of genres and, 46, 80, 124; Creator and, 219; debates on value of, 7; garden design and, 166–168, 173–175; innovation and, 30; instrumental vs. literary uses of, 91; Liu Xie on, 207–208; materialist vision of, 11; Ming-Qing dynastic transition and, 78–79, 82–83; remodeling and, 133; reproducibility and, 207–208; terms for, 92; *xu/shi* interplay and, 12, 166, 167. *See also* playwriting
Wu Bing, *The Green Peony (Lü mudan)*, 45, 46
Wu Weiye, 67, 170–171, 175, 310n83
wudi (no-place), 106, 107–108

Xianqing ouji. *See Leisure Notes*
xiaopin genre, 40, 41, 80, 239–240
Xu Fuzuo, *Discourse on Drama (Qulun)*, 112
Xu Wei, 313n50
Xu Xicai, 15, 16–17
Xu Zhen, "Manual of Beautiful Women" (Meiren pu), 253
Xu Zhi, 15
xu/shi interplay: body remodeling and, 254; buildings and, 8, 11, 142, 154, 167; concept importance, 299n3; fashion and, 248; fiction and, 119–120, 122, 133–134; interactivity and, 2–3; intermediality and, 8; *kongzhong louge* and, 119–120;

literalization and, 182–185, *183*, 323n56; playwriting and, 108; remodeling and, 8, 276–277; theater and, 11, 12, 277; *Tower in a Mirage* and, 8, 11; in *Twelve Towers*, 134, 141–142, 154, 182; writing and, 12, 166, 167

xu/shi interplay in garden design: aesthetic theory and, 164; clutter and, 177–178; fiction and, 164–165, 183–184; intermediality and, 174; literalization and, 182–184, *183*, 323n56; metafiction and, 180–181, *180*; novelty and, 190; scale and, 184–185; writing and, 166–168, 321n18

xylography. *See* woodblock printing

Yan Guangmin, 281, 334n1
Yan Shigu, 332n48
Yang Yunyou, 42
Yang Zhu, 262, 333n53
"Yao Dizhu Flees from Disgrace Only to Incur More Disgrace; Zheng Yue'e Uses a Mistake to Advance Her Own Interests" (Ling Mengchu), 212
Ye Xiaoluan, "Yanti lianzhu," 252, 331n25
Yi Hill Estate, 16, 17–18, 39, 162, 165, 166, 192
Yin Hao, 88
yinxialai. *See* print as metaphor
Yishengtang, 5, 23, 34, 282–283, 284, 286, 287, 296
You Tong, 167–168, 322n20
"Young Ladies Enjoy a Swing-Set Party" (Ling Mengchu), 123

Yu Tianxi, *Wang Dingchen, the Woodcutter, and the Fisherman on a Snowy Eve* (*Yuqiao ji*), 204
Yuan dynasty, 203–204
Yuan Hong, 44
Yuan Jun, 311n8
Yuhua xiang (Shi Chengjin), 317n18

zaju genre, 8, 203–205, 208, 214
Zang Maoxun, 314n56; *Selected Yuan Plays* (*Yuanqu xuan*), 204
Zeitlin, Judith T., 108
Zhang Cai, 67
Zhang Caixia, 164
Zhang Chao, 64, 175–176, 177
Zhang Dai, 308n52
Zhang Fengyi, 67
Zhang Gangsun, 66
Zhang Jinyan, 20–21, 292, 303n45
Zhang Lian (Nanyuan), 169, 170–171, 175–176
Zhang Liang Fetches a Shoe from Beneath the Bridge (*Zhang Zifang yiqiao jinlü*) (Li Wenwei), 204
Zhang Pu, 67
Zhang Yong, 165, 321n14
Zhong Xing, 67
Zhou Lianggong, 63, 65, 193, 309n72; *Chidu xinchao*, 65
Zhou Liangjie, 35
Zhu Sansong, 322n24
Zhu Sheng, 289–290
Zhu Xi, 219, 239
Zhuangzi, 128–129, 131, 239, 312n22, 312n27, 318n29
zhuodao ren (person who holds the sword), 43, 46, 47
Zito, Angela, 243, 278, 327n43

GPSR Authorized Representative: Easy Access System Europe, Mustamäe tee 50, 10621 Tallinn, Estonia, gpsr.requests@easproject.com